Witchfather

A Life of Gerald Gardner

Volume 2

From Witch Cult to Wicca

By the Same Author:

Skyways and Landmarks Revisited
    (with Jimmy Goddard and Paul Baines) (1985)
Earth Mysteries: An Exploratory Introduction
    (with Brian Larkman) (1985)
Tony Wedd: New Age Pioneer (1986)
The Elements of Earth Mysteries (1991)
Secret Places of the Goddess (1995)
Earth Mysteries (1995)
Mirrors of Magic (1997)
Magical Guardians: Exploring the Spirit and Nature of Trees
(1998)
Leylines: A Beginner's Guide (1999)
Wiccan Roots: Gerald Gardner and the Modern Witchcraft
    Revival (2000)
Gerald Gardner and the Cauldron of Inspiration (2003)
Newland Avenue School 1896-2006 (2006)

Witchfather

A Life of Gerald Gardner

Volume 2

From Witch Cult to Wicca

by

Philip Heselton

THOTH PUBLICATIONS
Loughborough, Leicestershire

Published by Thoth Publications
64 Leopold Street, Loughborough, LE11 5DN

EAN: 9781913660154

web address: www.thoth.co.uk
email: enquiries@thoth.co.uk

For Hilary, Owen and Aidan

CONTENTS

ACKNOWLEDGEMENTS

A book of this sort is far from being the work of only one person. Indeed, I have had help from a very large number of people. Some have given me great assistance over many years; others may have provided a small but useful snippet of information. To all who have helped me I give my thanks: there is no doubt whatever that this book would never have been written without you.

I give thanks to Mike Allen, Jo Anderson, Bridget Archer, M.Y. Ashcroft, Paul Atkin, Pat Badham, Suzi Balls, Hilary Bartle, Lesley Barton, Helen Bassett, John and Julie Belham-Payne, Ian Bell, Simon Bennett, Bali Beskin, Geraldine Beskin, Gavin Bone, Adrian Bott, Desmond Bourke, Lois Bourne, Roger Bristow, Jane Brodley, Ray Buckland, Fran Burgon, Cora Burke, Hilary Byers, Francis Cameron, Kenn Capps, Philip Carr-Gomm, Keith Chisholm, Else Churchill, Marilyn and Trevor Clark, Ann Cook, Rory Cook, Jerry Cornelius, Zach Cox, Phyllis Croft, Barbara Croom, Angela Crow-Woods, Patricia Crowther, Nick Culpeper, Mags Currie, Anne Dacre, Karen and Evan Dales, Morgan Davis, Dayonis, Roger Dearnaley, Kim and Tracey Dent-Brown, Peter Dickens, Elizabeth Doria, Lalita du Peron, Beverley Emery, Peter English, Janet Farrar, Michael Farrar, Jani Farrell-Roberts, John Ferguson, Ben Fernee, Alan Franklin, Ken and Marita Freeman, Don Frew, Adrian Gardner, Gay Gardner, Robert A.Gilbert, Kate Gladstone, Lynne Sydelle Gordon, Clare Goulder, Kenneth Grant, Simon Green, Paul Greenslade, Clive Harper, Christina Oakley Harrington, Melissa and Rufus Harrington, Lizzie Harris, Ralph Harvey, Jeanne Heaslewood, Nigel and Susan Heselton, Trevor Hildrey, Martin Hinchcliffe, Gillian Hodges, Michael Hodges, John Hopkins, Beryl Housley, Michael Howard, Nick Howson, Ronald Hutton, Nigel Jackson, Deric James, Richard and Tamarra James, Larry Jones, Prudence Jones, Steve Jones, Suzanne Josefowicz, Aidan Kelly, J Elwyn Kimber, Graham King, Richard Knight, Anna Korn, Fred Lamond, Andrew Lee-Hart, Ian Lilleyman, Ray and Lynda Lindfield, Grevel Lindop, Carey Littlefield, Catherine Lloyd, Nagia Lombardo, Chris Lycett, Beverly Lyon Clark, John and Kitty Macintyre, Jonathan MacQueen, Mary Kay

Mahoney, Laurence Main, Maria Malo, Carolyn Maunder, Gareth Medway, Hugh and Beryl Midgley, George Monger, Alan Moorhouse, Levannah Morgan, Marian Mozley, William Mullan, Tony Naylor, Paul Newman, Sue Newman, Jeremy Newson, Andy Norfolk, Caroline Oates, Dáithí Ó Geanainn, Jo Pearson, Julia Phillips, Doug Pickford, Joy Piper, Carol Price, Richard Price, Shelley Rabinovich, Jon Randall, Ken Rees, Andrew Robertson, Caroline Robertson, Jean Rose, Penny Rudkin, Jane Rutter, W.F. Ryan, Olive Samuel, Edward Saunders, George Schrager, Melissa Seims, Eleanor Sergeneson, Elizabeth Silverthorne, Geoffrey Basil Smith, Tony Steele, Ian Stevenson, Tim Stimson, Jean Stirk, Derek Stokes, Andrew Stoodley, John Tait, Jonathan Tapsell, Keith Thompson, Anthony Thorley, Helen Thorne, Kevin Tingay, Jane Estelle Trombley, Jean Tsusima, Julie Venner, Miranda Vickers, Bill Wakefield, Chris Wallis, Gareth Watkins, Sibyl Webster, Martin Westlake, Iseult Weston, Nicky Westwood, Roy and Grace Wheadon, Cerys Williams, Jean Williams, Steve Wilson, Caroline Wise, Allyn Wolfe, C.M. Woolgar, Jim Wright, John Yeowell and Kalisha Zahr.

I would also like to give my thanks to all those who wish to remain anonymous.

It is inevitable, with such a large number who have contributed their assistance, that I will have missed someone. This is no reflection on the value of their contribution: it is merely due to my failing memory!

My thanks to you all, and to those who will read this book.

PICTURE AND TEXT CREDITS

Bridget Archer 41; Boscastle Museum of Witchcraft 30, 38; British Federation of the International Order of Co-Freemasonry, Le Droit Humain 21; Patricia Crowther 40, 44, 45; Adrian Gardner 1-7, 11, 12; Rufus and Melissa Harrington 34, 46; Gillian Hodges 10; Richard and Tamarra James 9, 14, 15, 16, 29, 39; Larry Jones 48; Jonathan MacQueen 13; Sefton Libraries and Information Services 8; Ian Stevenson 22,23; Keith Thompson 17-20, 42, 43; Miranda Vickers 31, 32; Westminster Libraries 25. All other illustrations by or in the collection of the author. The author has made every effort to identify copyright holders and to obtain their permission but would be glad to hear of any inadvertent errors or omissions.

I must thank Ian Bell for his skills with Photoshop in improving many of the photographs included in this book. I must also thank Grevel Lindop and Gareth Medway for valuable detailed comments on the text.

My thanks go to John Belham-Payne for permission to quote from Doreen Valiente's published works. He has asked me to mention his websites www.doreenvaliente.com and www.paganismstudies.org which are both very good and informative.

I would also like to thank Graham King for permission to quote from letters and other documents held in the Boscastle Museum of Witchcraft archives; and to Richard and Tamarra James for permission to quote from various documents in the Toronto collection.

I would like to thank Pat Badham, Barbara Croom and other members of Five Acres Club for permission to quote from letters in their archives; and to Adrian Gardner for permission to quote from documents in the Gardner family archive.

Many others mentioned in the Acknowledgements section have given me permission to quote from documents in their possession, or which they have written, and I am most grateful to all of them.

ILLUSTRATIONS

Between pages 524 and 525:

A NOTE ON USAGE

I have used the names and spellings of countries and towns as they were when Gerald Gardner was living in or visiting them, so I refer to Ceylon, Borneo, Malaya, Johore and Gold Coast, for example, rather than the current Sri Lanka, Sabah, Malaysia, Johor and Ghana. This also applies to the boundaries of English counties and to organisations such as the Folk-Lore Society, which changed its name to the Folklore Society in 1960. Lois Bourne is referred to by that name when I am quoting from her book *Dancing with Witches*, but by the name Lois Pearson, when referring to the time when she knew Gerald Gardner. The building which was known as the Witch's Cottage while at the Abbey Folk Park, I refer to as the Witches' Cottage after rituals started to take place there in the mid-1950s. The naturist club of which Gerald was a member was known as both Fiveacres and Five Acres. I have preferred the latter form, partly in order to distinguish it from the former Fouracres Club. I have used the terms 'the Wica', 'the witch cult' and 'the Craft' as interchangeable. I have generally referred to Gerald Gardner by his first name because, as explained elsewhere, whilst I never knew him in this life, I feel I have got to know him very well in the process of writing this biography. I have also often referred to others, such as Edith Woodford-Grimes, Cecil Williamson and Frederic Lamond by their first names. Where I quote directly from Gerald's letters or other writings, I have preserved his somewhat idiosyncratic spelling, as I feel that in some way it enables us to get closer to him. For year dates, the suffixes 'CE' and 'BCE' are used in preference to the specifically Christian 'AD' and 'BC'.

≫ PART III ≪

Intense Cultivation

CHAPTER EIGHTEEN

Skyclad Philosophising

Gerald was restless by nature: it wasn't in his character to settle down. Certainly he seemed to take little notice of the wartime exhortations to limit one's travel. The posters asking "Is your journey really necessary?" had little effect on his actions. One manifestation of this is that from when he moved down to Highcliffe in July 1938 he had, for most of the rest of his life, two homes. He kept on the flat at 23a Buckingham Palace Mansions until at least March 1939, which is when he applied to be a member of the Folk-Lore Society. He had, however, given it up by autumn 1939, when it was occupied by Air Commodore Ronald Graham and his wife, perhaps the origin of the 'requisition' story.

The first years of the war at Highcliffe were perhaps too exciting for Gerald to think about moving away. His initiation, friendship with Edith, Rosanne's marriage, the ritual to try to stop the invasion and his roles in the ARP service and the Home Guard were probably enough to keep him in Highcliffe for quite a while.

However, things began to change. The New Forest Club was bombed in September 1940 and was thereafter closed permanently. And Major Fish was moved with his unit to Malvern in November 1942. Gerald got on with him very well and missed their discussions. Also, the same month, Rosanne became pregnant and her

son was born in August 1943. Edith took a lot of the work in looking after him while Rosanne was working as a Clerk in the Ministry
of Supply. The threat of invasion had also receded and I think Gerald began to feel restless and longed for the activities in London.

I think it likely that Gerald was doing at least three things
during that period. Firstly, he was researching witchcraft, in particular its history, at the British Museum, possibly under an
assumed name. Secondly, he was writing the book which would
become *High Magic's Aid,* or at least preparing notes towards it.
And he was visiting naturist clubs.

We know that Gerald was in the habit of staying in the London area throughout the war because Iseult Weston, who was
born and brought up in Spielplatz naturist club, remembers seeing him there as a day visitor. Gerald had probably started going
to Spielplatz because, according to Rex Wellbye, Fouracres ceased
operations in 1940. Iseult Weston, however, says that it kept open
throughout the war. Perhaps people did continue to go and use
the facilities but on a less formal basis.

However, Gerald was certainly a regular visitor to Spielplatz,
and that *did* stay open throughout the war. This was also in Bricket
Wood, one of the so-called 'Hertfordshire Nuderies', only about a
mile from Fouracres. It had been founded by Iseult's parents,
Charles and Dorothy Macaskie, in 1930. Iseult has written a history
of Spielplatz[1] and she still lives there. She remembers Gerald Gardner being a regular visitor to Spielplatz during the war, describing
him as an "old windbag" and "always ready to expound upon his
views on the subject in question".[2] Philip Carr-Gomm writes:

> *On talking to Iseult to try to pinpoint the exact years she
> remembers Gardner visiting Spielplatz, she is sure he visited
> throughout the war years, and can remember distinctly him
> being present on a memorable day in 1943 when the club-
> house caught fire ... She remembers Gardner standing in
> front of the blaze with his friend (and fellow Druid who
> later joined OBOD) Mary Dowding.[3]*

1. Iseult Richardson, *No Shadows Fall,* (Coast and Country Naturist Publications, 1994).
2. Letter, Iseult Weston to the author, 8 December 2002.
3. Philip Carr-Gomm, *I am Tough, Fantastic and Old: The Life of Ross Nichols,* (unpublished manuscript, 2001) footnote 28, 532.

According to Iseult Weston, Mary Dowding was in her late twenties at the time. She had a caravan at Spielplatz, later moving to Five Acres. She remembers her visiting Spielplatz a few years ago, when she seemed to be in her 80s. Neither Philip Carr-Gomm nor I have yet been able to find anything very much about Mary Dowding, but the fact that she was a Druid suggests that Gerald may have become involved with Druidry at least as early as 1940. Mary probably got to know Gerald in the 1936-1938 period, when she was probably also a member of Fouracres. She certainly knew Edith and Rosanne, probably via Gerald, and gave Rosanne a book as a wedding present. Indeed, it seems possible that Gerald was staying with Mary during his time in London, as they seemed to be good friends, or he may have already occupied the flat at 47 Ridgmount Gardens earlier than had previously been thought.

One of the people that Gerald met at Spielplatz was Ross Nichols (1902-1975). He is known today as the founder of the Order of Bards, Ovates and Druids (OBOD), and it now seems likely that it was Gerald who introduced him to Druidry.[4] Born in Norfolk, Nichols' attitude to life was in part formed by his experience of family and boarding school and living through the First World War. This encouraged an unorthodox approach, always challenging the status quo, expressed from a young age through poetry.

He read History at St. John's College, Cambridge, from 1921 to 1924. As a socialist and pacifist, he was rather out of step with the conservative atmosphere of the place, but his inspirations included the philosopher, Bertrand Russell, and the poet, T.S. Eliot.

A major influence on Nichols was John Hargrave who in 1913 had published a manual entitled *Lonecraft*, which led on to the formation, in 1920, of the Kibbo Kift Kindred, which combined elements from the Scout movement with Seton's Woodcraft, but also had a spiritual dimension with an acceptance of karma and what Philip Carr-Gomm describes as "the universal religion of the great spirit".

While at Cambridge, Nichols developed an interest in mysticism and mythology and was much influenced by Sir James Frazer,

---

4. Philip Carr-Gomm, *In the Grove of the Druids: The Druid Teachings of Ross Nichols*, (Watkins, 2002).

author of *The Golden Bough*. Nichols went into teaching for a living, but continued to write poetry, much of which was published.5

We do not know where Nichols derived his impulse to naturism, but certainly by the mid 1930s he had joined Spielplatz and had his own wooden chalet. According to Iseult Weston, he spent weekends and several weeks each summer at Spielplatz.

It is likely that Ross Nichols and Gerald Gardner would have known each other at Spielplatz, probably spending many hours in deep philosophical discussion on topics such as mythology, folklore, witchcraft and Druidry. Although they were of different political persuasions, the fertility of ideas during these sessions would have been of benefit to both men and would later have fruitful outcomes in several different directions. Philip Carr-Gomm has described Spielplatz as "an idyllic environment where alternative thinkers could meet in a natural setting". He concludes:

> *It is ... likely that the two seminal forces in the revival of Western Paganism in the twentieth century met, swam and talked together skyclad in the woods and on the lawns of a Hertfordshire naturist resort, whilst not far away the German and allied forces battled against each other grimly for year after year.*6

⚜

Gerald still spent at least some of his time in Highcliffe and took an interest in a variety of local organisations, including the Historical Association, of which, in June 1944, he was elected Co-President of the Bournemouth and Christchurch branch. The following month he gave a talk to the local Adult School on "A Museum for the Borough of Christchurch". At that date, Christchurch had no museum. Herbert Druitt, the local notable, had opened one at his own expense at the Red House in 1919, but this had closed. Gerald described the typical museum of the time, such as the one in Bournemouth:

---

5. See *Sassenach Stray*, (Fortune Press, 1941); *Prose Chants and Proems*, (Fortune Press 1941); *The Cosmic Shape*, (with James Kirkup), (Forge Press, 1946); *Seasons at War: A Cycle of Rhythms*, (Forge Press, 1947).
6. Carr-Gomm, (2001), 36.

*His first impression had been that there was "no decent system of labelling: no one to tell you anything: a door-keeper, whose answer was, "look what the label says." If there wasn't a "label", or the label was upside down or on the wrong article, it didn't then seem to be anybody's business to put it right.*7

He went on to say:

*Museums, called by the Greeks, "The Temples of the Muses", ... should be places to foster love of learning and beauty, the love of country and liberty: places which would inspire youth to defend these things.*8

He was obviously pleased with this pronouncement as it is reproduced in *Gerald Gardner Witch*. He recommended the museum at Salisbury, which he said was:

*... beautifully run. They concentrate on local things and, with the aid of models, showed exhibits in a way that were easy to understand. "It is possible to see, at a glance, how beautiful and well designed many things were in the past: and you realise that houses needn't be ugly or ill-planned," he said, adding that he could not imagine a boy who had been interested in Salisbury museum designing or allowing to be put up a badly designed house."*9

There was some correspondence in the *Christchurch Times* as a result of Gerald's talk, and it published a letter by him to local councillor, Donovan Lane, which read:

Mrs. Woodford Grimes has raised the question of a Museum at several of her lectures to various women's societies in Christchurch (the women's branch of the British Legion among others) and they had all said the same thing, viz. they didn't want museums, because the only thing they were interested in was in getting better houses built, and

---

7. *Christchurch Times,* 29 July 1944.
8. Ibid.
9. Ibid.

that the local museums were so uninteresting. So I took this for my theme, showing that local museums were only uninteresting because they were put in charge of a door-keeper who was only interested in drawing his pay and who, sure of a fixed job, discouraged visitors; people coming in meant answering questions and being bothered. No people meant no work and steady pay. So they made the place uninteresting while, where museums were made interest-ing, they were full of people and children, and were so good for education: and that if a museum was properly organised to show the local types of buildings by models showing good and bad construction, they would be able to get the good houses they were clamouring for and not get the bad types of construction they were complaining about.[10]

Gerald was unable to do much more of a practical nature to encourage the re-establishment of a museum in Christchurch as, particularly when the war had come to an end, he was spending more and more time in London. However, the Red House opened once more as a museum in 1952 and it was surely one which Ger-ald must have visited and, I imagine, approved.

Gerald came back to live in London some time in late 1944 or early 1945 if not earlier, moving in to 47 Ridgmount Gardens, a superior apartment in purpose-built "mansions" close to Totten-ham Court Road. This was very conveniently located for the British Museum and for a lot of the activities in which he was involved.

Meanwhile, when Fouracres closed in 1940, Wellbye had bought the site from Major Griggs, together with adjoining land fronting onto Oakwood Road and Woodside Road. Shortly after-wards, again with financial help from Griggs, he bought several acres of adjoining woodland which was on sale for housing devel-opment. He did it partly to preserve the privacy of the site because it was on the facing slope of a little valley. To have had houses built there would seriously compromise the extent to which the site could continue its naturist activities without over-looking. This land would later form the basis for 'Five Acres'. In respect of this, he wrote:

---

10. *Christchurch Times*, 12 August 1944.

I took this last on in the hope that people would be found willing to reside there, "respectable" in front, with back doors into club ground. Unfortunately such people never materialized, and I surrendered most of that strip of frontage. It was a pity as now I think the idea wd work.[11]

When the war ended, Wellbye wanted to start up a naturist club again on his land. What was still for some purposes known as "The Camp" (probably Rex had nostalgic memories of its earlier years) was still owned by two of the early landowners, Rex himself and 'Dek', who was J. M. Walker of Cheltenham. During 1944, Rex negotiated to buy Dek's share in the land, though this was only completed in 1945.

The first person to set up on the site was Douglas Powell, who had had a hut at Spielplatz by the name of 'Sun Tan'. He had a group of friends who used to cater for themselves rather than use the communal facilities at Spielplatz, so were already rather 'semi-detached'.[12] Powell wanted to move from Spielplatz, however, and his negotiations with Rex were obviously successful, for his purchase of a plot of land from him went through in May 1944. Anyway, in April 1945, Powell and his group moved 'Sun Tan' onto Wellbye's land and established what they initially called "The Sun Tan Club".

It was probably these land transactions that gave Gerald the idea of buying a plot of land himself from Rex, and probably more than a plot, as Rex wrote to Walker in January 1945:

The man who is buying the plot in The Camp, Gardner, was very anxious to help Powel's new venture to a further extent, to prevent his not having breathing room, + told him to buy anything else I might be willing to sell.[13]

It was not until July 1945, some six months later, that the sale to Gerald was confirmed. The problem we have with all the various land transactions which have taken place over the years is that, whilst there is a lot of written material, there seems to be a

11. Letter, Rex Wellbye to Hugh Shayler, 11 August 1954 (in British Naturism archives).
12. I am indebted to Iseult Weston and Philip Carr-Gomm for this information.
13. Letter, Rex Wellbye to J. M. Walker, 18 January 1945.

lack of plans showing exactly which pieces of land are being referred to. However, in a letter to his solicitors in August 1945, Rex refers to "the sale to Dr. Gardner of part (No. 29 Oakwood Road) of what was known as the Camp" and to the northern boundary of that land being indicated by a pencilled loop. This suggests that this is indeed the same land upon which Gerald later erected the Witch's Cottage and is thus close to the Oakwood Road entrance to the site.

There are several ongoing themes in the often voluminous correspondence between Gerald and Rex. One is the expressed desire to have the Club run as some sort of Trust where all members would have a say, rather then be proprietorial. The next is the undoubted financial stake in the enterprise that Gerald soon acquired. Rex very quickly became exasperated with Gerald, but he could not be ignored because of his monetary input. The third theme was one of balance: neither Rex nor Gerald wanted the other to have control and there is a lot of correspondence over the years devoted to ensuring that this state of balance was maintained.

To help ensure his position, Gerald enlisted the help of Edith Woodford-Grimes, supposedly as a financial backer. Although later he had to reveal her full name, he refers to her as 'Elsie' in much of the early correspondence. Doreen Valiente[14] told me that Edith was also introduced to her as 'Elsie'.

Whilst undoubtedly Edith knew what was going on and, indeed, on at least one occasion, attended a meeting at the Club, I strongly suspect that the money which she was supposedly putting up actually came from Gerald. This was repeated several years later but with Doreen Valiente in the supposed role of benefactress. Rosanne's second husband, Alfred Maguire ('Mac'), was also the supposed purchaser of a plot of land, as we shall see.

Gerald appears to have gone down to Highcliffe in mid-December 1945 to spend Christmas and the New Year. At what stage he sold 'Southridge' I do not know. The electoral register for 1945 indicates a couple by the name of Forshaw living there, with no mention of Gerald or Donna. The 1946 electoral register shows a different couple, the McElderrys, in residence. I suspect that

---

14. Letter Doreen Valiente to the author 24 August 1998.

this means that for about a year Gerald let the house on a short-term basis, but that he sold it some time in 1946.

Yet Gerald wrote a letter on Southridge headed notepaper to Rex as late as 17th December 1945, by which time the Forshaws were definitely in occupation. Perhaps he did not let the whole house but retained accommodation there for when he needed it. As late as 14th June 1947, Gerald wrote a letter, to Aleister Crowley, on Southridge headed notepaper, although someone has drawn a pencil line through the address. At first I thought this must have been Crowley, but it was probably Gerald, who must have had a stock of old notepaper, and who might have just wanted to impress Crowley with the grandness of his address (just "Southridge, Highcliffe" - no mention of Highland Avenue: it could be a great country mansion in its own grounds for all any-one receiving a letter from Gerald might know). He may have continued to use the headed notepaper, for reasons of grandeur, giving the impression of a "country seat", but perhaps also to mis-lead people whom he didn't want to give his real address until he trusted them. He may have arranged with the Forshaws and the McElderrys to forward any mail promptly.

The letter to Rex of 17th December 1945 refers to a piece of land known as 'the Bulge', probably in the vicinity of but addi-tional to the land which Gerald had already bought. He clearly wanted to acquire it as well. The letter is rather complicated: I certainly don't understand all the machinations, but he seems to me to be using Edith ('Elsie') to help him achieve what he wants. To quote from the letter:

> ...she feels she should have some valued security, if she helps a Club she's never seen + probably never will see. Its her idia to get the Bulge in my + her name, + thinks the con-dition on which she required to put up the Money I may persu ... Her idia was to get the Bulge quietly then appear out of the clouds, a sort of Lady Bountiful, buy a nice gift for the Club. That's why I didn't want it talked about. If she got her way she was prepared to go further + probably

would have payed for I believe the Pond or putting up Din-
ing Room + Kitchen + Bathroom in the Club House. But
here I have to keep jollying her on. The trouble is, when they
know Mother has any money, Daughter + Son in law come
round, so Im so afraid that if there's a long delay, well, it
will be, so sorry but no money. Actually, she's been asking
for her money back, but I keep stalling her. ...what about
letting Elsie buy the Bulge ... Shes heard of you, + will trust
anything you do + it would be nice to have the Kitchen +
Bathroom, etc. + the Pond enlarged Now instead of waiting
for years. I feel I have such a short time left, that makes me
impatient + want to get a move on. As I say, I'm so afraid
someone will come with a Hard Luck Story + Elsie (she's an
Easy Mark) will give it them ... [15]

It certainly seems as if Gerald is using Edith's possible financial involvement as a way of putting some sort of pressure on Rex.
Gerald obviously wants 'the Bulge' and is really bribing Rex with
the promise of improvements to the Club facilities if he will
agree, and quickly! He is using several salesmanship ploys, such
as "agree quickly or the money won't be available" and sympathy
("I feel I have such a short time left"). Of course, Gerald survived
for another 18 years!

The Club seemed in its emphasis to be the spiritual successor
of Fouracres, as a note published in Spring 1946 recounts: ... *a spe-*
cial feature of Five Acres is its "cultural" side - in connection with
which a programme of talks and discussions was adopted last sea-
son [i.e. Summer 1945], *with such success that a further series is*
planned for this year. [16] An advertisement of the time referred,
more formally, to 'lectures' and also to dramatics.

By January 1946, the Woodside Close Property Company had
been set up to own the land on which the club was sited. The
shareholders were Rex, Gerald, Powell and his son, and Herbert
Senior Fothergill, who was also the company secretary.

In July 1946, Fothergill produced a report which revealed that
there was "a clear crisis in the company", which blamed Powell

---

15. Letter, Gerald Gardner to Rex Wellbye, 17 December 1945.
16. Survey of the Sun Clubs 1946 in *Sun Bathing Review*, (Spring 1946), 15.

for issuing shares to himself. Gerald and Rex agreed that Powell should be paid to leave the company, that each should take out debentures and should have an equal number of shares. At an Extraordinary General Meeting on 28th July 1946, Rex was made Secretary to the company and was responsible for the active management of the Five Acres Club, and a resolution was passed:

> *The following persons shall be Directors of the Company, viz: Gerald Bressau [sic] Gardner, and Reginald Wellbye. They shall be Permanent Directors of the Company, and each of them shall be entitled to hold such office so long as he shall live ...*

In August 1946, Gerald set out his vision for the future of the Club in a letter to Rex:

> *I think the simplest + best thing will be to carry on as we arranged, buy the land + transfer it to the club. If it issent strangled with rents + sinking funds, the club can pay the debenture interest all right if the land, buildings &c are transferred to the Co, people wont be frightned any more, + we can go ahead. We must try + enlarge the Club House as aranged + make it comfortable for people to stay the night in, so folk can arrange, We can go down to the Club, + if weve booked we can will get beds, + be warm. I'd like to start on enlarging the Pool this winter if possible, Then we will get the right sort of Members, but we must show them the goods, + we must try + make the club attractive in winter. The White House did it, + we can do it too, but, it means places to sleep, where they will be warm, + entertainments, + Dances ...*

In March 1947, Rex reported on the state of the company. The main consideration seemed to be to get more members ("of the type desired") for the Club: at that time they numbered about sixty.

Certainly by Spring 1947 the Club was being referred to as having just been reorganised, presumably at least partly as the result of Gerald's financial involvement. Its distinctive character was, however, still being emphasised:

> This club ... aims at breaking new ground, making nudity a cultural agency, and so appealing to many not ordinarily attracted, or apt to be bored by "just nudism". As a social, recreational and cultural club on a nudist basis, it has as its object the bringing together of thoughtful and well-informed people for play, conversation and such cultural activities (e.g. discussions, talks, dramatics, etc.) as can be most pleasantly associated with social nakedness.[17]

Gerald's old friend, Ross Nichols, seems to have become a member of Five Acres, perhaps in part because of its philosophy and Gerald's involvement. Arnold Crowther, Cottie Burland and James Laver were also members.

Rex was 74 and Gerald was 63 in 1947 and both were thinking in terms of a Trust which would take over the Club when they retired from active involvement.

The process by which the Powells were bought out and by which Gerald and Edith invested in the company should have been reasonably straightforward, but in fact the arguments and negotiations went on for years, much faithfully chronicled in the correspondence still resting in the archives of the Five Acres Club. Unless one is fascinated by accountancy and legal proce-dures, it is a somewhat tedious enterprise to read through all of this sixty year old correspondence, but for one thing: it provides an insight into Gerald Gardner's character and some of his thought processes that is unequalled in any other correspon-dence that is currently available. So, for this reason alone, the series of letters that travelled back and forth between Rex and Gerald over several years is worth studying.

At a Board Meeting of the Company held on Tuesday 25th November 1947, a note from Gerald was considered which read:

---

17. Survey of the Sun Clubs 1947 in *Sun Bathing Review* (Spring 1947), 16.

I hereby appoint Mrs. E. Woodford-Grimes (Elsie Kerr) to be my substitute as Director in the Woodside Close Property Co. Ltd. She already holds my power of Attorney and a proxy to vote for me at any Company Meeting, and any act of hers may be taken as an act of mine. (Signed) - G.B. Gardner (date) 20/11/47

This was because four days later Gerald and Donna set sail from Liverpool on their way to the United States. By May 1948, after their return, the relationship between Rex and Gerald had deteriorated sharply. Gerald was critical of Rex in several respects:

Ive always said my memory was bad but, now Rex, issent yours a little bit hasey too? ... Now Rex, Do I understand from this. That when Mr. Hopkins wrote to me saying you had instructed him to write to me, & ask me to appoint somone to act for me in my absence, & to perpare papers so that a meeting should be held to pass such a resalution. That this was all false. That you had never given him such instructions, that he had acted entirely off his own bat as it were, a sort of Neni goat transection, in fact? Now will you please let me have a letter saying that you have never instructed him to do this, & autherise me to write to him for an explanation, I sincerely appologise for being fooled by him. I promise I will never believe anything he says in future, unless the letter is countersigned by you & that all letters I have sent him are utterly void. Does that satisfy you? I cant do more.[18]

This is typical of Gerald. He clearly doesn't believe Rex, but rather than accuse him, he goes to extremes in the other direction (a technique used many years later by Doreen Valiente against Gerald himself). Gerald goes on:

I know you said that the money was as much in my keeping as in yours, but I dident understand it then & I dont now,

18. Letter, Gerald Gardner to Rex Wellbye, 14 May 1948.

how is the money in my keeping? you wont tell me where it is; is it in the bank or Where. You never showed me any branch reciepts or anything. Now you say, Quote, You know you are safe over the land. & thats exactly what I dont. Youve never shown me the slightest evidance, I dont say at all that it dosent exist, But, if so, why mayent I see it, Now Rex, you say a lot of hard things to me. but. if the position were reversed, would you be content with my just saying, evrythings all right. & never showing you anything?[19]

There are other accusations, but Gerald ends up by saying:

Anyhow, promise me this Rex, If we have to fight in public, dont let it affect our friendship at the Club. If Churchill & Atlee can call each other names in the House, all day, & go home to dinner together. surely we can have our week ends in peace. & so lets agree, that we will never argue at the Club.[20]

This again is typical of Gerald. He was genuinely fond of Rex and didn't want to sacrifice the enjoyment which he obtained from many happy hours discussing philosophy with him. Rex defended himself vigorously:

Your letter is confused, incoherent and illogical, monkeying with dates, making what happened last the cause of what happened first, inventing "facts" and giving quite fictitious accounts of incidents. It is an extraordinary letter from a man who is supposed to be taking a share in managing a business. If the whole thing were not too clumsy and if your obtuseness & simplicity were not well known, it would appear to be the letter of one who was trying to get the better of his partner, while accusing the partner of doing the same.[21]

Rex proceeded to answer the various issues which Gerald raised in his letter, to my mind decisively and convincingly. He is clearly exasperated with Gerald, as he continues:

---

19. Ibid.
20. Ibid.
21. Letter, Rex Wellbye to Gerald Gardner, 19 May 1948.

... how can I answer the incoherent nonsense -- for such it is -- with which you blur the whole thing. It does not even make sense. ... How is it possible to work with anyone who cannot grasp a simple point...[22]

He sums up how he sees Gerald's approach:

Whatever you knew at the time you will forget; whatever the true facts you will concoct a false story, you wont trouble to check up, you are far too unbusinesslike to see the improbability, and too unmethodical to take the trouble to check up.[23]

A subsequent letter from Rex ended with an ultimatum to Gerald:

This is the end so far as our joint control is concerned, and the situation must be cleared up, to my satisfaction, by June 21st. Whether you buy me out, whether we wind up, or whether you can propose some satisfactory scheme -- I am leaving you to propose something.[24]

There continued concern on the part of both Rex and Gerald about the balance of power between the two of them. The position of balance in the shareholdings was clarified in an agreement signed on 28th June 1948 by all three directors:

IT IS HEREBY agreed that the shares of Dr. Gerald B. Gardner added to those held by Edith Woodford-Grimes shall be the same in number as the total of those held by Reginald Wellbye and H. Senior Fothergill, and that the shares to be received from Mr. and Mrs. Powell shall be distributed so as to maintain this parity.

This resulted in a resolution at an Extraordinary General Meeting of the Company on 10th November 1948 when one of Gerald's shares was deemed to have no voting rights.

---

22. Ibid.
23. Ibid.
24. Letter, Rex Wellbye to Gerald Gardner, 20 May 1948.

In mid-November 1948, Gerald went down to Christchurch, staying until after Christmas. He was probably staying with Edith, but he gave as his address Maguire's consulting rooms at 49 High Street, presumably in order to keep Edith's address from Rex.

The arguments between Gerald and Rex continued, however, and in early December, Fothergill wrote a letter to both of them. Part of it states:

> It is most pathetic to me that two people for whom I have a real regard and respect, and both of whom I believe only wish to behave with the utmost integrity, should each suspect either the sanity or the straightforwardness of the other.[25]

He suggested a meeting of all parties, which Rex agreed to, stating:

> The first step must lie with Gerald. I have a fear he may be reluctant, as he has shown a preference for independent action.[26]

He further emphasised the difficulty of his relationship with Gerald:

> G's proneness to take independent action (as from the beginning, when he offered E shares, despite knowing my views); his bad memory (as when he claimed that it was I who offered her them), and his unwillingness to discuss or reconsider any idea he may press upon me, and his general extreme difficulty in understanding business matters - all this makes it quite impossible for me to work with him."[27]

Writing to Gerald, Rex states:

> All this correspondence is just stupid. It not only does not get us anywhere, it actually makes things worse, for after

---

25. Letter, H. Senior Fothergill to Rex Wellbye and Gerald Gardner, 2 December 1948.
26. Letter, Rex Wellbye to H. Senior Fothergill, 3 December 1948.
27. Ibid.

every letter there is more to be cleared up than there was before it was written![28]

Rex's attitude is summed up in a letter that he wrote early the following year:

Reading through G's letter I can't help the impression that he is picturing himself as really the boss, due to his having put in most money.[29]

Gerald wrote to Rex about another naturist club known as Aesculapius, which was reputed to have 800 members, as opposed to less than 100 at Five Acres. In his reply, Rex wrote:

I've talked with one or two people re your envy of the Aesculapians, but so far no one seems to want that sort of crowd. ... If people only come because they are drawn by dancing, and so on, they don't make much of a club. Its quite different if people who have come together for something else get up festivities ...[30]

Several things were happening at the same time during the years immediately following the war, and we will examine these in the next two chapters. We look at Gerald's relationship with John S.M. Ward, the Abbey Folk Park and his acquisition of the Witch's Cottage, and at the various organisations that Gerald was involved in, from the Folk-Lore Society to the Ancient Druid Order.

---

28. Letter, Rex Wellbye to Gerald Gardner, 5 December 1948.
29. Letter, Rex Wellbye to John Pinches, 5 January 1949.
30. Letter, Rex Wellbye to Gerald Gardner, 7 December 1948.

CHAPTER NINETEEN

Folk Park, Church and Cottage

John Sebastian Marlow Ward (1885-1949) was one of those strange characters whose lives intertwined with Gerald's for a while and who influenced him greatly. He was born in British Honduras (now Belize) on 22nd December 1885, the son of an Anglican clergyman, Herbert Marlow Ward.[1] The family returned to England in 1888 and Ward was educated at Collet Court, Merchant Taylors and Charterhouse. He was a graduate in History from Trinity Hall, Cambridge. He had travelled extensively in eastern Asia, became the head of a Church of England school in Burma, and was subsequently Principal Officer of Customs in Lower Burma. During that time, Ward had acquired considerable knowledge of Chinese secret societies and was the co-author of a book which was a standard reference work for many years.[2] In fact, he had over 30 books published on such subjects as mediaeval history and Oriental theology. He returned to England in 1918 and was appointed Director of Intelligence for the Federation of British Industries. He was also a Freemason, according to Tillett[3]

---

1. I am indebted to Keith Chisholm for much of the biographical detail about Ward.
2. J. S. M. Ward and W. G. Stirling, *The Hung Society: or the Society of Heaven and Earth* (Baskerville Press, 1925).
3. Gregory Tillett, "Gerald Gardner: Some Historical Fragments", *The Australian Wiccan*, no. 14, n.d.

"one of the best-known authorities on Freemasonry in England", having written several books on the subject, including *Freemasonry and the Ancient Gods*[4] and *Who was Hiram Abiff?*[5] His brother, Reginald Lucien Ward, was killed in the First World War, and this seems to have started an interest in Spiritualism and led to his books *Gone West*,[6] and *A Subaltern in Spirit Land*,[7] which had a preface by Arthur Conan Doyle.

His first wife having died, Ward married a headmistress, Jessica Page, in April 1927. The following year they both began to have revelations that it was the end of an age and that civilisation was doomed. They had to prepare for the Second Coming of Christ and started to lecture about it.

In early 1929, under the guidance of the 'Angelic Guardian' of this work, they founded the Confraternity of the Kingdom of the Wise, and a book was published that year entitled *The Kingdom of the Wise: Life's Problems*,[8] which detailed their beliefs. Jessica Page became the Reverend Mother and the community changed its name to the Confraternity of Christ the King.

By 1930, they had bought property at 89 Park Road, New Barnet, to the north of London, and had established an Abbey there. This was a rambling old Georgian manor house known as Hadley Hall, in five acres of its own grounds. Initially, it was a lay Order, under the auspices of the Anglican Bishop of St. Albans, and had been dedicated by him on 14th February 1931. To start with, a local clergyman came in on a regular basis to celebrate Communion. The community was, however, somewhat unorthodox, with a number of men and women, including unmarried couples, who had taken religious vows. All possessions had to be handed over to the order, a new name was taken and the community was as self-sufficient as possible. Gerald mentions a revealing aspect:

In the Abbey Church at New Barnet, on the right side of the altar, is a large picture of Christ, and on the left is a large

4. J. S. M. Ward, *Freemasonry and the Ancient Gods*, (Simpkin Marshall, 1921).
5. J. S. M. Ward, *Who was Hiram Abiff?*, (Baskerville Press, 1925).
6. *Gone West: Three Narratives of After-death Experiences Communicated through the Mediumship of J. S. M. Ward*, (Rider, 1917).
7. J. S. M. Ward, *A Subaltern in Spirit Land*, (Rider 1920)
8. Baskerville Press, 1929.
.

picture of the (feminine) Holy Ghost, shown as a woman in white, the White Goddess. The priests of this church told me some years ago that Christ was born of the Father, conceived by the Holy Ghost, and that only a woman could conceive. They had a number of proofs of this being a very ancient doctrine.[9]

The ceremonies were colourful and seemed to lean towards the Greek tradition. This was obviously all too much for the new local vicar, who persuaded the Bishop to withdraw Church of England support and approval. Ward writes that, following its foundation in 1930:

... for five years it had struggled to remain in communion with the Anglican Church. But towards the end of 1934 the Bishop of St. Albans broke the one slender link which connected the Abbey with the Anglican Church by refusing to renew the licence for a Chaplain, on the grounds that the Rev. Father Superior [Ward himself] *had no authority to Minister the Word and yet had done so by Opening the Abbey Church to outsiders.*[10]

Ward was undaunted by this, and the fact that the Bishop's actions, which were seen by Ward as an "attack on the work of the Abbey", were based on the question of "authority" led Ward to "study carefully the whole question of the validity of Anglican Orders and therefore the right of an Anglican Bishop to make such a claim". These investigations led him to the conclusion that:

... in the ecclesiastical sense the Anglican Church has no valid Orders, and therefore no Priests and no Bishops, and that the gentleman who calls himself a Bishop is only a layman given the name of a Bishop by Act of Parliament, and appointed by the State like any other State Official.[11]

9. Gardner, (1959), 58-59.
10. J. S. M. Ward, *The Orthodox Catholic Church in England*, (Showing its History and the Validity of its Orders), (1944), 37-38.
11. Op. cit., 39.

During these investigations Ward had made contact with those who felt the same, as a result of which, he wrote: "At length the Abbey of Christ the King sought union with a branch of the Church which unquestionably had valid Orders, and ultimately, in October 1935, the Abbey joined the Orthodox Catholic Church." This had been established in 1929 under the leadership of John Churchill Sibley. Ward was re-baptised and confirmed by Sibley, admitted to the Minor Orders, ordained Deacon and Priest, consecrated as a Bishop and had conferred on him the office of Chancellor of the Province, all within a few days! Following Sibley's death three years later, Ward was elected Archbishop of the Orthodox Catholic Church on 19th December 1938.

The Orthodox Catholic Church was just one of a variety of separate churches all of which were under the umbrella of what might be called the Old Catholic movement. They had names like The Gnostic Catholic Church, The Ancient Orthodox Catholic Church, The Catholicate of the West, The Independent Catholic Church, The Catholic Apostolic Church, The British Orthodox Catholic Church, The Old Catholic Orthodox Church, The Western Orthodox Catholic Church, The Holy Orthodox Catholic Church of Great Britain and Ireland, The Ancient British Church, The Liberal Catholic Church and The Ancient Universal (Orthodox Catholic) Church. And these are just a few of them. In fact, some were alternative names for the same organisation, though there were still quite a lot of them.

It all started in the 18th Century when the Pope suspended the Bishop of Utrecht for supporting the views of Bishop Jansenius, which were contrary to the opinions of certain Roman theologians of the day. The rift resulted in the formation of the Old Roman Catholic Church of Holland, which believed that it embodied the true Catholic tradition as against the Roman church which had introduced innovations of doctrine and discipline. Such a movement was strengthened by reactions to the dogma of Papal Infallibility, which was introduced following the first Vatican Council in 1870. The Old Catholic movement admitted only Jesus Christ as the infallible Head of the Church.

According to Morgan Davis,[12] other characteristics of the Old Catholic movement were that services were held in the vernacular rather than in Latin, there was no fasting or confession, there were fewer compulsory feast days and the sacraments of Eucharist and Baptism were elevated above the others.

In time, various different churches grew up within the Old Catholic movement, each with their own distinctive lines of Apostolic Succession derived from a variety of different traditions dating back to the Patriarchs of Antioch, the Armenian Church and other historical lines. There seems to have been something of an obsession with Apostolic Succession among these men (no women are ever mentioned!), with the same names cropping up time and time again. However, I will limit my own enquiry to the extent to which Gerald was involved.

Gerald's Library[13] contains a diploma dated 29th August 1946 ordaining Gerald "to the Holy Office of Priest of the Ancient British Church". It is signed by Dorian, Bishop of Caerleon and witnessed by W. Ohly and M.S. Sanders. Tillett, who had been investigating Ward, seems to confirm this when he writes:

> ...*amongst the signatures on one document from 1946 was that of one "Gerald Brosseau Gardner, Priest, Ancient British Church". Gardner was a regular visitor to the Abbey, and frequently appeared wearing a clerical collar...*

What was all this about? Why was Gerald, who was supposed to have been initiated as a witch in 1939, becoming ordained as a priest? And what was the Ancient British Church?

To try to answer this, we must imagine Gerald's situation in the immediate post-War period. He had just moved back to London and, for the first time for several years, was not in day-to-day contact with Edith. He was the sort of person who always wanted to explore new things and over his life he joined a variety of societies. He had met Ward some time between 1936 and 1939. With his interest in museums, particularly of the progressive sort, Gerald

12. Morgan Davis, *From Man to Witch: Gerald Gardner 1946-1949*, (www.geraldgardner.com 2002).

13. www.newwiccanchurch.org/gglibrary/index.htm

could well have heard about the Folk Park which Ward had set up and decided to pay it a visit. Then again, with his interest in Freemasonry he may also have read some of Ward's books, particularly *Freemasonry and the Ancient Gods*. Gerald had certainly met him by early 1939, as he mentions him as having examined a collection of witchcraft relics in Gerald's possession in an article which appeared in *Folk-Lore* later that year.[14]

On his return to London, Gerald would undoubtedly have re-established his pre-war friendship with Ward and, very easily, been drawn into the various activities Ward was involved with, most obviously the museum and exhibits, but also his other interests such as freemasonry and folklore. Ward would undoubtedly have talked to Gerald about the Old Catholic movement and the various churches of which he was a member. As we have seen, in their desire for valid and unchallengeable Apostolic Succession, they became inextricably intertwined, with the same individuals being ordained in some cases into several different Old Catholic churches.

Joanne Pearson is quite clear that "... contrary to claims made by Davis, he [Ward] did not ordain Gardner".[15] She adds a footnote to the effect that Gerald did own a copy of the "Liturgy of the Orthodox Catholic Church in England" which was published in 1938. That copy, which is now in the Toronto collection, is annotated with notes in Gerald's handwriting which make it quite clear that he was learning how to perform the ritual. Even though he was not ordained by Ward, he may have been working towards it but circumstances intervened to prevent it.

Probably initially because of its name, Gerald was attracted to the Ancient British Church. This was the second organisation of that name and was in the charge of Dorian, Bishop of Caerleon. It seemed particularly willing to accommodate those from a wide range of religious backgrounds within its fold. For example, Dorian seems to have established the Fellowship of the Holy Grail, of which he was the Prior. It was stated to function "within the jurisdiction of the restored Ancient British Church" and not in any way subject to the authority of the Church of England, the Roman Catholic Church or any other Christian Communion.

---

14. G B Gardner, *Collectanea: Witchcraft: Folk-Lore*, 50 (June 1939), 188-190.
15. Joanne Pearson, *Wicca and the Christian Heritage*, (Routledge, 2007), 50.

One of the purposes of the Fellowship is described as the "unity around the Holy Chalice of all, irrespective of religious attachments, or differences of philosophic or doctrinal interpretation". This is emphasised by the requirements for Associate Membership:

> *It matters not ... whether you be a Roman Catholic, Freemason, Anglo-Catholic, Protestant, Orthodox, Nonconformist, Trinitarian, Unitarian, Jew, Literalist, Rationalist, or whether you are a member of a non-christian religion; provided that you can conscientiously declare that you acknowledge THE ONE TRUE GOD, and are prepared to share the common Chalice of holy brotherhood you may, at least, become an Associate of the Fellowship of the Holy Grail.[16]*

Much is made, however, of ordination:

> *The Royal Priesthood (Keeper of the Temple) is inherent in every soul, and is not necessarily the prerogative of a specially privileged professional class of persons. ... application may be made by Members (not by Associates) of the Fellowship of the Holy Grail ... for appropriate Ordination for the exercise of the religious offices or services in their respective private oratories or public chapels.[17]*

It is further stated that, as well as Associates, the Fellowship is composed of:

> *Members, being those who, by making the Caerleon Declaration, voluntarily enter into full communion with the restored Ancient British Church. Each member has the privilege of recognition, under Charter of the Bishop of Caerleon, of his, or her, individual (a) cell for study, (b) private oratory, (c) (in the case of those ordained) chapel for public devotions.[18]*

Gerald must clearly have accepted this in order to be ordained. Why was he ordained? I think he probably looked upon

---

16. *Fellowship of the Holy Grail*, (British Church, n.d.).
17. Ibid.
18. Ibid.

it as rather a status symbol. Indeed, expanding on Tillett's state-ment above, I have no evidence that Gerald took an active part in any of these churches.

⁂

Ward's most lasting legacy was undoubtedly the Abbey Folk Park. The idea of a folk park had long been discussed in museum circles, but following a decision by The Chapter of the Abbey of Christ the King to make this its educational work, progress was rapid. Eveline Marlowe has defined it as follows:

> *A Folk Park is a kind of open air museum which sets out to show the evolution of the everyday life of the folk or people of a country. In the grounds are erected old buildings or replicas of old buildings, which are then furnished appro-priately.*[19]

This is all very familiar to us and there is now a multitude of excellent examples to visit. But it was all very new in the early 1930s. There were examples in Scandinavia and America, but, when the Abbey Folk Park opened on 28th June 1934, it was reputed to be the first in the whole of the British Empire.

Ward was very much a pioneer in the rescue and subsequent conservation of historic buildings of all types. Whenever he heard about an old building which was about to be demolished, several members of the community would arrange to dismantle the build-ing carefully, numbering all the pieces, and re-erect it in the grounds of the Abbey. The same with furniture and other antiques, on which Ward was an expert. He attended auctions all over Eng-land, often obtaining pieces for a lot less than their true value.

When fully operational, the Folk Park consisted of a range of buildings and displays from prehistoric to Victorian times, all fur-nished to provide an idea of what life was like in the period con-cerned. We are so familiar with this approach, adopted by virtually every present-day museum, that it is difficult to appreci-ate the impact which the Abbey Folk Park had in its day. It

---

19. Eveline Marlowe, "Barnet's Folk Park", *Hertforshire Countryside,* (1981), 32.

attracted crowds of visitors, including coachloads of school parties, Prime Ministers (unspecified) and even Queen Elizabeth II
as a young girl.

Ward had constructed the likeness of a prehistoric village,
with examples of a Magdalenian Hunting Lodge, a Neolithic Pit-
dwelling, a Lake Dwelling and Bronze Age and Iron Age huts.
Doubtless much speculation was involved, but for the time, and
on a limited budget, it was undoubtedly an amazing achievement. The most prominent building on the site was The Abbey
Church which was used for several years as the chapel for the
Abbey. It was originally a 13th Century tithe barn from Birching-
ton in Kent. Other buildings and displays included a 16th Century
Armourer's Shop, an Elizabethan bedroom, a 17th Century Pottery Shop, an Apothecary's, a Jacobean dining room, an 18th Century weaver's shop, a Victorian jeweller's, a Carriage Shed and
Harness Shop, and a wheelwright's shop and smithy.

By 1936[20] there was also a 16th Century witch's cottage. It
started life somewhere in the vicinity of Ledbury in Hereford-
shire. In the early 1930s it was in use as an apple store on a large
farm. Ward had furnished it appropriately. He says of it:

*A most interesting building this, of half-timber work,
thatched with reeds and with a central hearth and a louvre
instead of a chimney. It is furnished with the pottery and
furniture of the period and all the appurtenances of a witch,
including blasting rods, magic staff, dowsing rod, and the
like.*[21]

Arthur Mee adds the further bizarre details that it had: "... a
stuffed crocodile and other monsters hanging from the beams, and,
of course, the witch's broom."[22] In another article, Ward adds:

*... all the furniture is of the sixteenth century. Hanging from
walls and roof are weird emblems and the grim implements*

20. Jennie Cobban, "The Witch's Cottage (Part I)", *Hendon and District Archaeological Society Newsletter* 245, (1991).
21. J. S. M. Ward, "The Abbey Folk Park, New Barnet", *East Herts Archaeological Society
Transactions*, Vol. IX, Part III, (1936), 320.
22. Arthur Mee, *The King's England: Hertfordshire*, (Hodder and Stoughton, 1939), 77.

*of her trade: a stuffed crocodile, a human skull on a shelf,
the magic staff, blasting rods, the sword of exorcism and
the Magic Circle on the floor.*[23]

The Folk Park had stayed open throughout the war, although
the number of members of the community gradually diminished.
In early 1945, however, Ward was in trouble. He was being sued
by an irate father, Stanley Lough, who claimed that Ward and his
wife had enticed his 16-year-old daughter, Dorothy, away from
her family to live in the Abbey. The court case took place over a
period of 11 days in May 1945 .[24] Although it seems clear from the
evidence that Dorothy was acting of her own free will, the judge
found against Ward, awarding Mr. Lough £500 damages and
granting an injunction restraining the defendants from continuing to harbour Dorothy Lough. In his judgement, Mr. Justice Cas-
sels did say that he "… realized that such an award was probably
a mere formality, because the defendants had put it out of their
power to possess so sordid a thing as money."[25] However, Keith
Chisholm informs me that: "Ward was, by design, a bankrupt
when judgement was delivered against him in court and was
hence unable to personally pay the £500 ordered - although it
may subsequently have been paid by the Trustees of the Confraternity."[26] The only way that these damages, plus costs, could be
paid was to put the Abbey and contents up for sale, the liabilities
being discharged in September 1945.[27]

In fact, it seems quite likely that Gerald would have at least
contemplated acquiring the whole of the Folk Park as he almost
certainly by this time had the idea of running a museum himself,
partly inspired by the example of Ward and partly by his long-
standing passion for collecting artifacts. However, his interests
seem to have been more specifically witchcraft and magical practice and so he limited himself to the Witch's Cottage, which he
had probably coveted for some years.

---

23. J. S. M. Ward, "Homes of Our Ancestors From Mud Hut to Victorian Parlour", *Homes and Gardens,* (August 1939) xviii.

24. *The Times,* Law Reports, 1st-5th, 8th, 11th, 12th, 15th, 16th and 19th May and 20th September 1945.

25. *The Times,* Law Report, 19th May 1945.

26. Email Keith Chisholm to the author, 1 April 2002.

27. *The Times,* 20 September 1945.

Michael Strong describes the end of the Folk Park:

Broken in health and by adverse publicity, as well as a mounting financial debt due to court costs, Ward began to dismember his enormous collection. A small selection was packed away in crates and the remainder including many of the larger and most important items, dispersed to dealers and other museums.[28]

Ward pondered on the possibility of moving to Canada, but this proved impracticable without adequate resources. Gerald suggested that the plot of land that he had bought in Cyprus might be suitable and he made a deal with Ward whereby Gerald acquired the Witch's Cottage in exchange for the land in Cyprus. Ward liked this suggestion. He was in sympathy with the beliefs and rituals of the Greek Orthodox Church, which was the predominant Church in Cyprus. Baker notes that: "On 13 July 1946, the Reverend Father, Reverend Mother and the more devoted of their followers disappeared from New Barnet, without informing anybody but a few intimate friends".[29] Edith Cuffe told me that Gerald: "... apparently had connections and arranged with someone in Customs for the Community and their museum collections to leave England on the same boat in 1946".[30]

The land at Gastria in Cyprus was totally unsuitable for the community. It turned out to be a fisherman's hut on a pebble beach. The Confraternity sold it, with Gerald's encouragement, almost immediately for £800 and bought a small block of land with a mudbrick house, an outside domed oven and a few olive trees along the south coast from Limassol. This was where Ward died in 1949.[31]

The Folk Park was offered to Ward's friend, William Ohly, who founded a museum and art centre. The museum opened in March 1947, with Cottie Burland as the Honorary Curator. Ohly was one of the witnesses to Gerald's ordination as a Priest of the Ancient British Church in August 1946.

꧁꧂

28. M. Strong, "Custodian of the Past", *Australian Collectors Quarterly*, (November 1991), 78.
29. Antony R. Baker, "The Scholar the Builders Rejected: The Life and Work of J.S.M. Ward", *Transactions of Quatuor Coronati Lodge*, Vol. 116, (2003), 127-192.
30. Email, Edith Cuffe to the author, 2 October 2006.
31. Ibid.

As soon as Gerald heard that Ward was having to sell the Folk Park, in the summer of 1945, he probably expressed interest in the Witch's Cottage, with the hope in the back of his mind that he could use it for witchcraft rituals. Ward was probably only too pleased to 'offload' it, or let it go to a 'good home', and so was delighted when Gerald offered his land in Cyprus in exchange.

I do not really know when the cottage was moved from New Barnet to Bricket Wood. The court case awarding costs against Ward ended on 18th May 1945 and the liabilities were discharged by 19th September that year. It seems as if Ohly allowed Gerald to keep the Witch's cottage in situ from the time when he acquired it legally, probably June 1945. This was the time when Gerald was interested in the Ancient British Church, having been ordained in August 1946, and he may have used the cottage as a "chapel for public devotions" for members of the Ancient British Church or associated organisations. His American niece, Miriam ('Mimi') stayed with Gerald and Donna while she was attending school in London for a year in 1946, and she told Morgan Davis: "He had a little Witch's Cottage set up, as a matter of fact, with the Greek Orthodox reform group (this is how Miriam identified Ward's group)."[32]

But Gerald was then faced with the problem of dismantling the cottage, finding some land on which it could be re-erected, transporting it and then reconstructing it - a major undertaking. I imagine that he had in mind some land at Five Acres and he immediately asked Rex for the area of fairly dense woodland, known as 'the Bulge', approximately half an acre in extent, close to the entrance to the site on Oakwood Road. Certainly in Gerald's eyes (and, it must be said, those of many others), the land and the cottage were clearly meant for each other.

The winter of 1946-1947 was the most severe in living memory, with snow on the ground until April. I am sure that Gerald would have wanted to have "wintered abroad", as he had done before the war, but travel was very difficult in the immediate post-war period and I doubt whether he went anywhere, particularly as he attended the January and February 1947 meetings of the Folk-Lore Society. A vivid picture of Gerald at this period is provided by Mimi, who told Davis: "... my uncle ... was usually

---

32. Email, Morgan Davis to the author, 10 February 2002.

fully clothed in about fifty things of clothing because he was freezing to death!"[33]

Whilst the cottage was probably moved from Barnet to Bricket Wood in late 1946, there are rumours of the timbers lying around for months waiting to be re-erected. Contact with a waterlogged ground and a cover of snow-drifts would hardly have helped the condition of the timbers. It was probably not until May 1947 that the cottage was re-erected. In doing so, the building was "modified" to some extent, partly on purpose and partly by accident.

The cottage originally had wattle and daub infill panels of the traditional sort, and it seems likely that Ward replicated this when the cottage was re-erected at the Folk Park. The roof was thatched with reeds, but had a louvre rather than a chimney, above a central hearth.

I doubt whether there was a lot of supervision in the process of demolition and re-erection, certainly not on Gerald's part. Some at least of the timbers were numbered but by its very nature none of the wattle-and-daub panelling could be re-used, and nor could the roofing thatch. When it was re-erected there was likely to have been no-one around with the necessary skills to re-create the wattle-and-daub panels. So Gerald replaced them with concrete panels, which was really the only practicable solution at the time. He got the outside cement rendered and the interior whitewashed.

With regard to the roof, thatching would have been an expensive process, even if he could get someone to do it, and I think Gerald decided against re-thatching the cottage and opted to use second-hand clay tiles instead. These were available in large numbers relatively cheaply from buildings in nearby London that had been damaged or destroyed by bombing during the war. They would also comply more readily with the fire regulations.

The windows were diagonally leaded lights, one large one in the gable-end elevation and several smaller ones along the walls. The timbers were painted black. The door, of solid oak, is reputed to be from the old St. Albans Gaol, which was in the Abbey Gateway until the new prison on Grimston Road was built in 1867. At what stage it was acquired, and by whom, is not known.

---

33. Email, Morgan Davis to the author, 10 February 2002.

The cottage was nearing completion towards the end of May, as a memo from Rex to members of the committee, Gerald, John Pinches and Boris Stelp, refers to: "… Gerald's suggestion for a Midsummer Eve's "do" round his Witches Hut to give it a house-warming."[34] Rex wrote further in a rather tongue-in-cheek tone: "Hope you will be present next weekend - - I expect you know we plan midsummer day revels combined with housewarming party of the Witches Hut, and Gerald is getting up rites and cere-monies, incantations and, I believe, a human sacrifice."[35] Rex was obviously rather amused, or bemused, by Gerald's activities, as the reference to human sacrifice shows! Exactly what the rites, ceremonies and incantations consisted of I do not know, but I would imagine that they would mostly be from such books as *The Key of Solomon*. I also do not know whether, in mid 1947, he would have had anyone to help him. If so, they would be likely to be other members of Five Acres and other naturist clubs in the vicinity, such as Arnold Crowther, Mary Dowding, Eda Collins and Ross Nichols. I am fairly sure that at that stage there wasn't a coven centred on Five Acres.

To those who are at all familiar with books, articles and tele-vision programmes on witchcraft over the last 40 years, the half-timbered cottage in the middle of the wood has taken on an almost iconic quality. Those who have seen its image have often said that it's what a witches' meeting place *should* be like. To quote Ronald Hutton: "Until the reality of the New Forest coven or of any earlier group is securely established, this spot in Hert-fordshire is the best-documented place on earth to bear the name of the birthplace of modern pagan witchcraft".[36]

The cottage has played an important role in the history of the modern witchcraft revival and, for that reason alone, is worthy of preservation. It is good to be able to report that it is currently being renovated and there are hopes that it will eventually be capable of being used by Craft members again.

Gerald probably used the cottage to sleep in when staying at Five Acres. Several more recent commentators, such as Patricia

34. Memorandum from Rex Wellbye, 28 May 1947.
35. Letter from Rex Wellbye to 'Ernest', 16 June 1947.
36. Ronald Hutton, *The Triumph of the Moon*, (Oxford, 1999), 214.

Crowther and Lois Bourne have mentioned the presence of a four-poster bed in the cottage, only used, in their experience, for the depositing of coats. Could this, however, have dated back to the time when Gerald might have used the cottage to stay overnight, even if only in the summer? In the 1947/48 period accommodation at Five Acres seemed to be limited to members' caravans and, rather than go to the expense of acquiring a caravan, I suspect that Gerald made use of what he had - the cottage - as soon as it had been reassembled on his own land.

It has long been rumoured that Gerald registered the cottage as a place of worship under the name of the 'Ancient British Church'. This idea probably originates from an article which appeared in early 1959:

> ... *they have had the effrontery to register their temple as a place of worship. I have seen the form sent to the local Registrar in St. Albans. It describes the cottage in Bricket Wood as "The Ancient British Church" and the "congregation" as "undenominational".*37

On the face of it this seems fairly specific and likely. The Registration would have been under the provisions of the Places of Worship Registration Act 1855. However, when I approached the local Superintendent Registrar's office, neither they nor the Office of National Statistics38 had any record of such registration.

Perhaps the form was never sent. Or perhaps the publicity caused by the newspaper articles resulted in the application being withdrawn or turned down. In any case, the relevant point here was Gerald's intention, which I think was merely that he liked the name "Ancient British Church". He was no longer (if he ever had been) actively involved in the Church, but thought it a good "cover" for the witchcraft activity which was going on there, or that he hoped would be going on there in the near future. For Gerald, I think that after a while, the name "Ancient British Church" lost all its original associations and was merely another, slightly humorous, name for witchcraft.

---

37. Peter Bishop, "'Now I will lose my job' says girl who revels in nude rites", *The People*, 11 January 1959.
38. Email from Lesley Barton of the Office of National Statistics to the author, 22 October 2001.

CHAPTER TWENTY

An Environment of Ideas

Gerald was never the sort of person to limit himself to one particular philosophical path. His mercurial personality was such that he was open to inspiration from a variety of sources. And certainly witchcraft, which appeared to him to be mostly practised by a few elderly individuals in the Highcliffe area, was not enough on its own to hold his enthusiasm when he was away from there. Following his initiation, he continued his long-held interests in anthropology, archaeology and folklore and sought out books, groups and individuals who were concerned with subjects which threw a light on witchcraft, such as magic, unorthodox religious movements, spiritualism and psychic research. Having returned by 1945 to the heart of occult and other activities in London, Gerald clearly participated fully, not just in the Five Acres Club but in a range of organisations, most of which were associated, even if distantly, with witchcraft.

One path that has parallels with witchcraft is Druidry. Gerald had undoubtedly read about the ancient Druids and their modern revival and this attracted his attention. From what he had heard about them they had a similar philosophy to the witches but with more of the grand ritual that he so liked.

Whilst it is uncertain when Gerald became involved, he had ample opportunity to meet Druids. The first definite date we have for his involvement is December 1946, but as early as 1938 at the Crotona Fellowship gatherings in Christchurch, he had met Irene Lyon Clark, who was a prominent member of the Ancient Druid Order. By 1940, he was friendly with Mary Dowding, who later became a member of the Order of Bards, Ovates and Druids (OBOD).

Modern Druidry is a re-creation of the ancient Celtic mystery tradition of poetic inspiration, divination and sacred mythology. What has been called the Druidic Revival began in the late 17th and early 18th Centuries, when small groups began to arise spontaneously. Several different Druidic traditions developed.

The Order that Gerald became involved with was the Ancient Druid Order, otherwise known as An Druidh Uileach Braithreachas, the British Circle of the Universal Bond, or simply The Druid Order. The Order started to claim in the 1950s that it originated in 1717 and produced a list of "Chosen Chiefs" which included such notables as William Stukeley and William Blake, but the Order probably only started in 1909 when George Watson MacGregor Reid became Chief.[1] He was a naturopath by profession and Editor of *The Nature Cure* journal. He travelled in India and elsewhere and incorporated Hindu and Buddhist concepts into Druid rituals, translated into a Western form.

The alternative title of The Universal Bond was introduced by Reid as a reflection of his strong universalist beliefs, which emphasise the similarities between world religions, the recognition of value in all religions and denial of the doctrine that one had to choose between them. Ever since knowledge of Eastern religions had been brought to the West in the early 19th Century there had been a growing recognition of this, culminating in the formation of the Theosophical Society in 1875. As Ithell Colquhoun writes: "Perhaps more ardently than the Theosophical Society itself, the Universal Bond desired the union of East and West: a Druidism stretching from the Celtic Fringe to Persia, India and beyond."[2] This approach is undoubtedly one

---

1. Email, Ronald Hutton to the author, 11 May 2009.
2. Ithell Colquhoun, *Sword of Wisdom*, (Neville Spearman, 1975), 124.

about which Gerald would have been enthusiastic, in view of his experiences in the East and his contacts with Buddhism and various native traditions.

MacGregor-Reid died in 1946. His son, Robert, was persuaded to put himself forward and was installed as Chosen Chief at the Winter Solstice 1946. There were 17 members present at that meeting, which was held at Leamington Spa,3 one of whom was Gerald Gardner. Whether Gerald was formally on the Council I do not know. I suspect that the meeting was open to all members and that all those present signed. As well as Gerald, these included R.J. Innis, W. Bromley, Ivy Arthur, H. Chellew, J.C. Duncan, Pat Soul, Marie Soul, Lyon Clarke, C. Trelawny, William Evans, C.D. Boltwood, John Clee, R. Millard and H. Neil. Also present was Anne MacGregor Reid, who is described as "the oldest living member of the Mother Lodge GAIRDEACHAS".4 At least two of the individuals on that list had links with Gerald in ways other than Druidry.

Irene Margaret Lyon Clark (1899-1947) could well have been the first member of the Ancient Druid Order that Gerald met, for she had been an active member of the Crotona Fellowship, performing in several of their plays and designing and making most of their costumes. She had been born Irene Margaret Guy on 28th November 1899, at Walsingham in Norfolk, the daughter of the schoolmaster, William Guy. Until she moved into a bungalow which was built for her near the Rosicrucian Theatre at Somerford, she had lived at Ballard Lodge, New Milton, possibly in association with the school at Great Ballard. During her time with the Crotona Fellowship she wrote a series of articles for the local paper on "Literary Links with Christchurch".5 Less than a year after the Winter Solstice 1946 meeting, however, she died in Ipswich in December 1947 at the comparatively young age of 48. Gareth Medway has pointed out that the 1951 issue of the Druid magazine *The Double Circle* was dedicated "to the memory of our esteemed companion Irene Margaret Lyon Clarke [sic]".6

---

3. Gareth Medway informs me that the meeting was held at 57 The Parade, Leamington Spa, probably in an apartment above the hairdressing salon run by Miss Allan Steer, who chaired the meeting.

4. Letter, Gareth Medway to the author, 29 November 2002.

5. Irene Lyon Clark, 'Literary Links with Christchurch", *Christchurch Times*, 2nd, 9th and 16th October 1937.

6. Gareth Medway, *The Ancient Druid Order: a Preliminary Survey*, (unpublished manuscript).

Charles Dennis Boltwood (1889-1985) was another of the sig-
natories at the Winter Solstice 1946 meeting. His Druid name was
"Wayland". He had also been consecrated a Bishop in the Ancient
British Church and it is thus highly likely that Gerald would have
got to know him through his friendship with J.S.M. Ward, any
time from 1936 onwards.

Gerald seemed to relish the midsummer rituals at Stonehenge
after they had been started up again in 1946 after the war. He
probably attended them each year, and we certainly know of
three which he went to. A booklet published in 1951, which is
described as a Festival Souvenir Brochure and had the alternative
titles *Stonehenge and the Druids* and *The Double Circle* contains a
description of the midsummer ritual which took place at Stonehenge that year, some time after the solstice, on the weekend of
9th-10th July. This seems to have been because the Ancient Order
of Druid Hermetists had booked the actual solstice with Stonehenge's owners, the Ministry of Works.7 The booklet states:

> *The Noon Ceremony saw the arrival of the delegates from
> the Isle of Man led by Dr. C. [sic] B. Gardner, carrying the
> ancient sword and oak leaf crown which he had constructed
> himself; he was in Scottish attire.*

The oakleaf crown (or wreath) is mentioned in Ross Nichols'
description of the 1946 ritual, so it had obviously become traditional (as it still is in midsummer celebrations for many Wiccan
and pagan groups today). Ronald Hutton informs me that "... it was
donned in succession by every full member of the order present at
Stonehenge at the summer solstice, as a sign of the essential
democracy of the order (so that all wore the crown as equals)".8

The sword which Gerald brought was apparently of a size
which fitted exactly into a cleft in the Heel Stone, from which it
was pulled out as part of the Noon ceremony. This obviously
made him feel an important part of the whole process, not that
he was only invited because of his sword! In 1959, the American
writer, Daniel Mannix visited Gerald in his museum on the Isle of

---

7. Email, Ronald Hutton to the author, 11 May 2009.
8. Ibid.

Man. In a subsequent article he wrote that Gerald had told him about a "very fine ritual sword" which they had lent to the Druid Order "for their annual midsummer ceremony at Stonehenge because it fits exactly into the cleft of the Hele Stone".9 The Museum Guide published the previous year, in 1958, says of the former owner of some objects in a display case:

> *She had a very fine ritual sword, which for many years was lent to the Druid Order which holds the annual Midsummer ceremony at Stonehenge, because it fitted exactly into the cleft in the Hele Stone.*10

In late April 1951, Gerald wrote in a letter to Cecil Williamson:

> *"The Druids wrote as they* [want] *me to come to Stonehenge this Midsummer + they hinted they could borrow the Sword and Bugle again. I wrote telling them of the Museum, saying the sword was a Witch sword, but I thought the museum would lend it for the occasion. Had no answer so far. I expect it gave them a scare. I know its the only one that exactly fits the hole in the stone + it has a sheath, + they must have a sheath for the ceremony."*

We know from the extract from *The Double Circle* which I quoted above that Gerald did indeed lend the sword again in 1951, and in fact took it himself. The quotations sound very much as if lending the sword had, contrary to the impression given in the museum guide, not been a regular event and that perhaps it had only been lent for the first time the previous year, at any rate *by Gerald*. The phrase "for many years" in the 1958 guidebook may have merely indicated the nine or ten years since Gerald had started lending it. We will examine the various possibilities for the identity of the previous owner of the sword in due course, but it is of interest as a definite link between Gerald and the Ancient Druid Order.

The sword is still in existence. It is in the possession of the North London coven that is the direct descendant and continuation of

---

9. Daniel P Mannix, "Witchcraft's Inner Sanctum", *True Magazine* (August 1959), 78.
10. G. B. Gardner, *The Museum of Magic and Witchcraft: The Story of the Famous Witches' Mill at Castletown, Isle of Man,* (Photochrom 1958), 17.

Gerald's original coven at Bricket Wood and who used to meet in the Witches' Cottage there prior to 1963. This coven knows little about the sword, apart from the legend that it was Dafo's, which seems to me to be an indication that it was in all likelihood passed on to Gerald by Edith but I suspect that it was not originally owned by her. All that was known for certain was that it has been in the possession of the coven since Gerald Gardner was a member.

The sword has had three stages of development. The blade is the oldest, probably from a 19th Century officer's sword, which has been remade with a new hilt and pommel, based on the design in *The Key of Solomon*. Subsequently, the symbol of the Wiccan third degree had been cut into the pommel. The design based on *The Key of Solomon* suggests that the sword was remade by or for someone who was involved in ceremonial magic or with a magical order such as the Golden Dawn, probably, in view of the method used to grind the blade, in the early 20th Century. As Gareth Medway says:

> *... this sword was certainly made in accordance with the instructions in the Mathers version of the Key: Mathers included a cross piece with two crescent moon shapes, which is not in any of the manuscripts he used, and was presumably his own innovation; so the sword cannot therefore have been made earlier than 1888.*

Meetings of the Folk-Lore Society recommenced in 1945 and Gerald thereafter attended fairly frequently, except during his annual 'wintering abroad', until 1959. The Society still possesses the attendance book in which members and visitors "signed in" at each meeting. This reveals not only which meetings Gerald attended, but also an indication of who arrived with whom, and therefore possible friendships and acquaintances. On the basis of this, I think it likely that Elspeth Begg, Jacintha Buddicom, M.M. Banks, C. Ouless and Sydney Carter were particular friends of Gerald. However, he also clearly knew quite well several other influential members of the Society including Walter Hildburgh and Margaret Murray.

Gerald wrote on various topics for the *Folk-Lore* journal, including 'The Hazel as a Weapon',[11] but he gave only one lecture during the twenty years he was attending the Society's meetings. This was on Wednesday 19th June 1946 at 21 Bedford Square, London, when he spoke on "Art Magic and Talismans". We do not have a report of the meeting, but four years previously he had an article on the subject published in *Folk-Lore*[12] and I think I may have located his notes for the talk.

Gerald started by remarking that, in his experience, charms, amulets and talismans have been used quite commonly in the East, but those using them did not usually talk to Europeans about them. He defined them as "objects specially made or assumed naturally to possess certain powers to avert danger, to protect against disease, to guard against material influences and their accompanying dangers, supernatural influences for evil such as witchcraft and generally to bring luck to their owner". This is interesting in that he refers to witchcraft in a negative sense, equating it with something evil. He was obviously at this stage not being open with his audience about being a witch himself and was prepared to make what is a disparaging statement about the Craft. Whether by 1946, when he gave his talk, he was able to be more open, I do not know.

The talismans used to illustrate the article are clearly based on illustrations in Barrett's *Magus* and appear later in substantially the same form in the endpapers to Gerald's novel *High Magic's Aid*. How Gerald came by them is interesting: one, "made for a Jupiter subject" he bought in Bournemouth and one was "borrowed from a shop in Christchurch". The following may well refer to one of his witch friends:

> *I know of one belonging to a lady friend, it is some sort of crystal, cut into all sorts of queer irregular facets, it is of such a shape and size, that it could not possibly be worn. It was given to her by a friend who had it especially made for her at a place in London, where she understands, this work*

11. G. B. Gardner, "The Hazel as a Weapon", *Folk Lore*, Vol. 55, No 4, (December 1944), 177.
12. G. B. Gardner, "British Charms, Amulets and Talismans", *Folk-Lore*, Vol. 53, No. 2, (30th June 1942), 95-103.

*is a speciality. I presume each facet has its meaning. It is
the odd or rare, certainly. I have not seen anything like it
before and should very much welcome information as to the
system on which the cutting of the facets is done, so as to
apply to the individual owner. The same lady showed me a
tiny gold hand, in the shape of the Horns of Power. It is
probably of Italian origin, but as she told me that her father
always carried it and firmly believed that it warded off all
sorts of harm and brought him good luck, perhaps we may
call it a British charm.*[13]

Only fifteen people signed in for the talk, rather fewer than
normal, but Gerald seems to have rounded up his friends and rel-
atives, including Donna, who didn't usually attend, Donna's stepmother, Ida Rosedale and his American niece, Mimi, who at the
time was at school in London and staying with the Gardners.
There was also Betty Lumsden Milne, who had edited *Keris and
Other Malay Weapons* for Gerald back in 1936. She was still obviously in contact with him and living sufficiently near London to
attend the meeting.

Gerald was elected to the Folk-Lore Society's Council in February 1946 and attended its first meeting the following month.
However, he did not take a particularly active part in the Council's activities, attending only 36 of the 97 meetings held between
1946 and 1959.

This is typical of Gerald and is repeated several times in his
life: the enthusiastic taking on of status and imagined honours
which, when it comes to work, responsibility and commitment, is
plainly not sustained for very long.

In May 1947, the Council considered a letter from M. André
Varagnac informing them that an International Institute of
Archaeo-Culture had been established to "cover the field of
research where archaeology, the history of religion and folk-lore
meet". He also told them that an International Conference of
Folk-Lore was to be held in Paris on 12th and 13th July. Whilst the
Council was somewhat equivocal and decided not to commit
itself to the Institute, Gerald announced that he would attend the

---

13, Op. cit., 103.

proposed conference. After giving a report on the conference at the November 1947 Council meeting, Gerald was appointed at the June 1948 meeting the official representative of the Society at the follow-up Congress on Folk-lore, Ethnography and Archaeocivilisation that was to take place in Paris the following month.

At the October 1953 meeting, the Council considered a letter from UNESCO asking for nominations for a conference on folklore which was to be held in Brazil in September 1954. Gerald said that he would be willing to go at his own expense but that he was not well-informed on the subjects of discussion at the congress. It was also reported that Miss Alford was suitable, and willing to go, but could not afford the cost. What was decided is not clear, but Gerald mentions the meeting in a letter to Cecil Williamson:

> By the way, I have been asked to go as one of the two Delegates from Great Britain to the Big Conference at S. Paulo in Brazil, + there is a small joke connected with this. Miss Alford + myself were nominated but she wrote saying Belgium had cleaned her out + she couldnt afford it, + did not attend the meeting. At the meeting, the Rev. Professor James spoke long + loudly. "Miss Alford must be persuaded to go. She must be helped. She must be there as she speaks Spanish." No one said anything, then I was asked. I said "my Portuguese is rusty, but I think I can brush it up." (The Rev. Proff. James no longer loves me). If you don't see the joke, Gwen will tell you."[14]

In the end, however, Gerald did not, in fact, go to the conference. Whether Miss Alford went, I do not know.

Members of the Council soon became rather sceptical about Gerald, and particularly of his claimed academic degrees, as, incidentally, did members of other societies as well, and we have already seen Gerald's response to John Yeowell asking him about his degree. Katherine Briggs told James W Baker that:

> Gardner, although recognized as possessing a wide if miscellaneous knowledge of anthropological literature, was notorious as a flamboyant crank who would bring imposing

---

14. Letter, Gerald Gardner to Cecil Williamson, 30 October 1952.

knives to meetings (which intimidated some people) and Miss Briggs was rather sharp about his influence on "young people". She was firm in her opinion that it was all "moonshine".[15]

It has been mentioned to me that Gerald was also in the habit of passing round photographs of naked young ladies, which evoked some disapproval in certain quarters!

Frank Smyth[16] points out that, despite Gerald having been a member of the Society's Council for 18 years, its journal did not publish any obituary for him. One reason was given by Christina Hole, a former editor of the journal:

Dr Gardner had a very curious personality. It did not inspire confidence - at least not in me, nor in a number of people interested in witchcraft and kindred matters. His theories were in themselves somewhat peculiar. I remember a meeting when the composition of the Council for the following year was discussed, and the question was raised as to whether his presence on our Council was really advantageous to the Society. Nothing was done about it, and his name was allowed to go forward as before, but the doubt was clearly felt and expressed.[17]

The Council did, however, stand in memory of Gerald, whose death had just been announced, at its meeting on 19th February 1964.

If the Society was sometimes wary of Gerald, then he was also on occasions frustrated with the Society. He wrote to Gerald Yorke:

I am on the Council of the Folk Lore Society, twice Ive said at a council meetings Ive a couple of witches coming to tea tomorrow. Do some of you drop in casually & meet them, I cant be sure theyll tell you anything, but they may, & no one would come.[18]

---

15. In James R Lewis, *Magical Religion and Modern Witchcraft*, (SUNY Press, 1996).
16. Frank Smyth, *Modern Witchcraft*, (Macdonald, 1970), 28.
17. Smyth, 32.
18. Letter, Gerald Gardner to Gerald Yorke, 24 October 1952 (Yorke Collection, Warburg Institute).

Even Margaret Murray comes in for criticism from Gerald: ... *the Folklore Society, Dr. Hildburgh & the Rev. Proffessor James, are being very obstructive in London, & unfortunately Magret Murray, instead of being pleased that all her Therys are proved Right, is most Damnably jealous that she didn't make the discovery.*[19] Later, she seems to have relented, as she did agree to write the Introduction to Gerald's book *Witchcraft Today*.

Dr. Walter Hildburgh (1876-1955), MA, PhD was the one who proposed Gerald for membership of the Society. Whether they knew each other beforehand is not clear: it may be that Hildburgh was chosen to propose Gerald formally merely because he was a long-established member of the Society, or they may already have known each other as they had both been members of the Royal Anthropological Institute for several years previously. Hildburgh was an anthropologist who donated a collection of Buddhist religious material to the American Museum of Natural History which is named in his honour. One of his specialisms was the iconography of Mediaeval English Alabaster Carvings, and he gave at least two lectures to the Folk-Lore Society on the subject. He was the third holder, in 1952, of the Society's Coote Lake Medal, which is awarded for outstanding research and scholarship. Even if they had not met before 1939, they certainly seem to have become friends subsequently. Gerald seems to have made a special effort to attend the meetings where Hildburgh was speaking and they were also sufficiently close for Gerald to mention to him in 1951 that he was thinking of transferring his collection to Williamson's newly-established museum at Castletown.

Elspeth Begg frequently signed in next to Gerald, including the first meeting he ever attended, in March 1939. She lived in Bournemouth, probably Boscombe,[20] and had first attended a meeting of the Society in January 1938, having become a member by November of that year. This coincidence of place and date suggests strongly to me that she may have known Gerald prior to that first meeting and that it may well have been she who introduced him, somewhat belatedly knowing his interests, to the Folk-Lore

---

19. Letter, Gerald Gardner to Cecil Williamson, 1 May 1951, (Document 48, Boscastle Museum of Witchcraft archives).

20. Her address in the List of Members published in the November 1938 issue of *Folk-Lore* is given as "c/o Westminster Bank, Boscombe".

Society. It is interesting that the only article that she wrote for the Society's journal is about witchcraft in Dorset. This relates to cases of witchcraft in the Woodlands and Verwood area in the late 19th Century told to her by a local farmer.[21] The article appeared in 1941 and raises the intriguing possibility that she may have been associated in some way with the group into which Gerald was initiated in 1939. Gerald was still in touch with her as late as 1953, when they seemed to be bidding against each other at an auction: "... I got a very fine Toad Stone Ring. Elspeth Begg was after it, but I beat her by a short head".[22] Toad Stone is a precious stone supposed to have been formed inside the body of a toad and said to have magical properties.

Jacintha Buddicom was one of the 14 people who attended Gerald's talk in June 1946, when she signed in next to him. She had attended meetings of the Folk-Lore Society back in 1938 and had become a member in 1945. She had also been a member of the O.T.O. (Ordo Templi Orientis) and been friendly with Aleister Crowley. She was born on 10th May 1901 in Plymouth and in her childhood (mostly spent in Shiplake-on-Thames in Oxfordshire) she was friends with Eric Blair, who became better known as the author, George Orwell. In her book *Eric and Us*,[23] there is a chapter entitled 'The Pagan', which is the title of a poem which Eric wrote for her in 1918. This was occasioned by an incident when she was at school in Oxford. Her parents were agnostics and had taught her about many different mythologies and pantheons. When the girls in the school were about to set out for a Christian church for the fourth Sunday in a row, Jacintha objected, asking: "Surely in a place the size of Oxford there must be a Temple of Astarte or somewhere we could go for a change?"

We do not know whether it was just coincidence that Jacintha attended Gerald's talk, but she clearly had pagan sympathies. She could well have conversed with Gerald after his talk and perhaps been instrumental in introducing him to Crowley the following year.

21. E. J. Begg, Collectanea, "Cases of Witchcraft in Dorsetshire", *Folk-Lore*, Vol. 52, (1941), 70-72.
22. Letter, Gerald Gardner to Cecil Williamson, 23 December 1953, (Document 89, Boscastle Museum of Witchcraft archives).
23. Jacintha Buddicom, *Eric and Us: A Remembrance of George Orwell*, (Leslie Frewin, 1974; revised edition Finlay Publisher, 2006).

The reality of the survival of the individual following the death of the physical body had been accepted by Gerald ever since he read Florence Marryat's *There is No Death*[24] as a boy. His experiences with the native peoples of Borneo and Malaya certainly convinced him and, on his visits to England in 1927 and 1932, he made efforts to seek the guidance of a variety of mediums, as we have seen.

Gerald had become a member of the Society for Psychical Research by May 1946. He seems particularly to have made the acquaintance of Dr. Alexander Cannon, writer on hypnotism and eastern mysticism, for he writes to Cecil Williamson in April 1951 that Cannon had a large house in Douglas in the Isle of Man where Williamson was living. Gerald's comments indicate that he was somewhat sceptical about Cannon's claims to carry out healing, make himself invisible and become immune to fire. Cannon was, indeed, a controversial figure, having treated King Edward VIII with hypnosis back in 1936.

Another prominent member was Dr. E.J. Dingwall, who was also a naturist. He seems to have been acquainted with Gerald, for in a letter to Williamson, he writes: "I met Dr Dingwell at the Soc for Phyecal Research meeting the other night ... [he] solemnly warned me against having anything to do with Witchcraft ..."[25]

Gerald obviously discussed witchcraft with various members of the Society, for in *Witchcraft Today* he implies that he put a suggestion of an experiment to a witch from a member of the Society for Psychical Research, about which the witch was rather scathing, saying that "...states of mind cannot be switched on or off at will to please the S.P.R."[26]

As one might expect from his mercurial nature, Gerald joined various different organisations, flitting from one to the other as his interests fluctuated, never being fully committed to any of them. There are probably far more than I have indicated in this chapter, such as the Flying Saucer Society, to whom he gave a talk in 1955. I think it highly likely that he was a member of several other organisations in the general area of his interests - archaeology, history, weapons and psychic studies.

---

24. Florence Marryat, *There is No Death*, (Kegan Paul, 1891).
25. Letter, Gerald Gardner to Cecil Williamson, 14 December 1952, (Document 76, Boscastle Museum of Witchcraft archives).
26. Gardner, (1954), 139.

On 26th January 1957, the rank of Chevalier was bestowed upon Gerald by the Illustrious & Knightly Order of the Crown of Stuart, which was a Jacobite monarchist organisation.

On 20th December 1957, Gerald was awarded honorary membership of the Centro di Relazioni Artistiche, Culturali e Sociali Latinitas in Milan, Italy. How significant this was, I do not really know, and the organisation does not seem to still exist. It is probably just another example of Gerald collecting perceived honours.

And, of course, he met individuals who had an effect on him in various ways. He undoubtedly welcomed contact with other people in furthering his interests, ideas and knowledge. Clues to the influences on him in the crucial post-war period might be provided by looking at the people he was friendly with, their interests and activities, and this is a theme which runs throughout this book. Some of these people may well have been crucial in the development of Gerald's ideas, but more research is needed to determine how it all fits together.

The writings of one such individual were undoubtedly very influential on Gerald Gardner - his name was Aleister Crowley.

CHAPTER TWENTY-ONE

Meetings with Aleister Crowley

Gerald had probably been aware of the writings of Aleister Crowley long before they met in person. As Doreen Valiente found when Gerald let her read the rituals that he was using when she first met him in 1952, there was a lot of Crowley material included in them. So, did Gerald ever meet Crowley and, if so, what emerged from it?

Edward Alexander Crowley (1875-1947), was born in Leamington Spa and was probably the most significant and controversial ritual magician of the twentieth century. His parents belonged to the strict Plymouth Brethren sect but were reasonably wealthy, having made money from the brewing industry. He attended Cambridge University but failed to obtain a degree. He did, however, acquire there his life-long interest in magic and the occult. In 1904, while in Egypt, he received from an entity called Aiwass the text of a document entitled "The Book of the Law", which presaged the start of what he called a 'New Aeon'. Crowley also joined the magical order, the Golden Dawn, founded in 1887. He had disagreements, however, with the leaders of that order and in 1912 joined the Ordo Templi Orientis (O.T.O.) an order which had been founded by the German occultist, Theodor Reuss in 1906.

Crowley became its leader in 1922, remaining so for the rest of his life. According to Sabazius X° and AMT IX°, the O.T.O.:

> ... *draws from the traditions of the Freemasonic, Rosicrucian and Illuminist movements of the 18th and 19th centuries, the crusading Knights Templars of the middle ages and early Christian Gnosticism and the Pagan Mystery Schools. Its symbolism contains a reunification of the hidden traditions of the East and the West.*[1]

Crowley wrote prolifically and well. He was a colourful character, undoubtedly treating some of his friends very badly, but as well as his magickal writing, he was an accomplished poet and mountaineer. He was, however, also a great leg-puller, with a purpose - to enable those seekers after truth to realise that the answers lay within themselves.

It was through his longstanding friend, Arnold Crowther (1909-1974) that Gerald had the opportunity to meet Crowley. Gerald had first met Arnold back in 1939 at a lecture on folklore given by the well-known author, Christina Hole. This was, incidentally, not a meeting of the Folk-Lore Society, but may well have introduced Gerald to that Society. Arnold told Doreen Valiente that he came across Crowley in a rather unusual way, towards the end of the war, when working as a stage magician with ENSA (Entertainments National Services Association).[2] Patricia Crowther tells me that her husband became interested in Crowley through reading his book on "Magick":

> *At one of the army camps where he was performing, a soldier was unpacking a crate of old books which had been collected by a church organisation for the lads in the forces. Having seen Arnold performing his conjuring act the previous night, the soldier handed him a book. "This will be more useful to you than to us," he said. "You may find some new tricks in it."*[3]

---

1. Sabazius X° and AMT IX°, "History of Ordo Templi Orientis", www.otohq.org/oto/history.html.
2. Doreen Valiente, *The Rebirth of Witchcraft*, (Robert Hale, 1989), 58.
3. Patricia Crowther, personal communication with the author.

Arnold expected it to contain something like card tricks, and so was rather puzzled by the title - *Magick in Theory and Practice* by the Master Therion - Aleister Crowley. It quickly became clear to Arnold on starting to read it that this was no manual about producing rabbits from hats or suchlike, but a treatise on ritual magic, which he read through, slowly, for it was hard going, but with growing interest. The volume was actually very rare, having been privately printed in Paris in 1929 and available only to subscribers. Gerald later managed to acquire a copy of his own, however, which was a four-part work in soft covers. He later gave it to a fellow member of Five Acres Club, who not long ago showed it to me. Unfortunately it has no inscriptions: Gerald was not one for writing in books, apart, of course, from the willing duty of signing them for those who requested it following the purchase of a book.

It was after the war, in April 1947, when Arnold was giving a private performance of his magic act, that a lady came up to him saying that she knew a magician with a similar name to his. It turned out that the lady knew Aleister Crowley and gave Arnold his address. Crowley was living in Hastings at the time, in fact his last residence before he died. He had moved in 1945 to Netherwood, a large house in 3½ acres of grounds, no. 379 on a road called The Ridge, a long road of mostly superior villas which, as its name implies, runs along a ridge which cuts across the northern part of the town. The house was surrounded by trees, approximately 2½ miles from the town centre and 450 feet above sea level. The building, which was demolished in 1968, dated from the mid 19th Century and seems to have been run as a sort of residential home, by the proprietor, Vernon Symonds, and his wife Kathleen ('Johnny').[4]

Arnold wrote to Crowley the following day and, about a week later, received a letter saying that he would be delighted to see him for tea at 4 p.m. the following Thursday. This turned out to be 1st May - Beltane - an auspicious and fruitful date for a first meeting. Did Crowley suggest it on purpose or was it just by "chance"? When Gerald heard that Arnold had arranged to see Crowley, he asked whether he could go along too. Arnold got in touch with Crowley again, who agreed: "Bring him along!"[5] It is

---

4. Letter from Roger Bristow, Information Services Librarian, Hastings Library, to the author, 7 February 2001.
5. Patricia Crowther, personal communication with the author.

interesting to note that another of Gerald's acquaintances, James Laver, who wrote the foreword to *Gerald Gardner Witch*, had visited Crowley only two to three weeks previously, at the end of March 1947 and one can well imagine Laver's account of his visit inspiring Gerald to ask Arnold whether he could go along with him to see Crowley. Indeed, it is possible that it was Laver who provided the key information about where Crowley was living. Laver was interested in naturism and it is likely that he had originally met Gerald before the war, at Fouracres.

There is much of Crowley's work incorporated into the Book of Shadows, the book of rituals and guidance which is copied by each of Gerald's initiates. What is not so clear is when they were incorporated - before or after Gerald's visit to Crowley. It is, however, likely that Gerald was familiar with a least some of Crowley's works before they met, even though he probably had little knowledge of Crowley's life and his order, the O.T.O., beforehand. Gerald's admiration for some of Crowley's writing probably both predated and provided a reason for their meeting.

To divert from the story for a moment, it has been suggested at various times that Gerald actually knew Crowley before 1947. One piece of evidence is provided by Allen Greenfield, who states:

> *My informant, Col. Lawrence, tells me that he has in his possession a cigarette case which once belonged to Aleister Crowley. Inside is a note in Crowley's hand that says simply: 'gift of GBG, 1936, A. Crowley*[6]

Of course, Gardner was in the habit of giving cigarette cases - his first gift to Donna was a silver cigarette case. But it was just the sort of thing which people did give each other in those days. However, I have another explanation for the note. There was a magical order, founded by one C. F. Russell, which seems to have taught a variation of the O.T.O. which advocated distinctive techniques of sexual magic. It was known as the G.B.G., which stood for "Greater Brotherhood of God", and I think that this Order, which was in existence from 1931 to 1937, is a much more likely

---

6. Allen H Greenfield, "Wicca and the Ordo Templi Orientis", *Lashtal*, Vol. 1, No 1, (1988), 47.

source for the cigarette case than Gerald who, from the evidence in Crowley's own diaries, did not meet him until 1947.

To return to the May Day visit, an extract from Crowley's diary for 1st May 1947 states the following:

"Thurs 1 May: Miss Eva Collins, Dr. G.B. Gardner Ph D Singapore, Arnold Crowther prof. G. a Magician to tea. Dr. G. R. Arch."[7]

This is the first mention of Gerald Gardner in Crowley's diaries. The "R. Arch" refers to Gerald's holding of the Royal Arch, a Masonic degree. The wording used also seems to imply strongly that this was the first time that Crowley had met Gerald because he is given a formal title and qualification, which one only does on the first occasion that one meets someone (leaving to one side for the moment the fact that he did not actually possess a PhD Singapore, and probably not a Royal Arch either).

The 'Eva Collins' mentioned in the diary entry is very likely to have been Eda Collins, who had been a member of Five Acres Club from at least July 1946. Perhaps Gerald and Arnold had talked with her about Crowley and she expressed an interest in coming along with them. Or perhaps she had that rare mode of transport, a motor car, and she was more in the nature of a 'chauffeuse'.

Patricia Crowther has relayed to me something of what Arnold told her had happened at that meeting. Crowley seemed to know a lot about witchcraft, but said that it was really a woman's cult and that it wasn't suitable for him, as the rites had to be conducted by a High Priestess and he wasn't the sort to be bossed around by women. He talked a lot about magick and about how it could never be done under test conditions. The important thing was to really want to achieve a particular result. The trappings and paraphernalia of Ritual Magick would not of themselves achieve anything. Practical experience was far more important than reading about Magick. He said he had no idea that anyone was still interested in Magick, and he explained to them that he no longer needed magical tools as he could contact the masters direct. Before they left, his visitors joined Crowley in

---

7. MSS 21-23, Yorke Collection, Warburg Institute.

an adoration of the setting sun ritual. He then presented Arnold with a signed copy of his book of poems, *Olla*, which is still in Patricia's possession.[8]

Bracelin also recounts Gerald's impressions of Crowley:

> *Once handsome, he was now reduced to a little, frail, gentle and archdeaconish figure, very bent. Could this be the Great Beast who had once boasted so many followers; who had thundered his way through life, determined to make his mark and leave a powerful organisation behind him? The fire was not quite all gone, however, even though he took heroin all the time.*[9]

Gerald also wrote about the meeting to John Symonds, Crowley's first biographer: *He was very interested in the witch cult, & had some idea of combining it in w. the Order, but nothing came of it. he was fascinated with some snaps of the Witches Cottage.*[10] Gerald gave further details of the conversation to Cecil Williamson:

> *By the way Alister Crowley was in the Cult, but left it in disgust, He could not stand a High Priestess having a superior Position & having to kneel to Her, & while he Highly approved of the Great Rite, he was very shocked at the nuedaty. Queer man, he approved of being nude in a dirty way, but highly disapproved of it in a Clean & healthfull way. Also he disapproved of the use of the scurge to Release Power, for the practical Reason if you teach a pupil the use of the Scurge, he can get a mate & do it on his own. If you have a highly paying pupil, if you teach them the Concentration & Meditation method, they go on paying you for years. But he didn't scruple to pinch lots of the Witches Ritual & incorporate it in his works. he claimed that he Re Wrote the Ritual for them but I doubt this. He did re write some Masonic Rituals, & made an awfull hash of them.*[11]

---

8. Patricia Crowther, personal communication with the author.
9. Bracelin, 174.
10. Letter, Gerald Gardner to John Symonds, 12 July 1950 (Scrapbook EE, Yorke Collection, Warburg Institute).
11. Letter, Gerald Gardner to Cecil Williamson, 8 February 1951, (Document 49, Boscastle Museum of Witchcraft archives).

This also puts a new light on the oft-repeated passage in *Witchcraft Today* where Gerald states:

> *The only man I can think of who could have invented the rites was the late Aleister Crowley. When I met him he was most interested to hear that I was a member, and said he had been inside when he was very young, but would not say whether he had rewritten anything or not. But the witch practices are entirely different in method from any kind of magic he wrote about, and he described very many kinds. There are indeed certain expressions and certain words used which smack of Crowley; possibly he borrowed things from the cult writings, or more likely someone may have borrowed expressions from him.*[12]

Rather than being duplicitous, I think that Gerald here is actually referring to the texts as they were presented to him, rather than the text as it was when he wrote *Witchcraft Today*, to which he freely admitted he had added much Crowley material. Note that in his 1951 letter, Gerald says that Crowley claimed to have re-written the rituals for the witches, but in *Witchcraft Today* (1954) he claims that Crowley would not say whether he re-wrote them or not. Bracelin also records Gerald's recollection: *At Oxford, Crowley said, he had been on the edge of witchcraft. Why had he not followed the way of the witches? Because he 'refused to be bossed around by any damned woman'.*[13]

Now, it must be remembered that this account by Gerald is from a period after he had distanced himself from Crowley and does not necessarily represent his own feelings at the time they first met. (Incidentally, it should be pointed out that Crowley was at Cambridge rather than Oxford, but perhaps we may excuse this as a lapse of Gerald's memory in the intervening years.) However, Thelemic scholar, Adrian Bott, remarks that:

> *The idea that [Crowley] was offered membership of such and rejected it because 'he didn't want to be bossed around by any damn woman' is particularly ludicrous if one knows*

---

12. Gardner, (1954), 47.
13. Bracelin, 174.

anything about what Crowley was actually like. He was
quite happy to prostrate himself before the Female Principle
and its representatives in the context of magic or religion.
He considered himself to be the Beast upon whom the Great
Whore rides - far from rejecting being bossed around by a
'damn woman' he positively dreamed of it.[14]

In contrast, Gerald Yorke, who knew Crowley well, and was one of his literary executors, says that this comment was "in character".[15] Perhaps Crowley, making the whole thing up to impress Gerald, had to give some reason why he left and on the spur of the moment mentioned that he didn't like being bossed around by women, even though in other spheres he did. The claim has certainly been disputed by Professor Ronald Hutton on the grounds that there is no mention of such involvement in Crowley's diaries, which were usually very revealing even of things which never appeared in his published writings.[16]

It is not, however, completely impossible, since Clive Harper draws our attention to the fact that Crowley's book, *Jezebel* (1899) contains "a small skull and crossbones crossed with an arrow and scythe", which is a characteristic symbol of the Traditional Craft.[17]

The most likely explanation is that Crowley pretended to Gerald that he *had* been involved, in order to retain the upper hand in their conversation and not to appear ignorant on the subject. He had previously told the same story to Louis Wilkinson[18] so it was fresh in his mind. Doreen Valiente also took this view, for she writes: "… I always took this with a grain of salt, thinking it probably just a piece of 'one-up-manship' on Crowley's part."[19]

Gerald was obviously much taken with Crowley, as he visited him three further times in the next month. On Wednesday 7th May, less than a week after the first meeting, he visited Crowley again. It seems that on this occasion Gerald must have asked about membership of Crowley's magical order, the O.T.O. and, I

---

14. Email, Adrian Bott to the author, 13 August 2001.
15. In a note on a statement by 'Ameth' (Doreen Valiente), Yorke Collection, Warburg Institute.
16. Hutton, (1999), 218-221.
17. Clive Harper, "Aleister Crowley and the Witch Cult", *The Cauldron*, No. 126, (November 2007).
18. Francis King, *Ritual Magic in England*, (Neville Spearman, 1970), 177.
19. Doreen Valiente, *Witchcraft for Tomorrow*, (Robert Hale, 1978), 15.

suspect, been accepted into it, because the entry in Crowley's diary is as follows:

Wed 7 May: Dr. Gardner about 12. Tell him phone Wel 6709[20]

The telephone number is that of Gerald Yorke, who at the time was living at 5 Montagu Square, London and who was able to supply Gerald with books. Crowley wrote to Yorke two days later asking him to send Gerald a copy of the *Equinox of the Gods*. This was a book published by Crowley and the O.T.O. in the 1930s. It includes a reproduction of *The Book of the Law*, and tells of how he received it. Clive Harper calls it: "... a handsome book, most copies being printed on japon and bound in cream buckram with gold blocking - and it sold for one guinea."[21] Crowley mentioned to Yorke that Gerald had already bought his own stock of four copies. This was presumably to distribute to others and this is confirmed by further correspondence.

It is probable that on this occasion, Crowley may have offered initiation to Gerald. In the Toronto collection there is a copy of "The Book of the Law" which is inscribed by Crowley: "To fra. :Scire P.I. from Baphomet X° O.T.O. on his affiliation". Morgan Davis states: "Karl Germer, who was the O.T.O. treasurer at that time, also made note that Gardner had paid the requisite dues and fees."[22] Gerald clearly wanted this, as did Crowley to have carried it out so quickly. Greenfield says:

> *Crowley referred to Dr. Gardner and his OTO encampment in private correspondence almost to the time of his death, and spoke of it with optimism and enthusiasm. ... Crowley, and his immediate successor, Karl Germer, who also knew Dr. Gardner, likely set 'old Gerald' on what they intended to be a Thelemic path, aimed at reestablishing at least a basic OTO encampment in England.*[23]

I think that Crowley initially saw Gerald as a means of reviving the rather moribund state of the O.T.O. in Britain. Bill Heidrick

---

20. MSS 21-23 Yorke Collection, Warburg Institute.
21. Letter, Clive Harper to the author, 17 June 1998.
22. Davis, 27.
23. T Allen Greenfield, *The Secret History of Modern Witchcraft*, (1996).

says that "The Order was certainly not much in England in the 40s, probably less than a dozen members still in touch with Crowley and resident."[24] Doreen Valiente considered that it was "existing more on paper than in actuality".[25] As a result, Crowley may have rather "buttered Gerald up", flattering him by bestowing degrees within the O.T.O. which were the equivalents of what he already had, or what Crowley thought he had. Clive Harper comments:

> I don't think Gardner understood the OTO degree system ... In High Magic's Aid *he refers to himself as "4=7 OTO" which confuses A A (or GD) grades with OTO degrees.*[26]

Ben Fernee clarifies this:

> ... in High Magic's Aid *Gardner confuses his OTO degree with the A A grade of 4 = 7. He mentions ... that he has the rituals of the OTO up to Perfect Initiate a.k.a. Prince of Jerusalem or P.I. (the "I" and "J" being equivalent) which is an appendage to the 4th degree, the OTO equivalent of the Royal Arch.*[27]

One possibility is that, in accordance with his practice, Crowley bestowed on Gerald what he considered to be the equivalent of his Royal Arch Masonic degree. Morgan Davis says of the Prince of Jerusalem:

> "This degree is also described as "Companion of the Holy Royal Arch of Enoch". Since OTO ritual parallels Free Masonry, it seems likely that Crowley admitted Gardner to the IV° under a process of affiliation, because Gardner had identified himself as a Royal Arch Mason."[28]

There seems to be no records of Gerald having attained the degree of Royal Arch. This could be another case of him claiming more than he should, or it could be that Crowley misheard Gerald when he mentioned the Johore Royal Lodge, of which he had been a member, and Gerald not correcting him.

24. Letter, Bill Heidrick to Clive Harper, 9 September 1992.
25. Valiente, (1989), 59.
26. Clive Harper, personal communication with the author, 5 June 1998.
27. Ben Fernee, personal communication with the author, 4 June 1998.
28. Davis, 29.

Greenfield comments that Prince of Jerusalem (4th degree Perfect Initiate of the Order) normally takes years of training but also admits that Crowley "may have given Gardner an 'accelerated advancement' in his order".[29] Harper writes: *Gardner, as a Royal Arch mason, would have been treated by AC as being equivalent to IV degree OTO. In "Magick Without Tears", AC specifically refers to a lady Co-mason [Anne Mackay] joining OTO at the degree equivalent to her Co-masonic degree.*[30] This seems to be somewhat equivalent to the practice of academic and professional institutions, where a system of exemptions operates, particular qualifications exempting you from certain examinations.

By the time that his *High Magic's Aid* (1949) was going to the printers, it is likely that Gerald had lost interest in being actively involved with the O.T.O. Crowley had died over a year previously and I suspect that Gerald put something on the title page that sounded impressive without worrying too much about its strict accuracy. Gerald Yorke, in an inscription in his own copy of *High Magic's Aid*, states:

> "Gardner was given a charter by A.C. to work Minerval and
> 1 to 3 degrees of O.T.O. He has not got the higher degrees,
> and at date of publication [July 1949] had not begun to
> work these degrees. He was never in the A.A. + is not enti-
> tled to call himself 4°=7°"[31]

Gerald wrote back to Crowley on 14th June asking for a list of the Minerval fees, reminding him that he had paid 10 guineas up to the 7th degree.[32] Ben Fernee comments on this:

> *Perhaps the reference to 7th degree in his letter to Crowley re
> dues is Gardners confusion, mixing 4th and P.I. with 4=7 A A
> with 7th OTO. ... He probably had the Minerval initiation
> with Crowley & Wilkinson ... and was read through the oth-
> ers which require 3 officers of the appropriate degree.*[33]

---

29. Greenfield, (1996).
30. Clive Harper, personal communication with the author, 5 June 1998.
31. In Yorke Collection, Warburg Institute.
32. MSS 21-23 Yorke Collection, Warburg Institute.
33. Ben Fernee, personal communication with the author, 4 June 1998.

I think it unlikely that Wilkinson attended Gerald's initiation, though Dr. Geoffrey Basil Smith informs me that 10 guineas was indeed the going rate at that time for the Seventh Degree.

According to Adrian Bott, this "reading through" would only take place "when there are not officers available to perform the ritual in full and *only* if the Candidate is affiliating across from Masonry or Co-Masonry". It would seem that Gerald met these criteria and that this was just what Crowley did in his case.

Gerald's letter is signed 'Scire', from the Latin for "to know", and this, together with the Charter already mentioned, seems to be his first known use of the name, which suggests that it was a magical name bestowed on him by Crowley during Gerald's visit on 7th May 1947. Bott states:

> *"Scire is one of the four Powers of the Sphinx - to know, to dare, to will and to keep silent. These are mentioned by their Latin names (scire, velle, audere, tacere) and made much of in the Second Degree of OTO; also in the Third."*34

This bestowing of degrees obviously worked with Gerald, and he began to see an important role for himself in the O.T.O. As was his nature, he could have sudden enthusiasms for things, and it certainly appeared to be true in this case. I think it fair to say that both men had something that the other needed at that time. Gerald was perhaps somewhat in awe of the 'great man' and certainly enjoyed the thought of being given an accelerated initiation and of being appointed what he imagined to be head of the O.T.O. in Europe. Crowley, in failing health, was gratified to find someone who seemed enthusiastic enough to take over the operation of the O.T.O. in Britain, which was on its last legs. But both overlooked the likelihood that Gerald's enthusiasm would come to nothing and that the seed would soon wither and die.

To understand the significance of this properly, it is important to realise their respective ages at the time of their meeting. Crowley was 71, in ill health and had just seven more months to live. Gerald was 62, in the twelfth year of his retirement and suffered, like Crowley, from asthma. He usually wintered abroad for the

---

34. Email, Adrian Bott to the author, 14 August 2001.

benefit of his health, and was shortly to have a severe bout of illness that necessitated his recuperation with his brother's family in America for several months. He was far from being a bright young spark ready to take over and revitalise a moribund O.T.O. but an ailing and ageing asthmatic who was set in his ways and, when it came to it, unwilling and unable to give the level of commitment that such a post demanded. Gerald was a bad choice, but Crowley was desperate.

※

For many years, Gerald displayed a Charter in his Museum of Magic and Witchcraft at Castletown on the Isle of Man. It purported to be from Crowley authorising Gerald to begin his own encampment. The O.T.O. had various bodies of the order: Chapters were run from the Fifth Degree, Lodges from the Third and Encampments were run from the lower degrees.

A Charter certainly exists. After the contents of the Museum were sold to Ripleys in 1973, the Charter passed through various hands and was subsequently acquired by Dr. Allen H. Greenfield, DD in 1988. In his will he directs that it be turned over to the O.T.O. on his death. Its wording is as follows:

> *Do What thou wilt shall be the law.*
> *We Baphomet X Degree, Ordo Templi Orientis*
> *Sovereign Grand Master General of all English*
> *Speaking Countries of the Earth do hereby Authorise*
> *our beloved son Scire (Dr. G.B. Gardner) Prince*
> *of Jerusalam, to constitute a camp of the Ordo*
> *Templi Orientis, in the degree Minerval.*
> *Love is the law, Love under Will.*
> *Witness my hand and Seal*
> *+ Baphomet X°*
> *seal   seal*

It is on parchment, supposedly written on the back of a land document or will from the County of Surrey for the year 1875 and is fixed with four wax seals and ribbons which bear inscriptions and designs. It is in Gerald's calligraphic hand - a similar style to that which he used for his Book of Shadows. This writing is very distinctive, particularly the thin stroke up towards the top right with which he finished many letters, showing that he must, unlike many witches, have been right-handed. Parts of it are written in red. There have been suggestions that this was blood, but I have examined good photographs of the originals and there is no evidence that this is the case. The copy is certainly much less neatly written than the calligraphic parts of Gerald's Books of Shadows, which indicates to my mind that he wrote it in a hurry.

With regard to the wording and layout of the Charter, the general style is unlike anything that Crowley ever wrote. Jerry Cornelius confirms this:

> Nowhere, in any archive world-wide, is the style of the likes of such a document found being used by Aleister Crowley. It's definitely NOT his style. He wrote or typed out everything and usually on regular paper ... at no time in his entire life did he allow others to write out 'the' authority he was granting.[35]

The wording is also rather unusual. As Clive Harper says concerning the Thelemic salutations:

> It is extremely unlikely that Crowley would have written 'Do what thou wilt shall be the law' and 'Love is the law, Love under will' rather than his customary 'Do what thou wilt shall be the whole of the Law' and 'Love is the law, love under will.'[36]

Cornelius is even more adamant. He says that Crowley:

> ... would never have allowed, and I mean never allowed all the use of capitals in the Thelemic greetings. This is forbidden in Thelemic circles and something he would have reprimanded a student very severely for doing. To sign his name to such a document would have been blasphemous. Also, he would never, never have signed his name to something

---

35. Letter, Jerry Cornelius to the author, 12 September 1999.
36. Clive Harper, "Gerald Gardner and the O.T.O. Part I: The Charter", *Nuit Isis*, No. 10, (1991), 9.

which began 'Do what thou wilt shall be the Law'. The ulti-
mate sin is misquoting Liber AL vel Legis.[37]

In contrast, Greenfield says that the misquotation from "The
Book of the Law": "... got by me for some months and probably
got by Crowley when it was presented to him for signature ..."[38]
In addition, Cornelius points out that the term "Sovereign Grand
Master General" is not one that was ever used in the O.T.O. and
the authority to rule "all English speaking countries of the Earth"
would also never have been appropriate because, as Outer Head
of the O.T.O., Crowley would have ruled all countries regardless
of language. Adrian Bott also points out that Gerald is using a
term from the Minerval initiation itself: 'I declare this Encampment open in the degree of Minerval, for the Quest of Peace and
Wisdom'. He says that one did not have a Camp in Degree Minerval as a chartered body: "It would have been far more likely for
Gardner to have been chartered as Master of a Lodge or an Oasis
with authority to initiate up to the Third Degree, if he had been
chartered at all".[39] Harper goes on to say:

> ... the term 'beloved son' is uncharacteristic of Crowley and
> the charters known to have been given by him in the 1940s
> tended to be handwritten on standard paper. Also in O.T.O.
> terms the degrees quoted are surprisingly humble. Prince of
> Jerusalem is only a side degree to IV° and Minerval is the
> introductory degree that precedes I°. [40]

Bott, whilst not disagreeing with this point, states that Prince
of Jerusalem is not a side degree, but a sequel, and the completion of a series.[41]

There are gaps in O.... T.... O...., indicating to my mind that
Gerald drew it up but did not really have any idea of what the
initials stood for, leaving spaces to be filled in by Crowley when
they next met. Clive Harper says that "... someone has filled in
'..rdo ..empli ..rientis' after the letters OTO - the handwriting is

---

37. Letter, Jerry Cornelius to the author, 12 September 1999.
38. Greenfield, (1988), 43.
39. Email, Adrian Bott to the author, 13 August 2001.
40. Harper, (1991), 9.
41. Email, Adrian Bott to the author, 14 August 2001.

intriguingly similar to Crowley's".[42] But was the signature Crowley's? There seems to be a genuine difference of opinion about this. His sigil seems different - cruder than usual, and Harper confirms this when he says that "... the Baphometic cross and signature are very different from Crowley's usual style.",[43] which he illustrates in his article. Yet Greenfield says "the signature and seals are certainly those of Crowley".[44] And Cornelius says that "real close examination, under a magnifying glass, convinces me that it is Crowley's signature."[45] Harper also said to me that Crowley had several distinct styles of writing, which seems to be the case. Bill Heidrick gives a different view:

> I saw the charter on display back in San Francisco in the early 1970s, and was struck with the fact that Crowley clearly did not write or sign it ... it is not unlikely that Gardner prepared his surviving charter to replace a more informal document actually signed by Crowley.[46]

The seals are a further complication. Clive Harper has said that:

> For formal documents AC always used his Ankh-f-n-khonsu seal ring. I feel certain that AC would never refer to his "hand and seal" unless he used this seal ring.[47]

I have seen photographs of the seals and they do seem very similar to this. Greenfield also confirms that they are Crowley's.

And what actually was the Charter supposed to be for? Greenfield makes this clear:

> ...not only was this not a simple initiation certificate for the Minerval (probationary-lowest) degree, but, to the contrary, was a Charter for Gardner to begin his own encampment of the O.T.O., and to initiate members into the O.T.O.[48]

---

42. Clive Harper, personal communication to the author, 5 June 1998.
43. Harper, (1991), 9.
44. Greenfield, (1988), 43.
45. Letter, Jerry Cornelius to the author, 12 September 1999.
46. Letter, Bill Heidrick to Clive Harper, 9 September 1992.
47. Clive Harper, personal communication with the author, 5 June 1998.
48.Greenfield, (1988), 43.

Cornelius adds:

*Crowley was notorious for doing everything very similar. I don't doubt that he [did] scribble a quick note off giving Gardner some sort of authority ... However, Gardner's ego might have wanted something 'more' or maybe what he purchased didn't look impressive enough to flaunt (if stories are correct about money being exchanged). There is no way he could have known that this was all anyone ever got out of Crowley. In other words, Gardner might have felt cheated for the money he spent by getting a one-page hand-written document scribbled on a regular piece of paper. He may well have copied Crowley's signature from his 'real' document onto the parchment simply to impress people, possibly believing that this would have been his charter had it not been [for] Crowley's failing health. Of course it's not like anything AC had ever previously used.*49

I think what happened is that at Gerald's request, Crowley wrote out a charter on a normal piece of paper. Or, more likely, Crowley dictated the Charter to Gerald, who copied it down hurriedly, and possibly wrongly. In any case, this would not have been good enough for Gerald, so in the week before their next meeting he found the most impressive document that he could in a hurry, which turned out to be a 70-year old land record. He copied down Crowley's charter onto the document, making mistakes as he went along, and adding little bits that he thought sounded good.

On balance, I think the correct explanation is that Crowley did sign and seal the document, filling in the blanks left by Gerald, but that he was clearly in failing health which meant that not only did he not spot the errors of wording but that his signature and Baphometic cross were not as elaborate as usual. Sutin confirms this when he states: This [the first meeting between Crowley and Gerald Gardner] was roughly six months before Crowley's death, and for most of that time, Crowley was in a state of severe decline.50

---

49. Letter, Jerry Cornelius to the author, 29 September 1999.
50. Lawrence Sutin, *Do What Thou Wilt: A Life of Aleister Crowley*, (St Martin's, 2000), 409.

Gerald is mentioned two further times only (making four in total) in Crowley's diary:

Wed 14 May: G.B.G.
Tues 27 May: Gardner here

It is interesting that for the first of these entries, Crowley uses Gerald's initials - GBG. This probably amused Crowley because they are the same initials as those of the magical order, the Greater Brotherhood of God, which I mentioned earlier. Anyway, these are the last entries that refer to Gerald, but there is only one further page of the diary, presumably because of Crowley's poor health and, of course, he died in December the same year.

It was therefore possibly at their meeting on 14th May that Crowley added to and signed and sealed the Charter prepared by Gerald. At what was probably their last meeting, on 27th May, it seems likely that Crowley agreed to Gerald overseeing the Minerval degree, for a letter from Crowley to W.B. Crow, dated just three days later, on 30th May 1947, states:

I suggest that you refer all your following in the London district to Dr Gardner so that he may put them properly through the Minerval degree, and some of them at least might help him to establish the camps for the higher degrees up to Perfect Initiate or Prince of Jerusalem.[51]

Crowley had annotated the letter, stating "A Camp, very good, will be ready in a few weeks". Rodney Orpheus[52] notes that Crowley wrote to his second-in-command, Karl Germer on 30th June:

England in particular is beginning to look up very brightly: we are getting a Camp of Minerval started during the summer if plans go as at present arranged.

Gerald had obviously written to Crow informing him of what was going on, probably because Crowley had referred to him in their conversation, and Gerald realised that he already knew him, through his friendship with J.S.M. Ward.

---

51. Harper, (1991), 9.
52. Rodney Orpheus, "Gerald Gardner & the Ordo Templi Orientis", *Pentacle* 30, (Autumn 2009), 14-18.

Crowley then started to send any enquiries about the O.T.O. to Gerald. Copies of letters sent by Crowley to prospective candidates still exist. Indeed, Crowley wrote to Gerald on 10th June, probably setting out more details about the Minerval degree, and enclosing a list of people for him to contact. He told him that there was only one active O.T.O. member, and that was a 90-year old woman.

There is also a handwritten note on one of Crowley's letters to Gerald, currently in the Ripleys' collection: "Put your witch in touch with Dion Byngham". This is clearly Edith, who lived within easy travelling distance of Byngham, who was at Langton Matravers in Dorset. Crowley had had some dealings with Byngham and suspected that his ideas would have resonance for the Craft. Gerald, if he had met Byngham at Fouracres, had obviously lost contact with him during the war, and had clearly not mentioned their previous acquaintance to Crowley.

Orpheus states that:

> ... *on the 14th June, it seems that Crowley raised Gardner directly to the VIIº (Seventh Degree) of the O.T.O., issuing him a receipt for 10 guineas, which was the fee for that initiation. This is significant in light of Crowley's letter to W.B. Crow, since the O.T.O. system requires an initiator to be at least VIIº in order to initiate new members to the Degree of Prince of Jerusalem. The implication of this is that Crowley and Gardner had discussed their plans further and had agreed that Gardner should be elevated in order to ensure his ability to initiate up to that Degree.*[53]

This is strange in that there is no record in Crowley's diaries of a meeting on 14th June, so this probably happened at an earlier meeting.

Gerald wrote back on 14th June asking for a list of the Minerval fees, and reminding Crowley that he paid 10 guineas up to the 7th degree. He also enclosed a stick for Crowley. This is obviously something they had previously discussed. He called it the 'Clonmel stick' and it may have had some connection with Clonmel in

---

53. Orpheus, (op. cit.).

County Tipperary, where there had been a witch burning in 1895. On 21st June 1947, Crowley thanked Gerald for the stick, saying that, as Gerald had Royal Arch (even though he didn't actually have it!) he wouldn't be required to pay for O.T.O. initiation.

⚜

It has been a persistent rumour that Gerald paid Crowley to write his Book of Shadows for him. Francis King says unequivocally: "He ... hired Crowley, at a generous fee, to write elaborate rituals for the new 'Gardnerian' witch-cult ..."[54] Gerald Yorke seems to have started this rumour and quoted a figure of £300, but really, there doesn't seem to be any evidence for this. Probably Gerald Gardner paid Crowley for the Charter and for various books and papers, but that is all. There is little in the Book of Shadows that 'smacks of Crowley', to use Gerald's phrase, which cannot be identified in one or other of Crowley's published works. In other words, there is no evidence that Crowley wrote anything *specifically for Gerald Gardner*, which is not to say that there is no Crowley material in the Book of Shadows.

£300 is probably the equivalent of upwards of £5000 today, which undoubtedly Gerald could well afford. This amount has been queried, for example by Morgan Davis who, knowing that Crowley left only £18 on his death apart from his property and effects, argues: "It would have been an impressive feat for an ill old man to spend £300 in a matter of six months just before his death ..."[55] However, it is clear from his diary entries that he was relying on contributions from his supporters in order to buy drugs: £300 from Gerald would thus have been very welcome and enough to permit any "bending of the rules" that might have been required. Nevertheless, whilst Crowley was meticulous in his diary entries about noting down these contributions, there is no mention of £300, or indeed any amount, from Gerald, so the story must be doubted on those grounds alone. Doreen Valiente says:

> *It has been alleged that a Book of Shadows in Crowley's handwriting was formerly exhibited in Gerald's Museum of Witchcraft on the Isle of Man. I can only say I never saw*

54. King, 180.
55. Davis, 31.

*this on either of the two occasions when I stayed with Ger-
ald and Donna Gardner on the island. The large, handwritten book depicted in Witchcraft Today is not in Crowley's
handwriting, but Gerald's...*[56]

In fact, rather surprisingly knowing his public persona, Crowley's handwriting is actually not very distinctive at all: it doesn't
stand out in any way. Gerald's script, in contrast, particularly
when he was writing out rituals to be seen from a distance or,
indeed, the Charter, is very distinctive. What might have happened is that someone saw the Charter on display at the museum,
noted the distinctive character of the writing and, not unreason-
ably, assumed that it had been written by Crowley. Also on display was Gerald's Book of Shadows in the same script and the
individual concerned therefore quite reasonably, but wrongly,
deduced that Crowley had also written the Book of Shadows. And
that is how rumours start!

⁂

The descriptive pamphlet for the Museum of Magic and
Witchcraft says:

*The collection includes a Charter granted by Aleister Crow-
ley to G.B. Gardner (the Director of this Museum) to oper-
ate a Lodge of Crowley's fraternity, the Ordo Templi
Orientis. (The Director would like to point out, however,
that he has never used this Charter and has no intention of
doing so, although to the best of his belief he is the only person in Britain possessing such a Charter from Crowley himself; Crowley was a personal friend of his, and gave him the
Charter because he liked him.)*[57]

This distancing of himself from Crowley is something which
Gerald did increasingly over several years, as interest in witchcraft and the museum grew. As Greenfield puts it:

*The explanation for the curious wording of the Text, taking,
as Dr. Gardner does, great pains to distance himself from*

---

56. Valiente, (1978), 17.
57. Gardner, (1958), 24.

Crowley and the OTO, may be hinted at in that the booklet [museum guide] suggests that this display in the 'new upper gallery' (page 24) was put out at a relatively late date when ... Gardner was making himself answerable to the demands of the new [sic] witch cult and not the long-dead Crowley and (then) relatively moribund OTO[58]

It seems as if Gerald did very little to establish an Encampment following his meetings with Crowley. Davis suggests that the two may have quarrelled, but the most likely reason lay in Gerald's health, which was still badly affected by his asthma. A note from his doctor, Edward A. Gregg, dated 26th April 1947, states:

Dr. Gardner, 47 Ridgmount Gardens WC1, is a patient of mine. He suffers from chronic bronchitis and asthma with much breathlessness on exertion. He is quite unfit to climb stairs and should <u>always</u> use a lift on medical grounds. It is a very dangerous thing for him to undergo the exertion of walking up a flight of stairs.

What the purpose of this note was I do not know. Perhaps he was after a ground-floor flat and wanted medical support. In the summer of 1947 he was 63 years old and he became fairly ill. Rex Wellbye told John Pinches, a member of the Fiveacres committee, about this:

Did I tell you that Gerald had been very ill indeed. He went down in August with asthma, and had to be pumped with oxygen, and fed with penicillin. It was touch and go for several weeks, but he won through, though is left very weak. Is just beginning to get out again a bit. He wants to winter with a brother in Tennessee, but is not hopeful about getting permission. Nothing but new forms to fill in, he says.[59]

Gerald may have been well enough to attend a bonfire night at the Club on Saturday 8th November 1947 when a conjuring

---

58. Greenfield, (1996).
59. Letter, Rex Wellbye to John Pinches, 4 November 1947.

show by one of the Club members who was a professional (almost certainly Arnold Crowther) took place.[60]

Gerald and Donna were intending to stay with his younger brother, Douglas, to whom he had been very close in his youth. Douglas was involved with the family timber industry on the Mississippi and had settled in Memphis, Tennessee with his wife Miriam and their daughter, Mimi. Mimi had stayed with Gerald and Donna in London the previous year. Morgan Davis gives details of Douglas' life:

> *In 1916, Francis Douglas Gardner moved to America as Secretary and Treasurer of the Anchor Sawmill Co., which had offices in New Orleans and Memphis. During the first portion of his life in America, Douglas lived in Louisiana. At some point, Douglas married Miriam Flemming and, around 1930, they had a daughter whom they named Miriam and called Mimi. In 1938, the family moved briefly to England and then returned to Memphis, Tennessee, where they took up permanent residence. In Memphis, Douglas led a quiet life, raising his family as Episcopalians. He enjoyed hobbies of semi-professional golf and tennis. Douglas also took pleasure in the arts, frequenting operas and painting prolifically, just as Gerald did.[61]*

Gerald had arranged a convalescent trip lasting several months from late November 1947 until March 1948. But it was touch-and-go as to whether Gerald would be well enough to travel. Indeed, only a week before he was due to go, Rex wrote: "Gerald writes today that his doctors won't let him come – its all they can do to get him well enough to get to the boat at L'pool."[62] But Gerald managed it, and on 29th November 1947, Gerald and Donna left Liverpool on the *S.S. Charles Lykes* bound for New Orleans. They arrived at Galveston on 15th December 1947. Davis gives further details:

> *Gardner and Donna arrived, in late 1947, to the small brick house his brother owned on 282 Strathmore Circle in midtown*

60. Letter, Rex Wellbye to John Pinches, 4 November 1947.
61. Davis, 25.
62. Letter, Rex Wellbye to John Pinches, 22 November 1947.

Memphis. The neighborhood was just off a main thorough-
fare and, across the street, there stood a wood of old growth
trees and a park. The street was filled with a number of
small eccentric houses built in the '20s, and flowers and
trees lined the road. Such a setting was ideal for Gardner to
convalesce in. Unfortunately, Douglas was not doing well.
His health was failing and, by then, he was nearly blind.
Miriam remembers that Gerald spent much of his time
between the fall of 1947 and March of the following year
helping his brother carry out daily tasks. The family lived
cozily in the winter months, and Gerald and his wife made
frequent forays to different cities.[63]

This included a trip to New Orleans, as Memphis was only
some 400 miles from that city and he wanted to find out about
Voodoo, which was obviously a living thing. His questions were
parried, however, and nobody claimed to know anything. Others
dismissed it out of hand as foolishness. Some tried to put him off
with talk of previous investigators who had been struck down
with mysterious fevers!

Eventually he met someone who pointed him in the right
direction. She was a lady who had been born on a plantation and
she advised Gerald to talk again with someone who had previously denied that voodoo existed. So he went back to see him,
lent him a copy of *A Goddess Arrives*, and told him something
about the witch cult into which he had been initiated.

Gradually Gerald was told something about the practice of
voodoo. He could see the connections between it and witchcraft,
reporting that "though the method of raising power differs, they use
it in the same way".[64] It was an active movement and he was told
that as many as a thousand people could be gathered together to
work particular types of magic. He noted that the graves of the old
High Priestesses were still tended and offerings left. He writes: "...I
noticed some suspicious resemblances which made me think that
Voodoo was not solely African in origin but had been compounded
in America of European witchcraft and African mythology ..."[65]

63. Davis, 25.
64. Bracelin, 174-175.
65. Gerald Gardner, *New Light on Witchcraft*, (manuscript), 87.

It has been suggested that Gerald also went to California to meet Jack Parsons, who was running an O.T.O. chapter (the Agape Lodge) at the time Gerald was in Memphis. It was, indeed, to this chapter that Crowley's ashes were sent. Parsons had had published in 1946 *Liber 49 - The Book of Babalon* which forecast the revival of witchcraft in covens of 11, which was the Thelemic number of magic, rather than the traditional 13. He followed this up with *Magick, Gnosticism and the Witchcraft*. However, Jarving says, and I agree with him in this matter:

> *As for Parsons essays on witchcraft, dating from that same period, they bear no resemblance whatsoever to anything in ... "High Magic's Aid" or any other of his writings. Of course GBG coud've sparked off an interest in Parsons, without there being any similarities, but it seems as likely that Parsons may have been inspired by Leland's "Aradia", from the phrases he uses. If he had been in correspondence with GBG, or even in cohorts with him to raise Wicca, there would've been similarities somewhere. But there's none.* [66]

I think it is highly unlikely that Gerald went to California to meet Parsons, or even to see him closer to Memphis. I suspect strongly that there was very little if any contact between the two.

If Gerald had been hoping for an amenable climate while he was in Memphis, he would have been disappointed. Having heard from Gerald in late January, Rex wrote:

> *[Memphis] is only 100m [sic] N. of New Orleans, and in the warm winterless zone. But the blizzardy weather they have been having up N. has spread southwards, even to New Or., and G. reports snow, blizzards and tornadoes, and perpetual wind. Not exactly a winter resort for an asthmatic. He says the sea trip set him up well, but that he is "rotten" now, and kept in by weather.* [67]

---

66. Letter, Stein Jarving to Bill Heidrick, 9 February 1993.
67. Letter, Rex Wellbye to John Pinches, 3 February 1948.

Gerald had only been two days out from Liverpool on his journey to the USA when Crowley died. When he heard about this, I do not know, probably by letter when he had reached Memphis. Gerald immediately began to have in his mind the idea of taking over the O.T.O. in England and, indeed, the whole of Europe. Only a few days after arriving in Memphis, Gerald wrote to Vernon Symonds, making it clear that he considered himself to be Head of the O.T.O. in Europe and trying to gather material together. The letter is dated 24th December 1947, i.e. just over three weeks after Crowley had died. It says:

> *... Aleister gave me a charter making me head of the O.T.O. in Europe. Now I want to get any papers about this that Aleister had; he had some typescript Rituals, I know. I have them, too, but I don't want his to fall into other people's hands, I'll buy them off the Executors at a reasonable price, together with any other relics they may be willing to sell.*[68]

It was clear from this that Gerald hadn't really got to grips with things. For example, he referred to Crowley in his letter as 'Aleister', effecting a presumed familiarity, but one which seems at odds with how others closer to Crowley actually referred to him, usually as 'A.C.'. Gerald seemed to know very little about the O.T.O. and its history and was trying to find out what material there was. It is also clear that Gerald was keener on collecting papers and other material than he was on reading and understanding them. He was certainly, as usual, concerned about information falling into the wrong hands, or rather wanting to consolidate his position and become the main source of information.

It was true that the O.T.O. was in a moribund state in England when Crowley died, and some people seemed to acknowledge that Gerald, virtually by default, was head of the O.T.O. in Europe. Bracelin reports that : "...Gardner found that many people seemed to regard him as Crowley's successor: though he was nothing of the sort."[69]

An example was Frieda Harris, who, in a post-script to a letter to Germer (Crowley's actual successor) dated 2nd January 1948,

---

68. Letter, Gerald Gardner to Vernon Symonds, 24 December 1947.
69. Bracelin, 174.

stated clearly that Gerald was the head of the OTO in Europe,[70] even though in a letter less than a month before to Frederick Mellinger, she was writing as a post-script: "Are you the head of the order here or was Gerald Gardner. I can't find him, I fancy he died?".[71] This was during the time Gerald was in America, which might explain why she failed to find him. Obviously in the intervening month someone, possibly Vernon Symonds, had enlightened her about him. Her letter to Germer continued:

> *G.B. Gardiner, 282 Strathmoore Circle Memphis 12 Tenn. is head of the O.T.O. in Europe – Dr W.B. Crow, 227 Glenfield Road Western Park Leicester has authority from A.C. to work the O.T.O. & the Gnostic Catholic Church. Would you write to him. Also Noel Fitzgerald 24 Belsize Road N.W.6. seems to have been asked to initiate Mr. Gardiner & may be a member.*

Orpheus comments:

> *From the date and tone of this letter it appears that she may have been quoting information given to her directly by Gerald Gardner the previous month – I am assuming that Gardner had told her that he was head of the O.T.O. for Europe, and we know that Gardner had been in contact with W.B. Crow. The mention of Noel Fitzgerald, who was a high-ranking IX° member of the British O.T.O., as possibly being Gardner's initiator is interesting. It was commonplace during this period for Crowley to initiate new members by putting them through all of the initiation rituals of the early Degrees of O.T.O. in one day, or over the space of a few weeks, and it is tempting to speculate that Noel Fitzgerald may have assisted Crowley in this.*[72]

I think it unlikely that Fitzgerald took any active part in initiating Gerald Gardner. Gerald did not return to England until the end of March 1948, by which time it was clear that he had lost enthusiasm for the O.T.O.

---

70. Thelema Lodge, OTO Newsletter, (November 1992).
71. Ibid.
72. Orpheus, (op. cit.).

Gerald was intending to sail back to England from New York on 19th March 1948 and wrote to Germer, who lived in New York, asking to visit him. Germer was obviously not very familiar with who Gerald Gardner was, for he wrote to Frieda Harris on 18th January 1948 asking about him:

> I received today a letter from Mr. Gerald Gardner, who says he is sailing from New York on March 19th and would stay in New York for a few days. I may either see him then, or, if I would have to go to the West Coast on a several months' trip, I might arrange to visit him on my way there. Did you ever meet him?

Gerald obviously told Germer that he was head of the O.T.O. in Europe and Germer was thus quite prepared to put himself out in order to meet him. Bracelin reports that the visit did in fact take place:

> In New York he met 'Saturnus', the enormous, hearty yet somehow seemingly humourless German who was, if anyone, Crowley's successor. He was interested to start a Crowley museum, and was looking for a house for it which he eventually found.[73]

But, as Morgan Davis says:

> What actually happened between Gardner and Germer in New York is ultimately a mystery. ... Germer could have endorsed Gardner's claim and instructed him to continue his plans to start an encampment in England, but this encampment never materialized.[74]

Kwaw states that: "After Crowley's death, Gardner wrote to Crowley's solicitor claiming that as "Head of the OTO in Britain" he, Gardner, was rightful heir to Crowley's goods and papers."[75] Nothing came of this, however. Dr. Geoffrey Basil Smith confirms that:

---

73. Bracelin, 174.
74. Davis, 34.
75. Quoted in email, Ben Fernee to the author, 18 January 2000.

"In order to be "Head" of the OTO ("in Europe" [sic] or any-where else) Gardner would have had to be a X$^{\underline{o}}$ at least (i.e. a National Grand Master) - but there was no such post! (i.e. a continental 'Head')" [76]

Galen confirms this:

The O.T.O. Charter that Crowley issued for Gardner (as "bought" IVth degree) (or better "signed") was "to constitute a camp" – "in the degree Minerval" which (at that time) included the first 3 degrees (of 10) in the O.T.O. structure (in the Oriflamme from 1912 the degree "Minerval" is 2nd degree).

With that Charter Gardner could have never become head of the English O.T.O. ... [77]

It appears that Gerald was really getting out of his depth. He was asking others for papers and suchlike, but he really didn't have any idea what to do and, following his return to England in March 1948, things ground to a halt. He didn't have the enthusiasm for the O.T.O. rituals and philosophy, insofar as he understood them, and, I imagine, was not prepared for the discipline and flexibility which working with other members of the O.T.O. entailed. Gardner wrote to John Symonds:

I tried to start an order, but I got ill, & had to leave the Country, After his [Crowley's] death word was sent to Germer that I was head of the order in Europe, & Germer acknowledged me as such, But owing to ill health I so far havent been able to get anything going. I had some people interested, but some of them were sent to Germany with the Army of Occupation. & others live far away. & so far nothing has happned. Actually, I havent all the rituals. The K.T. ritual has been lost, Gerald York thinks it may never have been writen. I have up to Prince of Jerusalam. You dont know about the lost degrees I suppose? [78]

---

76. Letter, Dr. Geoffrey Basil Smith to the author, 15 May 2001.
77. Galen, personal communication with the author, 11 May 2005.
78. Letter, Gerald Gardner to John Symonds, 12 July 1950 in Scrapbook EE, Yorke Collection, Warburg Institute.

Gerald claims in this letter to be head of the order in Europe (not just in Britain), but also makes it clear that he was never active in setting anything up, probably partly due to his health. He said: "I had neither the money, energy nor time".[79] Gerald Yorke confirmed that "Gardner never opened a camp".[80] Dr. Geoffrey Basil Smith says:

> "Gardner ... had not time to run the O.T.O. 'camp' autho-rised by Crowley and when the then O.H.O. Germer got a request [in 1951] for a charter from Kenneth Grant, he, after checking that Gardner had no intention of activating his 'camp', gave Grant a charter also allowing him to work the first three degrees of the O.T.O. system."[81]

Galen quotes Germer's correspondence with Grant: *If we want to get the OTO properly going again, we need a competent leader, not only for England but for the whole world. It must be somebody who knows the thing inside out: I have often thought that you might well be chosen for the job...*[82] On 5th May 1951 Germer issued a Charter to Kenneth Grant.

❧

This story of his involvement with Crowley and the O.T.O. illustrates how Gerald's enthusiasms could wax and wane very quickly. The latest interest took all his energy until something else arrived to take it over. I think that Gerald wanted to meet Crowley when the opportunity arose because he was impressed by what he had read of Crowley's writings. At their meeting, Crowley clearly "buttered Gerald up", probably partly because he saw in him someone who might revive the O.T.O. in England, but perhaps also because he felt he could persuade Gerald to part with money which he needed badly for drugs. Gerald liked the idea of being "Head of the O.T.O. in Europe" and agreed to what-ever Crowley suggested, in the way of financial contributions.

---

79. Bracelin, 171.
80. Inscription in Yorke's copy of *High Magic's Aid*, Yorke Collection, Warburg Institute.
81. Dr Geoffrey Basil Smith, *Knights of the Solar Cross*, (1981-83), 26-27.
82. Galen, (op. cit.).

However, Gerald was unrealistic and when he realised that he would have to do some work organising an O.T.O. encampment, he wasn't prepared for it. Indeed, he still had a very hazy understanding of O.T.O. beliefs and practices. As time went on, it became clear that Gerald had neither the will nor the ability to solve the numerous problems which he encountered. This was in part because of his illness and subsequent convalescent trip to America.

Gerald Gardner and Aleister Crowley were two very different personalities and working within a magical order would never have suited Gerald. To start with, he was not happy working within an existing structure where he was not free to indulge his own fantasies. He was certainly not prepared for the disciplined study which was needed to fully familiarise himself with the O.T.O. teachings. He was far too eclectic and mercurial. He was also not prepared to be given work to do - the organisation of an encampment was really beyond his ability. I also suspect that he contrasted what seemed to him to be the male orientation of the O.T.O. with the greater emphasis on the feminine which the Wica had shown him.

Gerald returned to England in March 1948 probably rather disillusioned with the reality of what involvement with the O.T.O. would mean. Crowley was dead and his attraction, for Gerald, seemed to die with him. During his stay in America, he had had time to think. Why was he getting involved in a magical order whose rituals and practices seemed to be leading him in a direction away from his natural inclinations? After all, he had a tradition of his own - the Craft of the Wica - and he had a witch's cottage to perform rituals in. His enthusiasm for witchcraft returned and his sights turned towards his next project, a book which he had been writing, off and on, for several years, a novel which had as its theme the beliefs and practices of the witches themselves.

CHAPTER TWENTY–TWO

High Magic's Aid

When he first asked Edith whether he could write about what she had told him, Gerald met with a straight refusal. But he was up in London, and away from her influence. He needed more people, younger people, and his mind turned again to the blank refusal his suggestion for publicity had met in the early days. Perhaps he should try again. As Patricia Crowther says:

> ...having been a close friend of Gerald's, I knew he could be very persuasive and convincing in his ideas. ... he had not wanted to see the Craft die out. And how were people to become interested in it, if they did not know it still existed?[1]

The idea of fiction as a medium to put over certain principles of the Craft probably came to Gerald after the initial refusal. He had some experience of writing fiction - *A Goddess Arrives* had been published in 1939 and I suspect that there may have been earlier manuscripts now lost. It is highly likely that he would have given each of his new friends a copy of the book, so they were familiar with his skills in that direction, which were considerable,

---

1. Patricia Crowther, Foreword to *High Magic's Aid*, (Pentacle Enterprises, 1993), 1.

even though the book had probably been substantially edited by Edith. Also, he had written about witchcraft in *A Goddess Arrives*, and he was now anxious to correct some of the false ideas which he had put forward on the subject by writing about the witches as he now knew them to be.

Gerald had probably secretly started work on what became *High Magic's Aid* at odd moments throughout the war years. He wasn't sure at that stage how much he would be allowed to say about the witches' beliefs and practices, but he had, I suspect, quite a good idea of the story and got quite a bit of writing done before he got permission to go ahead and publish it. He had a freer hand in a work of fiction to give details of witch beliefs and practices without it being obvious that they were other than pure invention. Unless the hint was given that it was something more, the book could be read as a simple historical adventure story with elements of magic and witchcraft woven into it. At the same time, it could perform the function of an introductory guide to the 'Craft of the Wise' - the only one available - and Gerald could give copies to those whom he thought ready to receive it.

Gerald wrote about *High Magic's Aid*: "A.C. [Aleister Crowley] read part of the M.S. & highly approved. He wanted me to put the Witch part in full."[2] This must have been no later than June 1947, the last time that Gerald met Crowley, so parts at least of the manuscript must have been in a state to read at that date, over two years before publication. Indeed, it is likely that the manuscript was substantially complete by then, for Gerald left a copy with Crowley, who commented in a letter to Gerald dated 10th June 1947 that the book should be two-thirds of the length. Whether Gerald took any notice of this literary advice, I do not know.

Edith's restrictions on writing about witch magic propelled Gerald into investigating other systems of magic in order to incorporate them into the manuscript of *High Magic's Aid*. This seems to have happened at a fairly late stage, as it was in June 1947 that Gerald Yorke lent Gerald a manuscript (probably in facsimile) copy of *The Key of Solomon the King*. This was during the period when Gerald was going down to Hastings regularly to see Crowley.

---

2. Letter, Gerald Gardner to John Symonds 12 July 1950 (Scrapbook EE2, Yorke Collection, Warburg Institute).

I think it was after one of those meetings, and certainly after receiving the copy of *The Key of Solomon* from Yorke, that Gerald had one of his 'Mr Toad' moments and became suddenly enthusiastic about ceremonial magic, putting everything else out of his mind. In 1947, there were few magical texts published and it was before the days of photocopiers, so if Gerald wanted a copy of some of the key texts he would either have to acquire them second-hand or would have to copy them out for himself. He certainly took the opportunity to buy a variety of printed texts on magic from book dealers in London with whom he had registered an interest. However, he could not guarantee that he could acquire what were considered to be key texts and he therefore fell back on borrowing them where he could and then laboriously making copies of them. He had a rather fine calligraphic hand and I think the first thing he copied was Crowley's version of the Goetia of the Lemegeton, or Lesser Key of Solomon the King.

He then started on a grander written project, and its title, "Ye Bok of Ye Art Magical", reveals Gerald's original intention, which was to copy all the magical texts he could into one volume. In wartime and the immediate post-war years, good quality paper was difficult to obtain, but Gerald managed to acquire some fine paper, identified by its watermark as being made by Grosvenor Chater and Co. The book is made from folded sheets of 12½ins x 16ins professionally sewn into sections and then bound, rather amateurishly into a brown leather cover which was originally on a copy of *The History of the Council of Trent* dating from 1676. Allen Greenfield describes his first impression of it: "At first glance it appeared to be a very old book, and it suggested to me where the rumours that a very old, possibly mediaeval *Book of Shadows* had once been on display in Gardner's Museum had emerged from."[3]

There are some 335 pages (12½ins x 8ins), most of which are folded sheets, but some are individual pages, neatly inserted and bound in. It was in Gerald's handwriting and had initially been prepared with blank pages between the original text. The book had been gradually added to by putting additional material on those pages. By looking at the pattern, and also the neatness of

---

3. T. Allen Greenfield, *The Secret History of Modern Witchcraft*, (1996).

the writing, Aidan Kelly,[4] who was the first researcher to study the book systematically, was able to determine the approximate order in which things had been written or copied into the book. His findings accord with my own thoughts on the subject. It had originally been intended, as its title suggests, as a book of ceremonial magic, with material taken from Mathers' version of the Greater Key of Solomon, published in 1888. A large part of 'Ye Bok' is an abbreviated transcript of "The Goetia", "The Lemegeton", "The First Book of the Lesser Key of Solomon the King", copied by S.L. MacGregor Mathers from manuscripts in the British Museum. This is confirmation that 'Ye Bok' originated from a time when Gerald had become very interested in ceremonial magic. He also copied extracts from several of Crowley's works.

Knowing Gerald's character, I think that almost certainly he never tried to use this material in rituals or magical workings. He was aware of the old mediaeval grimoires and, as he was going through his 'ceremonial magic' phase, he attempted to construct something similar, and this appears to have survived in the guise of this volume.

It was only later, probably in 1949, when for the first time he had someone to initiate, that Gerald copied witch rituals, mostly from the manuscript of his novel *High Magic's Aid*, and other witchcraft material into it as well. Much of this is in a large and very ornate script intended to be seen at a distance during rituals. There are some idiosyncratic spellings, which I believe have no significance beyond demonstrating that Gerald was very bad at spelling, probably partly because he was self-taught. He had never been to school and tended to spell words phonetically.

It has been claimed, for example by James Davies, that 'Ye Bok' was created by Gerald purely as a 'prop' for a display in his museum. Whilst it seems likely that it was displayed in such a context, this could not have been the original reason for its creation, since that occurred in 1947 and the museum was not set up until 1951.

By 1950, by which time Gerald's interest in ceremonial magic had lapsed, he copied the witchcraft bits into a thinner, more portable book. This was a foolscap size fibre-board backed ledger

---

4. Aidan A Kelly, *Crafting the Art of Magic Book I: A History of Modern Witchcraft, 1939-1964*, (Llewellyn Publications, 1991).

book – probably all that was available. It is known to researchers as 'Text A' and is in the Doreen Valiente collection. 'Ye Bok' was then relegated to serving as a rough note book where Gerald was using the blank pages for whatever he wanted. I am informed that, certainly for a while, it was in use as the witch's volume in the 'witch's cottage' display at the museum on the Isle of Man. Subsequently, 'Ye Bok' seemed to have been hidden, either deliberately or accidentally, in the back of a cabinet and was only found after the museum contents were sold to Ripleys in the 1970s. It is now in the Toronto collection.

Gerald had been familiar with the Theban alphabet (which seems to have been first widely publicised in Barrett's *The Magus* published in 1801) since at least 1939, since this was "Cornelius Agrippa's private code" which he used when he made the bracelet which I refer to in Chapter 15. A major feat of Gerald's was the transcription of the magical text known as the Grimorium Verum into Theban, some 104 pages of it, which must have taken him a considerable time. This document, and much more, is currently in the Toronto collection.

It is important to consider Gerald's state of mind when he was carrying out all this calligraphic work. It was his new enthusiasm and he was prepared to spend long hours at his desk at 47 Ridgmount Gardens doing this copying. I don't think he really had any idea of what he was doing it for, nor any real understanding of what it was all about.

In August 1947, he fell ill with asthma and couldn't do any more copying. By the time he had recovered and returned from his wintering abroad in America, it was April 1948 and it is my guess that it was in the Spring of that year that he dropped the copying of magical documents and took up his as yet unnamed manuscript again. And in May 1948, Rosamund Sabine died. I don't think Edith told Gerald of this, since five years later he thought her death had been 'recent', but it clearly affected Edith's attitude to publicity, as she seems to have relented somewhat and Gerald finally got the permission he wanted:

So, against their better judgement, they agreed to let me write a little about the cult in the form of fiction, an historical novel where a witch says a little of what they believe and of how they were persecuted.[5]

This permission was certainly qualified, as Gerald told Symonds: "... I was only given permission to publish things as fiction, & they [i.e. the witches] could cut out what they liked."[6] In fact, by the time he got this permission, it seems likely that the book was actually substantially complete, since he must have started it in at least 1946 and possibly before. Yet, what had Gerald been allowed to say? Edith had been very strict about what could and couldn't be included, as he makes very clear in a letter to a Mr. Gordon Bay dated 6th August 1952:

> *...Actually, I wanted to write about a witch + what she'd told me, + she wouldn't let me tell anything about Witchcraft, but I said why not let me write giving to the World the Witches point of view. You are always persecuted + abused + never answer. So she said I might if I didn't give any Witch Magic, + it must only be as fiction. So, as I had to give some magic, I simply copied it from Jewish Ritual Magic, chiefly "The Key of Solomon the King". It was taught that King Solomon could command the spirits + make them work for him. + if you know these words + sigils you could do the same. This key is usually in Latin or Hebrew, but there is an English translation by MacGregor Mathers. But personally I don't believe that it works. It's all very difficult + complicated ....*[7]

It was following Gerald's acquisition of the manuscript copy of *The Key of Solomon the King* from Gerald Yorke in June 1947, and probably mainly in 1948, that he incorporated material from it into his book. Fred Lamond states: *...Don Frew ... claims to have seen a letter, sent by Gerald to a friend around 1948 explaining why he had used a kabbalistic initiation ritual in his description of a witch's initiation in* High Magic's Aid: *"I don't like it and find it too heavy and ceremonial for a witch's initiation. But what can I do,*

5. Gardner, (1959), 11-12.
6. Letter, Gerald Gardner to John Symonds, 12 July 1950, (Scrapbook EE2, Yorke Collection, Warburg Institute).
7. Patricia Crowther, Foreword to *High Magic's Aid*, (Pentacle Enterprises, 1993), 1.

since I have been forbidden to reveal the actual initiation rite!"[8] He certainly tried to put the genuine 3rd degree ritual in because he tells Symonds: "I wrote the third degree of the Witch Cult, but they went up in steam, & cut it out entirely."[9] He continues: ... *of course things have been changed a little in the ritual, but Ive got it as nearly as thay do it, to the great scare of the publishers, but no one has objected in the slightest so far.*[10]

Gerald seems to be saying here that things have only been changed a little, yet in the previous letters referred to he admits having put a lot of the Key of Solomon material in rather than the actual initiation rite. I suspect that he probably did not include very much witch ritual but probably managed to sneak some of the wording through without being spotted.

When Gerald had more or less finalised the text of *High Magic's Aid*, he copied the ritual parts into "Ye Bok of Ye Art Magical". It was his habit to leave batches of blank pages, so this was fairly easy to do. I think the idea behind the calligraphy, in this and in some of the earlier texts, was so that the book could be placed on a stand and consulted during a ritual.

But what did Gerald want to say in the book? In one way, it was an advantage to be writing a work of fiction. As Dion Fortune says: *Writers will put things into a novel that they daren't put in sober prose, where you have to dot the Is and cross the Ts.*[11] Theoretically, Gerald was not limited to what the witches had told him: he could embellish and add exactly what he wanted to. He could make things up, alter traditions and beliefs and the reading public would be none the wiser. They would think of it as a good (or not so good!) story and that would be that. But he wasn't satisfied with this. The whole purpose of this book was to tell something of what the witches that he had met believed and did.

Since it had to be a work of fiction, he couldn't actually say that witches still existed, however much he might have wanted to, so it had to be set at some time in the past. However, he would

---

8. 'Robert' (Frederic Lamond), *Witness to Wicca*, (manuscript copy in the Boscastle Museum of Witchcraft archives), 3/5.
9. Letter, Gerald Gardner to John Symonds, 12 July 1950, (Scrapbook EE2, Yorke Collection, Warburg Institute).
10. Ibid.
11. Dion Fortune, *The Goat-Foot God*, (Williams and Norgate, 1936).

be able to include something about witch beliefs and practices, although no witch magic. This restriction probably gave him one of the main themes for the book, as well as its title. He included ceremonial magic and the title of *High Magic's Aid*, probably fairly late in the process because he wasn't allowed to put in any witch magic. So Gerald used magic derived from various grimoires, including the Key of Solomon, turning the restriction into a key theme, that of high magic's aid, in other words how ceremonial magic can help the simpler magical techniques of the witch.

Or rather, it is perhaps an example of "mutual aid", for, despite its title, one essential theme of the book is how witchcraft can assist 'High Magic' rather than the other way round. The protagonists are wanting to carry out magical working, which they can only do with the aid of a witch's consecrated tools and, indeed, the witch herself. As Gerald told Symonds, High Magic needed a medium to make it work, "which is best obtained from witches"[12] In the letter to Gordon Bay, quoted above, Gerald went on to say:

> *"... The Witches have a Tradition that all the ... sorcerers used to hire a Witch, as a sort of Medium, + in this way only did they get results. Actually I think some sort of Spiritualist Phenomenon is induced, but I doubt the spirits Power to do anything practical. In my book I tried to make this clear. A Witch (a ... medium) is necessary, + even then, you only get good advice but the advice is realy good."*[13]

The presence of the witch character in the story, Morven, allows Gerald to introduce some witch philosophy, rituals and other witch practices in the guise of fiction. An advertisement which appeared in *The Occult Observer* described the book as follows:

> *Here is a book of medieval witchcraft and magic in fiction form. The author has made thorough investigations into the rituals and ceremonies of magic circles with formulae and invocations. It is exceedingly readable and many have expressed their appreciation of its approach to the study of this fascinating subject. It is an exciting tale carrying the*

12. Letter, Gerald Gardner to John Symonds, 12 July 1950, (Scrapbook EE2, Yorke Collection, Warburg Institute).
13. Patricia Crowther, Foreword to *High Magic's Aid*, (Pentacle Enterprises, 1993), 1.

reader through an historical period when worship of the secret witch-cult was practised in spite of the persecution of the Church.[14]

High Magic's Aid is an adventure story set in 13th Century England, of which the central theme is the use of magic and witchcraft to recapture land and property which had been usurped by a Norman baron. It has been described as a pastiche of Sir Walter Scott's *Ivanhoe*, which, perhaps significantly, Gerald had been familiar with from his earliest years. As Ronald Hutton notes:

Its basic structure bears marked similarities to that of A Goddess Arrives: a tale of adventure set in times of political and military turmoil, in which a hero joins forces with a witch to achieve his ends. Once again, he is the more powerful figure, setting the pace and directing the events of the action, and she defers to him. Once again, she is repeatedly shedding her clothes to work ritual, ... [15]

The young heroes, Jan and Olaf, are seeking to reclaim the land stolen from their father, Edgar Bonder, by the hated Norman Fitz-Urse. They seek the help of Thur Peterson, a medical practitioner, or 'leech', who is also adept at ritual magic, having learnt this at Cordoba in Spain. The main magical theme is that in order to work their magic they need properly consecrated tools, which can only be made with other consecrated tools. They thus needed to find either another ritual magician or a witch. An elaborate ritual, based on *The Key of Solomon the King* is enacted, which results in the message "Seek the Witch of Wanda".

They search for the hamlet of Wanda and find Vada, a young half-starved and persecuted woman living on her own whom Thur recognises to be a witch from certain comments which she makes. The witch-hunt are following close, however, and the four have to depart in haste, just giving Vada enough time to dig up her mother's ritual knives which had been buried for safety in the garden. They have a narrow escape and are forced to keep under cover

---

14. *The Occult Observer*, Vol 1, No 3, (1949).
15. Hutton, (1999), 224.

during the day, travelling only at night. To protect her identity, Vada uses her witch-name of Morven and gradually assumes a rounder appearance through better nourishment.

After a stay in London, where it was easier to mingle with the crowd, Thur returns to his home town of St. Clare-in-Walden, with Morven, who assumes the identity of his niece whom he has taken under his wing following the death of her parents. Morven sets up home in Thur's house under the eye of Alice, Thur's housekeeper.

Further magical rituals take place to consecrate the necessary magical tools, but Jan is keen to raise an army to claim his inheritance. To help in this, Morven travels with the brothers to their home village wearing the red garters which indicate a high position within the Craft. These act as a sign to those who are members and she is invited to speak before a gathering which is assembled in the forest at the next full moon. She introduces Jan and he is accepted by those assembled as leader of a force to win back the castle usurped by Fitz-Urse. Later, magical ritual is again used to find the one individual, Even Gull's Egg, who knows the way into the stronghold.

In the meantime, Thur, Jan and Olaf are initiated into the first degree of witchcraft by Morven, and then Thur and Jan are taken through the second degree initiation.

The story ends with Fitz-Urse being defeated, the castle and lands being won back, and with the death of Thur in battle.

The one historical figure in the story is Stephen Langton, who seems to have been sympathetic to the Craft and who, perhaps by magical means, became Archbishop of Canterbury overnight from being an "utterly unknown man", according to Gerald.

High Magic's Aid should not be judged by its literary qualities: its importance lies in its author and what he revealed through it. But accepting this, there is a wide range of opinions about the book. Francis King[16] called it "long and almost unreadable", whereas Patricia Crowther has referred to it as "An exciting atmospheric novel ... its author ... has encapsulated fascinating magical rituals which draw the reader into the scenes, as though actually experiencing them."[17] I certainly found it a good story and vividly written, although I am not competent to comment on

16. King, 180.
17. Patricia Crowther, Foreword to *High Magic's Aid*, (Pentacle Enterprises, 1993), 1.

its historical accuracy. I am informed, though, that there are several anachronisms and errors of fact.[18]

If the main reason that Gerald wrote *High Magic's Aid* was to give an indication of what witches believed and did, which parts of it provide that information? Bracelin states that: ...*only the words used by the witch who is its heroine were claimed to be truly authentic.*[19] Patricia Crowther, commenting on this, says: *This is interesting in view of what Gerald said when he presented me with a copy of "High Magic's Aid" in 1960, "Darling, take notice of Morven's words, they will teach you much."*[20] It is interesting that he said this, even after *Witchcraft Today* and *The Meaning of Witchcraft* had been published, so there may be something revealed in Morven's words which are not in the other two books. We may expect that Gerald would put a description of the beliefs and practices of the witches into the mouth of the witch who features in the story, and an examination of Morven's words does indeed give a picture of what he calls 'the witch cult' in terms of its history, the powers of a witch, and numerous insights into the rituals which form part of the story.

Gerald wrote: *The witchcraft parts are chap xIv Dearleap, & XVII The Witch Cult.*[21] And, in *Witchcraft Today*, he states: *They [i.e. the witches] showed me one queer trick with music which I described in my novel High Magic's Aid, in the chapter called 'Music Magic'.*[22] So, taking into account these three chapters, plus Morven's words where they occur throughout the book, what can we deduce about what Gerald wanted to convey about witch beliefs and practices?

The story Morven tells is of a young girl brought by her mother into a thriving faith where the members have magical and mystical powers. There are themes which are repeated in Gerald's first non-fiction book on witchcraft, *Witchcraft Today* - an emphasis on rebirth, the hereditary principle and nudity. Another is that the Craft came originally from the East. Also, the witches believed their gods were not all-powerful.

---

18. Gareth Medway, personal communication with the author, October 2009.
19. Bracelin, 183.
20. Patricia Crowther, Foreword to *High Magic's Aid*, (Pentacle Enterprises, 1993), 1.
21. Letter, Gerald Gardner to John Symonds, 12 July 1950, (Scrapbook EE2, Yorke Collection, Warburg Institute).
22. Gardner, (1954), 142.

They believed in rebirth: *"Why,"* said she, *"having rested for a while in the lovely country on the other side of life, we come back again, and are reborn on this earth. We ever progress, but to progress we must learn, and to learn oft means suffering. What we endure in this life fits us for a better existence in the next, and so we be heartened to endure all the troubles and trials here, for we know that they but help us to higher things. Thus the gods teach us to look forward to the time when we be not men any more...but gods!"*[23]

Gerald seems to some extent to have ignored Edith's ban on the mention of any witch magic, as there are actually some very interesting magical and divinatory techniques described which are not repeated in his subsequent non-fiction books. Morven speaks about a range of magical techniques as practised by the witches, which contrasts markedly with the ceremonial magic which also features prominently. These include divination by Drawing Down the Moon, the use of herbal cures, the scourge, trance mediumship, scrying and 'psychological' techniques such as those for invisibility.

The main magical theme of the book is that Thur, the magician, needs some tools that have been properly consecrated, particularly the knife. He is told to seek out a witch for these, which he does, but he finds that she herself can act as a catalyst for magical workings. Gerald has her saying: *"... they said that I helped by giving power from my body. My coming was likened to the opening of the sluices of a water-mill for the power it gave to work marvels."* [24]

Their divinatory techniques seemed to have a shamanic element. Morven is quoted as saying:

"They also said that the witches' learning came secretly from these same old gods [Greek]. The Greek witches could draw down the Spirit of the Moon." "Artemis?" She flashed him an admiring glance. "Truly you are a learned man, Thur. Yes, Artemis. She could reveal the future and help gain the love of men. We used to invoke Ardrea, the daughter of Artemis." "How was that done?" "By sitting in a circle with a little drum we used for dancing. This was placed in

23. Gardner, (1949), 84.
24. Op. cit., 120.

the centre, and we laid our fingers lightly on the skin and asked questions of Ardrea. She answered Yes, or No, by tilting the drum. We had warnings of danger and much good advice that way."[25]

A well-established witch divinatory technique is scrying, as indicated in the following passage, which also reveals Gerald's attitude to spiritualism:

"Some witches there were who could read the hour of death on the face, or the future fate. Always they promised me sorrow, to be followed by joy...and sorrow I have had aplenty. ... Others there were who would fall into a sleep and the spirits would enter their bodies, speaking with the lips but not the voices of the sleepers. Women would speak with the voice of a man, and men with a woman's pipe."
"Ah," cried Thur more hopefully, "and what said they?" She shrugged. "Little, I fear. Warnings of danger or sorrow. What they foretold would come to pass, but methinks how to avoid direness would have been more to the purpose. When they wakened they knew naught of what they had said. ... Some there were who would look into a pool of water or a magic stone, and see visions of what was happening at a distance, and so we would be warned of approaching danger. ..."[26]

There were also techniques of the mind, or what might popularly be called 'psychology':

"Many of the farm folk who see us may be 'of the brotherhood'. Let us each wear a bit of white cloth behind us, like rabbits' scuts. ... Any brother who sees us wearing them will know that we wish to travel unseen, and even under torture will swear that they saw nothing but four rabbits on the road. *Long ago we found that if a man swore under torture that he saw none, his eyes betrayed him,* but if he believed that in some mystical way we are transformed

25. Op. cit., 118-119.
26. Gardner, (1949), 119-120.

into rabbits, he will maintain that he saw naught but rabbits to his death! *Aye, 'tis queer, but 'tis so.* "27

There is also a section on the way that witches became invisible, which is largely a matter of having the confidence to play a part convincingly:

"Thus do we witches, ever bearing in mind that invisibility is not a lack of sight in all beholders, but lack of observation. Any but the blind may see, but he who carries the spell is not marked by all about him."

"Your witchcraft, it seems, is very much a thing of the mind...the dominance of the witch's mind over her surroundings."

"Truly. A thing of much accurate observation, and knowledge of what people do, and may do in certain events. The witch holds the mind of those she would influence. 'Tis simple. An old woman with a load may come and go unnoticed, so long as her behaviour is that of an old woman with a load.."

"So if she hurry, or stop to glance about her, she would be marked?"

*"Yes, always one so disguised wears the charm of the Talisman with such confidence that she knows none may note her. As she sees herself in her own mind, so do others see her. But if she trusts not in the powers she wears and lets fear taint her mind, then does she impart fear to those about her. They see her furtiveness, mark her, remember her, question her, and take her."*28

Gerald also gives a hint of the relevance of the chapter on 'music magic' when he writes in *Witchcraft Today* that it was based on something which happened to him:

27. Op. cit., 77.
28. Gardner, (1949), 140.

They told me they could make me fighting mad; I did not believe it, so they got me to sit, fixed in a chair so that I could not get out. Then one sat in front of me playing a little drum; not a tune, just a steady tom-tom-tom. We were laughing and talking at first ... it seemed a long time, although I could see the clock and knew it was not. The tom-tom-tom went on and I felt silly; they were watching me and grinning and those grins made me angry. I did realise that the tom-tomming seemed to be a little quicker and my heart seemed to be beating very hard. I felt flushes of heat, I was angry at their silly grins. Suddenly I felt furiously angry and wanted to pull loose out of the chair; I tugged out and would have gone for them, but as soon as I started moving they changed their beat and I was not angry any longer.

I said: 'It is just suggestion,' but they insisted it was something more - that it was an old secret and could be used to make men fighting mad before a charge.[29]

Chapter XIV is entitled "Dearleap", the title of which refers to a place in the forest where the witches met. Gerald describes it thus:

... they saw an outcrop of high rocks at one end of a big clearing. On closer view it proved to be a natural amphitheatre, grass grown, wide at the base, upon whose boulder-strewn sides many people were assembled.[30]

This is clearly not in the New Forest, as there are no rock outcrops of any sort, and it seems to be a product of Gerald's imagination - a sort of ideal meeting-place, perhaps, but there are many places in England and elsewhere where such a landform can be found, and Gerald may have come across such a place in his travels and remembered it. 'Dearleap' does not appear on any Ordnance Survey map, as far as I am aware, but 'Deerleap' does, and it seems to make more sense as well, as deer are apt to leap. One suspects a spelling error on Gerald's part which never got corrected! There is certainly a Deerleap Inclosure on the north-eastern edge of the forest not far from Lyndhurst and it may well

29. Gardner, (1954), 142
30. Gardner, (1949), 220.

be that Gerald was telling us indirectly to look closer at it, or perhaps he just liked the name.

The 'Dearleap' chapter is about a large gathering of the adherents of the Old Religion in the woods at night at which Morven speaks to those so assembled. There are certain elements which seem significant because they have become part of the modern Craft. Firstly the gathering is held at Full Moon. Margaret Murray does not appear to mention this, but it is certainly prominent in Leland's *Aradia*. Secondly, nudity is much in evidence and Morven appears naked amongst the assembled gathering. Other motifs that feature in this chapter are the use of the athame (the witches' ritual black-handled knife), chanting and harps (something which has not generally survived into the modern Craft) and a follow-my-leader dance, which Gerald also refers to in *Witchcraft Today*.

The most remarkable section in the book, Chapter XVII, consists of Morven taking the male characters through the first and second degree initiation rituals, which she calls the triangle and the pentagram respectively. The rituals are familiar to those who have read of them in books such as those of the Farrars. It is striking to find the first printed versions of them in virtually the same wording.

Apart from the general influence of Masonic practice, and the Golden Dawn, the only known source of any part of these rituals is the Key of Solomon.

Yet, could there be something of Gerald's own initiation in the initiation rituals in *High Magic's Aid*? If so, then it would be more likely to be actions rather than words and those elements which are not taken from the published sources referred to above.

The third degree ritual is barely hinted at in the book, presumably all that Gardner felt able to write after the witches 'went up in steam':

"There is but one degree more," she said. "Where you take an oath and are made to use the working tools, but after that, there is what is called a degree. There is no oath, and all who have taken the second degree are qualified to work

it, but 'tis the quintessence of Magic, and 'tis not to be used lightly, and then only with one whom you love and are loved by, may it be done, all else were sin."[31]

To some extent, the inclusion of fight sequences in both *High Magic's Aid* and *A Goddess Arrives* may have been a substitute for the fact that Gerald never actually engaged in such activity in reality. It was certainly something he focused on, with his collections of weapons, and membership of the Legion of Frontiersmen, Ceylon Planters Rifle Corps, the Malay States Volunteer Rifles, and the Home Guard, and this is probably bound to come out in his works of fiction.

The immense power of search engines such as Google means that we can now identify in a moment a particular quotation, however obscure its origin. This has been particularly revealing when applied to Gerald's writings, for we can now see that some pieces are not his original work but come from already published sources. It is clear that Gerald was not above plagiarism in the case of *The Moon Endureth* by John Buchan,[32] which is a collection of stories, one of which is entitled "The Grove of Ashtaroth". It is a story of a sacred grove in Africa, where, following his part in its destruction, the hero finally realises that there is some virtue in the old beliefs and practices. The story includes the phrases "old secrets of joy and terror", "brush against the soul in dreams" and "delicate mystery of worship". These are very specific and occur within two pages of "The Grove of Ashtaroth". They also occur in both *High Magic's Aid* in a very short passage[33] and in one paragraph of *Witchcraft Today*[34] where Gerald is apparently reporting what a witch of his acquaintance had told him. It is clear that these phrases were obtained from Buchan and subsequently used by Gerald in *High Magic's Aid* and *Witchcraft Today*.

Another example comes from the book by Mark Twain entitled *A Connecticut Yankee in King Arthur's Court* in the U.S.A. and *A Yankee in the Court of King Arthur* in Britain, a copy of which

---

31. Gardner, (1949), 299-300.
32. John Buchan, *The Moon Endureth*, (Hodder and Stoughton, 1912).
33. Gardner, (1949), 299.
34. Gardner, (1954), 141.

was in Gerald's library.35 There are several similar sections, as, for example, one which concerns a Valley of Holiness, Twain writes:

> *Of old time there lived there an abbot and his monks. Belike were none in the world more holy than these; for they gave themselves to study of pious books, and spoke not the one to the other, or indeed to any, and ate decayed herbs and naught thereto, and slept hard, and prayed much, and washed never; also they wore the same garment until it fell from their bodies through age and decay. Right so came they to be known of all the world by reason of these holy austerities, and visited by rich and poor, and reverenced.*36

The equivalent passage in *High Magic's Aid* reads:

> *Morven said: "In my home town folks talked much of the Valley of Holiness."*
>
> *"I have not heard of it."*
>
> *"A tale of an Abbot and his monks. None so holy as they in the land of Egypt, giving themselves to the reading of pious books, denying themselves speech, both among themselves and with the outside world, lest the member offend God; eating only herbage, living in every discomfort, praying always and washing never, wearing one garment until it dropped off them from decay and old age, or crawled away, like Becket's. They became famous throughout the civilised world for their learning and Holy Austerities."*37

There are quite a few other passages in Twain's book that are closely paralleled by passages in *High Magic's Aid*. How did these passages appear in *High Magic's Aid*? The most obvious way is that Gerald had read them and liked them and included them in his book. He probably had a much more relaxed approach to using other people's work without attribution than we do today. He may just have thought: "I like that bit" and put it in his book.

---

35. I am indebted to Kate Gladstone for drawing attention to this.
36. Mark Twain, *A Yankee at the Court of King Arthur*, (Chatto and Windus 1921).
37. Gardner, (1949), 145-146.

The endpapers of *High Magic's Aid* are clearly drawn by Gerald in his neatest calligraphic hand and consist of illustrations of the following: the sword; the athame; the white-hilted knife; the layout of the Grand Circle; the burin; characters on sprinkler; characters on the ink horn; the layout of another circle; the sigil of Dantilion; Various talismans, including Mars in Aries for Jan, Jupiter in Sagittarius for Morven, Mercury in the Twins for Thur, the Sun in Leo for Olaf and Saturn in Aquarius for Stephen. Gerald has signed each leaf with his "monogram".

These drawings derive essentially, with minor variations, from Mathers' edition of *The Key of Solomon*, published in 1888, and Barrett's *The Magus*, published in 1801. They demonstrate, as does the whole book, that Gerald was heavily influenced by ceremonial magic. However, there are differences from the source material as given by Mathers and Barrett and these are quite revealing as possibly reflecting some of the practices of the witch tradition into which Gerald was initiated. There is the introduction of pentagram symbols, rectangular altars and two circular stools in the circles. Also, astrological symbols of the planets and zodiac signs are given on the talismans. All of this suggests an influence, either direct or indirect, from the magical order, the Golden Dawn.

Gerald drops various hints throughout the text giving information in a rather obscure and roundabout way, giving the names of people and places, either in a recognisable form or subtly altered. They rather suggest a pointing towards significant places for those who were "in the know" - places associated with witchcraft activity. First of all, the place where the witch lived was called 'Wanda' and the name by which she was known was 'Vada'. Combining these two names, I was reminded irresistibly of 'Vanda', who is mentioned by Patricia Crowther when she is writing about her husband, Arnold:

> ... *Gerald once took him to the home of a lady called Vanda. She frequently held soirees where various artistes, intellectuals and writers, were able to commune with their equals and let down their hair by 'peeling off', as Gerald put it, and sitting around sky-clad.*[38]

38. Patricia Crowther, *One Witch's World*, (Robert Hale, 1998), 18.

The name 'Morven' is equally interesting. It could have occurred to Gerald because of his contacts with Alexander Keiller, the archaeologist who had carried out excavations at Avebury and Windmill Hill. Keiller's Morven Institute was named after his family home in Aberdeenshire.

Several places in the vicinity of Christchurch are mentioned by name. Morven says:

> *"I have heard that the people of the Witch Cult band together at St. Catherine's Hill, and that is but a league beyond thy mother's farm."; and "... so say that you will ride with me to St. Catherine's Hill (as they call it now, though better is it known as Kerewidens Hill) and I will risk the night there."*39

In the last chapter of the book, almost as if Gerald was trying to cram all the names in that he could, the Abbot says:

> *"Mind you, I think we must charge special fees for holding the Court at such short notice. Those farms at Southridge, for instance, and the mill at Walkford ... If you want money, I will give you a good price for Highcliffe Farm or Sumer-ford."* 40

Southridge was the name of Gerald's house in Highland Avenue and Highcliffe was the village he lived in. Although there was never a Highcliffe Farm as such, it enabled him to mention Highcliffe without having to refer to a particular location. Somer-ford was the location of the Rosicrucian Theatre where Gerald claimed to have first met the witches. There was never a mill at Walkford, but there was one on the Walkford Brook - Chewton Mill. We have, of course, already come across this: it is none other than the Mill House, the home of Dorothy St. Quintin Fordham! Was this a subtle indication that witches met there as well, somewhere that Doreen Valiente would later reveal as being the place that Gerald told her he had been initiated?

---

39. Gardner, (1949), 170 and 171.
40. Op. cit., 348 and 349.

Other places are also indicated, but not quite so clearly. In searching for the Witch of Wanda, Thur, Jan and Olaf stopped for the night at a hamlet called Eyeford. It is surely more than coincidence that the next village over the River Stour from Christchurch is called Iford. Indeed, the River Stour itself is also mentioned by name. Other names seem totally invented, like the etymologically unlikely Hurstwyck.

❧

At some stage in the production of the manuscript, Gerald had to approach the problem of getting it published. It is highly likely that he had paid for the publication of *A Goddess Arrives* out of his own pocket. He was not short of money and I doubt if he would have been inclined to approach many orthodox publishers over *High Magic's Aid* and almost certainly be faced with a series of rejection slips, for it was not of the literary standard of most books published then. It was long and there was still a paper shortage.

After considerable negotiation with Edith as to what he could and couldn't include, Gerald was ready, towards the end of 1948, to look for a publisher. It was obvious that none of the mainstream publishers was interested, and he chose the occultist, Michael Houghton, who was the proprietor of Atlantis Bookshop. Gerald almost certainly knew Houghton already, probably by visiting Atlantis on a regular basis. Atlantis Bookshop is situated in Museum Street, very close to the British Museum, and is reputed to be the oldest occult bookshop in the world. It was founded in 1922 by Houghton, a refugee from eastern Europe, who wrote under the pen-name of Michael Juste. He ran the shop until his death in 1961.

It is fascinating to speculate whether Gerald visited Atlantis Bookshop during his leave in England in 1927 and 1932. As he had a reader's ticket to the British Museum in 1927, it is very likely that he did and, I am sure, became a regular visitor following his retirement. He probably knew Houghton sufficiently well by the late 1940s to ask him to publish *High Magic's Aid*. Atlantis Bookshop had become, in the words of Philip Carr-Gomm, a "... kind of salon to the occult intelligentsia of the 1940s and 50s".[41] It

---

41. Carr-Gomm, (2001), 50.

seems to have been used for formal and informal meetings of various kinds, and regular visitors included Aleister Crowley, Dion Fortune, Paul Brunton, Gerald Yorke, W.B. Crow, Ross Nichols, Cottie Burland and John Hargrave.

Out of this emerged several enterprises. Houghton ran one of the first occult correspondence courses, as well as a magical lodge called 'The Order of the Hidden Masters' from the basement which, according to Caroline Wise:

> ... was turned into a temple, dedicated, rumour has it, to a Sumerian dog-headed goddess. Murals in a Near-Eastern style decorated the walls. It was here the order taught, following Golden Dawn-type rituals and ran a healing group.[42]

However, the writer, Charles Beatty, considered that the Order consisted of a "most sinister, hard-headed bunch of occultists" who "aimed at power over people - preferably in high places".[43] Gerald had apparently wanted to be a member of this order but had been refused.

Another enterprise to emerge from Atlantis Bookshop was a magazine entitled *The Occult Observer*. Although only surviving regularly for six issues between 1949 and 1950, it was extremely influential, having some excellent writers and providing a focus for much of the occult revival which took place in the 1950s, not least the modern witchcraft revival. Houghton was editor and Ross Nichols was appointed Assistant Editor. I get the impression that the various regular visitors to Atlantis were called upon to contribute, including Julian Shaw, W.B. Crow, John Hargrave, Gerald Yorke, Mir Bashir, Bernard Bromage, Dion Byngham, John Heath-Stubbs and John Cowper Powys.

The character of *The Occult Observer*, which had the sub-title 'A Quarterly Journal of Occultism, Art and Philosophy', was intellectual rather than sensational and the aim seems to have been to attract high quality writing from experts in their respective spheres. It hoped to 'publish and review such subjects as may disentangle the vast phantasmagoria misnamed occultism and bring

42. Caroline Wise, "A Pagan London Landmark: The Legendary Atlantis Bookshop", *Pagan Dawn* 116, (Lammas 1995), 14.
43. Charles Beatty, *Gate of Dreams*, (Geoffrey Chapman, 1972), 178-179.

a sense of proportion to these secret sciences of the illuminated'. In some ways, it could be seen as the journalistic equivalent of the Fouracres Club - certainly at least Cottie Burland and Dion Byngham were associated with both. After the sixth issue, in 1950, production ceased. Possibly sales were not as great as had been expected or the work involved in producing it was more than Houghton and Nichols could cope with.

Houghton was also a book publisher, but on rather a small scale. Since 1935, when he had published a volume of his own verse under the imprint of the Atlantis Bookshop, he had published an average of one book every two years. At over 350 pages, *High Magic's Aid* was by far the longest book he had ever published. Printing and binding costs alone would have been considerable and it is virtually certain that Gerald paid the bulk, if not all, of the costs of production.

Gerald's manuscript needed quite a lot of work to make it suitable for publication. Houghton introduced him to Dolores North, also known as Madeline Montalban, who could use her skills as a journalist and writer to help him. Julia Phillips, who has studied Madeline Montalban's life and work, tells me that Madeline had practically to write the book herself. Gerald had approached her with "a mass of notes he had assembled and struggled with unsuccessfully to turn into something usable". Gerald paid Madeline a fee to edit and transform his material into a publishable book. Gerald implies, in a letter he wrote to Cecil Williamson, that Madeline actually worked for Houghton:

> *It's very funy. Mrs. North is 'Delores'. She used to work at the Atlantis Bookshop, + she typed + put the spelling right in High Magics Aid. She makes a living at Astrology + love philtres, on the quiet. I know she claimed to be a Witch; but got evrything wrong. But, she knows High Magics Aid + has a lively imagination.*[44]

Julia Phillips doubts that Madeline ever worked at Atlantis Bookshop: perhaps she was just there on a temporary basis while dealing with Gerald's manuscript, or perhaps he used to meet her

---

44. Letter, Gerald Gardner to Cecil Williamson, June 1951, (Document 42 Boscastle Museum of Witchcraft archives).

there rather than at her own home. She could have been just a frequent visitor.

Both *A Goddess Arrives* and *High Magic's Aid* are good competent novels, but questions have to be asked about the extent to which Gerald had help in writing them. Certainly it seems as if Madeline did more for *High Magic's Aid* than just putting the spelling right, as Gerald claimed. It seems to me that sorting out a pile of notes, writing or re-writing whole sections, putting scenes into order, correcting grammar and spelling is actually enough that *High Magic's Aid* could reasonably be said to be a joint effort between Gerald and Madeline.

If that was necessary in the late 1940s, it must have been even more so ten years earlier, and I suspect that the help that Edith gave to Gerald with *A Goddess Arrives* was again far greater than merely correcting the grammar and spelling.

Doreen Valiente writes that Gerald told her that he had first met Madeline in London during the war, when she had been wearing the uniform of a WRNS (Women's Royal Naval Service) officer,[45] so perhaps she had been visiting Atlantis Bookshop regularly for some time.

Madeline seems to have taken against Gerald at some stage, describing him as a fraud and 'ritually inept'. There were probably ideological differences and personality incompatibility, but Mike Howard, editor of *The Cauldron* and one of her former students, told me that she fell out with him following a ritual where she was "tied up naked and tickled with a feather duster". This sounds like a rather unusual description of the initiation ritual, with which she was presumably familiar, having worked closely with Gerald on *High Magic's Aid*. Anyway, she subsequently did not like Gerald's name mentioned in her presence.

High Magic's Aid was published in July 1949, at a price of ten shillings and sixpence. It was a finely produced hardback volume, in page size 7¼ ins x 4¼ ins and was 352 pages in length. It was the very month that paper rationing was finally abolished in England, thus allowing what was, in reality, a fairly long book. The dust cover has a very striking illustration, in black and lime-green on white, showing the main four characters of the story next to a censer from

45. Valiente, (1989), 49-50.

which much smoke is issuing forth. I do not know the identity of the artist, who is identified merely by the initials 'HD' or 'DH'.

The title page indicates the author as "Scrire O.T.O. 4=7 (G.B. Gardner)". "Scrire" is almost certainly Gerald's mis-spelling of "Scire", his magical name (Latin for "to know" and one of the four powers of the sphinx) which is spelt correctly on the spine of the book and the dust-jacket. This suggests that Gerald was not that familiar with the name, which is likely to have been conferred on him by Crowley. He possibly thought that it related to the divinatory technique of 'scrying' and that it was a way of spelling 'scryer'. It has also been pointed out that 4=7 is not an O.T.O. degree. Its use supports my conclusion that Gerald did not understand the O.T.O. or its degree system.

It makes me wonder whether the individuals back in pre-war Highcliffe ever had witch names. If they did, then surely Gerald would have used his witch name in a book about witchcraft in preference to the one given him by Crowley. I certainly have doubts as to whether 'Dafo' was a magical name, since she had been known as 'Daff' in her family from childhood. Gerald gave the heroine in his book a witch name – Morven – and it is, I am sure, significant that his first initiate, Barbara Vickers, was given 'Morven' as her witch name.

The book did not sell well initially. Francis King puts this more bluntly: "The book seems to have been a resounding flop - five years later I saw the publisher's shelves still groaning under the weight of unsold copies"[46] This was probably because there was no way for potential readers to realise the significance of the book, beyond that of a story of magic and adventure set in 13th Century England. Certainly distribution of the book does not seem to have been particularly effective, and it must have been given a low profile even within the shop itself if a tale recounted by Gerald in 1951 is to be believed. He was going into Atlantis, just as a man was leaving. The shop assistant was saying "No, there aren't any books that tell you how to do it." On enquiring what he had wanted, Gerald was informed that he had requested books on how to work

---

46. King, 180.

magic. "What about *High Magic's Aid*?" he suggested. The assistant replied that she hadn't thought about that! [47]

Those who bought or subscribed to *The Occult Observer*
would have known about the book and some may have contacted
Gerald as a result, perhaps particularly any who may have
belonged to an existing witchcraft tradition.

It was only after Gerald had started selling the book from the
Museum on the Isle of Man that he made it quite clear that
witches still existed and that he was one himself. The notice that
was on display there gives a good indication of his motives in
writing the book:

> *Though it is a novel it is the only book that tells how High
> Magic, Ritual or Kabalistic was worked & how the tools you
> see upstairs were used. It also gives things from the
> Witches point of view & tells all about Witchcraft that is
> permitted to be made public.*[48]

And it was really only after Gerald had "come out" following
the publication of *Witchcraft Today* in 1954 that the book could
be put in its rightful context, for in the very first chapter of
Witchcraft Today he admits that:

> *... as it is a dying cult, I thought it was a pity that all the
> knowledge should be lost, so in the end I was permitted to
> write, as fiction, something of what a witch believes in the
> novel High Magic's Aid.*[49]

But the very book which revealed the significance of *High
Magic's Aid* also put it "in the shade" because in *Witchcraft Today*
Gerald was telling of witchcraft's survival - a work of non-fiction
which claimed that witches still existed and which rather stole
the thunder from a mere story set in mediaeval times.

And yet we have already noted that he gave a copy of *High
Magic's Aid* to Patricia Crowther in 1960 telling her to look at
Morven's words particularly, so he must have considered it to be

---

47. Letter, Gerald Gardner to Cecil Williamson, late 1951 (Document 35 Boscastle Museum
of Witchcraft archives).
48. In the archives of the Boscastle Museum of Witchcraft.
49. Gardner, (1954), 18-19.

still relevant even after the publication of *Witchcraft Today* in 1954 and *The Meaning of Witchcraft* in 1959.

What was Gerald's intention in writing *High Magic's Aid*? I think really it was only to get something published, even though few who initially bought the book would have realised its significance. Perhaps he hoped that readers might decide independently to revive the Craft, based purely on the details given in the book. Or, more likely, he began to see it as purely an interim exercise, hoping all the time that he would be able to get a non-fiction book about the Craft published one day.

However, the book affected at least one reader strongly enough for her to make contact with the author, with significant and far-reaching effects, as we shall see in the next chapter.

CHAPTER TWENTY–THREE

Two Encounters in Atlantis

In December 1948 Gerald wrote to Rex: *...came to town. got hold of Pinches, found hed no word, so concluded meeting had been called off, & went back. London hotells arnt comfatable.*[1] It is interesting that the alternative to going back to Christchurch is staying in a London hotel. What had happened to 47 Ridgmount Gardens? I suspect that he had sub-let the flat to someone else, probably Donna's brother, Jacko. Gerald was intending to go straight from Christchurch to Antwerp, from where the boat was leaving for his usual "wintering abroad", so would be away from the beginning of December certainly until late February and possibly until mid-March, enough time to make a sub-let worth while. During this period, Donna probably stayed with her sister, Queenie, or may have remained in the flat if her brother had taken it on.

Gerald had already established his custom of "wintering abroad", usually from the beginning of January to mid-March, a period which usually coincided with the coldest weather in England. It was also the period when snow was most likely, and thus something that Gerald would want to avoid. Kenneth Grant made a revealing comment about Gerald's journeys: *Gardner was old &*

---

1. Letter, Gerald Gardner to Rex Wellbye, 23 December 1948.

*in failing health by the time we met him - in those days the medica-
ments that controlled asthma were less effective than now. A reason why he favoured sea cruises was that they enabled him to
breathe more easily.*2

In the period just after the war, passenger ships to the
Mediterranean were something of a rarity. Gerald usually preferred cargo ships - they were probably cheaper, had fewer cabins
and often went to places that the other ships didn't. Arranging
such a ship, however, was never straightforward, particularly in
1948 and, with Gerald, there was always an aspect of mystery. On
17th November, he wrote to Rex: *I have had some news of my boat
but no definite date. she is being repaired in Antwerp. there were
too many forms to be filled in in England so they got her over there
& will fix her up sometime.* On 6th December he wrote to John
Pinches: *My boat may be repaired in the near future, things are
uncertain nowadays.* On 23rd December, he wrote to Rex from
Christchurch: *My boat leaves Antwerp on 29th, according to latest
news, I have to leave here on the 27th at latest, possibly before.*
Another letter to Rex the following day revealed: *I still don't know
where Ime going, but beleive we have a cargo for the Lebenon. I
wonder if its arms? possibly thats why they wont touch England?*
And a last letter on 27th December to John Pinches: *Am just off…
I still don't know where the boat is going to.*

Apart from Gerald's hint about Lebanon, we also really don't
know where the boat was going. Rex wrote to John Pinches on 7th
February 1949, after Gerald had been gone for over five weeks: *No
one has had any news of Gerald. They say he never writes, not even
to his wife.* John has added "or to Elsie?" after this.

We know, however, that Gerald visited John S.M. Ward and
his community in Cyprus that year, before Ward died in July 1949.
He went to see how they were getting on. They seemed to be
managing and were on good terms with the local people, but the
political situation was having an impact, particularly with the
EOKA guerrillas. In the end things got too difficult for the community, so they left Cyprus, ending up in Caboolture in S.E.
Queensland, Australia, where they established the Abbey
Museum of Art and Archaeology.

2. Letter, Kenneth Grant to the author, 5 March 2007.

Gregory Tillett reports that:

Ward [sic - he obviously actually means Gardner] *was ordained to the Priesthood by Bishop Colin Mackenzie Chamberlain, whom Ward had consecrated; the precise reasons for his ordination were not made clear, but it took place at the direction of the Reverend Mother, much of whose authority derived from visions and revelations she claimed to receive from the Holy Spirit. Gardner was never actively involved in the work of the Orthodox Catholic Church or the Confraternity of the Kingdom of Christ, and made no mention of his Priestly status in his published works.*[3]

By 19th February, Gerald was in Spain, in Borriana, near Castelló de la Plana. He informed Fothergill that he would be back by the end of March. In fact, he was back by the second week in March, for Rex wrote to Pinches on 13th March: *Boris has just told me that Gerald is back -- has been back a little while, very bad on arrival, but better now (indeed he was out when B rang up Donna).*

❦

Some time in late 1949, Gerald probably received a letter which Houghton had passed on to him. It was from Gilbert and Barbara Vickers, who lived in Prestwich near Manchester. They had read *High Magic's Aid* and were interested in meeting him. It seems likely that Gerald wrote back and suggested that they come and see him at his flat in Ridgmount Gardens.[4]

Gerald subsequently claimed that Gilbert and Barbara were members of a traditional coven in Cheshire. There is really no evidence for this that has so far come to light and I am inclined to believe that this was just another little invention of Gerald's. He also claimed long witch lineages for Doreen Valiente, Dayonis and Lois Bourne to try to add authenticity to the Craft, and, unless further evidence comes forward, I am inclined to think the claims on behalf of Gilbert and Barbara fall within the same category.

---

3. Gregory Tillett, "Gerald Gardner: Some Historical Fragments", *The Australian Wiccan*, No. 14 n.d.
4. I am indebted to Gilbert and Barbara's daughter, Miranda Vickers, for much of the information in this section.

What I think happened is that Barbara was in the habit of coming down to London on a regular basis to visit her parents. Because of her interest in spiritualism and the occult, she probably also visited Atlantis Bookshop. As we have already noted, this was an "occult melting pot" and a favourite meeting place in the immediate post-war period when interest in such topics as witchcraft and the occult generally was much rarer and less well accepted than it is today. It seems to have been the custom for free coffee to be made available to customers, some of whom had travelled a considerable distance. When *High Magic's Aid* had been published by its proprietor, Michael Houghton, for Gerald Gardner in July 1949, copies would probably have been displayed prominently in the shop. Barbara may well have been sufficiently intrigued by the book to have bought a copy and later made contact with the author, or indeed may have encountered Gerald in the shop and started a conversation with him.

So, that afternoon in the autumn of 1949, Barbara probably told Gerald something about her life and her interests. She had been born Kathleen Marie Blake on 13th July 1922 in her parents' home just off Acton High Street in West London. Thomas and Elsie Blake were strict Catholics, Thomas having been born in County Cork, Ireland. I get the impression that Barbara's early life was rather restrictive and that the expectations of her family for her future were quite limited: she was therefore seeking every effort to escape. As a teenager she rebelled against Catholicism, taking the opportunity which presented itself when the Second World War became imminent and she joined the Army a year before she should have done, becoming a corporal in the Signals Corps.

It was while stationed at Catterick in Yorkshire that she met her future husband, Gilbert. He had been born in 1907 into a family of Manchester industrialists, Hedley Vickers and Co., Meat Manufacturers. They married on 23rd December 1944 in Kingston, Surrey, where they were stationed at the time. The Vickers family were strongly Protestant and Gilbert persuaded Kathleen to change her name to something more Protestant-sounding. So Kathleen Marie became Barbara Kathryn! She was also persuaded to take elocution lessons.

When the war ended, the couple moved north to the family home of Barnfield, Prestwich, Manchester. It was a large house and, in the days of austerity just after the war, they couldn't afford to heat it and just lived in the kitchen area: the rest of the house was closed off. They later tried to run it as a hotel, but it was not a success, partly because of the difficulty of getting staff.

It was here that Barbara first saw a ghost. She was searching for Gilbert one day and she entered one of the closed-off corridors, looking in all the rooms. She entered one and noticed a group of people dressed in very old-fashioned clothes, toasting crumpets by the fire. None of them looked up as she opened the door. She closed it quickly and then, suddenly realising that there should be no-one else in the house, opened it again, to the view of dust-sheets covering all the furniture. This is in many ways an unremarkable account, but it does indicate some psychic ability on Barbara's part. This ability seems to have survived her death, since a séance message from Barbara could well have saved her daughter from being murdered!

It is not clear when Barbara first met Gerald Gardner. From 1945 to 1953 Barbara and Gilbert were living "up north" and by at least mid-1951 became members of the North Western Sun Bathing Society, a naturist club that had woodland premises between Macclesfield and Congleton in Cheshire. It seems likely that they were introduced to naturism by Gerald.

There must have been something in *High Magic's Aid* that made Barbara aware that this was not just a story but something more. Being psychically sensitive, she probably had the knack of "reading between the lines". Anyway, after she had first met Gerald, he would have spoken at length about what he was probably still calling "the witch cult" and very soon Barbara had either asked for, or agreed to, initiation. Gerald was then faced with something of a dilemma. His memories of his own initiation, over ten years earlier, were full of deep and exciting feelings, but could he remember the words and actions that were necessary? He knew that he couldn't and that he wouldn't be able to get anything out of Edith either: she would have refused to speak about it. So he was, really by default, having to fall back on the ritual which he had written in *High Magic's Aid*, which was largely taken from *The Key of Solomon* together with material from Masonic and other sources plus what he could remember from his own initiation. I think it was at this stage that the volume known as 'Text A' really came into use. Gerald had copied the first, second and third degree initiation rituals into the book, which he could easily place on a stand so that he could read the ritual from a distance by candle-light.

At least he had something which could be used for the initiation, the date for which was rapidly approaching. Gilbert had also asked for initiation. Gerald felt it was important to keep up the tradition where a man initiates a woman and a woman initiates a man, so he planned to initiate Barbara first and then guide her through Gilbert's initiation. He carried out exactly the same procedure over ten years later when he initiated Patricia and Arnold Crowther.

The initiation is likely to have been some time between autumn 1949 and autumn 1950. Barbara told her daughter that Gerald had confided in her that it was a very important event historically, which she took to mean that she was one of the first, if not the first, to be initiated by Gerald. He gave Barbara the witch name of Morven, the witch name of the heroine of *High Magic's Aid*. This provides additional confirmation that she was indeed the first person ever to be initiated by Gerald, since it was the obvious name to give a woman initiate. It was also an implicit recognition that his claims that she had been a member of a traditional group had little foundation, as otherwise she would probably have already had a 'witch name'.

It was a momentous occasion for Gerald: perhaps after all there might just possibly be a future for the witch cult. What is certain is that by November 1950 at the latest, Gerald had initiated Barbara into the Craft, as two photographs taken by Gilbert have survived showing her skyclad, holding ritual objects in characteristic pose. In one, Barbara is holding a two-handled metal cup. There is also what looks like a dark mirror, circular, about 3ft 6ins in diameter, surrounded by a frame on which the names of the four archangels are painted, possibly in Gerald's own hand. This was later on display in the Museum of Magic and Witchcraft. Gerald describes it as:

... a large round mirror. This is a Magical Mirror, which has evidently been used by a practising magician or a magical fraternity. It is convex, and backed with a dark substance instead of the usual silvering. Around the frame are the names "Michael", "Gabriel", "Uriel", and "Raphael", the four great Archangels who are said to rule the four quarters of the universe. Such mirrors as these have been used for many centuries to summon up magical visions.[5]

Gerald had noticed the mirror in a rather run-down junk shop somewhere off the Tottenham Court Road in London. The shop was closed, but he was back there first thing the following morning and promptly acquired the mirror from the proprietor, who obviously had no idea what it was.

In the second photograph Barbara is seated, hands crossed and holding what look like a scourge and a wand. She is wearing a large metal bracelet similar to those which Gerald made for his other priestesses. She is also wearing a pendant on a necklace which contains what her daughter describes as "a lovely green stone". Beside her, on the bed on which she is sitting, is a book, page size possibly 8ins x 5ins, which appears to be handwritten, and which could well be what we would now describe as her Book of Shadows. We know that she did have such a book, since in the typed version of what is commonly known as 'Jack Bracelin's Book of Shadows' we have a handwritten annotation at one point reading "from B.V.'s book".

These photographs are of immense significance in that they are some of the earliest so far identified of anyone involved in what Gardner described as 'the witch cult', characteristically sky-clad with 'regalia' and postures.

Some have suggested that the photographs of Donna referred to earlier demonstrate that she was Gerald's High Priestess. I am not convinced, however, that these were other than simple nude photographs of a woman by her husband and therefore not connected to 'the witch cult'. Besides, the timing is wrong. The photographs of Barbara, on the other hand, are very specific with

5. Gardner, (1958), 29.

regard to both postures and equipment and show convincingly their connection with 'the witch cult'.

If I am right that Barbara was Gerald's first initiate, then the coven, if such it could be called, would consist just of Gerald, Gilbert and herself. We know that Gilbert was also an initiate, since Gerald, when writing to Cecil Williamson in 1953/54, says: *You quite agreed that you could not be told all the secrets of Witch-craft unless you joined + took the oaths. Barbara + Gilbert were willing at the time, but you would not.*

From press reports it seems likely that there was a coven which met at Fiveacres Club in Bricket Wood by late 1951. An arti-cle in October 1951 states: *I learned of a nudist camp where at mid-night rites were performed with nude devotees of both sexes.*

Doreen Valiente told Mike Howard, editor of *The Cauldron*, that when she started working with Gerald, there was a very pretty blonde woman in the coven who was called Barbara Vick-ers and who had obviously known Gerald for some time. This would have been the coven which met at Gerald's flat in Holland Road in early 1953 when Doreen was first involved. Presumably Barbara managed to fit in coven meetings with her visits to her parents in Acton.

It seems possible that Gilbert and Barbara did start some sort of a coven in Cheshire, probably based on the naturist club to which they belonged. Their daughter was born in Cheshire in March 1952, but by September 1953 the couple had separated and Barbara returned to London with her young daughter to live with her parents. This left her in an awkward situation: her parents were strict Catholics and would not condone their daughter being involved in what they called 'hocus pocus' while living with them.

Barbara managed as best she could, and when her daughter was old enough to be left with her grandparents, she got a flat in Basil Street, Knightsbridge, which was the venue for what seems to have been some sort of group which held séances on a regular basis. She also continued her membership of Gerald's coven. Ger-ald refers, in a letter to Cecil Williamson in March 1951, to Barbara having a 'Monomark' address, which is similar to a P.O. Box num-ber, and frequently used by occult magazines, organisations and practitioners. This suggests that she may have been involved in some sort of commercial enterprise, although her daughter told me that later, when she was living with her parents, Barbara retained the 'Monomark' address for privacy reasons.

By the end of 1954 it seems as if Barbara had ceased to attend meetings of the coven, because in mid-November of that year she mentioned[6] that she had seen Gerald and that he had become very thin, which suggests that this was the first time she had seen him for quite a while. The occasion was probably a launch party for his new book, *Witchcraft Today,* which had been published on 1st November. Barbara's copy was inscribed *To One from another. To Barbera with the Authors Love. Gerald. Nov 2nd 1954. Blessed Be* together with the usual scourge and pentagram symbols.

Probably the last time that Barbara ever worked with Gerald's coven was at the initiation of Jack Bracelin and his girlfriend, in March 1956. I think she came as a special favour to Gerald as Doreen Valiente, the coven's High Priestess, was not available for some reason, perhaps because she didn't approve of what Gerald was doing. Barbara wrote a letter to Gilbert in April 1956[7] in which she refers to her recent meeting with Gerald (which was obviously a rare event) and commenting again that he was looking very thin.

I think that Barbara probably felt that bringing up her daughter in the Catholic faith, which she agreed to do, was incompatible with remaining a member of the coven. Indeed, in later years she rather took against the Craft. In 1959, she saw an apparition of Gerald Gardner at the foot of her bed (probably this was during a period when he was very ill) and, for some reason, although she had seen ghosts before and attended séances regularly, it frightened her so much that the following day she took all her witch 'regalia', wrapped it up and put it in the rubbish which was to be collected that day. One can only hope that the dustmen were as perceptive of items of value as they are reputed to be and that somewhere the 'regalia' still survive!

Barbara died in 1973 and Gilbert in 1978.

⁂

6. Letter, Barbara Vickers to Gilbert Vickers, 11 November 1954, copy in the author's collection.
7. Letter, Barbara Vikcers to Gilbert Vickers, 4 April 1956, copy in the author's collection.

Gerald was a frequent visitor to Atlantis Bookshop since the publication of *High Magic's Aid* the previous year and, as we have seen, had met Gilbert and Barbara Vickers as a result. It was probably in November 1950 that Gerald encountered someone else there who would be very influential in his life in the course of the next few years - Cecil Williamson.

It seems as if Gerald and Cecil got talking (perhaps over a cup of coffee, or rather two cups!) and Cecil told Gerald that he was wanting to open a Museum of Witchcraft. He had accumulated over many years a large collection of material on the subject and was looking for a venue near London for such an enterprise. In fact, I suspect that, until he had met and had discussions with Gerald, Cecil was thinking of opening a museum not of witchcraft but of torture. In June 1950, before he met Gerald, he was enquiring of Louis Tussaud, great-grandson of Madame Tussaud, whether he had any torture material for sale.[8] And it is certainly true that, following Gerald's takeover of the museum in 1954, Cecil briefly set up a Museum of Torture at Onchan, in the Isle of Man.

Gerald immediately expressed an interest, said that he might be able to find somewhere suitable (he was thinking of Five Acres Club, as we shall see), that he had some suitable exhibits (primarily the 'Matthew Hopkins' box and its contents, which he had shown to the Folk-Lore Society in 1939, plus a variety of items that he had accumulated during his time 'out east' and more recently) and hinted that he might be able to help financially. Cecil gave Gerald his card and then left, both promising to keep in touch.

Gerald was very excited by this chance meeting, for he suddenly realised that he would very much like to be involved in opening a museum of witchcraft, in fact very much involved indeed. Museums were probably in Gerald's blood. We have seen how he bought a knife in the Canary Islands with his first pocket money, and his fascination for collection went on from there. *Gerald Gardner Witch* includes a photograph of Donna in their Johore bungalow in front of a wall on which all sorts of weapons are displayed. This developed into a detailed study of the keris which culminated in the publication in 1936 of *Keris and Other Malay Weapons*.

---

8. Letter, Louis Tussaud to Cecil Williamson, 17 June 1950.

It seems likely that Gerald had had the idea of a museum of witchcraft at the back of his mind possibly as early as 1939 when he acquired the box of witchcraft relics about which he wrote the article for *Folk-Lore* journal. We know from this article that by 1939 he was also in contact with J.S.M. Ward and was therefore undoubtedly familiar with his Abbey Folk Park, which opened in 1934. I am sure that Gerald would have approved of this pioneering venture in a form of display that has now become virtually universal. And we have seen how he became interested in techniques of display after visiting the museum in Salisbury during the war and how he spoke in favour of a museum for Christchurch at a time when it was lacking in that direction.

So Gerald was very keen to get involved with Cecil Williamson on this project. He invited him to attend a meeting of the Folk-Lore Society on 13th December 1950, when a Mrs Danielli was talking about "The Geomancer in China".

In the course of that meeting and the informal discussion afterwards, Gerald managed to learn something of Cecil's background and interests, though he later learned that many of Cecil's stories were just that - stories, and not to be taken literally. The problem was to decide which ones fell into that category!

Cecil Hugh Williamson (1909-1999) was born on 18th September 1909 in Paignton in Devon. His father had had a long and distinguished career in the Royal Navy and had later joined the Fleet Air Arm. One of the family homes was Newlands Manor, at Everton, between Highcliffe and Lymington, so he had a definite connection with the New Forest area. The other home was Carrington House, Shepherd Street, in the prestigious Mayfair area of London.

Cecil told Gerald that his first contact with witchcraft was at the age of seven when he was spending the summer with his uncle, who was Vicar of North Bovey, on the edge of Dartmoor. One afternoon, he tried to protect an old woman who was being attacked by local farm-workers for being a witch. A week or so later, Cecil said that he met the old woman again. She befriended him and taught him a lot of practical skills, like tickling for trout, as well as folklore and witchcraft, for she did indeed claim to be a witch.

There was a family expectation that Cecil would be going into the Navy, but at that time Dartmouth was not taking on any more pupils, so he was sent to Malvern College, following which he went to Southern Rhodesia (now Zimbabwe) to learn tobacco growing.

Returning to England in the early 1930s, Cecil was attracted to the growing popularity of the film industry. He worked for several studios as a film producer, and in 1933 he married his co-director's niece, Gwen Wilcox.

During this time in London, he built up contacts with individuals in the occult world. The list reputedly included Aleister Crowley, Montague Summers, Harry Price, Wallis Budge, Margaret Murray and James Laver, as well as practitioners of rural witchcraft - the characters he called 'Auntie Mays'.

In 1938, as war loomed, Col. E.F. Maltby, an old family friend, who worked for MI6, the Secret Intelligence Service, invited Cecil to meet him. He had learned of Cecil's knowledge of the occult and wanted him to find out the names of Nazis in the German military and government who were interested in the occult. Cecil supposedly made several visits to Germany under the guise of a folklore researcher, compiling a list of 2000 Nazi officials who were interested in astrology and the occult.

When the war started, Col. Maltby sent Cecil to work for Richard Gambier-Parry, who ran what later became the Political Warfare Executive, one of the objectives of which was to broadcast programmes on wavelengths near those used by German transmitters, so that some misinformation could be fed to those listening. At first, this was in Whaddon Hall and Wavendon Towers in Bedfordshire, but in 1942, the most powerful transmitter in the world, known as 'Aspidistra', was installed in Ashdown Forest in Sussex. Cecil lived nearby for the rest of the war, although later he became involved in Operation Fortitude, which fed misleading information to convince the Germans that the 1944 Normandy landings were merely a diversion from a major attack which was to take place in the Pas de Calais. Various methods were employed, including artificial airfields with papier-mâché aircraft! Cecil's role was to set up in a truck in the New Forest making broadcasts which simulated Army manoeuvres which gave the impression that they were concentrating their forces in Essex for a possible invasion from that location.

When the war ended, Cecil was demobilised: *I was without a job. My assets were a little cash in hand from wartime pay, and a large data file on the occult and the supernatural*[9] He decided to go back to the film industry, and in 1948 he made the film *Trophy Island* in the Isle of Man, which set the scene for the 1949 TT Races, including a piece featuring the last native speaker of Manx Gaelic.

However, Cecil sold his interest in the film company and was looking for another way of making a living. Like Gerald, he seems to have been a born collector and friends who were connected with London museums commented to him that his "stuff ought to be seen by the public as it was too good to be tucked away".

He was undoubtedly at a crossroads in his life and open to new ideas when he made that fateful encounter with Gerald in Atlantis Bookshop in the autumn of 1950.

⚜

The setting up of the witchcraft museum on the Isle of Man is an important part of Wiccan history, and its story reveals insights into the characters of both Gerald Gardner and Cecil Williamson.

We are fortunate in that Gerald's letters to Cecil, during the 1951 to 1954 period, are preserved in the Museum of Witchcraft archives at Boscastle in Cornwall. But it is an inevitable fact that correspondence only takes place when individuals are apart - letters are not usually written to the same extent when people are in daily contact. And, at the time (late 1950), Cecil was living (or at any rate working) at 2 Wardour Mews, D'Arblay Street, Wardour Street, London W1, and Gerald was at 47 Ridgmount Gardens, which were less than a mile apart.

The first item of correspondence between them is dated 4th January 1951, a note from Gerald which refers to Cecil as "Mr. Wilkinson", which suggests that they had not been acquainted long! Indeed, the way in which Gerald addresses Cecil is interesting and helps to date some of the letters. The earliest note calls him "Mr. Wilkinson", as mentioned above; then he is referred to

---

9. Cecil Williamson, "A Report from the Enquiring Eye of the Witchcraft Research Centre", (1991).

as "Mr. Williamson" (i.e. Gerald gets the surname right); then as "Cyril" (in other words, on first name terms, but he gets the name wrong!); then, finally, as "Cecil"!

So, the early discussions between Gerald and Cecil following their meeting in Atlantis Bookshop are not recorded or, at any rate, any correspondence does not appear to have survived. It certainly seems as if many different ideas were being discussed, and they mostly seemed to focus around the Witch's Cottage.

It seems that Cecil started his search for somewhere to display his exhibition material back in May 1950, for in the guide leaflet issued at the opening of the museum, he writes: ... *after nine months of persistent but fruitless endeavour the idea of trying to open in England was abandoned*.[10] We don't know exactly what efforts he made, but they seem to have been tied in with the Festival of Britain. 1951 was the centenary of the Great Exhibition of 1851, and an opportunity to publicise the cultural and industrial life of Britain emerging from the austerity of the Second World War was taken with the announcement of a Festival of Britain, to be held that year. Gerald and Cecil clearly had the idea of capitalising on the interest surrounding this event by making the Witch's Cottage available as an exhibition centre to show something of the history and practices of witchcraft. The idea was to dismantle the cottage and re-erect it temporarily, for the duration of the summer of 1951 (the Festival ran from 1st May to 30th September that year) wherever it was wanted. I don't think any detailed costings had been worked out and in practice the cost of moving and re-erecting it would undoubtedly have proved prohibitive, as Cecil was eventually to realise.

The main Festival of Britain site was on the South Bank of the River Thames in London, but there were also numerous local events taking place that summer. Cecil had written to several local Festival committees offering the cottage and an accompanying exhibition, which probably hadn't, at that stage, been put together. At the end of January 1951, he received rejection letters from Chelsea and Canterbury. A local doctor in Shakespeare's birthplace, Stratford-on-Avon, had agreed that he could use some garages at the rear of his garden, but press publicity was such that

---

10. The Folklore Centre of Superstition and Witchcraft, "An Introduction to Visitors", (1951).

the locals were very much against a witchcraft exhibition and nothing came of the matter.

⚛

For his annual trip abroad, Gerald went to Gibraltar by sea, as usual, embarking at the beginning of February 1951. He had arranged to stay at the Rock Hotel. Built in 1932 by the Marquis of Bute, it is still the most famous hotel in Gibraltar and has been host to many distinguished guests over the years.

He seems to have gone on a round trip from Gibraltar to Majorca and Ibiza. On 8th February he wrote to Cecil: *I go to Valencia in a week's time, then to Granada + Gib. – England beginning of March.* He was in Ibiza on 13th February, but he was a little vague about his future movements, for in a letter to Rex Wellbye he wrote: *I leave here on the 19th. My movements depend on other people, but a letter Co. Barkleys Bank, Gibraltar should reach me about the end of the month ... It depends on other people ... exactly when I get back to England.*[11]

The mention of "other people" suggests that he was travelling with someone else. In fact, his travelling companion was Edith who, in the passenger list for the return journey from Gibraltar on the *R.M.S. Orion*, is listed as "Mrs. E. Gardner". Avenue Cottage is given as the home address for both her and Gerald. This is particularly interesting, as it suggests, not only that Gerald and Edith had an intimate relationship, but that she may have accompanied him on more than one occasion when he wintered abroad.

Gerald was in Gibraltar again on 27th February and had booked on a boat on 1st March which was due back in England on 6th March. However, the following day he wrote to Rex:

> *I have been down trying to get a passage home, but Cooks are hopeless, the Spanish Travel Agencies are shut. Am trying all the Shipping Cos, But Government Controll everything + all say they are not allowed to Book unless by Govt. Order ... The weather has at last turned warm + I am sunbathing as I write on the Hotel Balcony*[12]

---

11. Letter, Gerald Gardner to Rex Wellbye, 13 February 1951.
12. Letter, Gerald Gardner to Rex Wellbye, 28 February 1951 (although he put 1950 on the letter, this is almost certainly a mistake).

However, Donna wrote and told him to stay a bit longer in Gibraltar because the weather was so bad back in England. Then, as Gerald reports in a letter to Rex, ...*the trouble started & travel bacame difficult.*[13] I don't know exactly what the trouble was, probably some workers' dispute, but it certainly disrupted travel plans.

He was home by 14th March, however, because he attended a meeting of the Folk-Lore Society on that date, even though he claimed in a letter that Rex received on 30th March that he had "just got home". Perhaps he didn't want to be caught up immediately in all the controversy surrounding the Club. He would probably have made a special effort to come back in time to attend the Folklore Society meeting on the 14th, since it was the Presidential Address by his friend, W.L. Hildburgh on "The Psychology underlying the employment of Amulets in Europe", a subject that was of particular interest to Gerald.

⁂

In Gerald's absence he left Cecil a note dated 4th January 1951, which stated, unambiguously: *To Whom It May Concern: I have give the Witch's Cottage to Mr. Wilkinson to Remove when he can get transport. G.B. Gardner.* This tells us that they expected that things would go fast and that the cottage might be needed for removal for the purposes of the Festival of Britain while Gerald was away.

There was quite a lot of correspondence between Gerald and Cecil. He had obviously told Gerald about the rejections from Chelsea and Canterbury (and possibly elsewhere) because Gerald makes the suggestion that Cecil puts in an offer for the half share in Five Acres Club not owned by Gerald and his friends and that he opens it as a museum and witchcraft study centre. Gerald writes:

> ... *there is a Row on at the Club where I took you that day, & one section say sell the damned place. There are supposed to be 5 acres there, & another 2 acres for £200/- some income from parts leased to people who own the Huts, a good Club House, which you saw. I'd value the land at £100/- per acre, Club House at say £300/-/-. Say £800/- more or less for the place, & an additional 2 acres for £200/-. The Club House wd*

---

13. Letter, Gerald Gardner to Rex Wellbye received, 30 March 1951.

make a lovely museum & Refreshment Room, Caretaker in adjacent Hut. Leave the Witchs Cottage where it is this year, take people to museum first, then to cottage by the entrance they came in. Move Witchs Cottage next year. We then could have the centre for a Study Group, who could stay out there in Huts if they liked. Being a Nudist Club no one could object to Nude Dances & Rites only the Actual Ceremonies wd have to be kept secret. But this is all in the air, & any breath of it would make them refuse to sell, & no mention of my name, or there be trouble, but think it over & see how it strikes you.[14]

Gerald was obviously getting enthusiastic about the idea of having the proposed museum at Five Acres and, almost certainly without receiving a reply from Cecil, wrote him another letter in which he sets out his ideas in more detail. The following is an early transcript of Gerald's original letter, which is now lost. The spelling is therefore corrected:

I have been thinking over what I wrote to you the other day re the Club land, always provided you like the idea. You might get in touch with M.D. Mackee ... The position is that the blighter who is giving me so much trouble is trying to wreck the Club and get it all in his own hands, but I and a friend of mine hold half the debentures and she says OK. That means that what ever the price only half need be paid. We take it in shares in the Museum. If the price is £800 only £400 cash need be found. If £1000 only £500. Of course, on top of that, it will need water laid on, nothing much and what decoration that needs doing, showcases and a Caretaker will have to live down there. But this is my plan. Have if possible a married couple, who will be caterer putting up lunches and teas.

If you run motor coaches from London, through the beautiful country past Elstree through Bricket Wood to Witch Hut and museum lunch there, then on to St. Albans Cathedral, Museum Roman remains and back to London another way I think it would be popular; or it could be St. Albans first, lunch

---

14. Letter, Gerald Gardner to Cecil Williamso, n 8 February 1951, (although he put 1950 on the letter, this is almost certainly a mistake).

at Club and visit Museum and Witches Hut or it might be an afternoon trip and tea at the Museum. Say you did this 5 days a week (I don't think it would run to more than 5 days a week), then the Club could use it on Saturdays and Sundays. (The Caretaker would have to be a nudist or at least not mind) but you would also have the profits on the nudists lunches, teas and dinners on Sat and Sundays – money for jam.

The Caretaker would have the big hut to live in, the big club room would be the museum, the smaller games room could be a tea room in cold weather, good weather, tea on the verandah. ... We can have the stuff out and study it, and try it, and try the old Witch dances, etc: the ones who take to it will be initiated and no one can say anything because they are all members of a Nudist Club. Next year, if possible, we can move the Witches Hut up to the group, but this year there's no time so leave it where it is.

Don't tell Mackee about the Cult, just say you want land for your Museum. It would mean that it could only function as a club on Saturday and Sunday. Of course, people could do what they liked on their own land, but must fence it off. You would have to put in water, but that's not a very big thing, there's a good kitchen, you would want a few more cups and plates, but the Club has a lot already. As you'd only have to deal with one coach load at a time, and possibly a few stray motorists, if it became popular you'd arrange things so that one coach came for lunch, one for tea, of course it would mean the catering people would have to work, but they'd get a house to live in. ...

If it could be managed we could I think get a good and strong cult going. We could probably have a meeting place in London. The Folklore Society can always borrow a Committee room from the London University and I think the Folklore Study Group could also get it, if the secret was kept. But it must be kept. Write to Mackee and see what he thinks.[15]

---

15. Letter, Gerald Gardner to Cecil Williamson, late February 1951, (Document 73, Boscastle Museum of Witchcraft archive).

It is clear from this that Gerald's relationship with Rex Well-bye had deteriorated markedly, and later that month he wrote:

I have told you of Rex Wellbye, my bad neighbour, he has been trying to get the Council to Dig Drains through my land to spoil it. ... If Wellbye wants the drains dug they should go through his own land which is the shortest way & would not spoil his land.[16]

From Wellbye's point of view, the problems looked rather different:

Our Sec. ... had to resign, and no successor has been appointed. ... We have very charming members -- but they just do not want to be bothered to do any work or even sit on a committee. When we took over it was a proprietary club, and so far my efforts have failed to make it a members' club, the only result being to let in an unrepresentative clique. This might have worked for a time if the additions to the Board had displayed energy, but the lethargy has been colossal, and the slowness and reluctance to meet unbelievable ... One of the enlarged Board has resigned, another is so ill and old that he is sure to resign, too, a third will only attend a meeting if he happens to be on the spot, while the fourth, to whom they all look for action, is procrastinating and unbusinesslike -- but wont let go! [This sounds like Gerald!] *I have now taken steps to end the situation one way or the other, but the position will not become clear for a few weeks more.*[17]

The comment about getting "a good and strong cult going" is interesting because it seems to imply that there was no witchcraft activity going on at Five Acres or at the Witches' Cottage at the time (February 1951). This is confirmed by a statement in the earlier letter when Gerald writes: "By the way, the Cult are very angry about my talking to the reporter". This was in the context of articles which were supposed to have appeared in the *Sunday Dispatch* and at least one other paper, though research has so far failed to

16. Letter, Gerald Gardner to Cecil Williamson, 27 February 1951.
17. Letter, Rex Wellbye to Ernest Virgo, 13 January 1951, (in British Naturism archives).

unearth these. Gerald seems to have been interviewed by a reporter from the *Sunday Dispatch*, presumably some time before he went away. Donna sent the cuttings on to him. He comments to Cecil:

> *Nearly everything is wrong. I told him that the Goddess had to do with the Moon, + the God seemed to have to do with Horned Cattle. + he makes them Sun Gods. I told him the Rites were performed nude, he says the main object of the Rites is to get into a frenzy + tear off your clothes, etc. etc. I told him things on condition that no address was given, + not even to mention that I lived in London, + he publishes this address. His name is Meyor. If he ever comes to you please refuse to see him, + tell him why[18]*

This was the first, but by no means the last, time that Gerald had trusted representatives of the press and been let down. However, he never seemed to learn from this experience and continued to give interviews in the hope and expectation of fair treatment, which was often not forthcoming.

When Gerald writes "...the Cult are very angry about my talking to the reporter", this was clearly someone who was in a position to be angry with Gerald; there was only one person in that position and that was Edith. The fact that he identifies her with 'the cult' suggest strongly that she and whatever was going on in Highcliffe constituted the whole of 'the cult' at that time. As Aidan Kelly says, Gerald *hadn't yet found the right mix of ingredients to keep the engine running steadily.*[19]

While he was away, Gerald wrote to Rex Wellbye about the Club, and I think it is indicative of the degree of his interest in the museum project:

> *... I only want to see the Club put on its feet + then wash my hands of it. you know I will help anyone who tries to do that, as I will fight anyone trying to harm the Club, but I have lost all interest in the place, + I have lots of work to do.* [20]

❧

18. Letter, Gerald Gardner to Cecil Williamson, 8 February 1951.
19. Message on Gardnerians_All, 5 November 2006.
20. Letter, Gerald Gardner to Rex Wellbye, 13 February 1951.

Gerald's enthusiasm about opening a museum at Five Acres was not shared by Cecil. Whilst Gerald was trying to persuade him to make the cottage at Bricket Wood into a tourist attraction, there is the first indication, at the end of February, that Cecil had turned his sights elsewhere. Gerald asked him: *Do I understand that you will open the museum in the Isle of Man, & do you want to transport the Witches Hut up there?* [21]

Cecil Williamson had learnt from his experiences in Stratford. He began to look for somewhere where the environment for opening his exhibition might be more congenial. It would have to be a tourist area, but he had been rather discouraged by the bureaucracy involved with local government in England, particularly the need to get planning permission, which had been introduced universally four years earlier, in 1947.

His thoughts began to be directed towards the Isle of Man, where he had directed the publicity film for the Tourist Department and had kept in touch with some of the staff. He approached them informally and they were enthusiastic about his project. Perhaps in part because of his established contacts, Cecil found the attitude of the authorities on the Island much more positive than in England, and he received help and encouragement from the Castletown Board of Commissioners and the Chief Executive Officer of the Publicity Board. Anticipating objections, and with the wisdom of hindsight, Cecil recounted: *This time I took good care to play down all mention of that awful word witchcraft.* However, rather illogically, he continues: *All the documents concerned with the project bore the style "The Folk-lore Centre of Superstition and Witchcraft.* [22] He drew their attention to the relative absence of displays on witchcraft, magic and superstition in national and municipal museums.

He went over to the island to look for suitable premises. Those in Douglas proved to be too expensive and so he spread his net wider. He finally found what he was looking for in Castletown, the ancient capital of the island. Cecil's eye was caught by Windmill Farm, on the outskirts of the town, a ruined mill, with a collection

21. Letter, Gerald Gardner to Cecil Williamson, 27 February 1951, (Document 38, Boscastle Museum of Witchcraft archives).
22. Cecil Williamson, "The Witchcraft Museums", *Pentagram* 6, (Candlemas 1967), 27.

of outbuildings which seemed fairly sound. The farmstead and immediate curtilage, consisted of approximately four acres, which was probably the old farmyard and gardens. It was off Arbory Road, in the vicinity known as Red Gap, next to the present-day Castle Rushen Secondary School, and it appeared to have been disused for some years. It consisted of a dwelling house, two former millers' cottages, several stone barns each over 40 feet long, another large range of detached stone outhouses, a large 3-storey limestone granary and a 60 foot high derelict windmill tower open to the sky.

Cecil could see the potential of the place, which was available on lease at a price which he could afford. The dwelling house was habitable and the granary would be ideal for the museum. There was also a large area suitable for car and coach parking.

The site had an interesting history. The first mill on the site was certainly in existence by 1611. Windmills are rare on the Isle of Man, possibly because watermills were cheaper to build and also because of the frequency of very high winds and gales which make their operation impractical. There are records of only 12 having existed on the Island. The Castletown windmill dates from 1828, though its history, right from the start, was full of misfortune, being destroyed successively by storm and fire.[23] Gerald tells the story that:

> ... when the old mill was burned, they used the ruins as a dancing-ground, for which it was eminently suited; being on the edge of town, close to the Arbory road, and being round inside to accommodate the witches' circle, while the remains of the stone walls screened them from the wind and from prying eyes.[24]

There were trials of witches in Kirk Arbory in the 17th Century, but there is no written evidence that there was ever a coven operating there. I thought it was likely to be purely Gerald's wishful thinking, but I have been told recently by a reliable source that there was an Arbory line of witches on the Island. Certainly, the ruined mill tower probably suggested itself to him as a ritual place

23. J. K. Qualtrough, "The Windmill, Castletown", *ProcIoM NH&ASoc*, Vii, No. 2, 248-263.
24. Gerald Gardner, "Magic, Witchcraft and Fairies in the Isle of Man", manuscript in the Toronto collection.

immediately he saw it and he was clearly keen to perform rituals there. Whether he ever did I do not know, but there is a photograph showing Monique Wilson preparing for a ritual there.[25]

When Cecil took over the mill and buildings in 1951, his strategy in approaching the authorities seemed to work, because all the necessary permissions were granted. He then proceeded to convert the buildings into a museum and living accommodation. He moved to Castletown and started work on the buildings in April 1951. The property included a small house, which he renovated and occupied, probably in early May 1951, followed by his family later the same month.

Cecil only told Gerald that he was interested in opening a museum in the Isle of Man in late February 1951. Immediately Gerald got back from wintering in Gibraltar he tried to make arrangements to meet Cecil on the island. Gerald was always one to do things on impulse and he was clearly itching to see the old windmill and buildings that Cecil had acquired for the Museum. He was trying to fit in a visit with a Committee meeting of the Club. He wrote to Rex:

> *I have a lot of work to do in connection with the Festaval of Britain. If I don't hear from you by tomorrow, I'll conclude that it's not for this week, Sun 8th, & so will go off to the Isle of Man. my address will be the Folk Lore Centre, Casseltown, I Of Man. If youve called the Committee for the next week end. Sunday 15th, Ill be down for it.[26]*

On Wednesday 4th April he wrote to Cecil saying:

> *Ive booked things on Friday. 10.30 from Euston + catch the afternoon plane from Liverpool. Please will you book me a single room at the George Hotel, or elsewhere. I'd come to the George Hotel to find out. I don't know what time I'll get to Castletown, but the hotel people will know.*

Whilst there had probably been some loose arrangement with Cecil to go up there that weekend, Cecil had clearly not appeared,

---

25. Colin Cross, "The Witches Ride Again", *The Observer*, 1 December 1968.
26. Letter, Gerald Gardner to Rex Wellbye, 2 April 1951.

for the next we hear is a telegram from Castletown on the morning of Saturday 7th April from Gerald to Cecil at his Herne Bay address in Kent: *At George till Tuesday. Are you coming. Gardner.* Whether they ever did meet on that occasion, I do not know!

⁂

Cecil had obviously notified his contacts that a museum was in the offing because in February he was approached by the BBC who were interested in producing a 10-minute television programme about witchcraft. Gerald had approached Barbara about taking part, asking her to contact Cecil direct. He wrote to Cecil: *If she fails me I have another one who I think I can get but she doesn't look as good as B. But her speaking voice will be good.*[27] This alternative was obviously Edith, who was an experienced actress and teacher of elocution. Whether Edith would have been as willing to appear as Gerald seemed to think is open to considerable doubt. Gerald gave details of the intention of the programme in a letter to Gerald Yorke:

> *The idea was we, Williamson and self, would talk about the Museum, & witchcraft, ending with "Would you like to see a witch? Well, here's one." Id arranged with a very pretty one, who was rather thrilled, the conditions being they'd not let any reporters know, & would see she got away immediately afterwards, & was not followed.*[28]

However, there were problems, as Gerald recounts:

> *A few days after they rang up saying, unfortunatly, Roman Catholicks were so strong in the B.B.C. they wouldent allow it at any price, & would I go on alone. I refused, then they worried & worried, they wanted me, & got on to Donna. Williamson wanted publicity for the Museum, so I did it...*[29]

27. Letter, Gerald Gardner to Cecil Williamson, 27 February 1951 (Document 38, Boscastle Museum of Witchcraft archives).
28. Letter, Gerald Gardner to Gerald Yorke, 24 October 1952, (Yorke Collection, Warburg Institute).
29. Ibid.

A letter to Cecil Williamson from Peter Hunt, acting on behalf of the BBC, confirmed the decision not to have Barbara on the programme but was rather circumspect as to the reason: *We are not having the lady from the north as there are difficulties which you will appreciate and which I have explained to the good Dr.*[30]

The programme was broadcast live on Saturday 14th April 1951 and, whatever the reason for the BBC not wanting Barbara to appear (and it may well not have been quite as Gerald surmised), in the event Gerald went on alone, being interviewed by Leslie Mitchell and Joan Gilbert and showing various witch tools.

Gerald gave his thoughts on how the programme had gone:

The Catholic influence prevented Barbara being shown on Television. So they made me do it alone. Of course B. being out, it was not half as striking, + we could not show her beautiful Tools. But Hunt, + Joan Gilbert seemed quite pleased, + two or three people who heard it say it was good, so we'll hope for the best.

... They put me down for a trial, just my stuff, + Lesley [Leslie Mitchell] had a heart attack, + it didn't come off. After tea, he just ran through it with me, said that's O.K., + that was all. Just when we were to go on, news came of Bevin's Death [Ernest Bevin], + we all got the jitters, + I got asthma waiting. When we did go on, Joan got up + spoke some time, introducing us. I thought she was telling about the Museum, but she faced away from me, + I couldn't hear what she said, then they asked me my questions, + I answered.

Actually, when they cut out Barbara, I refused to go on alone. Hunt said he was [illegible word] with you, then on Friday he come here, + said I must do it as you couldn't come. I thought he was saying just what you wanted done, + thought Joan Gilbert had done it. Actually, she was in an awful state of tension over the delay, + probably forgot her lines. The thing now is for you to come + give a broadcast now as a follow up.[31]

---

30. Letter, Peter Hunt to Cecil Williamson, 9 April 1951.
31. Letter, Gerald Gardner to Cecil Williamson, 17 April 1951.

There was an amusing follow-up a few days later, when Gerald wrote:

> *I've just seen a man who said "Why on Earth did you let yourself be put on Television as an advertisement for Dracula? I said, I wasn't, It was for the new Museum in the Isle of Man, + he said yes, they talked hot air about a Museum, + then put on that moavie fellow Dracula just afterwards. I never connected the two things up, + of course didn't know till almost the last minute that I was going on. But issent it funy how people take things.*[32]

---

32. Letter, Gerald Gardner to Cecil Williamson, (Document 41, Boscastle Museum of Witchcraft archives).

CHAPTER TWENTY–FOUR

Making a Museum

Gerald Gardner ran the Museum of Magic and Witchcraft at Castletown on the Isle of Man for almost ten years, from April 1954 until his death in February 1964. He described it, probably with justification at the time, as being the only museum of its kind in the world. The story of how Gerald came to be Director of such a museum needs to be looked at in some detail. A witchcraft museum was something which combined two of Gerald's greatest interests and at some stage he had probably had a similar idea himself. He clearly didn't want Cecil to beat him to it, so I suspect that on the spur of the moment he decided to get closely involved in the project, which included a financial commitment.

Cecil had obviously asked him about his box of witchcraft relics, for Gerald wrote: *Of course you can have Mat Hopkins Box & anything else you want.*[1] Cecil took him up on this, and clearly arranged with Gerald that the bulk of his collection should go to the museum.

Not everyone was as enthusiastic, notably Walter Hildburgh, long-standing member of the Folk-Lore Society, and Gerald's sponsor in his application for membership back in 1939. Gerald wrote to

---

1. Letter, Gerald Gardner to Cecil Williamso, n 27 February 1951, (Document 38, Boscastle Museum of Witchcraft archives).

427

Cecil in March 1951: *Donna told Dr. Hildburgh I was giving my collection to a museum in the Isle of Man & he's furious "They mustnt
be allowed to leave England, etc. etc." Donna said, England has
known about Them & won't let them be Exhibited, so what!!! ...*[2] It
seems that this uncharacteristically vehement grievance of Donna's
was shared by Gerald as, on 15th July 1951, just a fortnight before the
opening of the museum, he wrote a codicil to an earlier will, revok-
ing an earlier bequest to the Victoria and Albert Museum and
expressing the hope never to set foot in England again![3]

Gerald wanted to be closely involved with the museum project.
He had a great interest in museums and if there was the chance of
setting up a museum of witchcraft then he would definitely not
want to be left out. He felt he could help by donating artefacts
which he had built up over the years, by helping with the construction of the special displays and, crucially, helping financially.
It is clear that Gerald kept a keen eye on how things were going,
offering advice by letter and coming over to the island on several
occasions, usually staying at the George Hotel in Castletown.

Cecil thought that the granary was the most promising building for the exhibition, but he had been carrying out research into
what factors helped a museum to be successful, and started by
planning a restaurant. This was his wife's suggestion, for *...on
inquiring into the ways and means of the museum trade had hit on
the hard fact that, whereas there were about 700 museums in the
British Isles, not more than a score of them showed a profit or paid
their way. As my wife wisely suggested, "At least we will be able to
eat on the firm." This restaurant we called "The Witches Kitchen".
It was to prove an instant success and the revenue from it allowed
me to stay in business with the museum in its first unprofitable two
years.*[4] And so plans were prepared to open the restaurant at the
same time as the exhibition.

When it first opened, it was known as "The Folklore Restaurant", though it very quickly changed to "The Witches' Kitchen".
It was located on the ground floor of the granary building and is
described as being 'primarily for the enjoyment and refreshment

2. Letter, Gerald Gardner to Cecil Williamson, 11 March 1951, (Document 37 Boscastle Museum
of Witchcraft archives).
3. In the Ripleys' collection.
4. Williamson, (1967), 27.

of the visitors to the Centre'. But there were originally other aims as well, namely to "bring back and offer to the public many of the old country dishes associated with the numerous feast and festival days which are found throughout the calendar". Particular emphasis was to be given to old Manx dishes and 'those of a superstitious nature'.[5] It is uncertain whether this aim was realised, as the menu card has nothing which would be out of place in most ordinary cafes of the period. However, the fare in the evenings may have been more elaborate, for in the first season the premises stayed open from 10am until midnight. A poster for the restaurant produced shortly after its opening stated "We are famous for our superb Home Baked Cakes in the old Manx farmhouse style", adding "To Drink? What better than the Original Witches Brew?" This was said to have a rum base. Whether it was ever made, or whether the establishment ever actually got a licence for the sale of intoxicating liquors, I don't know. Certainly, after Gerald took over, it didn't, much to his regret.[6]

From the evidence of surviving photographs, the restaurant appears to have had a very strong atmosphere with large beams and simple but heavy timber furniture. Teare describes it as having: ... *blackened beams bedecked with relics from the past ... solid unpolished wooden tables, a feature in themselves, spotlessly clean with their uneven contours following the shape of the tree trunks from which they have been hewn.*[7]

When Cecil took over the building, there was no staircase between the ground and first floors, probably because there had been an external timber staircase that had been removed when the granary closed down, perhaps for use elsewhere. In his view, the upper floors would be ideal for the exhibition, so he pondered on where to put the staircase. Gerald advised:

Would it not be better to have the staircase inside, instead of outside the building? It will be warmer. Also, if it comes on to rain, People won't want to go out in the Rain to go to the Museum, or from the Museum to the restaurant.

5. The Folklore Centre of Superstition and Witchcraft, "An Introduction to Visitors", (1951).
6. Letter, Gerald Gardner to Cecil Williamson, Spring 1962, (Document 31. Boscastle Museum of Witchcraft archives).
7. T. D. G. Teare, *Folk Doctor's Island*, (Times Press, Douglas, 1964), 192.

*What is wanted is for People from the Restaurant to think
'Oh, it's showery. I'll go up to the Museum for an hour till
it's over...'* [8]

In the end, this is what happened: the staircase rose from
the middle of the restaurant up to the exhibition areas on the
upper floors.

Cecil intended to start on a fairly modest scale in the first season, with an exhibition on the first floor. The central feature was
to be a reconstruction of the magic circle as used by the Elizabethan magician, Dr. John Dee:

*The main feature will be Dr. Dee's magic circle, of which he
produced carefully drawn plans. The circle must be constructed to a complicated formula of dimensions and there
are constituents involving an altar carved with innumerable
cabalistic signs each with a separate significance; inscriptions of the names of Hebrew gods; nine candlesticks each
in the form of a different symbol; black earth (to be specially imported), the eye of Horus; the magician's wand and
cup and four white swans' wings.* [9]

He received the help of ceremonial magician, Kenneth Grant's
wife, Steffi, in the design and construction of this display and the
artefacts within it. It is clear that Williamson wanted the circle to
be "live", as he described it, "not just a waxworks". He intended to
invite witches to the island to use it: "When it is completed, members of the only sect in the world who can endow the circle with
power are coming here to do so."[10] He involved the local community in this work, not just in obtaining construction materials from
local contractors, but in commissioning the Douglas School of Art:

*In the preparation of Dr. Dee's magical circle, Mr.
Williamson encountered difficulty in having a series of
brightly coloured and extremely intricate emblems - which
are an essential part - executed. Commercial firms would*

---

8. Letter, Gerald Gardner to Cecil Williamson, 17 April 1951, (Document 40, Boscastle Museum of Witchcraft archives).
9. E. W. Kinrade, "There's Something Brewing in Castletown!", *Isle of Man Examiner*, 20 April 1951.
10. Ibid.

*not tackle the job, and he was stumped until the students of
the Douglas School of Art stepped in. By arrangement with
Mr. W.H. Whitehead, the principal, the students carried
out the work very successfully - they painted the Hebrew
characters and Thebian [sic] outlines perfectly, completing
the Tree of Life, Calvary Cross, the seals of Saturn, Luna
and Mercury, and the Devil's Head without fault. It is probably the strangest job they will ever have.*[11]

At the time he was being interviewed, in April 1951, Cecil clearly
still had hopes of bringing the Witches' Cottage to the Island for a
period, though he gives a rather romanticised view of its history,
for he says that it is: *...a genuine Elizabethan witches' hut in which
the cult of witchcraft has been practised since the 16th century.*[12]

Apart from the centre-piece of the circle, the main exhibits
were from Gerald's and Cecil's existing collections. Cecil's material consisted of magical items from a variety of cultures in all
parts of the world, particularly talismans and items designed to
protect from the 'evil eye'. Gerald had lent the contents of his box
of witchcraft relics together with assorted vessels and knives,
including what was reputed to be a "500-year old sorceror's
sword". There was also a shrine to the memory of those who had
died as a result of witch persecutions over the years.

Gerald worked closely with Cecil during this period, collecting and making appropriate items for display as well as advising
on where certain items might be acquired. He had built up skills
in making things and improvising, probably forged through the
many practical problems he had had to solve working in tea and
rubber plantations over many years. His skill at making ritual
items and his contacts with likely manufacturers were acknowledged and appreciated by Cecil.

※

Gerald was still in regular touch with Edith during the time
that he was involved with Cecil in setting up the museum and
during the period when he was moving to the Isle of Man. After

11. E. W. Kinrade, "Introduction to a Witch", *Isle of Man Examiner*, 20 July 1951.
12. Kinrade, (April 1951).

the television appearance, Gerald seems to have arranged to go down to Highcliffe to stay with her. The plans for the museum were obviously a major talking point and Gerald was trying to persuade Edith to go up and visit the Isle of Man to see the Mill buildings and progress on renovation. She had probably mentioned to him that she had certain witchcraft items including some that were previously owned by Rosamund Sabine, and Gerald was also trying to persuade her to lend these for display. He wrote to Cecil:

> I'me trying to get one of them to come up to the Isle of Man with me + see the place for herself. She can't come on the 10th, but may come about the end of the month. What Ime after is to borrow some of her things. So you can advertize that Both the Northern Coven + the Southern Coven have lent some of their Magic Tools, for the Festival of Britain, to make the Museum a Success. That's a thing to Broadcast in America.[13]

In the same letter, Gerald wrote:

> There was a very nice little May Eve Rite down here last night, but the people are not at all pleased with me or with a cutting about you that appeared in a Sunday paper a little while ago. I'd not seen the cutting + they cant tell me the paper. They say it's making a joke of the whole thing. I've swatted them down, saying that the Reporters will change things round + make fun out of anything. ...[14]

The newspaper cutting was likely to have been an article entitled "He Plans a Jamboree for the Witches of the World" by Barrie Harding, which appeared in the *Sunday Pictorial* on 29th April 1951. It is a report of an interview with Cecil Williamson in which he announces a forthcoming "international gathering of witches, wizards, sorcerers and witch-doctors". The works in progress at the Mill are mentioned, as is the fact that Cecil would be "sending out hundreds of letters of invitation to all parts of the world". The

---

13. Letter, Gerald Gardner to Cecil Williamson, 1 May 1951.
14. Letter, Gerald Gardner to Cecil Williamson, 1 May 1951.

article concludes: *The witches who accept will be allowed to prac-tise their rituals in the old windmill without hindrance, giving its owner an opportunity of first-hand research.*

The part of the article which probably upset Edith and the others was a section which read: *When it* [the exhibition] *is com-plete, he* [Williamson] *will send out a clarion call to a coven of witches practising in the south of England. Who are these witches? One is a woman school-teacher, another a Civil Servant. "I know of one very attractive girl in the coven" says Mr. Williamson. This coven is concerned solely in calling on spirits who can bring good will. But some witches lay too much stress on sex, according to Mr. Williamson. He says: "At certain times in the year they observe the fertility rituals, prancing and dancing in the nude. It is rather pathetic in a way, because some of them are quite old."*[15]

These are clearly Edith, Gerald and Rosanne and it seems obvious that Cecil is only relaying what Gerald had told him about them. One can understand Edith being displeased with Cecil Williamson for his personal comments, but also with Gerald for revealing certain details, though I think it likely that Gerald did not know that Cecil had given the interview.

Gerald's letter is interesting in that it mentions a "May Eve Rite". Whether it was anyone more than just Edith, Rosanne and himself I do not know, but it does indicate that Edith was still involved in rituals as late as 1951.

Gerald clearly kept Edith informed about the progress of the museum preparations, but she was obviously still concerned about the publicity that such an enterprise was generating. Ger-ald was still trying to get Edith and Barbara to visit him on the Isle of Man but he had not succeeded in persuading either of them to visit. In an undated letter to Cecil towards the end of May or early June 1951, Gerald writes:

> ... *the Witch* [Edith] *wants me down to talk to the Coven. Theyre angry about things, + I must smooth them down, + incidentally try + get some more out of them ... I saw the Witch's Daughter* [Rosanne] *the other day. She says mother*

15. Barrie Harding, "He Plans a Jamboree for the Witches of the World", *Sunday Pictorial*, 29 April 1951.

is better but she'll not come up to the Island. Couldn't say why so I must go down + try + find out what is the matter.

In the same letter, Gerald wrote:

Ive written to Barbara, trying to get her to come across to the Island, + hinting at an invite up to her place. But no reply, so she may be away. Anyhow, its awfully hard to get a letter out of her in any case. I want the stuff she promised. She has a lovely Ritual Sword, that would look well in the Circle, if we can't get anything else.

Some time later, Gerald wrote to Cecil: *The Witch is sending a car to Fetch me on Tuesday, so I have to go down & sweeten the coven. Will come to the Island as soon as I can.*

What are we to make of this correspondence about coven activity in the spring and summer of 1951? It seems as if there were two covens: the Northern and Southern covens. I am fairly certain that these are not their actual names (if they had any) but titles given by Gerald to refer to the two covens that he knew of. The first (the "Southern Coven") was based in Highcliffe and consisted of Edith, Rosanne and possibly some others. Gerald still referred to Edith as "the Witch", the first one that he met, and the one who still had a lot of influence over him. The "Northern Coven" could have been Gilbert and Barbara's group in Cheshire, although Gerald later used that term to mean the coven that had been formed in the Isle of Man following the opening of the museum.

And that was the total sum of 'the witch cult' on the eve of the opening of the museum. Directly or indirectly that museum would change that situation to a much greater extent than Gerald would ever have thought possible.

෴

Gerald had had the idea of taking more permanent accommodation in the Isle of Man as early as April 1951, when he wrote to Cecil: *...if theres any sort of small house or flat or cottage for rent or sale please let me know & Ill come up.*[16] This had been made more

---

16. Letter, Gerald Gardner to Cecil Williamson, 17 April 1951, (Document 40, Boscastle Museum of Witchcraft archives).

definite by 1st May 1951 when he wrote: *I want to see about getting a cottage or somewhere to stay, where my wife can come. If there's anything reasonable for sale or leese or of course lodgings. Furnished rooms would do, but they're sure to be full for the summer.*[17]

He kept in touch with Cecil by letter and on his return seems on a sudden whim, probably mid-May 1951, to have arrived unannounced on the Williamsons' doorstep:

> *... he suddenly appeared without warning; I turned around to find him standing in my doorway. He had arrived on a flying visit "to see how things were going" - with his overnight things stuffed into an old, battered music case. Gardner planned to return to London a couple of days later, but what he saw changed all that! When he left for London it was to make final arrangements for moving his home to a house in Castletown's Malew Street, a mere stone's throw from the museum.*[18]

During that visit, Gerald definitely began to look seriously for a place to live. Initially he did not find it easy, as house prices were very high. It must not be forgotten that Gerald was by birth a Lancastrian, and the Isle of Man has a particular fascination for inhabitants of that county, particularly for those who live or have lived on the coast. It acts as a sort of 'Shangri-La', 'El Dorado' or 'Tir-na-nOg' - that ultimate destination in the west that is ever strived for. To visit it was something which had to be undertaken, like the Muslim's pilgrimage to Mecca: to live there was to reach that which was attainable only by the very few.

It was going to be very difficult to buy or lease a house on the Island. There were few houses available, and those were over £6,000. With Cecil's help and local contacts, Gerald eventually found somewhere which seemed ideal. It was at the junction of Malew Street and The Crofts in Castletown. No. 77 was a 400-year old stone-built house with a stone barn attached. It was vacant but the owner was unwilling to sell. Gerald fell in love with it, and turned to his fellow witches, and magic, to help:

---

17. Letter, Gerald Gardner to Cecil Williamson, 1 May 1951, (Document 48, Boscastle Museum of Witchcraft archives).
18. Williamson (1967), 28.

My secret friends helped me to get my house in Castletown, Isle of Man. I could not find a house within my means on the island. I had to live in digs, apart from my wife. There was an empty cottage but the owner would not sell. He had refused every offer since its last occupant, his brother, had died.

Eight other witches helped me to cast a spell. We danced round a priestess of the Moon Goddess. Charcoal, herbs and incense burned in a cauldron. We chanted phrases and made signs handed down to witches for generations ... A strange spirit filled the circle ... I trembled, lost all sense of time as the power radiated from my body ...[19]

The result was striking. Half an hour after Gerald had arrived back on the Island, he received a visit from a gentleman acting on behalf of the owner. He had agreed to sell, but it would be as well for Gerald to see him quickly before he changed his mind. The two met, and the old man told Gerald that someone he knew needed a holiday, which would cost a certain sum. If Gerald agreed to pay that, then he could have the house. He agreed, and the deal was done. Gerald added: *The owner was quite resigned to selling the cottage ... he had quite suddenly CHANGED HIS MIND. It took us only 10 minutes to clinch the deal.*[20]

In a letter to Cecil probably dating from June 1951, Gerald is referring to his "new home" and to dealings with a house agent and lawyer, so it is likely that things moved quickly after his initial enquiry in April 1951 and that the events surrounding the acquisition of 77 Malew Street took place in May and early June that year. The house was probably bought in early June. Certainly on 9th July 1951, Gerald wrote to Rex Wellbye on the new Folklore Centre headed notepaper saying: "I have baught a small farm house up here, but it has no bathroom etc., so I don't know exactly when I shall move in."[21] Gerald set out his feelings about moving to the Island in a letter to Rex:

Of course I have very important + interesting work here, + so don't feel so cut off. Its a lovely place, what I have seen.

19. Gerald Gardner, "I Am A Witch", *Weekend*, 24-30 June 1957.
20. Ibid.
21. Letter, Gerald Gardner to Rex Wellbye, 9 July 1951.

Ive been to busy to see much yet, Actually your not so cut off, as it <u>seems</u>. In Summer, you leave London Airport at 1.20 + arrive at Castletown at 3.20. Just two hours. It always took me about 2 hours, Train + Bus to get to Bricket Wood, In winter its different. You have to go to Liverpool 50 minutes + take the Train about 4 hours. But in Winter, I'll be in Spain. Anyhow, I'm glad to be out of the Club quarrels.[22]

I don't know exactly what works were necessary to the property before Gerald and Donna could move in. Certainly a new bathroom was needed and Gerald probably took the opportunity to make a doorway through to the barn direct from the bathroom, as Patricia Crowther and others have mentioned. Gerald records that he was still "trying to get the house ready" in December 1951, and he probably did not move in permanently until his return from wintering in Italy in March 1952.

⚜

While the house buying was going ahead, Gerald was active in trying to get the new museum displays ready. One thing he was trying to get was a suitable sword, as he wrote to Cecil:

I took my sword to Commander Ward's and left it there, but he was out. Ive been several times and at last I found him today. He says he told you that it was very unlikely that he could make it, as he didn't know where he could get the 3 brass balls unless he took them off a bedsted, + anyhow the Hilt was an impossible shape. So I said "I left a Ritual Sword for you to see, that has been used for ages". He said yes but the balls are not equidistant. I said well can't you cast some in brass on these lines that will be equidistant? He said Fred's away!!! I said can't you get someone else to cast it? He said No!!! We can't ask another firm to make a thing. We make things for other people. He suggests that I try some Theatrical Costume people. He gave me a name but no address. I'll try + contact them + let you know what they say. The only other

---

22. Letter, Gerald Gardner to Rex Wellbye, 14 July 1951.

thing I can think of is, can you get one made in Castletown? There's an old Ex-Army blacksmith, the father of the One Armed Artist. I should think he could make one. He lives at the Victoria Hotel, just opposite my new home. Making a further comment about a sword for the display, Gerald writes: *You'll see the Golden Dawn book says any kind of Cross Hilted sword will do if you can write on it. I can get you one for about £2/10/- I think that we could write on nicely.*[23]

Gerald was obviously keen and wanting to be very fully involved in the setting up and furnishing of the museum, and was trying to locate and arrange for the manufacture of items for it. It is interesting that, even before he had moved to the Island, he was already in contact with local artists and craftspeople.

He was trying to arrange to move some items up that were in the Witch's Cottage in Bricket Wood. He doesn't say what they are, but they were obviously fairly bulky:

Ive been trying to get things up from the Cottage, but can't go far. Carter Pattersons and the Railway say yes, if I have someone down there waiting to give them the goods. When they fetch them it will be all right but can't say to a week when they will go there, + I cant wait a week at the gate for a lorry that may never come. Ive been trying to get someone with a car, but so far without result.[24]

Cecil had obviously asked Gerald about a silver bell for one of the displays: he had initially asked Gerald whether he could make one himself, knowing of his skill in that direction, but he replied:

No, I'm afraid I can't make the flatish silver bell. Is it discribed anywhere? The kind of silver I have doesn't ring when struck. I think something must be done to make silver ring. I'll try + find out. Is it pictured anywhere? You have my Book 4. it may be there. If so I'll have a look when I come up. ... I'll try for a Church Lamp, but I don't know what sized one you want, a Sanctuary Lamp or what. They have

23. Letter, Gerald Gardner to Cecil Williamson, May/June 1951, (Document 42, Boscastle Museum of Witchcraft archives).
24. Letter, Gerald Gardner to Cecil Williamson, May/June 1951, (Document 42, Boscastle Museum of Witchcraft archives).

them all sizes, but mostly for Electric Light unless its for a Sanctuary Lamp, + they're very small. ... Ive no polished steel chain. You can get silvered chain + black stuff. Ive been all morning trying to get some sheet brass, but the Government have organised a shortage so well that theres none to be had. I've been combing Clerkenwell. I can get silver sheet but not brass.[25]

However, when Gerald thought that Cecil was asking unnecessary questions, he was quite prepared to say so:

I can't do anything about a Robe. You have Book 4. Cant you make it up there? I seem to remember something like a white shirt or old nightgown would do. ... I can make a crown, I think, if I can get some brass. I can get you a genuine Chreus snake, from an Egyptian statue, but it costs £3/-/-, or I may be able to fudge you up something, out of the brass sheet, if I can get it, when I have time. do you know how wide the Crown should be? My idea is about an inch wide, but it may be more (or less). Let me know. ... Ime working hard at the picture of a witch burning for the Sanctuary, + I think it will be good."[26]

I suspect that this is the picture that appeared in the first edition of *The Meaning of Witchcraft*, the caption of which reads: "Margaret Ine Quane and her son, burnt alive for Witchcraft in Castletown, Isle of Man, 1617. From a picture in the Witches' Mill". It shows the couple chained to a stake on top of a pile of logs which are about to be lit. Castle Rushen, in Castletown, is in the background.

I can fix you up with a Dagger all right. Must the Hilt be any special form? I can make a scurge all right - but Raw Hide thongs are difficult to get. Possibly you could get some up there. Anyhow Ill do my best. ... Have you got the Circle Painted in yet? It should be properly consecrated you know.[27]

25. Ibid.
26. Ibid.
27. Ibid.

In a subsequent letter Gerald reported to Cecil on the progress he had made:

> My dear Cyril [sic]. I got a catalogue sheet from the Catholic Supply Shop. Opposite the Westminster Catholic Cathedral. they say thats enough to address. Ive marked the one I like ... Ive been to sevral Theatrical Costumers, but they all say they cant make a sword up. Ill try some more. The trouble is partly the Governments orgonising a scarcity of metals + partly no Craftsmen. ... I for the same reason cant get any strip brass, but hope to get some in time. Let me know what you want me to do re the snake Chreus Head. Shall I try to buy the Egyptian one? Or shall I make one? Again, shall I buy the Golden Dawn Hilted Sword? Or shall I try + make a wooden one (Golden Dawn type) or will you get one made up there? Wood, gilded, will look all right if you not too close. ... You might have a try in Castletown for sheet brass. For my purpose I want a sheet of Muntz Metal. But there's none to be had ... Muntz Metal is what they use to sheath boats with + in a small fishing village they may have it. So you might get me a sheet or two. Its about 4' x 2' 4 feet by 2 feet. Its a sort of brass. ... Ive been trying to get a blank book to write a grimoire. But cant get the right sort so far. ... By the way, a Practising Magician says that its all Rot about having the balls equidistant, as the hand should not be in the triangle. If you want a triangle, make the hilt thus [there followed a diagram] so the hand is outside. ... Daggers + Scurge O.K. Will bring them when I come.[28]

Gerald went down to stay with Edith in Highcliffe some time before the Summer Solstice 1951. The next letter to Cecil is headed "Stone-Henge", in other words, he doesn't want him to know exactly where he is staying. It starts: *Dear Cyril* [sic - he still gets his first name wrong, even though they've been involved in a lot of joint activity over several months!] *I am down here with the Druids Winding up the Sun.*[29] This is his slightly humorous way of

28. Letter, Gerald Gardner to Cecil Williamson, May/June 1951, (Document 46, Boscastle Museum of Witchcraft archives).
29. Letter, Gerald Gardner to Cecil Williamson, early July 1951, (Document 47, Boscastle Museum of Witchcraft archives).

referring to the Summer Solstice ritual which the Ancient Druid Order performed every year at Stonehenge and which I described in Chapter 20.

Gerald stayed with Edith until the following day, Monday 9th July 1951, when he returned to London and caught the 10.30 train on the Tuesday from Euston to Liverpool and then the 3.30pm boat, arriving at Douglas at about 7.30pm, whence he would catch a bus, rather optimistically hoping to arrive in Castletown by 8pm. He tells Cecil:

Now, I'll have a lot of weight. Can you possibly meet me with the Car at Castletown Brewery, where the busses stop, Tuesday 8pm, as I have been having a lot of asthma, + cant possibly carry the stuff up to the George. Otherwise could you get a man to meet me with a barrow or somthing.[30]

Whilst staying with Edith, Gerald obviously managed to placate her to the extent that she agreed to lend some items. He told Cecil:

Ive ben trying to squre this Witch + she promises she'll come up about the 15th. Ive got a most Priceless Old Gong out of her, + some other things, but its heavy. I'm sure youll love it, + it will be an attraction.[31]

The saga of the sword continued: *Ive been to sevral more Theatrical People, but none of them will make the sword. So Im bringing up 2 swords for you to see, + I think we can fake them up.*[32] There was progress to report on some, though not all, of the other items as well:

Ive made the Chreous Crown, + got some chain - will have to burnish it, but your wall cleaning thing will polish it up. I couldn't arrange with a lorry to meet me at the Witch Hut, so can't get the chain + pot yet, but I have a bacon spit of my own I'll bring. Ive made the picture for the shrine + I have written out a lot of the Grimoire. Dr Dee's in Enochian language, you know. How he evoked the Spirit in what he said

---

30. Letter, Gerald Gardner to Cecil Williamson, early July 1951, (Document 47, Boscastle Museum of Witchcraft archives).
31. Ibid.
32. Ibid.

was the language of the Angels or what Enoch spoke. ... I think it will look quite imposing when its stuck up. Binding it is a trouble, but will fake up somthing. It seems absolutely impossible to get a blank book anywhere nowadays. They say Government prohibits these being made, excepting printed account books. So I got an old album, nice paper, but the covers were impossible. ... Re Silver Bell. Ime told that to get silver to ring it must be cast. Ive got a dentist who thinks he could cast one. Only, I cant remember what the bell in Book 4 looked like. You say a flat bell, is that like a cow bell? We could send him drawings + trust to luck, or there are bell founders. I dont know if they would take a small job on.[33]

The dentist is likely to be Alfred C.H. Maguire ('Mac'), Rosanne's second husband, who practised in Christchurch. Gerald had obviously had a word with him while staying with Edith.

Do you need robes for show? The Theatrical People can make them, but they say it takes time nowadays. ... Im bringing 2 daggers up to choose from + a lot of other stuff. So please do try + meet me.[34]

Cecil had obviously asked about the Golden Dawn, as Gerald writes:

I sent off the Golden Dawn books before I left. Hope they arrived O.K. + you can get what you want out of them. The man who works the Golden Dawn Rituals showed me a lovely manuscript coppied from some of Dee's, but he wont sell.[35]

Gerald finishes his letter with a note of caution:

I trust you are all well up there + that everything is going well + the Restaurant is ready. Ime trying to spread the news, but everyone says it's so far off.[36]

---

33. Letter, Gerald Gardner to Cecil Williamson, early July 1951, (Document 47, Boscastle Museum of Witchcraft archives).
34. Ibid.
35. Ibid.
36. Ibid.

CHAPTER TWENTY-FIVE

A Grand Opening

July 1951 was a particularly appropriate time to open a museum devoted to witchcraft, since the last of the witchcraft acts had been repealed the previous month: it was no longer illegal to proclaim oneself to be a witch or to practise witchcraft. Of course, at the time when the exhibition was first being proposed, the practice of witchcraft, strictly speaking, was still illegal, under the Witchcraft Act 1735. This was not just of theoretical and historic interest. As recently as 1944, the spiritualist medium Helen Duncan had been sentenced to nine months imprisonment, prosecuted under the 1735 Act for carrying on her normal mediumship activities.[1] There was outrage at this sentence, from more than just Spiritualists, and as a result of pressure on Members of Parliament, the Fraudulent Mediums Act[2] was passed, and became law on 22nd June 1951. This Act abolished the Witchcraft Act of 1735 and, instead, made it an offence for anyone to "act as a spiritualistic medium or to exercise any powers of telepathy, clairvoyance or other similar powers" *with intent to deceive*. It also prohibited the use of any "fraudulent device". Thus did the law

1. Malcolm Gaskill, *Hellish Nell: Last of Britain's Witches*, (Fourth Estate, 2001).
2. 14 Geo VI, cap. 33.

for the first time recognise genuine mediumship and distinguish it from deliberate deception.

This was very important for the witches. For the first time in many hundreds of years they could practise their Craft without fear of prosecution. The fear of *per*secution did, however, remain, and most witches preferred to continue to practise their religion in secret. So, by the time the Folklore Centre opened, in July 1951, it was no longer illegal to be a witch, which was just as well, because in the publicity Cecil Williamson made much of the fact that he knew witches and that a witch would perform the opening ceremony.

Cecil was a good publicist. He had supplied both national and local papers with material for several months before the opening. Two pieces appeared in the *Sunday Pictorial*. On 29th April 1951, was the article by Barrie Harding[3] about which Edith was not very happy. On 29th July 1951, the same paper published an article by Allen Andrews entitled "Calling All Covens", which made mention of the Grand Opening that same day of what was called The Folklore Centre of Superstition and Witchcraft. The opening ceremony was to be performed by Gerald Gardner, who is described as "the resident witch". Articles also appeared in the local *Isle of Man Examiner* with an interview of Cecil on 20th April 1951 and a piece about Gerald entitled "Introduction to a Witch" on 20th July. The Grand Opening was set for Sunday 29th July 1951 and the place opened to the public the following day. The *Isle of Man Examiner* reported the event as follows:

> *Dr. Gerald Gardner, 67-year-old, white-haired "resident witch" at the witches' den at the Old Windmill Farm, Red Gap, Castletown, performed the first ceremony in the magic circle of power on Sunday. Three young women, first visitors to enter the magic circle, knelt before him as he read part of the ritual contained in his grimoire (textbook of witchcraft practice) to promote a spell of good fortune for them. ... Dr. Gardner stood by the altar in the centre of the mystic circle to perform the initial rites. He held a witch's "thaim" - ceremonial dagger - in his hand as he read from his grimoire.[4]*

3. Harding, (1951).
4. "The Witches' Den Opened", *Isle of Man Examiner*, 3 August 1951, 4.

The opening of the Centre was reported in the London *Daily Mail* on Monday 30th July 1951 under the heading "2 Girls Ask Witch to End Curse" and the sub-heading "First Centre in Britain". The report began:

> *Two young women went to Britain's first folk-lore centre of superstition and witchcraft at Red Gap Windmill, Castletown, Isle of Man, yesterday and asked to be "de-cursed" ... They asked if anything could be done to end their run of bad luck ... Dr Garner [sic] read passages to them from his grimoire - textbook of witchcraft - before a cabalistically inscribed "altar" ... The women listened intently as Dr Garner [sic], standing over them with his flowing white hair and bronze face, emphasised the passages with his atham [sic] or witches' knife."*[5]

The report also included an interview with Cecil Williamson, who said:

> *The two girls asked if we could break a spell and I told them it was comparatively easy. It is a question of science of witchcraft and belief in sorcery. Before the end of the year I shall have added a 17th-century witches' kitchen ready for the working of magic, and an alchemist's den.*[6]

The report concludes:

> *Because of a revival of white magic which, according to Mr. Williamson, is seeping over Britain and Western Europe, the centre has been opened as a clearing house for information. Mr. Williamson has collected from all over the world 300 relics of magic. There is a human hand on which is growing a fungus or skull moss, which witches years ago used to treat many ills. There are also fingers, skulls, mummified heads, and masks leering from behind glass showcases.*[7]

---

5. "Girls Ask Witch to End Curse", *Daily Mail*, 30 July 1951.
6. Ibid.
7. Ibid.

Cecil had obviously tipped Gerald off that the article was to appear, for Gerald writes as follows:

> My dear Cyril [sic]. I went round and got a couple of copies of the Daily Mail. I don't know what you think, I think it is a disgusting performance. It is mostly lies. Did you hear anything about taking this curse off. He said he wanted a photo of some girls, so Laura Aclem [sic] + 2 girls from the Cafe were planted in the circle + I read something to make them laugh. I was not holding an athame, + he spells it wrong, Atham, he says we have only 300 magic relics, when we must have nearly 3000 three thousand if we count those not on show. I should think we must have about 1,500 on show."[8]

It seems as if the reporter had, perhaps, embroidered the truth a little to make a good story, but nothing out of the ordinary. And for Gerald to accuse others of bad spelling ...!!! Strangely enough, he didn't comment that his name was spelt wrongly. Anyway, Gerald was determined to do something about it. He continues:

> I went + fought the Editor, but he says What can I do? That's the report he put in. But he seems a very decent bloke + was very interested in what I had to tell him. He collects old things himself. I Thought if you were to write in, as head of the museum, correcting the impression that we do curse people + that its a serious show (+ what the Editor said was a good bit of News, an existing Coven of Witches had lent us a lot of stuff) you might get a bit more publicity out of it.

It is clear from this account that Gerald had returned to London shortly after the opening ceremony. He seems to have felt a bit guilty about doing so since in a reply to Cecil's report on how things were going he is quite conciliatory:

> Im awfully glad to hear that you have had more people. do tell me who the Experts were? + do you mean Expert Occultists, or Museum folk, or Witches or what? I was sorry I had to bunk off + leave you but so many things were

---

8. Letter, Gerald Gardner to Cecil Williamson, early August 1951 (Document 35, Boscastle Museum of Witchcraft archives).

pulling me down, + my return ticket had nearly run out. I do hope your feet are all right now. Edith is most distressed to hear about them. So is Donna, + they both send the best of good wishes for your feet + the Museum, + in that order."9

This was something that Gerald had always wanted: he was heavily involved in a museum that he hoped would interest many people. He could hold his head up high amongst folklorists and museum curators the world over. His thoughts naturally began to turn towards the forthcoming International Congress of European and Western Ethnology, which was to be held at the Nordiska Museet in Stockholm and Uppsala from 27th to 31st August 1951. Gerald told Cecil about his intention to attend the conference:

Donna wants to go to Sweden, + possibly Denmark on the way back. I think, taking the long view, it will be such an Advertisement for the Centre. There will be 150 Delegates, + sure to be lots of Yanks who will spread the story at home. That its worth my being away for another 10 days. So please will you write me a letter on the paper as Curator of the Museum, saying I represent the museum.[10]

Shortly after writing that letter, in part probably due to his exertions leading up to and during the opening ceremony, Gerald caught a cold, as he tells Cecil: ... *we both got bad flu, + are feeling like chewed string. We should have been up long ago if it were not for that. We have booked a flight for next Sunday, 19th, arriving at 10 to two P.M., 13.50. If you can meet us Id be thankfull, as Ive got somthing for the Museum thats very breakable.*[11]

Gerald probably only went back to Castletown for a few days, since the conference in Sweden started on 26th August. He wrote subsequently to Cecil: We go off to Sweden on the 25th, + have been asked to go to Copenhagen on the way back. So I hope to spread the News on the Continent. This travels, it will take time to bring results, but I think by next year should bear fruit.[12]

9. Letter, Gerald Gardner to Cecil Williamson, 9 August 1951.
10. Ibid.
11. Letter, Gerald Gardner to Cecil Williamson, mid-August 1951 (Document 81, Boscastle Museum of Witchcraft archives).
12. Letter, Gerald Garder to Cecil Williamson, mid-August 1951, (Document 44 Boscastle Museum of Witchcraft archives).

The International Congress of European and Western Ethnology was held in the Great Hall of the Nordiska museet (Nordic Museum), Stockholm from Monday 27th August to Friday 31st August 1951. It was attended by some 225 delegates from 18 countries. It was a follow-up to the Congress on Folk-lore, Ethnography and Archaeocivilisation that took place in Paris in 1948 and which Gerald attended. At that congress he made the acquaintance of M. André Varagnac and he renewed their friendship in Stockholm, where Varagnac was one of the speakers.

The opening speech to the Congress was given by Professor S. de Madariaga, President of the International Commission on Folk Arts and Folklore (CIAP). The main point he made was that: *You ... have rendered an immense sense* [sic] *to the knowledge in turning the attention of people from the doings of men as they ought to be, to the actual doings of men as they are."*[13] This is a point which Gerald took up in *Witchcraft Today* when he wrote: *...I am an anthropologist, and it is agreed that an anthropologist's job is to investigate what people do and believe, and not what other people say they should do and believe."*[14]

Whilst Gerald did not read a paper at the Congress, there must have been some mention of the recently opened museum on the Isle of Man, and that he was an expert on witchcraft, as he was interviewed by at least one Swedish newspaper. Donna was with him for at least the visits after the main conference, and she also gave an interview, which was quite revealing:

> *"I know the most delightful young witch, 27 years old. Her mother is a witch, and she has a male relative in a prominent position within English industry who is also a witch, however odd it may sound." It is Mrs Dorothea Gardner, wife of the well-known ethnologist Dr G B Gardner speaking, and her spouse nods in agreement. "That's quite true," he says. "A man can be a witch, too, but most of them are of course women."*

---

13. "Papers of the International Congress of European and Western Ethnology", Stockholm 1951 (International Commission on Folk Arts and Folklore: Stockholm 1956), 12.
14. Gardner, (1954), 18.

Dr Gardner has for many years researched magic and folk superstitions, black masses, magicians and other occult practices. A few years ago he came into contact with a group of witches who still exist in England. Later he made contact with a further circle of witches, and now he knows personally 18 of them, young and old. They have inherited qualities from generations of forefathers across hundreds of years. It is thought possible to trace their origins right back to the stone age." [15]

The "delightful young witch" and her male relative are probably Barbara and Gilbert Vickers, but the idea of her mother being a witch seems to have originated purely in Gerald's mind. I also doubt whether Gerald knew eighteen witches by the summer of 1951.

On Wednesday 29th, the whole Congress moved to Uppsala, an old university town and documented centre of ancient paganism, after which Gerald and Donna spent several days visiting historic sites in Sweden. From photographic evidence it would appear that they visited Visby on the Baltic island of Gotland. And it was certainly Gerald's intention to go to Copenhagen on the way home to visit his friend Holger Jacobsen. Whether this happened I do not know.

Gerald went over to the Isle of Man again on the afternoon boat on 13th September 1951. The Restaurant and Exhibition were only open during the relatively short tourist season in the Isle of Man. They closed at the end of September for the winter and Gerald returned to his flat in London, 47 Ridgmount Gardens. He wrote to Cecil: *We got down safely. Very calm passage. The boat was cramd full of people getting away. It had been rough for two days before, so theyd all stopped over.* [16]

He told Cecil about a trip which he had just attended as a member of the Historical Association, which had been founded in 1906 and which he had been a member of for many years:

Ime just back from the historical soc trip, had a very good time, but it was hard work. Ive spread the news round a lot.

---

15. Unknown newspaper and date. Translation by Julie Venner.
16. Letter, Gerald Gardner to Cecil Williamson, 1 October 1951.

They are nearly all School Teachers + though a bit anti, I got them by saying Do you believe in teaching the truth, or in suppressing the truth, to suit the prejudice of any certain party? + they all said "we want to teach the truth", then I said, then why not admit what you know to be true. 300 years ago people believed in magic + did or did not do certain things because of this belief. Its not saying that there's anything in magic, only that people did or did not do certain things because they believed + if you admit that, what is wrong in showing the instruments that were used in magic, if it is right to show the instruments they used for Cooking or navagation at that date. Showing an Astralabe + a backstaff does not make children try to navagate an Ocean Liner with them. Nor showing a huge cooking pot does not make people scrap their gas stoves. Their great criticism was that it was all right for adults to see magical instruments, but that we should not admit children. Anyway, Ive spread the news ...[17]

Gerald had arranged a trip to Paris, starting on Monday 8th October 1951. He had got to know Professor André Varagnac quite well and had been invited over to Paris. Gerald and Donna has arranged to stay at the Royal Condé Hotel. Before he went he wrote to Cecil:

Please drop a line to any French papers you think would be intrested, as I'll be too busy to go round to see them. Ive ordered enlargements of the Photos I took of the Museum (with the flash lights) so I hope they come out good. They'll be good advertisements. Ive contacted some Americans in London. Hope it will come to somthing.[18]

The close season provided the opportunity for further improvement in the museum and, in this, Gerald and Cecil were still working fairly closely together. Gerald liked the dramatic and putting over ideas to people in an attractive way, using what we might today call "multi-media presentation", as we can deduce

---

17. Undated letter, Gerald Gardner to Cecil Williamson (Document 44, Boscastle Museum of Witchcraft archives).
18. Letter, Gerald Gardner to Cecil Williamson, 1 October 1951.

from his earlier comments about Salisbury Museum. And witch-craft and magic in particular cannot be fully comprehended by static displays: they involve activity and ritual. They had obviously discussed the possibility of incorporating special events, including live rituals, into the Museum programme, and Gerald makes some perceptive comments to Cecil about the difficulties of performing rituals in public:

> *... the trouble with them* [rites] *is, no one will perform the Rites of anything of which he is a member, in public, but they will often go through the Rites of a society of which they are not members.*[19]

In fact, during the whole of the 1951 season, Gerald and Cecil had not discussed the ritual practices that each were carrying out. In a December 1951 letter, Gerald writes:

> *How exactly are you working, what system I mean? You speak of getting results, & answers, somhow it seems as if Ive never had a yarn with you since weve been on the Island, always too busy, or somthing. I know its proberbly my fault. Ime always on the rush, trying to get the house etc ready, next year Ill have more time.*[20]

It is clear that Cecil Williamson was interested in the practice of ceremonial magic. His headed notepaper and the first introductory guide for visitors include sigils and quotations from Dee's *Of Spirits and Apparitions*: "Who so bears this sign about him, all spirits shall do him homage" and "Who so bears this sign about him, let him fear no one but fear God". In a letter to Gerald Yorke dated 7th August 1952, Cecil wrote about forming some sort of magical group. He claimed to have received a message from Crowley, though he was anxious to distance himself from spiritualism. He seemed to be in the process of developing rituals for some group of which he claimed to be a member and wanted Yorke to lend him some of Crowley's books to assist in that. I

---

19. Letter, Gerald Gardner to Cecil Williamson, 20 February 1952, (Document 25, Boscastle Museum of Witchcraft archives).
20. Letter, Gerald Gardner to Cecil Williamson, December 1951 (Document 28, Boscastle Museum of Witchcraft archives).

doubt whether this ever amounted to anything: nothing else that I have seen of Cecil's refers to it further, and I can only suppose that it was overtaken by events. It does, however, belie his future claims that he was only actively interested in the "village wise woman" type of witchcraft.

In preparation for the second season, Gerald makes the suggestion that Druid ceremonies might fit the bill, probably because they were more public than witchcraft rituals, and therefore could be performed without compromising oaths of secrecy. As we have seen, Gerald had been a member of the Ancient Druid Order since at least 1946 and knew the Order's Chosen Chief, Robert MacGregor Reid, well. An undated note signed "RMR" states:

Re the Isle of Man Druid Lodge. It wants a Founder. That is yourself. And three who are interested. We will assist in all other matters except - at present - financial. It wants a Name and a date for its inauguration meeting, at which you could defect the Mother Lodge.

Gerald wrote to Cecil in November 1951:

I have been trying to get a Charter from the Druids. Apparently they will give me one if I can get 3 other members to make a start. Now do you know any likely people? And is there anything in this neighbourhood where we could perform any ceremonyes? I could take it on, then resign and hand it over to you if you like. Being a Crowned Druid, they will give me a Charter to start with, and that gives us some sort of legal standing, so to speak.[21]

Cecil obviously replied positively for Gerald states:

I wrote to Macgregor Reid, asking him to come & see me as soon as I got your letter. It was waiting for me when I got back. but have had no reply yet, only four days so not much time yet, I asked him to grant me a Charter, & to get me copies of the Rituals. They are always so Piso [I don't know what this word means. The letter is typed, so there's no

---

21. Letter, Gerald Gardner to Cecil Williamson, 6 November 1951, (Document 32, Boscastle Museum of Witchcraft archives).

scope for misreading. In the context it seems to mean something like "secretive"] *about them. I tried to get copies before & they wouldent let me, but if Ime to have a Charter, I must have them.*[22] In fact, there is a copy of a Druid initiation ritual dated 1948 filed away with Gerald's letters to Cecil, so it looks as if he managed to get something!

Gerald went on to express a certain degree of disillusionment with the Ancient Druid Order rituals, for he says:

Actually, Ive a very poor opinion of what Ive seen. but, we must have somthing to start on, I think we can rewrite them to cut all the false Christanity & silly sentiamality out of them & get some of the truth that is behind it out to the light, if its been cut out, we can put some back.[23]

He had ideas about the sort of performance that could be put on; which didn't seem to involve too much input from the Druids:

I dont think the Druids would expect much of our Lodge, we may have to pay some small sum to be in communication with them. They're very hard up, so will be content with anything, if we can make up some sort of show that they can boast about.[24]

Cecil had suggested to Gerald that the inside of the derelict windmill be used as a 'dancing ground'. This may be the origin of Gerald's perpetuation of myth that the Arbory Witches used the burnt-out tower for that very purpose in the mid-19th Century.

As far as I have been able to discover, nothing came of the proposed Isle of Man Druid Chapter and it remains just one of the many ideas which never came to fruition.

꧁꧂

Gerald 'wintered abroad' in the early part of 1952 in Italy. The first place he stayed was Naples, at the Pension Westend in the

---

22. Letter, Gerald Gardner to Cecil Williamson, December 1951, (Document 28, Boscastle Museum of Witchcraft archives).
23. Ibid.
24. Ibid.

Salita Piedagrotta, and he quickly went to visit Pompeii, the Roman town that had been destroyed (and preserved!) by the eruption of Vesuvius in 79 CE. Excavations had been taking place there and it is likely that his old friend, Ross Nichols, who had been there the previous year, had told Gerald that it was well worth seeing.

Of particular interest to Gerald was the so-called 'Villa of the Mysteries'. Otherwise a typical villa, it contained what some have called an "initiation chamber". On its walls were frescoes illus-trating what seems to be the initiation of a young woman. To Ger-ald's delight, the scenes include both nudity and flagellation. As he wrote on Monday 14th January on a postcard to Cecil showing this scene: *This shows the Veiled symbol on the Altar in the fresco of the Villa of the Mysteries, Pompei. It wasn't discovered when I was here last. P.S. The kneeling figure is unvaling it.* He later wrote: *... when I visited the Villa of Mysteries at Pompeii I realised the great resemblance to the cult.*[25]

He then spent some time on the island of Ischia before embarking on a tour of Sicily: *Have got a little information out here, but, the Italian Government is the Communist + the Pope + both are persecuting fiercely, so everybody is hiding, + I can't make contacts I want. Funnily enough, you know the badge of Sicily is the 3 legs like the Isle of Man. Tried hard all over Sicily to get one. None to be had, they're banned. Pope says it's magic, Communists say its nationalistic, not international, so banned.*[26]

On 25th February 1952, Gerald went on to Rome, where he stayed at the Albergo Diana on the Via Principe Amedeo. Gerald probably chose this because of its name, the headed notepaper including a drawing of Diana the huntress with her bow and two dogs. There is one incident while he was in Rome which Gerald recounts in *Witchcraft Today:*

> *I believe ... that sometimes the Black Mass is performed. Once I doubted it; but in February, 1952, I was in Rome and was told that some unfrocked priests and nuns celebrated it at times. My informants said they could arrange for me to see it done properly by these unfrocked priests and nuns, but that it would cost me about £20; I had not enough foreign*

25. G B Gardner, "New Light on Witchcraft", (manuscript), 87.
26. Letter, Gerald Gardner to Cecil Williamson, 20 February 1952.

exchange or else I would have gone, so as to settle the question to my own satisfaction. I think it was probably a show put on for the tourists, though I was assured by responsible people that it was not.[27]

On 7th March 1952, Gerald left Rome for Visso, in the March region of Italy. On telling Rex this,[28] he adds "Worse luck", so it sounds as if he didn't want to go there, which is strange if he was on holiday. I think the most likely explanation is that he was with someone who wanted to see Visso, and that that someone was Edith, who had accompanied Gerald on at least one previous occasion.

Gerald continued to emphasise in his letters to Rex the value that he put on the museum and his role in setting up and running it: ... *I have very important + interesting work here ...*"[29] *I ... am engaged in important work ... I'm a very busy man. I'm doing work that may be of great value to Posterity + I get sent about as people want me + I don't know where I'll be next week.*[30]

While he was away, Gerald carried on a correspondence with Cecil about the future of the Museum. In January 1952, Cecil had written to Gerald reporting that the enterprise was not doing at all well financially and that he needed some money urgently to continue to pay the rent to Barclays, who were acting on behalf of the owner, J J McArd of Port Erin. Gerald, who was by that time in Italy, wrote to Cecil sympathising:

This is bad news indeed. I was dubious about any customers in Winter. Unless, as we have often talked about, if people can dance & enjoy themselvs somhow they will come, but they won't come out in the cold simply & have lunch & then go home again. ... I'll write to Mr Moore [Gerald's solicitor]... asking him to see if he can fix up somthing. Funnily enough, Edith wrote me two days ago asking about you.

---

27. Gardner, (1954), 28.
28. Letter, Gerald Gardner to Rex Wellbye, 2 March 1952.
29. Letter, Gerald Gardner to Rex Wellbye, 14 July 1951.
30. Letter, Gerald Gardner to Rex Wellbye, 28 February 1952.

*Saying that of course you couldent possibly make a place
like that pay in the Winter unless there was some attrac-
tion. ... She also said why dosent he contact the teachers?
School, Elocution, & Music, & sugest that they should give
Recitals, & possibly they could link up with their local
Drama League. Something to attract the Local Talent. ...
Edith speaks as if there are lots of stray Music Teachers &
Elocaution Teachers about, not in schools but in private
practice. I don't know if there are. Anyhow, good luck & see
what Mr Moore can fix.*[31]

If I am right about Edith accompanying Gerald, then she would
have seen Cecil's letter and commented directly to Gerald about
the points raised. If so, then Gerald was trying to hide this fact by
writing "Funnily enough, Edith wrote to me two days ago ...".

Gerald wrote further on 20th February 1952 saying that he
would arrange for £200 to be forwarded to Cecil as soon as possible. Gerald also reported that his bank had suggested that he purchase the Windmill Farm buildings and that he offer them to
Cecil on a mortgage. He also wrote that his bank would be willing
to forward £400 to Cecil and would be amenable to forwarding
further sums if the money was spent on buildings and land.

This is a very different picture from that presented by Cecil
Williamson in his various accounts of the relationship, and shows
that Gerald was the benefactor whose actions enabled the
museum to remain open.

Cecil obviously agreed to this, because on 29th February 1952
Gerald wrote to his solicitors asking them to prepare a mortgage
for £2100. The money was transferred to Cecil at the end of June
1952. The interest was to be at 4%, but Gerald had the discretion
to charge 5% if payment were more than one month in arrears.
The mortgage was repayable with 6 months' notice on either side.

⚜

Gerald was back in England by 15th March 1952 and he found
that his house on the Isle of Man was finally ready to move in to

---

31. Letter, Gerald Gardner to Cecil Williamson, 5 February 1952, (Document 34 Boscastle
Museum of Witchcraft).

after the substantial building works had been completed earlier that month.

Gerald quickly made himself at home there, with Donna joining him a short time later. In the context of acquiring 77 Malew Street, he decided to relinquish his flat at 47 Ridgmount Gardens. However, he was reluctant to give up a place in London altogether:

> *We're trying to get a smaller flat. None to be had in the ordy. way, & we're trying to do a three legged swap (being a Manx man now it should come natural). It's an awful job packing, when you don't know where you're going.*[32]

He acquired a flat at 145 Holland Road, near Shepherd's Bush in West London. He described this as a "pied-à-terre", in other words a small flat that would enable him to visit London regularly without having to book accommodation. In this, he was carrying on a tradition which I suspect he kept up during the war. Interestingly, the Electoral Register entry for 145 Holland Road had a "John and Mary Gardner" living there. This seems to have been another example of Gerald's sometimes apparently pointless and inappropriate mystification. He frequently used "John" and "Mary" as archetypal names in his stories.

Even though he was there only part of the year, the new flat in Holland Road didn't really suit Gerald. After only nine months he was writing: *I get so damned tired it takes such a time to get anywhere these days, being out here is so different from Goodge Street.*[33] Goodge Street Station was the nearest underground station to his previous flat at Ridgmount Gardens. It must be remembered that Gerald was 68 when he wrote that letter and suffering from chronic bronchitis and asthma.

Gerald settled in to the house in Malew Street very easily and it seemed to most who visited him as if he belonged to the house and had grown old with it. Various descriptions have been given of him at home, those by Bracelin and Teare being remarkably similar:

---

32. Letter, Gerald Gardner to Cecil Williamson, 24 March 1952, (Document 8, Boscastle Museum of Witchcraft archives).
33. Letter, Gerald Gardner to Cecil Williamson, 14 December 1952, (Document 76 Boscastle Museum of Witchcraft archives).

Inside, the difference between this house and its neighbours is ... marked, for the walls of the low rooms, of the narrow staircase, of the huge study upstairs, are covered, encrusted with swords, spears, daggers, pikes; clumsy mediaeval blades and bright Toledo rapiers stand side-by-side with curved Saracen scimitars and snakelike kris from Malaya. This is the harvest of a lifetime's interest. Between dull or gleaming steel, books lean and lie in untidy groups - books on folk-lore, on archaeology, on weapons, on the Far East, on psychical research, on Magic, witchcraft, extra-sensory perception, secret societies.[34]

The walls were covered with swords, spears, daggers, cutlasses and pistols, the harvest of a collector's lifetime. There were books in every room, on folk-lore, on weapons, on the Far East, on archaeology, on magic, witchcraft, secret societies and suchlike, but these were not contained in showcases; they were used for daily reference.[35]

There was a barn leading back from the main building, the upper floor of which Gerald used as his magical temple or ritual area. Access was obtained from the main house via the bathroom. Patricia Crowther gives a vivid description of this:

A small door in the bathroom connected the house to a barn comprising of two stories. The top floor of the barn held Gerald's Magic Circle as well as hundreds of books which lined the rough stone walls. An ancient carved sideboard fashioned with many cupboards and secret drawers occupied a position between the small door and one of the windows, while old swords and pieces of armour decorated any available space on the walls. Beautifully wrought incense burners and lamps from distant lands hung from the great beams, and the aroma of incense permeated everything in this unique chamber.[36]

⁂

34.. Bracelin, 7.
35. T. D. G. Teare, *Folk Doctor's Island*, (Times Press, Douglas 1964) p 197
36. Patricia Crowther, *From Stagecraft to Witchcraft*, (Capall Bann, 2002), 142.

There was much enthusiasm on the part of both Cecil and Gerald to expand the exhibition into the top floor of the granary with a lot more exhibits for the 1952 season. What is described as the 'upper hall', or upper gallery, of the granary was a fine room, with the roofing timbers on display. They made some 17 airtight display cases arranged around a central circulation area. There were also two "tableaux", representing the interior of a 17th Century witch's cottage and the temple of a ceremonial magician.

Gerald gave Cecil some fairly detailed advice over setting up the Witch's Cottage display:

> *The Witches Cottage would be just a cottage of this period but the furniture would be just a bit better + it would be kept clean, which would be a bit unusual for the period. There would be a big box bed, wall hangings, a built up stone fireplace in the floor with a hole in the roof for the smoke to go out. The circle should be triple, being a clear 9 nine feet to dance round in. If the other circles are 6 inches apart. This would make it 11 eleven feet over all, but if there is no room, they can be squeezed together. A simple circle will do, but 3 three are usual. They usually had no words or signs painted round the circle. But somtimes the ones who were more fortune tellers + charlatans put things in because their clients expected them to have what they knew wizards + sorcerers had, + it made it look awe inspiring. She would have a few rough shelves, as in the Witches Cottage, + a lot of rough jars + pots, in addition to the usual cooking pots, + the big Chaldron.*

> *If you could get somebody to make one or two little clay ovens, for simmering potions over a lamp. Copy the ones in the Witches Loan Collection, it would be good. Have plenty of dried herbs hanging from the ceiling.*

> *Of course, the (some of the) early witch probably could not read. On the other hand she was the Hereditary Priestess, + so much better educated than the common herd. So I think we can take it, she was one who could read, so would have a few manuscripts, + probably a few books. In this case, she*

would have a stand to hold the Ritual Book, as in the Witch's Cottage, + like the one I made that's in the barn here, + this is important, a Church lectern is made for one priest to read standing up. But in the Cult you must do what witches call "Draw down the Moon" i.e. invoke the Goddess into someones body + so some of the work must be done kneeling so the stand must be so it can be read at various heights, by different people. If you will look at mine, you'll see what I mean.

Then the most important thing is the altar. This may be a table, or better a long box, as in the Cottage. But it must not be too long to interfere with the Dance, + it must not be too small so as not to hold all the tools at one time, + there must be somthing, a table, or Box of the same hight, so as to make the altar a full 6 six feet long for certain rites. But the altar must not be a high one! The altar must be low enough that the Priestess's vagina can be seen when she stands behind it.

A few stools + possibly a chair, + ordy. domestic tools, a wooden spade, a sythe, Anything old will do. The Witch's Working tools you know of, I think. The sword, 2 knives, wand, incense-burner, pentacle, scurge + cords.

If you can get somone to copy one of the pentacles that are in the cases. Any sword will do, provided it is cross hilted, i.e. of the old type. The knives must be single edged, + one have a black hilt, one a white one. (Note. A Witch neednt necessarily have a sword. But there is always one that the coven can borrow. They are only used in initiations, + in a certain eventuality which may not occur once in a thousand years, but, to make things complete a sword would be good). The Chief, "The God, or the Devil as the trials call him", always has a sword, a High Priestess is usually given a sword, as a sign of rank, making her a man in fact but scarcely ever uses it (except in initiations). Any old incense-burner will do. I can make a wand, + I can plat a scurge. A few old Candelsticks, which can be of wood.

A tall standard candel stick. You know the type. There's one in the Witch's Cottage, + I have one here in the Barn. You've seen it, beside the book stand. This is important as you must have light to read the book by. If they hadn't one, somone was told off to hold a candel to the book, hence "Holding a Candel to the Devil".

Have a Broomstick, but have a used one, one that's worn a bit so it look like a Phalus when held upright.

To make the Cottage, I think you could make a frame of planks, painted black, like half timber work, + fit in that thick white fibre boarding between, this would look like half timber work. Have little lattice windows (You used to be able to buy strips of lead at Woolworths, which you can cement on glass windows to look like lattice work) + a door, with old iron work + if possible a Judas, the tiny loophole with a cover, + an iron grill so you can look out + see who is outside.

In Denmark, they are very fond of having creepers growing up the inside walls of their rooms. So, a few creepers grow-ing up the wall would add a lot to the atmosphere.

If you could get a really pretty gay figure, it would be splen-did, but it must be one that looks natural, a poor one would spoil it.

Also, if you could get one of a Magician for the Dee Circle, with proper robes, it would look fine by the way. If you could get some Enochian Tablets made, they would be good. Unfor-tunately I havent the drawings of any. Are there any in Book 5? (You have my copy) Crowley gave them in The Equinox, but I haven't got this volume. Michial Just [Michael Houghton of Atlantis Bookshop] *could easily provide one, I think.*

In Witch's Hut, of course, any ordy. domestic articles, a few pewter, or even a silver spoon of the old shapes, pottery plates (Woolworth's ones painted would do) pottery or horn drinking mugs.

The Circle could be drawn on the boards in either black or dull red paint. Id favour red, as looking brighter. Put a few signs on the wall, not too many, but understandably have the Witch sign [drawing of pentagram with triangle above].

⁂

During the second season, from April 1952 onwards, Gerald helped in the museum selling copies of his book: *He became the 'resident witch' at the museum during the summer season and entertained old and young ladies in the teashop with colourful stories of his adventures in the Far East.*37 The book had not sold well and the publisher wanted to clear his stock shelves. Cecil agreed that these copies could be kept in the Museum and Gerald could sell them provided that he took a percentage of the profit.

Several commentators have observed that Gerald used to ride on a bicycle between his house and the museum. Patricia Crowther writes: "He could be seen free-wheeling down a steep street, his white hair streaming behind him in the wind."38 Cecil Williamson paints a vivid picture:

*Every day he would toddle over to the Museum around 11.30am, have coffee, chat up the tourists, lunch on the House. He had his own special table located on the left hand side of the wide set of steps leading up from the main entrance. He was decorative, looked the part of a Magician, and of course he was happy, and on to a good thing, for he was selling his book "High Magic's Aid" and of course signed every copy he sold. You can picture the scene - Gerald at a large elm wood Rustic Table, stacks of books, and a litter of letters, papers etc.*39

Edith seems to have visited the museum on at least one occasion. Cecil was very keen to meet her, but Gerald was equally keen that he should not. I'm not sure exactly why, probably just that

37. Michael Howard, "Gerald Gardner: The Man, the Myth & the Magick: Part Two", *The Cauldron* 84, (Beltane/Midsummer 1997), 20.
38. Crowther, (2002), 144..
39. Letter, Cecil Williamson to Michael Howard, about 1982, (Boscastle Museum of Witchcraft archives).

Gerald wanted to control the flow of information between the two. So Gerald played a trick on Cecil and got a friend of his who was a landlady in Douglas to pretend to be Edith, a role which apparently she rather enjoyed. The deception probably would have worked but, as is likely in the Island, the kitchen staff recognised her and told Cecil, who was upset at the whole charade.

At the height of the summer season in 1952, Gerald wrote to Rex: *...we're just crowded out with people + arnt the other Museums jealous?*[40] And Cecil was enthusiastic when he wrote to Gerald Yorke:

The formation of this "shop window" was deliberately planned to act as a magnet to draw to one those interested. The place was chosen because it suited my overall plan. So it is that now a year is passed. I look back and see the results of my efforts. These one time, and some what extensive Ruins are now well on the way to reestablishment. The Restaurant is well established. The Museum or Exhibition call it what you will is launched and as such is successful. In short then the entire project is under way and in being...[41]

He had accumulated quite an extensive collection of amulets and talismans and a large proportion of the exhibits consisted of these. A guidance sheet, which was sold or given to those looking round the exhibition, was largely devoted to an explanation of the philosophy underlying amulets and talismans. It stated:

Our aim is to please you with Good Food and Pleasant Surroundings and to interest you with our Exhibition of Superstition Magic and Witchcraft. So that together these two things combine to make your visit one that you can look back upon with pleasure.

The Exhibition is limited to the study of three subjects, namely: Magic, Witchcraft, and Superstition. Oddly enough, for one reason or another, these subjects are either completely ignored or at the best only lightly touched upon by National and Municipal Museums. One wonders why?

---

40. Letter, Gerald Gardner to Rex Wellbye, 7 August 1952.
41. Letter, Cecil Williamson to Gerald Yorke, 7 August 1952, (Yorke Collection, Warburg Institute).

Small as it now is, a start has been made to bring together, for the first time in one place, matter relative to this purpose. We have been here but a few months; our aim is to have over three thousand exhibits on display within three years. Behind the scenes we hold a mass of printed and written material. The whole combining to form a solid base from which in time future generations of research workers in this field, may build upon with confidence.[42]

The leaflet was undersigned by Cecil H. Williamson and Gerald B. Gardner, indicating that Gerald had become formally part of the establishment.

Cecil was intending to set up some form of membership organisation based on the museum, possibly what was later known as the Witchcraft Research Centre, but initially just called 'The Folklore Centre':

Anyone is welcome to apply for membership to the Centre. Election is subject to suitable references and payment of the small annual subscription. Members will receive periodically, a journal compounded of current news regarding the activities of the Centre; detailed descriptions of new additions to the collection; articles on a variety of subjects both from members and non-members; answers to members correspondence queries. Members will have free use of the Centre's library (postage extra). Members will be encouraged to help in extending the scope of the collection by themselves gathering items of interest from their own location, whether it be within the British Isles or in any other part of the world. Members may join the study group. The function of the study group is to examine in a practical way, the methods alleged to have been employed for the working of magic. Members will be invited to attend the Centre's annual "Witchcraft convention" held on June 24th of each year at the Folklore Centre, Castletown, Isle of Man.[43]

---

42. Cecil H. Williamson and Gerald B Gardner, "The Witches' Kitchen, Castletown, Isle of Man," (probably 1952).
43. "The Folklore Centre of Superstition and Witchcraft: An Introduction to Visitors", (1951).

I have no evidence that such a membership organisation actually started or that the witchcraft conventions were ever held.

Despite the visitor numbers, the 1952 season had not been particularly successful financially, and whilst numerous stories and allegations have grown up over the years, there definitely seems to have been a clash of personalities between Cecil Williamson and Gerald Gardner. Suffice it to say that, by late 1952 or early 1953, Williamson, quoting the short length of the tourist season on the Isle of Man, decided to go back to England, although, as we shall see, financial and legal matters were probably the determining factors.

CHAPTER TWENTY–SIX

Collection and Conflict

Gerald returned to London at the end of the 1952 season, keeping in touch with Cecil by letter. Two notable events occurred on the Island that autumn: they concerned the Bishop and the Storm!

Manx people generally had a relaxed attitude towards the topics of witchcraft and magic, and it was some time before there was any criticism of the museum. When it came, it came, perhaps predictably, from the Church. Cecil Williamson had been invited by the Bishop of Sodor and Man, John Ralph Strickland Taylor, to the Diocesan Conference being held in St. George's Hall, Douglas. The Bishop gave an address on the subject of sorcery and witchcraft, "chosen because people have been disturbed by an awakened interest in the subject in a certain part of the Island", an obvious reference to the museum. He said that the Bible presented witchcraft as something evil, declaring "The real answer which the Bible gives to these things is something positive and vital. It is the revelation of the true nature of God. Let in the glorious sunshine, and out go the ghosts and ghouls of darkness." Cecil was then invited to speak to the assembly, where he said that the Bishop "was absolutely right in stating that a light should be thrown on the subject", declaring that "there are still great natural powers that no one can understand".[1]

Gerald was not inclined to take the criticism by the Bishop very seriously and in his reply wrote:

> It's a scream. I should suggest that you write to the Bishop, asking him to come + see the Museum for himself. (I'd go through the cases first, Put the scurge away from the witchcraft case, + some of the Phalic charms away first). Then put it to him, "If you don't believe in Witches, what are you making all the fuss for? If you do believe in Witches, what do you believe, that they fly through the air on Brooms. Will you say you believe this for the Papers? If you simply object because it's the relics of a heathen cult, what about the Druid ceremonies at Stonehenge?
>
> Also say, "Don't you know that what the Bible realy says is "Thou shalt not allow a Poisoner to live". That either by mistake or by intention the word was wrongly translated in King James Ist time? as Witch, but all Bible scholars know the Word means poisoner."
>
> At the same time, I'd try as far as you can to get the National Press interested. Bishop denounces Witchcraft Museum!!! Diocesan Conference held to discourage scientific investigation!!! etc. etc. I think quite a lot of Advertisement (+ Amusement) could be got from this. The Bishop won't like it if the Papers say that he believes in Witches!!!
>
> I'll see if I can get some publicity this end, but you must get any funny charms + the scurge put out of sight before they come in, as they'd jump at them + say they were immoral. You can put them back afterwards ...
>
> John Wallace says we'd better change the notice under the Witches to nine million + two, as they'll be Burning the both of us.[2]

---

1. Letter, Cecil Williamson to Gerald Gardner, 18 December 1952.
2. Letter Gerald Gardner to Cecil Williamson 20 December 1952, (Document 77, Boscastle Museum of Witchcraft archives).

Donna gave her support to Cecil in a letter where she said: *My stepmother says she knows yr. Bishop so I have told her to suggest to him a more charitable attitude towards his small flock upon the Island!*3

Some on the Island, however, were a good deal more positive about witchcraft. Cecil wrote to Gerald about what seems to have been a talk by Gerald recorded earlier and which was then played back to the audience on Sunday 23rd November 1952. It was introduced by Dr. Alexander Cannon, the controversial writer on spiritualism and psychic phenomena who lived on the Island:

> *Thought that you would like to know that Sunday went off well. Full house in spite of quite heavy snow falling. Dr. Cannon gave you a truly wonderful introduction. But his introduction was mild to the boost he gave you at the end of the recording. He said words to the effect that he had spoken to the Head of the British Museum who had told him that he knew Gerald Gardner, that Gerald Gardner was undoubtedly the leading authority in the world today on witchcraft, that you had a tremendous and brilliant Brain. Then Cannon went on to say that though your voice was with us tonight, your body was thousands of miles away, that you were going on one of those great ventures in quest of knowledge, a venture fraught with danger and hardship into the dim shadows of the forbidding jungle ... how like so many great men you had gone off quietly with no more fuss than if you were to see a dear relative, that truly you were one of the great. Now, dear friend, you ought to take a Bow!* 4

One event which did not help matters was a severe storm on 17th December 1952. Cecil reported to Gerald on how it had affected the museum buildings:

> *Today broke my heart. We have had the most awfull gale or rather Hurricane. The B.B.C. say that the R.A.F. hut on Snaefell registered 130 m.p.h. winds today. The Airport I know registered 97 m.p.h. winds before lunch. Well, old*

3. Letter, Donna Gardner to Cecil Williamson, 1 February 1953.
4. Letter, Cecil Williamson to Gerald Gardner, 29 November 1952.

*man, it has been too much for the roofs. They have been breaking up all day long. There is a huge hole in the Museum Roof and the Big Barn on the left of the windmill tower is a shambles. No Boat could leave the Island. I have been trotting around like a mad man. Phone wires down so all told have had the Hell of a time. But I went down to your house. It was OK at 4.30 today .... Having a good look around your place the only damage I spotted was a broken pane in one of your studio windows. ... The floor under the two upturned bikes is very damp - looks as if flood water from the pavement has come in under the street door, flowed through and out the other door into your yard drain. Do you want me to move the clobber in that corner to the far end of the workshop.*5

⚮

Gerald was away because some time in the autumn of 1952 he had heard from his old friend, Dennis Collings, who was now living near Accra in the Gold Coast (now Ghana) in West Africa. He had been appointed to set up a new museum and invited Gerald to pay him a visit. Gerald had been wondering where to go for his regular "wintering abroad" and, as he was also now a museum curator (or so he described himself on the passenger lists), he decided that the Gold Coast would be ideal. Gerald had become interested in Voodoo during his trip to America in 1947/48. He wanted to explore its African origins and possible links with ancient Egypt and the Greek Mysteries. He booked his passage and set off on a cargo boat, the *Sulima*, from London on 30th December 1952. There were only two other passengers. The voyage had been delayed, as Gerald reported to Cecil: *... she was to have gone on the 13th, then put off to the 18th, then the 23rd, now 30th. It's all a matter of Cargo, and the Docker Union, + whether any of the cargo men will be sober a week after Xmas.*6

At the beginning of February, Donna wrote to Cecil: *Gerald has arrived safely at Achimota, says its lovely + hot, but muggy. I hope he + young Collings have a good time. He said the voyage was good. He*

5. Letter, Cecil Williamson to Gerald Gardner, 17 December 1952.
6. Letter Gerald Garder to Cecil Williamson probably, 23 December 1952.

had an awful week of dense fog ... + he began to get asthma again + was very chesty. I was thankful to see him go - sounds a bit heartless, but that fog put a lot of people under the sod.[7]

Gerald arrived in the Gold Coast and stayed with Dennis Collings at the University College at Achimota:

> *This is a queer place. It's an enormous College. Set up in the wilds with the special intention of preventing the students being able to get off + make whoopee. So its impossible to get out of. There is no museum. We have a very large room borrowed from the School of Geology about the size of our large room at the Mill, packed full of stuff, + a very large house is being built for the Department of Archaeology, which will be used as a temporary museum, will be finished in May. So we're busy packing everything ready to be transported. The room we're in belongs to the Geology people, + they're trying to heave us out. There's a very fine site for the Real Museum in Accra. But, Self Government has grabbed the funds for building it.*[8]

He recalled that this was not the first time he had visited Accra: his mind went back to the time when he and Com had caused something of a sensation some 60 years previously. Perhaps things had quietened down a bit in the meantime!

Cecil had obviously asked Gerald to see if he could obtain some Mau-Mau items for the museum. Gerald was not at all hopeful, the main reason being that the Gold Coast was some two thousand miles from Kenya, where the Mau-Mau uprisings were taking place:

> *I haven't seen any pictures of Mau-Mau stuff. Send me some + i'll see what I can do. Actually it will be impossible while I'm in the College here + the trouble is Collings can't get away till another man gets back + he keeps getting extensions of leave. Anyhow, I'll see what I can do.*[9]

7. Letter, Donna Gardner to Cecil Williamson, 1 February 1953.
8. Letter, Gerald Gardner to Cecil Williamson, 25 January 1953.
9. Letter, Gerald Gardner to Cecil Williamson, 25 January 1953.

As usual on his expeditions, Gerald wanted to make contact with the native peoples to find out about their beliefs and magical practices:

Am trying to get up some connections. Missionarys and Government have driven the Witch Doctor underground round here. They are good Christians of different denominations who fight, + burn each other's villages, + everyone says there are none, I must go right up country for them, but I think I can smell things. Anyhow, we'll see.[10]

Whilst he may not have been able to acquire any Mau-Mau artefacts, he was able to accumulate quite a lot of items that were said to have magical uses, totalling some £18, for the museum. He listed them as including knives, birds' skulls, a witch doctor's whisk, drums, assorted gourds, elephants' and mongooses' tails, axes, umbrellas, hooks, handcuffs, gongs, masks, casting bones, bull roarers, bracelets and many other items. Gerald had been led to believe that they had been used for various different types of magic, though I suspect that the individuals that he acquired them from may in some cases have seen the opportunity to get rid of some assorted junk for cash. Undoubtedly Gerald did make contact with local people who worked magic, and Dennis Collings introduced him to several "witch doctors" in whom he was most interested. It is clear that whilst Gerald was taken into their confidence to some extent, there were also things that they would not reveal to him, which is understandable despite his approach, which tended to encourage all manner of people to talk to him.

It was not straightforward transporting this material back to the museum:

They wouldnt let me send packets by air. Everything has to be vetted at the Head Custom House, + nothing odd will be allowed to Pass, now they have Self-Government, + the worst thing you can say is Museum Specimens. So I'me bringing items as luggage, + will try + send them from Liverpool .... most of the stuff I'm sending is fetish or witch doctor stuff, but it all has to be kept very dark, as the Various

---

10. Ibid.

Churches are very strong, as with Self Government they control so many votes.[11]

Gerald returned on the *S.S. John Holt* from Takoradi, arriving back in Liverpool on 17th March 1953.

⁂

The loan of certain items in the ownership of the 'Southern Coven of British Witches' (i.e. Edith) for display in the museum seems to have been first mentioned back in April 1951, at Gerald's request. Arrangements were made, with Gerald acting as a go-between, for Edith to send up 52 items for display and these were exhibited, probably at the opening of the 1952 season. It was these items that were to prove the catalyst for a growing sense of unease between Gerald Gardner and Cecil Williamson, ultimately leading to a complete rift.

The items which were lent to the Museum by the Southern Coven were listed on a schedule, probably, to judge from the spelling, by Gerald himself. An examination of this list is quite revealing. There are some 52 items in total, which can be classified as follows:

Preparation of Herbs: *Brass-handled knives; Brass pestle and mortar; Steel balance; Brass 14-section filter; Pewter filter vase; Pewter measures; Earthenware candle oven with bars; Ivory spatula.*

Storage: *Inlaid fitted wooden box with secret drawers; Boxwood and pewter boxes; Round horn ointment box; Small 8-sided incense box.*

Items for use in Rituals: *Dwarf wooden candlesticks; Incense burners; Gong, beater and ring; Candle snuffer.*

Magical Items: *Pinchbeck love charm; Necklaces (jet and amber); Wooden hand mirror.*

Miscellaneous: *Tinder boxes (wood and ivory and silver); Silver spoons; Pottery bowl; Pewter dish.*

This suggests that the cutting, preparation, weighing, grinding, filtering, heating and storage of herbal concoctions, ointments and incenses was a preoccupation of the former owner of these items.

---

11. Letter, Gerald Gardner to Cecil Williamson, probably late February 1953.

The Museum Guide in 1958 described this material as follows: *A collection of objects used by witches, lent by an existing coven of witches. Naturally, they have only lent articles which they are not using, hence the collection consists chiefly of implements for the making of herbal cures and charms; there is, however, one very fine ritual wand, and a curious old desk containing seven secret drawers, in which they used to hide some of their possessions.*[12]

Patricia Crowther gives a more detailed description of one of these items: *One case in the museum was of great interest to me. Among other items it contained a large wooden box with a mirror inside the lid and paintings of the God and Goddess on either side. It held a miscellany of vials, charms, talismans and knives, and the latter had curious signs incised on them.*[13]

The guide book description tells us, or at least strongly suggests that the Southern Coven was still in existence in 1958, that it previously had members who made herbal cures and charms, but that they no longer had such members, who had presumably died or left the coven, or those members who had previously been involved in such activity had ceased their involvement for some reason.

The "curious old desk containing seven secret drawers" sounds very much as if it is the same object as the "very nice little cabinet" of little drawers that Gerald had acquired which had originally belonged to "Mother Sabine".

At first, following the loan, all went well and the items were exhibited in a display case all to themselves, with an appropriate caption. Apparently, some members of the 'Southern Coven' visited the museum and were happy with how their material was being displayed; whether this was Edith or Rosanne or an invention of Gerald's I do not know.

However, after a few weeks, what seems to have happened is that Cecil rearranged things, using some of the items in other displays and taking other items out of the exhibition altogether. Gerald was not pleased with this course of action, and this seems to have been the source of the first conflict between the two of them which got more acrimonious as time went on. He obviously informed Edith, who requested the return of the items in April

---

12. Gardner, (1958), 18-19.
13. Crowther, (1998), 27.

1953. After what seems to have been repeated requests, Cecil finally packaged up the items for return to her in July of that year. On 5th August 1953 a receipt for the returned items was typed and sealed 'Dafo' in Theban script and posted in Christchurch.[14] It could, of course, have been that Gerald had taken them and hidden them away in his house, with Edith's agreement.

Michael Howard[15] comments that they were never returned to the 'Southern Coven' and that he saw them on display at Cecil's museum at Boscastle in 1967.

Cecil's account of the incident suggests that Gerald had deliberately chosen the middle of the summer season to request their return, to make things awkward for him. However, Gerald's letters make clear that the first request had been made back in April. In any case, by his own account Cecil had plenty of material in storage to replace the display.

There also seems to have been a disagreement which arose through a misunderstanding of the basis on which Gerald allowed some of his own exhibits to be displayed. On 1st August 1953, Gerald wrote to Cecil:

> *With reguards to my collection, it was offered to you &*
> *accepted on the clear understanding that it was a collection,*
> *& would be treated with the customary courtesey, & would*
> *not be broken up, but shown as a whole, this was in Donnas*
> *presence in London. It was to show the public what magic &*
> *witchcraft realy is, & not as ignorant & intrested people con-*
> *spire to make people think it is. You promised it would have*
> *a room to itself, with my portrait, called the Gardner room.*
> *Yesterday you complained that the case was so empty. I sug-*
> *gested that you should either return the many things that*
> *were formerly in this case which were removed without my*
> *knowledge or consent, or else you should put the various*
> *magical books of mine which you have put into another case*
> *in to fill up this case & make a good show such as it formerly*
> *enjoyed & you were not willing to do either. If you will only*

---

14. Letter, 'Dafo' to Cecil Williamson, posted 5 August 1953, (Document 1, Boscastle Museum of Witchcraft archives).
15. Michael Howard, *Modern Wicca: A History from Gerald Gardner to the Present*, (Llewellyn Publications, 2009), 105.

tell me clearly what you are aiming at, possibly I could help you, but it must be true, I will not co-opperate in making a Dennis Wheatly Montague Summers pack of lies. As you long ago agreed upon, my collection is only of value if unbroken, so I cannot sell any part ... As you said you did not wish me to show people round the Museum this year, I have kept away. If you wish my co-opperation in future I shall always be happy to assist you, but I must be allowed to understand what you are intending to do, a little discussion beforehand would have perhaps prevented this unhappy business with the Southern Coven, which has taken away nearly all the Scientific value of your Museum.[16]

Gerald wrote further:

I gather you now have a very large collection of your own & wish to exhibit this. This was all along understood. My stuff should have a room to itself, & yours should be the main museum, but this did not include my and my friends stuff being put away, or hidden, or mixed up to make it inchomprehensible. Anyhow, if youll explain to me what your new ideas are, we may agree that it is better that as space is limated it is better that your collection alone should be on show for a year or two, as I gather mine does not intrest the man in the street. I quite understand this, & agree to it.[17]

As you know, I have always been very dissatisfied with the presentation (from the museum point of view) because the things were not explaned. But I <u>knew it was your museum</u>, & realise you did not wish the things to be explained, so said little.[18]

As so often seems to be the case, it was in the financial arrangement between the two men that the relationship became fraught. The 1952 season was not a success financially and at one stage Cecil discussed with Gerald the possibility of moving the

16. Letter, Gerald Gardner to Cecil Williamson, 1 August 1953, (Document 30, Boscastle Museum of Witchcraft archives).
17. Letter, Gerald Gardner to Cecil Williamson, 2 or 3 August 1953, (Document 2, Boscastle Museum of Witchcraft archives).
18. Letter, Gerald Gardner to Cecil Williamson, 5 August 1953, (Document 3, Boscastle Museum of Witchcraft archives).

museum to Douglas, to see if that improved matters, but in the end nothing was done.

In December 1952, in reply to a query from Cecil, Gerald made clear his views on the future of his collection. He wanted it to be available for the public to see, but said he couldn't afford to donate it to the museum, as he wanted something to provide an income for Donna should he die first:

> I think the Museum should have the stuff when we pass on. We've no children or anyone dependant on us. Otherwise I think you cant blame me if I get a good offer from some Museum or from America, if I let the stuff go. But I'd be very sorry for it to go to America. Only Donna must be made secure she's about 60 now, so it's really a life interest for her. Of course I know so well you simply cannot do anything in the next two or three years, the top floor must be got open, & in working order, & if possible, the place made a centre for like minded people to meet.[19]

It is clear from this that Gerald intended that his share of the collection should generate an income for Donna when the museum started to make a profit, but that it would be left to the museum after they had both died. The comment "... I'd be very sorry for it to go to America" is rather poignant in view of the final destination of much of the museum's contents.

The relationship deteriorated during the 1953 season, partly because of the saga of the Southern Coven's artefacts, mentioned above, and in September 1953 Gerald's solicitors served formal notice on Cecil that repayment of the mortgage would be required in 6 months' time, as interest had not been paid on it. It is obvious that by this time Gerald was determined to extract all he could from him because, when Cecil paid the due interest at the end of September 1953, Gerald insisted on it at the 5% rate because it was not paid on time. In addition, he also asked for £19.15s for items that he bought in Africa in 1951 and £9 for swords that Cecil wanted to acquire. Gerald seemed to be wanting to

---

19. Letter, Gerald Gardner to Cecil Williamson, 14 December 1952, (Document 76, Boscastle Museum of Witchcraft archives).

make life difficult for him: the relationship had obviously deteriorated seriously in the course of the previous year.

All Gerald's grievances against Cecil seemed to surface in a series of letters which he wrote in the early months of 1954. He complained that, for the previous 18 months, Cecil had not kept a promise to pass all those who were enquiring about the Craft to him. Cecil was obviously generating a lot of ideas for making the museum more financially viable, none of which seemed to Gerald to be very sensible. He was not very keen on Cecil's ideas about changing the restaurant into a 'Road House', organising a travelling exhibition, or turning it into a plaster cast factory!

⁂

Gerald fulfilled his intentions of returning to the Gold Coast and took the *M.V. Accra* from Liverpool to Takoradi on 31st December 1953. He was again staying with Dennis Collings, but Gerald's relationship with Cecil meant that his letters from West Africa are mostly about issues to do with the museum and very little about what he was experiencing in Africa. Though some accounts state that Gerald "was popular with everyone ... from natives to university dons", he wrote:

> *I gave a lecture here on Witchcraft etc. in of all places the Young Men's Christian Association, + at last information is coming forward. I may have to stay out here longer than I expected. I have also been broadcasting. The missionaries don't love me.*[20]

Ralph Merrifield (1913-1995), the expert on folk magic and curator of the Guildhall Museum in London tells the story of when he was living in Achimota to arrange the displays in the new National Museum in the Gold Coast in 1956:

> *We were allocated a pleasant bungalow on the edge of Achimota, a few miles from Accra, and here we occasionally received visits from itinerant Hausa pedlars. A tall and*

---

20. Letter, Gerald Gardner to Cecil Williamson, 30 January 1954.

stately robed figure would appear on our verandah, followed by a porter with a bundle on his head as large as himself. The cloth container would be opened and the wares spread out to tempt us. On one such occasion we were entertaining for tea Dennis Collings, Curator of the University collection which it was my task to transform into a public museum. The Hausa became very excited when he saw Dennis, and begged to be given the address of that 'white master' who had stayed with him the year before - "he who never slept, but sat up all night talking to devils". In fact, as I subsequently learnt, Gerald suffered badly from Asthma, and could only sleep propped up in bed, as was observed by watchful African eyes. His visit had been made in the hope that the humid atmosphere of the West Coast of Africa would give him some relief. He made a great impression on the local population and the Hausa was anxious to obtain a charm from him. He had given a lecture on witchcraft at the YMCA in Accra, where the hall had been packed to capacity and there was nearly a riot among those unable to gain admission. When he visited the market he had been mobbed by the market-women, with cries of "Master, you give me baby" - to which the answer was "I'm too old!". With his little white beard and walking-stick carved with serpents he was a striking figure, and he undoubtedly had charm.[21]

At the beginning of February 1954, Gerald was in Benin:

At present "I go walk about bush". I'm in Nigeria. The lecture + broadcast produced good results, + information is coming in. I've seen magic worked, + am on the trail of something widespread, + its produced exactly as European Witches do. There's also an interesting cult of the double axe. Very interesting. I'll be back in the Gold coast to get my things before I go. Boats are difficult this time of year, but I'm down for several + so should click somewhere."[22]

21. Ralph Merrifield, "G.B. Gardner and the 20th Century 'Witches'", *Folklore Society News*, No. 17, (June 1993), 10.
22. Letter, Gerald Gardner to Cecil Williamson, 7 February 1954.

The journey home was somewhat eventful: *We had a Hell of a passage home, a Dutch boat to Cape Palmas, Monrovia etc. We had a deck cargo of mahogany logs. All chained down, of course, but in the storm they broke loose, the ship's carpenter + a deck hand went overboard + were drowned + lots of damage + this made us very late.*[23]

Gerald summarised his two visits:

> *The first year I had no luck; but after I had given a suitably watered-down lecture on witchcraft at Accra, Gold coast, in January 1954, in (of all places) a Y.M.C.A. building, followed by a smll wireless talk, information began to trickle in, and now I have seen magic worked in the Coast fashion. Of course I quite realise they don't tell me all their secrets; from what I have seen they do use two of the processes that witches use to gain power, but these two processes seem to be world-wide.*[24]

Gerald certainly expected Cecil to move imminently, perhaps back to London. To end his letter of 7th February 1954, from Africa, he wrote: *If you have moved on before I get back, let me know where to as I'd like to see your show.*[25]

At the expiry of the period of notice, in March 1954, Gerald's solicitors reminded Cecil that repayment was required or proceedings would be taken. Gerald also informed him, via his solicitors, that Edith Woodford-Grimes would be willing to take over the property with vacant possession for the amount due to Gerald on the mortgage. Cecil's solicitors warned him that this was less than the property was worth.

Two days before the deadline, Cecil sent a telegram to Gerald asking him to withhold legal action and requesting a telephone conversation. Gerald replied, telling him not to worry and immediately came up to the Island for discussions. We don't know exactly what was agreed, but on 7th April 1954, Gerald wrote a note accept-

---

23. Letter, Gerald Gardner to Cecil Williamson, 15 March 1954.
24. Gardner, (1954), 155.
25. Letter, Gerald Gardner to Cecil Williamson, 7 February 1954, (Document 27, Boscastle Museum of Witchcraft archives).

ing that Edith would take over the mortgage and stating that he would instruct his solicitor to draw up the necessary agreement.

Cecil claimed, almost certainly rightly, that Gerald carried on all the negotiations via Edith, trying to hide the fact that he wanted to take over the museum. But he also gives the impression that he was the one who wanted to move and he knowingly and voluntarily sold the museum to Gerald: *By the second year I had decided that I would go back to England. Gerald was very keen on the place so I told him that he could buy the place if he wanted to.*[26]

Cecil moved out some time in April 1954. He later wrote that Gerald had expected him to leave some of the exhibits. However, he makes it clear[27] that none of the exhibits were included in the sale. Much of the material that was previously owned by Gerald had been bought some time previously by him under pressure from Gerald, whose own collection was far from sufficient to provide enough material for a viable museum. According to Cecil, Gerald pleaded with him to let him have some material to fill the cases. It was only after Donna's intervention that he agreed to let Gerald have his collection of talismans and amulets.

There were subsequent disagreements following the move. Cecil had, according to Gerald, removed certain items that should have remained, and Gerald wanted the purchase price adjusted to take account of this. Cecil tells an unlikely story about removing the witch logos from the plates in the restaurant because Gerald wouldn't pay anything for the goodwill and that when Gerald found out what he had done he tried to stab him with his athame.[28] Lois Bourne told me:

> When he sold his property to Gerald he made so many difficulties and when Gerald and Donna took possession they found that every toilet and wash basin had been smashed and damage done to other parts of the property which had to be repaired and which cost quite a lot of money.[29]

I suspect that fundamentally the conflict arose because of a difference of approach between the two which did not surface initially

---

26. "An Interview with Cecil Williamson: Part 2", *Talking Stick VIII* (Autumn 1992).
27. Letter, Cecil Williamson to Graham King, 14 June 1997.
28. "An Interview with Cecil Williamson: Part 2", *Talking Stick VIII*, (Autumn 1992), 20.
29. Letter, Lois Bourne to the author, 19 May 1999.

because of the excitement of the whole thing and the activity of setting the museum up. It was only when cold financial consideration came into play that the differences surfaced. Gerald stepped in and bailed Cecil Williamson out. This is always a difficult circumstance and so it proved in this case. Cecil was the one who found the site for the museum and set it up. However, Gerald must have felt that his financial support gave him certain rights over the displays, as we can tell from the saga of the 'Southern Coven' artefacts, and his daily routine. It seems as if Cecil responded by making life difficult for Gerald, not just in rearranging the exhibits but by keeping back information about enquirers and so on.

It is clear that Cecil was more of a showman than Gerald. He wanted to emphasise the more sensational aspects of witchcraft, whereas Gerald tried to be more academic, giving more explanation of the exhibits. It was really inevitable that, as the financial crisis came to a head, they would go their own ways, with Gerald taking over the museum, and Cecil taking his exhibits, eventually finding a permanent home for them at Boscastle, in Cornwall. He ran this Museum of Witchcraft very successfully until his retirement in 1996 at the age of 87, when he sold it to the present owner, Graham King. It is well worth a visit.

For the 1954 season, Gerald had taken over the museum at Castletown completely. And, as if to seal the change, the name had become "The Museum of Magic and Witchcraft". On Saturday 5th June 1954, the museum opened for the summer season under Gerald's directorship. This change is emphasised in the advertising which was carried out. The Witches Mill (late Witches Kitchen) is first on the advertisement and is described as being "under entirely new management", offering morning coffee, grills, teas, suppers, snacks, ices, minerals, etc. Smaller lettering underneath refers to the Museum of Magic and Witchcraft which was "under the personal supervision of Dr. G.B. Gardener [sic - obviously the personal supervision did not extend to ensuring that his name was spelt properly in the advert!]. Open 10am to 11pm daily."

Both Gerald Gardner and Cecil Williamson were colourful characters and, although each had flaws in their personalities, between them they built up what was a major showcase for witchcraft - a religion emerging from the shadows of illegality.

The Museum achieved a lot in the way of publicity and it paved the way for an event which, more than any other factor, achieved Gerald's long-cherished hope that the Craft of the Wica would not die but gain new adherents: it was the publication of his first non-fiction book about the Craft: *Witchcraft Today*.

CHAPTER TWENTY–SEVEN

New Light and a New Witch

Whilst Gerald achieved a lot with *High Magic's Aid*, he was limited because it was a work of fiction from making the statement that he wanted to - that witches still existed and moreover that he was an initiated witch himself - though those visiting the museum would get a very clear idea about that. Some of the exhibits were specifically captioned as coming from present-day witch covens, and the notice that was on display at the table where Gerald was selling *High Magic's Aid* makes it quite clear that witches still existed.

The turning point was in January 1952, when a book was published, with the simple title of *Witchcraft*.[1] It was written by Pennethorne Hughes and in many ways it was just a typical history largely based on the works of Margaret Murray. However, the consequences of its publication were very far-reaching indeed. Hughes (1907-1967) had been a history teacher at a leading English private school for five years, after which he joined the BBC as a producer. He had had several books published on such topics as the history of modern Europe, Egypt in wartime, and the origin of surnames. This was his first (and only) book about witchcraft.

---

1. Pennethorne Hughes, *Witchcraft,* (Longmans Green, 1952).

By 1952, Edith was about the only member of the group which initiated him with whom Gerald was still in regular contact. She had probably seen reviews of the book while Gerald was away in Italy and acquired a copy. What she read must have disturbed her considerably, the following being a typical passage: ... *witchcraft, as a cult-belief in Europe, is dead. As a degenerate form of a primitive fertility belief, incorporating the earliest instructive wisdom, the practice is over. Conjurers, wisewomen, palmists, and perverts may be called witches, but it is using an old stick to beat a dead dog.*[2]

One can well imagine Edith's reaction to being equated with degeneracy, perverts and dead dogs, and how this would not exactly enamour her with Hughes! She was angry, indeed incensed by the way his book gave a totally distorted view of the witches' beliefs and practices, but what could she do? She was in something of a quandary. On the one hand, the Cult was secret and she didn't want people even to know of its existence. Yet, here was an author who was giving what appeared to be a most warped view of the Cult, which made her angry. What could she do?

She made up her mind. Since the publication of *High Magic's Aid,* Gerald had been pestering her to be allowed to write something of a more factual nature about the Cult. It would need careful thinking and a lot of talking about what could and could not be mentioned, but she decided that when Gerald came back from Italy she would agree to his writing the factual book on the Cult that he had long wanted to produce.

We don't know exactly when those discussions took place, certainly at the latest when Gerald went down for the Druids' Summer Solstice celebrations at Stonehenge in June 1952. He gives details of some of those discussions: *This* [Hughes' Witchcraft] *made some of my friends very angry, and I managed to persuade them that it might do good to write a factual book about witchcraft, and so I wrote* Witchcraft Today.[3] Unusually, Gerald annotated his copy of Hughes' book in ink, drawing attention to certain paragraphs which he found particularly interesting, frequently topics which eventually found their way into *Witchcraft Today*. I counted sixteen paragraphs which had been annotated and I stopped

---

2. Op. cit., 204.
3. Gardner, (1959), 12.

counting two-thirds of the way through the book. It is interesting that, rather than dwelling on the negative aspects of Hughes' book, Gerald has marked the paragraphs that provide useful information which he could use in his own book.

In the Foreword to *Witchcraft Today*, Gerald reports further on his discussions with Edith: *I have been told by witches in England: "Write and tell people we are not perverts. We are decent people, we only want to be left alone, but there are certain secrets that you mustn't give away". So, after some argument as to exactly what I must not reveal, I am permitted to tell much that has never before been made public concerning their beliefs, their rituals and their reasons for what they do ...*[4]

Edith was quite adamant about what she would allow and what she wouldn't. She particularly did not want Gerald to give details of any rituals which were definitely magical, nor did she wish it to be known how they raised power. Gerald described the situation: *... I soon found myself between Scylla and Charybdis. If I said too much, I ran the risk of offending people whom I had come to regard highly as friends. If I said too little, the publishers would not be interested. In this situation I did the best I could.*[5]

Gerald got down to writing quickly after receiving the initial permission from Edith, in case she changed her mind. This is reflected in an early version of his Foreword, where he writes: *"... I want to get it out before I am told: "It doesn't matter; let it go, don't write anything."*[6]

Gerald had certainly started writing the book by August 1952, as he tells Rex Wellbye that he is writing it. In fact, he had probably been accumulating material for such a book for several years and I have located some early notes that appear to be roughs for this. In a sense, his whole life, and his interest in and wide reading around a large number of topics, had been preparation for what in many ways would become his 'magnum opus'.

⁂

If Edith had been somewhat ambivalent about giving Gerald permission to write his book, I can imagine that she was made

4. Gardner (1954), 13.
5. Gardner (1959), 12.
6. Gerald Gardner, "New Light on Witchcraft", (manuscript in Toronto collection).

more determined that he should go ahead by an article which appeared in the autumn of 1952.[7]

Cecil Williamson and Gerald were always on the lookout for publicity opportunities for the museum and, in September 1952, after the close of the summer season, they thought of Allen Andrews, who had written the sympathetic article for the *Sunday Pictorial* the previous year which coincided with the opening of the museum. Andrews told them he would like an opportunity to write an article at greater length for a magazine, illustrated with photographs. They were enthusiastic about this, so it was arranged that Andrews would come over to the Island with a photographer. The magazine that he was to write the article for was called *Illustrated*, a weekly that was very popular, consisting largely of profusely-illustrated articles in an era when good quality illustrations were rare, particularly in colour.

Andrews interviewed both Gerald Gardner and Cecil Williamson and the article appeared in the 27th September 1952 issue under the title "Witchcraft in Britain". It starts by focusing on Cecil as a witchcraft consultant:

> *It is his full-time occupation. And when, for example, he receives an express letter imploring him to remove a spell set on the writer, he is sufficiently learned in the lore of witchcraft to compound a remedy.*[8]

The article then goes on to describe what Cecil told them was "a spell found in an old book". A woman had written to him asking for help in counteracting a spell which had been made against her, and enclosed what was described as a "malevolent screed, written in magical characters, which she had received from a former woman friend."

Cecil then describes in great detail how he made a "poppet" from various ingredients, some fairly unpleasant. It involved the burning the bodies of three black toads, a pregnant brown rat and a black cock. The ashes were then added to the poppet. The spell was completed as follows:

---

7. Allen Andrews, "Witchcraft in Britain", *Illustrated*, 27 September 1952.
8. Op. cit., 19.

He thrust glass splinters into the poppet, shrouded it, and dis-
patched it to his client. Her instructions were to bury it in a
shallow unconcealed grave near the witch's home, light a fire
*over it and intone a powerful, prescribed counter-spell.*9

This is illustrated by a series of no less than eleven photographs of Cecil gathering ingredients and making the poppet. It
is interesting that the malevolent woman at the beginning of the
story becomes a 'witch' at the end.

It is clear from the content of the latter part of the article that
Allen Andrews also interviewed Gerald Gardner, although,
strangely, he is not mentioned by name. Possibly this is because
he knew that Gerald would not like the article as published and
wanted to try and minimise likely recriminations. The article
gives details that make it quite clear that it was Gerald who was
being interviewed. There are quite a few new items of information and it was the first time that mention was made in print of
the working in 1940 to try to stop the threatened invasion. Some
very specific details of the ritual are mentioned, together with the
number of people involved. And there are details of coven organisation, seasonal festivals and deities. Equally strangely, the
Museum is not mentioned once in the whole article, which was
the probable reason they approached Andrews in the first place.

It was Cecil's contribution, which seemed to link witchcraft to
'black magic', that Edith objected to. Whilst it seems unlikely that
he actually used all the ingredients referred to and whilst it might
be good publicity for the Museum, it was just the sort of thing
that made her angry at its misrepresentation of witchcraft. It
made her more determined than ever to encourage Gerald in his
endeavours, though it is clear that she wanted to be very much in
the background, for the following month he wrote: *I may som-*
time be able to persuade some [witches] *to come forward, but the*
publicity that has happned, things like what was in Illustrated for
*instance, makes them angry, & they want to keep out of it.*10

I think that when Gerald read this part of the article, probably
only when it appeared in its published form, it was the first time

---

9. Ibid.
10. Letter, Gerald Gardner to Gerald Yorke, 24 October 1952, (Yorke Collection, Warburg Institute).

that he realised that Cecil's approach to witchcraft was rather different to his own. It was the start of the major conflict between them and an end to their working partnership.

I very much suspect, however, that a lot of the article is pure imagination, on either Gerald's part or the part of Andrews. At least eight covens are mentioned, with about half a sentence given over to each – the location of the group and one fact about each: it just doesn't quite sound right.

Aside from Edith, there were other responses to the *Illustrated* article, this time more positive. Gerald refers to one letter in *Witchcraft Today:*

> *...I received a letter dated September 29, 1952, telling me of a meeting held in a wood in the south of England about two months before, in the traditional nude (luckily the weather was warm). They cast the circle with the Athame, did the fertility dances on broomsticks, performed the proper seasonal as well as other rites, and had some of the old dances. The letter also mentioned three indoor meetings in the last few months where everything had been done very satisfactorily and spells performed which worked!*[11]

I do not know who this letter was from. The obvious answer is that it was from Edith, updating Gerald on latest activities. That it was from someone who was previously unknown to him may have been precisely the impression he wished to convey without actually telling an untruth!

⚜

The article also resulted in one of the most creative minds in the history of the Craft becoming involved: that person was a young woman named Doreen Valiente. She had been born Doreen Dominy in 1922, the daughter of Harry Dominy, architect, and his wife, Edith (née Richardson). She was sent to a convent school (reputedly the same one attended earlier by Arnold Crowther) and spent some of her teenage years with her grandparents in the New Forest, where her first inklings about magical working appeared. Her first marriage to a merchant seaman, Joanis Vlachopoulos,

---

11. Gardner, (1954), 54.

came to a tragic end when he drowned during the war. In 1944 she married Casimiro Valiente. By 1952 she was an office worker living in Bournemouth and interested in the occult.

In late September 1952, she saw in her local corner newsagent's shop a copy of the issue of *Illustrated* with the article 'Witchcraft in Britain'. She bought it and read it with fascination. Bournemouth was not far from the New Forest, so she surmised that there might still be witchcraft activity going on not far from her. She wrote to Cecil Williamson with a request to be put in touch with the witch cult. He passed her letter on to Gerald, who replied, and who, after a bit of correspondence, arranged to meet her at Edith's house. Doreen describes that first meeting vividly:

> *Thus it was that one sunny afternoon, as autumn was fading into winter in 1952, I found myself in Dafo's pleasant, well-appointed house shaking hands with a tall, white-haired man who rose to greet me as I entered the drawing-room. We seemed to take an immediate liking to each other. I realized that this man was no time-wasting pretender to occult knowledge. He was something different from the kind of people I had met in esoteric gatherings before. One felt that he had seen far horizons and encountered strange things; and yet there was a sense of humour about him and a youthfulness, in spite of his silver hair. He did not then have the beard which he grew later. The clean-shaven portrait of him which appeared in the first edition of his book* Witchcraft Today *is a good likeness of him at that time. His clothes were informal but of good quality – Harris tweed, if I remember rightly. He wore a large silver ring with some strange signs upon it, which I learned later represented his witch-name, 'Scire', in the letters of the magical Theban alphabet. On his right wrist was a heavy bronze bracelet, with symbols upon it denoting the three degrees or grades of witchcraft.*[12]

Edith told Doreen that of recent years her health had been such that she no longer took an active part in the Craft. She also had to be rather cautious because her job as a teacher of elocution would, she felt, be severely compromised if there was any

---

12. Doreen Valiente, *The Rebirth of Witchcraft*, (Robert Hale, 1989), 37-38.

whisper locally of her connection with witchcraft. This also applied to Rosanne's husband, 'Mac', who was a dentist. Doreen wrote: *I do not think she was really happy that Gerald had arranged our meeting at her house, though she made herself welcoming enough to me.*[13]

When she was about to leave, Gerald gave Doreen a copy of *High Magic's Aid.* He told her to read it carefully, as it would tell her a lot about the witch cult and mediaeval magic. Gerald apparently gave copies to likely initiates to judge how they reacted to his description of ritual nudity and scourging.

Gerald gave his own account of the meeting to Cecil Williamson:

I went down to the South coast and saw Mrs. Valiente but it was at the time when the weather + the fog was so awfull, so actually she came to see me at Christchurch. What I wanted was to go to her + have a meeting, + see how she worked, but apparently ~~they always~~ *the only place they can work is at a friend's flat, + he + it was not available when I was there.*

They have the Golden Dawn Rituals, + a lot of Golden Dawn instruments. they have been mostly using magnatized black mirrors, to get Prophetic Vissions, + she claims with success. But she says, the last time they tried it, in the middle the friend suddenly remembered had left something boiling on the kitchen stove, rushed wildly to take it off, thus breaking the circle, + a locked door violently burst open, + loud noises + almost [illegible word] *phenomena occurred, + they've done nothing since. Apparently neither seems to have realised that in this sort of work the circle is for protection + it is highly dangerous to break it (if you have succeeded in calling up anything, that is)*[14]

Doreen never seems to have been a member of any Golden Dawn temple, though she seems to have chosen the magical name "Ameth", after a symbol in Enochian magic, about this

---

13. Op. cit., 38.
14. Letter, Gerald Gardner to Cecil Williamson, 14 December 1952.

time. Her interest seems to have been aroused by the acquisition of some notebooks that had previously been owned by Dr. Henry D. Kelf, whose Golden Dawn motto was "Nisi Dominus Frustra". Kelf had died in December 1951 and Doreen had acquired his notebooks in a rather unusual way. She was talking to her bank manager who, knowing her interest in magic, mentioned that he had recently been valuing for probate the possessions of a doctor who had recently died. He told her that the doctor's widow had a lot of magical manuscripts which she was going to burn because she was afraid of them.

Doreen managed to find out from the bank manager the general locality where the doctor had lived and, making enquiries locally, soon found his address. She called round, but the widow was out. So in order to provide a psychic link she picked up a pebble that had fallen onto the grass from the wall. When she got home, she used it to visit the widow psychically.

The following day, the bank manager telephoned Doreen, saying that the widow had contacted him to say that she knew he had a lady friend who would take away the manuscripts. Doreen went round to the house and the widow gave her the manuscripts. As well as the 28 magical books, she also gave Doreen swords, pentacles, etc. The manuscripts were those given to initiates into the Golden Dawn. Doreen retained the swords but eventually gave Gerald the manuscript books for the museum. Most of them are now in the Toronto collection.[15]

Doreen kept in regular touch with Gerald for it was several months later, in July 1953, that she was initiated. This coincided with Gerald's visit to Edith in order to attend the Druids' Midsummer ritual at Stonehenge, which he had been doing for several years. Doreen's initiation was the night before:

> ... I went to the Stonehenge ceremony with Gerald and Dafo. I had never been to the great stones before, but it seemed very appropriate to me that my initiation (which had taken place the previous day) should be sealed, so to speak, by this visit to one of the great spiritual centres of Britain.[16]

---

15. See Bracelin, 179-180. I am also grateful to Melissa Seims for additional information.
16. Valiente, (1989), 40.

It was only later in 1953, well after Doreen was initiated, and probably after the summer season when Gerald returned to London from the Isle of Man, that he invited Doreen to his flat in London to meet the rest of the coven: *There were about eight or ten of them, mostly people who were fellow members with Gerald of a naturist club he was interested in* [Five Acres]. *They made me welcome, and I felt that a whole new life had opened up before me.*[17] We cannot be certain who these members were, but they certainly included Barbara Vickers and could well also have included James Laver, Eda Collins and Mary Dowding.

⁂

With Edith's strictly qualified permission, Gerald started work on the manuscript of a book which was initially entitled "New Light on Witchcraft". He was now free, within limits, to write what he wanted to, but, after the initial euphoria, he found fairly quickly that merely giving the witches' beliefs and non-magical practices resulted in a very short manuscript. The problem was that what Edith told him tended to slip through his fingers. Much was nonverbal and he probably forgot a lot. And by late 1952 and early 1953, when the bulk of the book was being written, he was living in the Isle of Man, away from regular contact with Edith, whom I suspect to be the only one of the original group with whom he was still in touch. Anyway, it became clear that he needed to supplement the text with other material. And Gerald was far from short of material. Here was a blank canvas on which he could speculate.

Gerald always needed help in bringing a manuscript to the stage where it would be suitable for publication. Betty Lumsden Milne polished his classic text on the Malayan keris that was published in 1936. Three years later, I suspect that Edith Woodford-Grimes performed a similar function for *A Goddess Arrives*. And in 1949, Dolores North edited and typed the manuscript of *High Magic's Aid*.

Gerald realised that he needed help with 'New Light on Witchcraft'. He was not in regular contact with Edith and he and Dolores had fallen out, so he approached his old friend Ross Nichols, who had acted as Assistant Editor for *The Occult Observer* and had also edited and revised a 19th Century French

---

17. Op. cit., 47.

work, Paul Christian's *The History and Practice of Magic*, which was published in two volumes by the Forge Press in 1952.

Nichols took on the job enthusiastically and also approached Gerald Yorke, whom he had met through *The Occult Observer* and who worked for the well-respected publishers, Rider and Co., who specialised in books on the occult and mysticism. Riders offered Gerald a contract and Nichols was appointed in 1953 to edit "New Light on Witchcraft" for publication. Doreen Valiente[18] has stated that "Riders were sticking their neck out" in publishing *Witchcraft Today*. Nichols' editing was needed. Francis King, referring to Gerald Yorke, considered that it was: ... *not at all a bad book, for the reader responsible for its acceptance, himself an occult scholar of distinction, managed to blue-pencil most of the more rubbishy passages.* It would be interesting to see the early version referred to in order to check whether the rejected passages were as "rubbishy" as King suggests.

In the Toronto collection there is a typed annotated manuscript of an early version of "New Light on Witchcraft" which differs to some extent from the final published version. Certain interesting personal comments were removed, which are worth reproducing. In the Foreword, Gerald makes a request, which appears in the first published edition but which is thereafter removed: "I should like to get in touch with people from other covens to discuss these matters." Why this was removed from subsequent editions I do not know.

There is a passage which is very revealing of what Gerald got from his association with the Wica:

> *In my own case, for instance, they well knew my views. I was intensely interested in the subject. I did not believe in their gods as such, but I believed in the change which we call death and in fertility, that biological urge which we see every day, and I loved the beauty of their stories, of the great spirits controlling these forces, and frankly enjoyed assisting at the rites in their honour ...*[19]

---

18. Talk to the Pagan Federation Annual Conference, 22 November 1997.
19. Gerald Gardner, "New Light on Witchcraft", (manuscript in Toronto Collection), 42-43.

Gerald also writes: *I know one coven nowadays, who elected a Maiden, as deputy for the High Priestess who is somewhat aged. The maiden does the work, but the H.Ps. retains the power.*[20] This is clearly the coven at Highcliffe: the High Priestess was Edith and the Maiden was Rosanne.

There are certain annotations by hand, which are in no case included in the final text, which suggests that these were made on a copy which never reached the publisher but remained in Gerald's hands. He certainly seems to have been involved in quite a lot of negotiation about the draft manuscript, with Yorke on the one hand and Edith on the other. Ross Nichols was also undoubtedly closely involved in the whole process.

An indication of the matters which were covered in this negotiation is provided in a surviving letter from Gerald to Yorke. He had obviously submitted a draft of the manuscript for comment, which Yorke had made, and this was Gerald's response. The topics covered in the letter included yoga, a hallucinatory drug called soma, the Knights Templars and certain details of the witch rituals. Gerald had obviously included quite a lot about yoga, which Yorke had persuaded him to cut out, presumably because it was not directly relevant to the subject.

I am sure that there must have been other correspondence between Yorke and Gerald, although much may have been carried out indirectly via Nichols. One thing that changed was the title, almost certainly at the suggestion of the publishers, from "New Light on Witchcraft" to the more punchy and informative "Witchcraft Today".

Margaret Murray agreed to write the Foreword to the book. Gerald had known her since before the war and was certainly well aware of her work on witchcraft. He usually called the Craft "the witch cult" following her usage of the term.

By late 1952, Gerald was clearly fully committed to the Craft. He was the author of the only book in existence (*High Magic's Aid*) which gave present-day witches' beliefs and practices, albeit in the unrecognised guise of historical fiction. And although not yet running it, he was spending a lot of time at the Museum at Castletown and had moved there earlier in the year. He had also

---

20. Op. cit., 49.

met someone who would not only help him with his forthcoming book but would become his High Priestess and make her own contribution to the development of the Craft - Doreen Valiente.

For Yule 1953, Gerald rather sprang on Doreen the task of writing part of the ritual. She adapted part of Carmichael's *Carmina Gadelica*.[21] The verse that she wrote is now well-known and Gerald reproduces it in *Witchcraft Today*,[22] albeit giving the impression that it was from an old witch ritual.

It seems to have been about this time, in early 1954, that Gerald and Doreen co-operated in compiling the book that researchers know as 'Text D'. It was one of the first books to actually have the title 'Book of Shadows' on its first page. It certainly included both material that had been extracted from the earlier books as well as material written specially for it. Gerald gave this book to Angus McLeod on the Isle of Man and it is now in the Toronto Collection.

We can imagine, perhaps, that this new spirit of optimism encouraged Gerald to look again at what material he had been given by Edith. The 13 years since his initiation had perhaps given him some sort of perspective so that he was able to see things more clearly when writing about what he was told and shown.

He was also probably being given material all the time. He certainly had an older book which he used to carry round with him contantly. It was probably given to him by Edith, but whether it was originally hers or she had acquired it from some-one else, I do not know. Anyway, that book was stolen, probably in 1952. Cecil Williamson gives further details:

> *How well I remember that little book ... it never left his side and it is a true fact that he even took it to bed with him ... tucked into the Book of Shadows Gerald had two large sheets of carefully folded very thin air-mail type paper. These were covered from top to bottom in closely-spaced hand-writing done with a pen and a fine steel nib. Much of it was like blank verse and the rest descriptive instruction. One sheet had the Crowley symbol ... in the bottom left-hand corner ...*

---

21. Alexander Carmichael, *Carmina Gadelica: Hymns and incantations with illustrative notes on words, rites and customs, dying and obsolete: orally collected in the Highlands and Islands of Scotland*, (Norman Macleod, 1900).
22. Gardner, (1954), 24-25.

Well, on that fateful day there was Gerald putting on the charm ... he left his table to take a small party of French ladies upstairs to see. His only exhibition stall was a showcase near the head of the stairway in which were displayed the Loan collection of artifacts as used by the New Forest coven.

This was around three o'clock on a Friday afternoon. Lunch was over and the staff had not reset the tables for the cream tea trade. Being Gerald, and being in charming company he did his stuff and treated his party to an extended tour of the Museum. In due time they descended and departed - Gerald was provided wit his usual afternoon tea, and later gathered up his gear to go back to his house. Only then was it discovered that his beloved "Book of Shadows" was missing. It was quite clear that some visitor had drifted in, browsed around and pocketed the "Book of Shadows" as a souvenir. All rather sad.23

Gerald also refers to at least two other witches' books, so there were sources of information available to him which he probably didn't have initially. He also may have met witches who made contact with him following the publication of *High Magic's Aid*. And, of course, museums always attract information and contacts, which he would have followed up where possible.

Witchcraft Today is not just an account of Gerald's contact with the witches and of their beliefs and practices. It isn't even *mainly* about that: in fact, probably less than 10% of the book is about the thoughts and activities of the witches that Gerald met. I think the problem was that, when he came to write about what they told him, he found it difficult because it had been in no sense a structured course of learning - more things told at odd times in a strange order and he wasn't very good at remembering. Anyway, he set things down as best he could.

Nevertheless, there wasn't enough material to make a book on its own, so Gerald gave himself a free hand to write about his own ideas and theories about the development of witchcraft, including much historical material. The information about the

---

23. Letter, Cecil Williamson to Michael Howard, about 1972, (Boscastle Museum of Witchcraft archives).

witches he had met was scattered about the book like plums in a pudding. In fact, just as plums might tend to sink to the bottom, so much of this material seems to be included in Chapter 13 - Recapitulation - which is almost an afterthought, as if he suddenly realised that there was material on the witches that he had forgotten about and hadn't included and that therefore he had to cram it in the final chapter, probably at the last minute.

Much of what Gerald writes about what he was told I give in Chapter 17. There is, however, some other material in *Witchcraft Today* which Gerald claims are the words of the Wica when speaking about their beliefs and practices. These are, however, almost identical to passages in his novel, *High Magic's Aid*. So, words which are fictional as part of *High Magic's Aid* become factual in *Witchcraft Today*. I think Gerald was pleased with those phrases when they appeared in *High Magic's Aid* and considering them the sort of thing a witch might say, he incorporated them, largely unchanged, in *Witchcraft Today*.

For example, in *High Magic's Aid*, Morven says: *When the brotherhood was strong, they ever picked out those who had a little natural power and they were taught, and practised one with another, and they developed their powers.*[24]

In "Witchcraft Today", this passage is as follows: *Another [witch] said: 'We ever pick out those who have a little inherent power and teach them, and they practise one with the other and they develop these powers.*[25]

The bulk of the book is really a summation of Gerald's reading on witchcraft and allied subjects over a number of years. What I think he was aiming to do was to provide an outline history of witchcraft, from the Stone Age onwards, at the same time showing the connections that certain religious or other groups may have had with the Craft. This gave him the opportunity to write about many of his favourite topics, including the Druids, the 'Little People', the Knights Templar, Ancient Egypt, the Greek Mysteries and much more besides. In many ways, *Witchcraft Today* is a record of Gerald's phases of enthusiasm, some of which I have chronicled in earlier chapters of this book.

---

24. Gardner, (1949), 297.
25. Gardner, (1954), 140.

Just as Gerald claimed anyone named 'Gardner' as part of the clan, so he was interested in anything which used the words 'witch' or 'witchcraft' even if there was no connection whatever with what he had been initiated into.

Gerald was an exponent of the idea that the fairies, or Little People, that were the subject of legend and folklore, particularly in the Celtic countries, were actually the older and original inhabitants of those lands, marginalised by later invaders. He presented as evidence the small size of many remains of dwellings and that the Little People were supposed to live in conical hills, in effect round-houses. He sums them up by saying:

> *All these people seem to be remembered by the same characteristics: good friends but dangerous enemies, very strong, able to disappear at will, having great festivals at night and making use of poisoned arrows.*[26]

Whatever the truth of this idea, (it has other exponents, but I am not sufficiently knowledgeable to pass judgement on it) Gerald then moves on to what is probably complete fantasy in linking the Little People with the witches. He seems to be suggesting that the Little People were the heath dwellers, or 'heathens', and that they were associated with much anti-clerical activity, including the Robin Hood legend, the May Games and sabbats attended by six thousand people! In the process they became known as witches.

Gerald saw certain similarities between the witches and the Knights Templar, such as wearing cords, the use of the chalice and the kiss at initiation. The one point where Gerald strongly emphasised the difference between the witches and the Templars was in who was able to initiate:

> *The witches tell me: 'The law always has been that power must be passed from man to woman or from woman to man ... (The reason is that great love is apt to occur between people who go through the rites together). They go on to say: 'The Templars broke this age-old rule and passed the power from man to man: this led to sin and in so doing it brought about their downfall'.*[27]

---

26. Gardner, (1954), 59.
27. Gardner (1954), 69.

Gerald also drew attention to the similarity between the witches' rituals and the rites and myths of the Greek and Roman mysteries such as those of Dionysus, Orpheus and Eleusis. He emphasised the importance of the discovery of the Villa of the Mysteries in Pompeii, which he had visited in 1952, as previously the secrets were kept and never revealed. There are wall paintings, containing 29 figures. Gerald quotes Professor Vittorio Macchioro:

> *It is evident that we have a single act divided into several episodes depicting the story of one draped female figure who reappears in all the episodes. The story is a series of liturgical ceremonies by means of which the woman is initiated into the Orphic Mystery and attains communion with Zagreus.*[28]

Gerald quotes Macchioro at length describing the story of the initiation into the mysteries as revealed in the wall paintings. He concludes: *I showed a picture of these frescoes to an English witch, who looked at it very attentively before saying: 'So they knew the secret in those days.'*[29]

There is a rather unusual chapter entitled "Out of the Land of Egypt" which quotes Pennethorne Hughes: *Studies of the magic and ritual of Africa have in the last few years established with some certainty that all the systems for the disturbance of consciousness practised by the African Negro are derived from ancient Egypt.*[30]

Gerald developed this idea somewhat and postulated that the European mystery cults had originated in Egypt and that the Voodoo practices which he had studied when he was in New Orleans were a mixture of European and African influences. I think Gerald was really trying to put forward what is known as diffusionism, although he also says that similar practices may have come into existence in different places independently of each other.

The chapter entitled "Irish Witchcraft" is really an amalgam of various seemingly unconnected items. Firstly, there is the story of Dame Alice Kyteler, accused of witchcraft in the 14th Century, which is taken from Margaret Murray's *The Witch Cult in Western Europe*.[31] There is then an interesting account of a witch cult

---

28. Op. cit., 85.
29. Op. cit., 88.
30. Op. cit., 93.
31. Margaret A. Murray, *The Witch Cult in Western Europe*, (Oxford, 1921).

which was "practising nowadays", meeting in a quarry, holding full moon rituals, sacrificing animals to the moon, with a high priestess called Diana. What this was has never been determined and whether it continued, and if so for how long, I do not know.

I get the distinct impression that much of this material is just 'padding' to eke out the relatively small amount of material which he obtained from Edith. Much of it can now be challenged academically and consists of little more than Gerald's ideas of some incidents in the history of witchcraft.

Witchcraft Today was published in November 1954. It sold well, his first book to do so, and it made Gerald Gardner's name. The difference was that for the first time he had not paid the costs of production. Moreover, a mainstream publisher such as Riders had a good distribution system, which is always a key ingredient in sales figures. Gerald Yorke, writing in April 1958, noted that the book had sold over 5,500 copies.

It certainly achieved reviews in several of the journals to which Gerald subscribed. He also subscribed to a cuttings service, Romeike & Curtice Ltd., after the publication of *Witchcraft Today*, to catch all the reviews of that book. They were rather mixed. That in *Folk-Lore*[32] is unsigned and refers to the book as 'an apology for witchcraft' and considers that it 'can hardly be regarded as a serious contribution to a very complex and highly controversial subject".

The reviewer for the *Journal of the Society for Psychical Research* takes up this theme, saying "Somehow, the apology is not quite convincing". He continues: *Some of his historical assertions resemble those of Dr Murray's in that they ignore other interpretations of a fact than the author's own.* The reviewer concludes by saying ... *it is greatly to be regretted that in what is in many ways a pleasant and interesting book there are so many slips, typographical and otherwise. ...One can only hope that when Dr Gardner and his witch-colleagues recite their incantations they prudently maintain a higher standard of accuracy.*[33]

---

32. Review of "Witchcraft Today", *Folk-Lore*, Vol. LXVI, No 2, (June 1955), 313-314.
33. Geoffrey B. Riddehough, Review of "Witchcraft Today", *Journal of the Society for Psychical Research*, Vol. 38, No. 690, (December 1956), 378-379.

Despite the mixed reviews, the book has been included in the permanent collections of most major public libraries in Britain and throughout the world, and for a generation was likely to have been an enquirer's first taste of the subject. It is still, for many, a classic text.

⚜

In the first edition of *Witchcraft Today*, Gerald made an announcement that he was hoping to arrange a small exhibition of witch tools at No. 3 Thackeray Street, Kensington Square, London. The address was that of Gerald's friend, Ivar Mackay, a member of the Golden Dawn. Whether the exhibition ever materialised I do not know.

Following publicity associated with the book, Gerald began to receive invitations to talk to various groups. Frank Smyth gave the following account:

> *Stewart Sanderson, M.A., Director of the Institute of Dialect and Folk Life Studies at Leeds University remembers his only contact with Gardner at the International Congress on Maritime folklore and Ethnology held at Naples in 1954.*

> *Describing him as 'that strange man Gardner', Mr Sanderson recalls: 'He appeared with his wife; wore an extraordinary copper snake bangle on one wrist, and one day I actually saw a fisherman on the Lungomare make the cornuto sign against the evil eye as Gardner crossed over from the tram stop.'*

> *Gardner read a paper which was later published in the proceedings of the congress. Its subject was the development of Manx fishing craft, and on the surface it was a scholarly piece of research.*

> *'However', says Mr Sanderson, 'the article gave no references and no acknowledgement was made to earlier studies of the subject. It is, in fact, a scissors and paste job with a sprinkling of folk lore beliefs at the end, based on Basil and*

Eleanor Mewgaw, "The Development of the Manx Fishing Craft", in Proceedings of the Isle of Man Natural History and Antiquarian Society, 1952, and also on an article in Mariner's Mirror, *April 1941.*'[34]

I have so far been unable to check the details of this account or the date of the conference, but it appears on the surface to be yet another example of Gerald using material without seeing the need to acknowledge his sources.

On Wednesday 30th March 1955, he gave a talk entitled "The Religion of the Witches", though to whom he gave the talk is not clear! The following week, on 6th April 1955, he spoke to the Marylebone Spiritualist Association on what seems to have been the same subject, and a long report was published in *Psychic News* on 9th April. He also spoke to the Psychic and Literary Club at a luncheon at the Rembrandt Hotel, South Kensington, to the Ghost Club which met at Over-seas House, Park Place, St. James', the Middlesex Hospital Medical Society and to the Flying Saucer Club.

Later the same month he attended the 8th International Congress for the History of Religions at Rome, which had the theme of "Sacral Kingship". Perhaps as a result of contacts made at that conference, Gerald had an article about the Museum published in the influential Italian journal *Humana Studia*.[35]

Gerald had a natural advantage when it came to giving talks: he was good at talking! Although he had actually given very few talks by the time the book was published (the only one I can think of being the one he gave to the Folk-Lore Society back in 1946), he seemed to enjoy doing it and accepted invitations to talk from time to time, probably more than we know about.

---

34. Frank Smyth, *Modern Witchcraft*, (Macdonald, 1970), 31-32.
35. G. B. Gardner, "The Museum of Magic and Witchcraft", Seie II Anno VII, Edizioni Mediche e Scientifiche, Roma 1955.

CHAPTER TWENTY-EIGHT

Magic!

Gerald had frequented Atlantis Bookshop on a regular basis since his return to London and certainly in the 1948-49 period when getting *High Magic's Aid* ready for publication. It was probably there that Gerald had come across the occultist, Kenneth Grant, and his wife, Steffi. Certainly by November 1949 they were in contact since Grant gives an account of a ritual involving Gerald which occurred in that month. After an afternoon spent at Gerald's flat in Ridgmount Gardens, he and the Grants walked over to Dolores North's flat off Tottenham Court Road. There was also a young woman, making five in total. Grant recounts the ritual:

> *Gardner explained that the purpose of the rite was to demonstrate his ability to 'bring down the power'. He intended raising a current of magical energy with the purpose of contacting certain extra-terrestrial intelligences with which I was, at that time, in almost constant rapport. The rite was to consist of the circumambulation of the five of us round a large sigil inscribed on parchment which had been specially consecrated. The sigil had been designed for my use by Austin Osman Spare who was, at the time, also engaged in contacting extra-terrestrials. The sigil would*

later be consumed in the flame of a candle set on an altar in the north quarter of the apartment.[1]

However, the ritual was interrupted by a caller who turned out to be Michael Houghton, the proprietor of Atlantis Bookshop. After this, the ritual was abandoned. Grant reports, wrongly, that several of the participants died shortly afterwards as a result of the abortive ritual.

Subsequently, Gerald had kept rather loose contact with the ceremonial magic scene in London since his involvement with the museum started in 1951. His focus was then firmly on witchcraft, with the museum in the Isle of Man and covens both there and at Bricket Wood.

However, he had kept up correspondence with Germer, Crowley's successor as head of the O.T.O., in New York and had sent him copies of his books. There are at least six letters to Gerald from Germer dated between 1948 and 1956.[2]

Francis King writes that: ... *when Germer received a request for a charter from a young English occultist named Kenneth Grant he, after checking that Gardner had no intention of activating his lodge, gave him a charter empowering him to work the first three degrees of the OTO System.*[3] Gerald had obviously satisfied Germer that he had no intentions in that direction, for on 5th March 1951, Germer issued a charter to Grant authorising him to open a camp of the organisation in London.

In 1954, Grant founded the New Isis Lodge, with the intention of "providing a conduit for the influx of cosmic energy from a transplutonian power zone known to initiates as Nu-Isis."

It was not until late 1954, when Gerald wanted the services of Spare that he re-established contact with Kenneth and Steffi Grant. Austin Osman Spare was born on 30th December 1886, in the City of London, the son of a policeman, Philip Newton Spare, and his wife, Eliza Ann Osman. He was largely self-taught in art, but by the age of 16 he was already exhibiting at the Royal Academy. He had strong psychic abilities and he developed a deep interest in the occult.

---

1. Kenneth Grant, *Nightside of Eden*, (Frederick Muller, 1977), 122-123.
2. Ripley's Collection.
3. Francis King, *The Magical world of Aleister Crowley*, (Weidenfeld and Nicolson, 1977), 177-178.

In August 1954 Gerald had arranged for Doreen Valiente to 'sound Spare out', as it were. Doreen seems to have been acting almost as a secretary for Gerald during the 1953/54 period. She told Spare that her name was Diana Walden, witch name Ameth, and that she was the head of the witch cult in Britain.4 Spare records the visit, in a letter to the Grants dated 25th August 1954:

> *Dr. Gardner of the Isle of Man sent along his deputy, a myopic stalky nymph ... with two magicial [sic] Knives that she insisted on showing me! Harmless & a little tiresome ... what she was* really *interested in I don't think she herself knew. She believed the 'Witches' Sabbath was a sort of Folk dance of pretty young things ... I agreed that a Maypole may have symbolism.*5

It was through the Grants that Gerald got to meet Spare. They informed him that Gerald would be in London in September, and offered to bring him along to meet him. On 20th September, Grant wrote to Spare asking whether he could bring Gerald to see him the following Friday:

> *Gardner is very keen to see your work and he is himself quite an interesting character. He is connected with some sort of Coven in the South of England and conceals his activities under the cloak of Folklore (he's president of some Society or other devoted to Folklore). I can't vouch for what he might be like when I bring him along but I know you're quite used to curious people. Actually, he's a charming old chap.*6

Anyway, the visit was arranged. Grant collected Gerald from his flat and they arrived at Spare's at about 2.45 p.m. on Friday 24th September 1954. After introductions, Gerald ordered a "flying saucer" for a guinea. These were magic plates, which Grant describes as follows:

> *... these enshrine a sigillized wish, e.g. "I desire ... (Sigil)"; this is adapted to the <u>nature</u> of the desire, as Tigers for Great Strength, Woman for Lust, etc. You can then "bury it, burn*

---

4. Op. cit., 95.
5. Kenneth and Steffi Grant, *Zos Speaks! Encounters with Austin Osman Spare*, (Fulgur, 1998) 86.
6. Op. cit., 94.

it, throw it, or do any bloody thing with it as long as you agree beforehand what process you intend subjecting it". He told Scire how, the other day, he had thrown one over the wall of a compound diagonally opposite his window.[7]

Spare promised Gerald he would make one and pass it on via the Grants.

Grant describes the meeting between Gerald and Spare as being "a screamingly funny interview":

> *ZOS and Scire had a fierce argument as to who had been to the Witches' Sabbath, what the Witches' Sabbath actually was, and so on. Scire drew his magical athame and showed ZOS the strange characters on the hilt. ZOS should have blanched before them but he didn't, saying he "knew all them symbols and more". Behind a mirror on his mantelpiece where stands his latest pictures, ZOS keeps a "Borneo Dyas", complete with nineteen human hairs sprouting at end, of victims that have died by its blade. The ghastly relic is supported by two metal picture-hangers flattened against the wall in an inverted position. This he brandished before Scire, who later gave him various Witch-Cottage pictures and Isle-of-Man 'literature': ZOS generously admitted that the Witch on the Broomstick* [possibly Gerald's black and white ink drawing of the Witches' Mill] *was "very nice".*[8]

At one point, Spare was recounting a dream he had had which was so different from everyday reality that he felt totally unable to reproduce it artistically. Grant recounts what happened next:

> *Zos said: "There y'are, not the sort o' dream a London spiv would have; 'e'd probably dream of fucking Mrs Brown next door, or something". Gardner tittered, wishing he could even dream the Spiv's dream, never mind Zos's*[9]

The following day, Spare wrote to the Grants: ... *through my usual absentmindedness I forgot the <u>Initials</u> of the chap Dr. Gardner*

---

7. Op. cit., 95.
8. Op. cit., 95.
9. Op. cit., 97.

thinks means trouble - is it P.M.?[10] What this is about, I don't know, but it is probably something to do with the talisman which Gerald had asked Spare to make for him. The Grants confirmed by return that these were the correct initials, but at present the identity of this individual, 'P.M.', remains a mystery. In their letter they also give their assessment of the meeting:

> *Gardner was greatly impressed by all he saw but I think he has a bit of a bias about witchcraft - as you yourself saw. I doubt if he's ever met anybody to come up to the Witch who taught you when young. But he's an interesting man and may possibly introduce others.*[11]

He is referring here to a lady called Mrs. Paterson whom Spare made contact with at an early age. She was probably just a family friend, a spiritualist who told fortunes with playing cards. However, over the years, and particularly following Spare's contact with Gerald Gardner, she seems to have transformed in his imagination into a witch named 'Yelg'. Nigel Jackson states that:

> *It's only around the 50s and the period of the Spare-Gardner encounter that she becomes embellished into a 'Witch' of old Salem stock – 'Mrs Paterson' seems to be a tale that grew in the telling, to put it mildly. ... the encounter with Gardner obviously inspired Spare to start incorporating Witchcraft imagery into his art and writing in a way that he hadn't before.*[12]

As Jackson commented to me: ... *after the Gardner-Spare meeting the scenes of the Witches Sabbath start appearing in Spare's work.*[13]

After receiving confirmation of the correct initials, Spare worked quickly and the following day forwarded a talisman to the Grants with an accompanying note:

---

10. Ibid.
11. Op. cit., 97-98 letter Grants to Spare, 26 September 1954.
12. Email, Nigel Jackson to Grevel Lindop, 29 January 2008.
13. Email, Nigel Jackson to the author, 30 January 2008.

Thought you would like to see what I've done for the Old Boy Dr. G. [It is interesting that Spare refers to Gardner as "the Old Boy" even though Gerald was only two years older than Spare himself! Grevel Lindop has noted that many people have referred to 'old Gerald', 'old windbag', etc. and he suspects that this is because Gerald always looked older than he was, with the bristling white hair and the goatee beard adding to this impression. Also, he says that Gerald "came across as a 'character' – garrulous, intent, full of weird knowledge and original ideas. He was clearly notably unselfconscious: self-absorbed, no shyness. I think it's this sense of eccentricity, of something odd or 'old-fashioned' about him that so often leads people to the word 'old'".[14]] *Will you be so kind as to forward on to him?*

I hope he appreciates - that it is through our friendship - nothing in it for me & don't desire that there is. About 2 days work with my present health.

He should make some sort of 'token sacrifice', so I suggest that he sends me a cheque for 10/- (no more or it spoils it) made out to the "Royal Society for the Prevention of Cruelty to Animals" (I'll explain that technique to you later) & I'll forward it to them for a definite purpose. ... Note: I've made everything (i.e. what Mr Gardner has to do) as easy as possible."

He then includes a note to be forwarded to Gerald, as follows:

Dear Dr. Gardner,

Herewith the magical formula we argued about. It works on the Boomerang principle. Any evil from that person returns and hits them.

Sorry I couldn't get hold of a suitable plate - I bought ½ dozen different kind but the glass on them simply prohibits drawing on them. Anyway the enclosed Stele even better. But one or the other - makes no difference re. its Powers.

---

14. Grevel Lindop, email to the author, 2 April 2009.

You will find the enclosed very potent indeed. Any way I can help - let me know.

Yrs sincerely Austin Osman Spare

P.S. The drawing has been waterproofed and may be varnished or polished. I've adapted some Nth American (about the only real primitives left) symbolism deliberately.

[Sigil] Carry this or a copy of same on you.

This is the sigil you must visualize (as near as possible) whenever the 'subject' enters your mind.

Expose this board for seven days then hide it for twenty one days - after which nothing from that 'subject' can harm you.

After this it's immaterial what you do with this magical Stele.

Abcreate (To yourself only, 'Self to Self') all your thoughts relating to the subject and write down inside this folder;

illustration:

I loathe [Sigil] because of his hatred towards me.

Then cross out as above.[15]

Gerald was obviously satisfied with the working of this talisman, against the mysterious "P.M.", because in early 1955, he approached Spare again for another talisman, this time one for 'restoring stolen property to its rightful place', a common phrase in ancient grimoires but, as we shall see, it meant something rather different from what would appear on the surface!

Following a series of articles in national newspapers and magazines, Gerald had received various enquiries from people interested in witchcraft who wanted to take it further. One of these was a young woman known as Clanda Fain (probably not her real name). She was clearly investigating different paths and had been interested in Gerald's witch cult.

---

15. Kenneth and Steffi Grant (1998), 98, letter Spare to the Grants, 27 September 1954.

What seems to have happened is that she had become disillusioned with the witch cult, "for she found that she was not making any progress towards realizing herself as a Priestess of the Moon" and had sought entry to the New Isis Lodge in the hope that this would be a more appropriate home for her.

Grant describes her as: ... *a tall woman of curiously squameous appearance, an impression conveyed by her long wavy hair which clung to her like seaweed.* "[16] He also writes that she "claimed to be a Water Witch"[17]

Gerald was determined to have her back. Whilst he wrote a lot about magical techniques it is clear that he did not feel sufficiently confident to work magic himself to achieve his objectives. So he asked the Grants and they may well have recommended Austin Osman Spare. In order to keep what he wanted to do secret, he used the phrase "restoring stolen property to its rightful place", another example of Gerald's deliberate mis-representation of what he wanted to do.

Grant sets out the background from his point of view:

> ... *Gerald Gardner had taken exception to Clanda's defection from his witch cult and was projecting a baleful current of thought towards the lodge in general and myself in particular. He had actually gone to the length of inducing a popular 'occult' magazine to publish a letter in which he expressed disapproval of New Isis Lodge and its activities. Behind the scenes, however, he had taken more drastic steps and had approached Spare, whom he asked to prepare a talisman for 'restoring stolen property to its rightful place'. Spare, of course, had no idea that Clanda was supposed to be the stolen property in question. He was always willing to oblige and in due course Gardner acquired his talisman.*[18]

It is rumoured that the "law of three-fold return" (that any magical working will bring returns, either good or bad depending on what was sent, three times what was sent) was invented by Spare

---

16. Kenneth Grant, *Images and Oracles of Austin Osman Spare*, (Fulgur, 2003), 30.
17. *Man, Myth and Magic*, 124.
18. Kenneth Grant, (2003), 30-31.

because he was beginning to be fed up with Gerald asking him to make curses for people. What truth there is in this, I do not know.

Things came to a head at a ritual of the New Isis Lodge attended by Clanda, according to some accounts at the house of an alchemist in Islington. Grant gives a vivid account of the proceedings:

> *On the night of the episode in question she lay upon an altar under an image of Nu-Isis designed by Spare as a back-drop for the lodge-room. ... she lay supine ... waiting to incarnate the Spirit of Black Isis. The air was thick with incense compounded of galbanum, onycha, storax, and olibanum based on a special preparation of moon-juice or menstrual fluid. It rose upon waves of unnaturally heated air to the star-spangled canopy above. Violet-stoled figures circumambulated Clanda as she lay entranced, and it was during this interval between invocations that the unexpected incident occurred. Instead of the magical descent of the Goddess, another, altogether different phenomenon began to manifest. Its onset was announced by a sharp fall in the temperature. Clanda sat bolt upright and stared at the heavily curtained window in the north wall of the room. She said later that the curtains parted and an icy wind bore down upon her, and with it a shadowy bird swooped into the room and - with its great webbed talons - lifted her into the air, through the canopied ceiling, and out into the night. She saw snow-covered roofs racing beneath her. The flight continued until they approached a wharf-like structure, when the bird began to lose height. She struggled against the creature with all the strength of her will, and was dropped back upon the altar like a stone.*[19]

> Grant concludes: *In actual fact, of course, Clanda had not levitated physically; most of her terrifying experience occurred astrally. But the window in the north, which was frosted over with the cold, showed unmistakable signs of claw marks, and a slimy substance emitting a strong odour of the sea lay on the sill, pullulant, as if breathing!*[20]

---

19. Op. cit., 32.
20. Op. cit., 33.

It was not long before Grant made the connection: *When I dis-covered that Spare had made a special talisman for restoring stolen property to its rightful place, I recognized Gardner's hand in the busi-ness. I asked Spare what sort of elemental he had bound into the tal-isman and he described it nonchalantly as a 'sort of amphibious owl with the wings of a bat and the talons of an eagle'.*

Clanda did not return to Gerald. In fact, it is rumoured that she was drowned at sea on her way to New Zealand. If so, this was strangely appropriate, for, as Grant comments: *Clanda was undoubtedly of the great deep; all the signs suggested it: her appearance (she reminded one of a mermaid, in some obscure way), her conviction that she was a priestess of the moon or of the sea, and the saline substance deposited on the window-sill. Spare had unerringly summoned the appropriate elemental.*[21]

Gerald probably became aware that his ploy had not only failed to work but that it had been discovered by the Grants and Spare. This is confirmed by Gerald's actions when they subse-quently met, on 25th October 1955 at a preview at the Archer Gallery in Westbourne Grove of an exhibition of Spare's paintings and drawings. Grant notes that: *Gardner arrived and was very furtive; he avoided us and left shortly after the speech.*[22]

This is odd in that a fortnight later, on 12th November 1955, Ger-ald received a letter offering him co-rulership of a new Isis lodge, Altair de Aquila. Whether this was an attempt by Grant to build bridges with Gerald or whether it was some totally different organ-isation formed as a result of Grant's expulsion from the OTO in July of that year I do not know, but in any case, nothing came of it.

Cecil Williamson has given an account[23] of another meeting between himself, Gerald Gardner and Spare, but I have consider-able doubts about this account for two reasons. Firstly, Williamson was wont to make up stories about Gerald, particu-larly to the latter's discredit. Secondly, and more importantly, the timing is all wrong. Gerald met Spare for the first time in Sep-tember 1954, by which time his break-up with Williamson had occurred and the two were not on speaking terms.

---

21. Op. cit., 33.
22. Kenneth and Steffi Grant, (1998), 142.
23. Letter, Cecil Williamson to Robert Ansell, 18 February 1987, (Boscastle Museum of Witchcraft archives).

Austin Osman Spare died the following year, on 15th May 1956. *The Times*' obituary read in part:

> *A dreamer of dreams and a seer of visions, he had that complete other-worldliness so often depicted in romantic fiction and so rarely found in real life. Money meant nothing to him. With his talents as a figure draughtsman he might easily have commanded a four-figure income in portraiture, but he elected to live quietly and humbly, rarely going out, painting what he wished to paint, and selling his works at three or four guineas each. Even in outward aspect he conformed to type - with his untidy shock of hair, small imperial, and a scarf instead of a collar. But for most of his life he did not mix in what are called "artistic circles". Not Chelsea, Fitzroy Street, Bloomsbury, or Hampstead claimed him, but for years a little flat "in the south suburbs by the Elephant," far removed from the coteries, deep-set in the ordinary life of the people.*[24]

Gerald Gardner and Austin Osman Spare probably only met on one occasion and it is my conclusion that, whilst meeting Gerald may have sparked Spare's imagination in the sphere of witches' sabbats and how he saw Mrs. Paterson, Spare did not really influence Gerald significantly, for they were totally different characters on different paths in life, which the unfortunate Clanda episode underlines perfectly.

The passenger lists show Gerald's usual 'wintering abroad' in early 1955 consisting of a round trip to Alexandria in Egypt on the *Bysanz*, of which he was the sole passenger, leaving London on 10th January. However, the Folk-Lore Society's signing-in book shows him as attending a meeting on 19th January, so I am not sure what was going on. Either he cancelled the trip at the last minute, someone signed in on his behalf or his magical advancement had reached the stage where he could be in two places at once!

---

24. *The Times*, 16 May 1956.

CHAPTER TWENTY–NINE

The Golden Age

The publication of *Witchcraft Today* took some time to penetrate into the collective mind of reporters in the mass media. Apart from reviews, none of which appeared in the mass-circulation newspapers of the day, the first mention of witchcraft occurred in a series of articles which appeared in The *Sunday Pictorial* during May and June 1955. The four-part series was presented by Peter Hawkins. It claimed to be the result of a 5-month investigation into 'black magic and devil worship in Britain'. However, it continues: *The* Pictorial *investigators have found evidence of a nationwide chain of witchcraft groups called Covens.*[1]

Having implicated witch covens (and the existence of a "nationwide chain" in 1955 was a pure figment of journalistic imagination) the series of articles goes on to recount the story of a woman from Birmingham who is described as an "ex-witch" but who seems rather to have become involved in some sort of voodoo group and rituals.

However, the fourth article in the series, published on 17th June 1955, is a report of an interview that Hawkins had with Gerald. It is headed "This man's whitewash is dangerous: no witchcraft is fun"

---

1. Sunday *Pictorial*, 22 May 1955.

and starts *Dr. Gerald Brosseau Gardner is an authority on witch-craft. It is through him that many people get their first mistaken ideas about witchcraft. ... He is a self-confessed witch and a practising devotee of a witch coven in Britain. But he is also a whitewasher of witchcraft. He puts around the, to my mind, dangerous idea that witchcraft is not evil."*

The article goes on in this vein. Hawkins complains that nowhere in *Witchcraft Today* could he find descriptions of any "horrible and degrading ceremonies". He does, however, find passages in *High Magic's Aid* which he finds "lurid" and which he describes as "foul bait", quoting a passage about using the living body of a woman as an altar. He concludes:

> *There is no doubt at all that there are satanic devil-worshippers in Britain who are ready to provide this type of sexual perversion to capture the men and women they wish to make their slaves. That is why I believe that his [i.e. Gerald's] books, in the wrong hands, can be dangerous. And there is no way of stopping them getting into the wrong hands."*

The whole article was such a distortion of the truth that Gerald was shocked. He had indeed seen Hawkins the previous week when the journalist had visited him on the Isle of Man. Doreen Valiente records Gerald's response when he read the article:

> *Gerald was completely taken aback. 'He seemed such a nice chap when he interviewed me', he told us. 'Of course he did', I replied. 'You didn't think they would send someone who would arouse your suspicions, did you? You were simply being set up.' However, Gerald soon recovered his usual jauntiness. 'It would have cost me thousands to get this sort of national publicity if I'd had to pay for it', he said. His wife Donna took a more realistic view. She confided to me when Gerald wasn't listening, 'You have no idea what we've suffered since that story came out.' She didn't go into much detail; but I gathered that many people whom they had hitherto regarded as friends suddenly hadn't wanted to know them.*[2]

---

2. Valiente, (1989), 67.

It is clear that the police carried out investigations following the allegations contained in the articles. Newman[3] describes the Birmingham woman as a well-known police informant who was considered garrulous and mentally unstable. He states that she claimed to the police that Gerald was national head of the cult into which she claimed to have been initiated and that he, together with Aleister Crowley's widow, had organised the murder of Charles Walton, a farm labourer, in 1945. It seems that the police were dubious about the allegations, and it is not clear whether they even interviewed Gerald: he never mentions it in his account of the affair in *The Meaning of Witchcraft*. Certainly no proceedings were ever brought.

However, the adage that there is no such thing as bad publicity proved true. The article stimulated interest in the Museum, as Gerald records:

> *During the next few weeks, the number of motor coaches which arrived at the Museum were almost more than we could cope with. I got as many copies as I could of the papers' attacks, and put them there for people to see; and to my huge amusement many people wanted to buy them, and several of them were stolen. I must give the papers the credit of having spelt my name rightly, and adorned some of their articles with an excellent photograph of me; but I had never thought it was so good that people would want it for a pin-up. However, devotion to truth compels me to record the fact!*

> *Not only did I achieve the status of a pin-up, but fan-mail started to come my way; our local postman had to give me a mail-bag all to myself one day, and the daily deluge of letters kept up for weeks.*

> *Many of the letters were evidence of the interest taken by people in all walks of life in what is generally known as the supernormal, and of their dissatisfaction with orthodox approaches to life and religion. Often, the writers gave per-*

---

3. Paul Newman, *The Tregerthen Horror*, (Abraxas, 2005), 102-104.

sonal experiences, and interesting scraps of folklore and tradition. I can only remember one letter which was hostile; this was from a clergyman, who said that I was quite as bad as the spiritualists and the Christian Scientists![4]

༄

When we come to look at the coven which was based in Bricket Wood, there are some members who are still alive. In one way, this is good in that we can hear from them directly about what happened and ask them questions. However, with this may come the responsibility of ensuring that names are not revealed unwittingly. There is still a strong tradition amongst the Craft of not revealing members' names and I have respected this as far as possible. The exceptions are where individuals are well-known through interviews or because they have written books. Also, where I know that the individual in question has died, I have given their name. I believe that this is important as a historical record, increasingly valuable as the years pass. Where individuals are, or may be, still alive, I have used only their first name or 'witch name' or other distinguishing characteristics such as their profession. I have not used pseudonyms.

One of those who read the article was a 28-year-old sales representative for a paint wholesaler living in Crossfield Road, Swiss Cottage, named Jack Leon Bracelin, a name now remembered as author of the biography *Gerald Gardner Witch*,[5] though his other contributions to the history of the Craft have been largely ignored. In his earlier years he had been a member of the Palestine Police Force and had been interested in ceremonial magic for some years and therefore knew a little bit about the subject matter of the articles. Lois Bourne describes him thus: ... *about 5'9", slim-built with light brown hair, blue eyes and a small moustache which gave him a military air. He appeared to have a degree of suppressed nervous energy. I felt he would be a good judge of character; he spoke in a very direct manner and gave the impression of honesty and integrity.*[6]

4. Gardner, (1959), 230.
5. J.L. Bracelin, *Gerald Gardner Witch*, (Octagon Press 1960).
6. Lois Bourne, *Dancing with Witches*, (Robert Hale 1998), 20.

Bracelin, like many others, was not taken in by the antagonistic tone of the article about Gerald. On the contrary, he noted down the name of the book that was mentioned, *Witchcraft Today*, and ordered it from his local library. When it arrived he read it through avidly and was most impressed. His girl-friend also read it. Fred Lamond says of her that she: ... *had an elfine face that looked as if she had come straight out of an Arthur Rackham drawing. Gerald told reporters that she came from a hereditary witch family* ...7 She told me that there was no truth whatever in this "traditional witch family" story, which was what she described as a "Geraldism".

Lois Bourne, referring to her as "Annis", describes her as: ... *a slight, slim girl ... with elfin features and long dark hair drawn back severely from her face into a pony-tail style; she was warm and friendly, articulate and self-possessed, and there was a charismatic quality to her presence.*8

Anyway, they both read *Witchcraft Today* and discussed it: she says they both thought "Aha! This is it!" I understand that response because it mirrors very much my own feelings five years later when I read *Witchcraft Today* for the first time. Crucially, however, Jack did something which I did not think of doing: he wrote to the author c/o the publishers expressing his feelings about the book.

Very quickly he got a reply, inviting him to visit Gerald at his flat at 145 Holland Road. This was followed up quickly by a joint visit by Jack and his girl-friend, after which they discussed what they had experienced. She said that they liked the concept very much and that it felt as if they had "come home", a feeling echoed by many over the years! Gerald gave them *High Magic's Aid*, to read and this confirmed that the Craft was definitely for them.

There were then a few more visits, but very soon a date was set for their initiations. No "year and a day", as was supposedly traditional: Gerald was far too much in a hurry for that! So, probably on the Saturday before the March Full Moon, 24th March 1956, four people gathered for the initiation which took place at Gerald's flat at 145 Holland Road. As well as Jack, his girl-friend and Gerald, there was a woman they had not met before called

---

7. Frederic Lamond, *Fifty Years of Wicca*, (Green Magic, 2004), 12.
8. Bourne, (1998), 20.

Barbara. Barbara Vickers had ceased working regularly with Gerald some time before, and I think this was probably the last time that she did work with him.

Jack's girl-friend (whom I will from now on refer to by her witch name of 'Dayonis' the heroine of Gerald's novel *A Goddess Arrives*) recalls that Donna used to prepare very nice meals for the meetings, including a wonderful lemon tart, but would then retire to her room (she and Gerald had separate bedrooms, according to Fred Lamond) to read detective stories and play patience while the rituals took place. Dayonis remembers that Donna was rather bewildered about the Craft, but that she was "lovely", "sweet" and "a real lady".[9]

Although Doreen Valiente had been Gerald's High Priestess since 1953, I get the impression that, probably mainly due to distance, she did not attend coven meetings very often and that there was not much love lost between her and the new initiates, Jack and Dayonis. They always referred to her by her magical name, Ameth, and Dayonis was in the habit of calling her "she who must be obeyed"! When Doreen did make one of her rare visits, Dayonis remembers that they "pulled out all the stops to make it nice for her": she likened it to "the Goddess come to earth"! I think it likely that Gerald never asked Doreen to approve Jack and Dayonis before he initiated them, which would be an additional reason for the "Proposed Rules for the Craft" which were produced prior to the forthcoming split.

From 1956 onwards, Gerald seemed to cut back a bit on his wintering abroad and I suspect that this coincided with the growing interest in the Craft and the initiation of new members into it. Although he usually continued to take relatively brief trips in Februarys, his year was really divided into a short summer season in the Isle of Man and the rest of the year spent in London with international trips to conferences.

Whether there was a regular coven meeting at that time, I do not know. Gerald Yorke, in a letter to Cecil Williamson in January the previous year wrote: *I shall soon know all about the old boy's coven. A friend has persuaded a friend to join it. The latter has done*

---

9. Discussion between Dayonis and Don Frew and Anna Korn, 1995.

so complete with wife. So soon I shall know all about it."[10] But in July that year he wrote: ... *Gardner's new London coven hardly ever meets now, so I have no gossip about it.*[11]

We do not really know who was in the coven at this stage. Barbara had already ceased to work regularly with Gerald, and it was before the influx of new members in 1956. Various people have been mentioned as having been members - Doreen Valiente, of course, James Laver, Dennis Collings, Ned Grove, Derek Boothby and a retired Army officer and his wife (possibly these were Yorke's spies)[12] I suspect, however, that it was only with the initiation of Jack and Dayonis that regular coven rituals started taking place.

Jack and Dayonis applied for joint membership of Fiveacres Club in April 1956 and I suspect that this was because Gerald was keen to use the Witch's Cottage for rituals and he could only do this if those attending the rituals were members of the Club. However, this only became possible following the 'takeover' of the Club in January 1957.

Gerald's old friend, Dennis Collings, was a member of the coven, but only attended rarely because he lived in the Gold Coast. I don't know when he was initiated, presumably while he was in London before going out there.

Ned Grove (Edward Thomas N. Grove, born 1891) was a member of the coven before Jack and Dayonis joined. She thought he may have had some connection with the Golden Dawn. Gerald first met him at a Folk-Lore Society meeting in 1939. He was fairly well-to-do, owning land in Ireland. In the Five Acres membership list his address is given as Knockkelly House, Fethard, Co. Tipperary. He lived in London quite a bit of the time: Fred Lamond describes him as a city financier, and Dayonis, more specifically, says that he was a director of a bank. She also adds that he was "a wonderful, delightful gentleman". He had a military career in which in 1918 he became the first district commissioner of the Opari District of southern Sudan.

---

10. Letter, Gerald Yorke to Cecil Williamson, 13 January 1955.
11. Letter, Gerald Yorke to Cecil Williamson, 1 July 1955.
12. Gareth Medway has suggested that authors Evelyn Eaton and Ithell Colquhoun be added to this list (personal communication October 2009).

On returning to England it seems that he became part of an artistic circle of friends on the fringe of the Bloomsbury set, including the artist Augustus John, whom he first met in 1919. Chamot, Farr and Butlin[13] report that John "had several shots at painting him" at that time. Another of John's subjects was an artist's model, Nina Forrest, better known as Euphemia Lamb, former wife of the painter, Henry Lamb. She is famously depicted in a 1908 portrait bust by Epstein. Ned and Nina married in 1934, but divorced nine years later. The following year, Ned married Gwyneth Owen in Oxford.

Augustus John had another shot at painting Ned in 1940. Chamot, Farr and Butlin note:

> He [Ned] wrote (21 October 1957): 'The portrait was painted during the late summer of 1940. I went down to Fryern [John's house at Fordingbridge on the edge of the New Forest] for about a week and sat for Augustus daily. We had met in London the week before & he insisted on my coming down to be painted - I had just finished my harvest and was the colour of a brown boot. He had some difficulty with the portrait, I remember, as the nightly consumption of gin at Fryern in those days was quite considerable & my complexion during the week slowly changed from brown to green which annoyed him very much. I thought the portrait had gone into discard as I never saw it again until it appeared in the Royal Academy. Whether he did any subsequent work on it I don't know. It certainly now seems a much more finished portrait than I remember in 1940'.[14]

The coven undertook a variety of magical working over the years. One of the earliest that Dayonis remembers was a working to help Ned Grove. Ned's farm in Ireland was suffering from drought and so the coven did a working to get some rain for him, which arrived soon after. Dayonis commented to me: "... that was such a clear picture of work. That was so good."

Major Derek Boothby (Frederick Alexander Cunningham Boothby) was born in 1909 in Weymouth, Dorset. His father,

---

13. Mary Chamot, Dennis Farr and Martin Butlin, *The Modern British Paintings, Drawings and Sculpture,* (Oldbourne Press, 1964), Vol 1.
14. Ibid.

24. Mill House, Highcliffe

25. Buckingham Palace Mansions, Victoria.

26. Ridgmount Gardens, Bloomsbury.

27. 145 Holland Road, Shepherd's Bush.

28. 266 Elgin Avenue, Maida Vale.

29. The Witch's Cottage at the Abbey Folk Park, New Barnet

30. An altar in the Witches' Cottage prepared for a ritual - 1950s.

*31. Gilbert and Barbara Vickers,
Oxford Street, London - 1950*

*32. Barbara Vickers with
ritual items - 1950*

33. 77 Malew Street, Castletown, Isle of Man. Gerald's home from 1952 until his death in 1964

34. Gerald at the Museum of Magic and Witchcraft, Castletown, Isle of Man, in 1954

35. The Restaurant at the Museum of Magic and Witchcraft

36. The Upper Gallery at the Museum of Magic and Witchcraft

37. The Southern Coven collection at the Museum of Magic and Witchcraft

38. *The Crowley exhibition cabinet in the Museum of Magic and Witchcraft. The Charter in Gerald's calligraphic hand is in the top right of the photograph.*

39. *Gerald's drawing of the Witches' Mill, Castletown*

40. *Doreen Valiente*

41. Monica English

42. Gerald in Highland Dress

43. Gerald Gardner in the early 1950s

44. Gerald with Arnold and Patricia Crowther on their wedding day - November 1960

45. Gerald Gardner - early 1960s

*46. Gerald in the Isle of Man -
early 1960s*

47. Donna's gravestone, Malew Cemetery, Castletown, Isle of Man

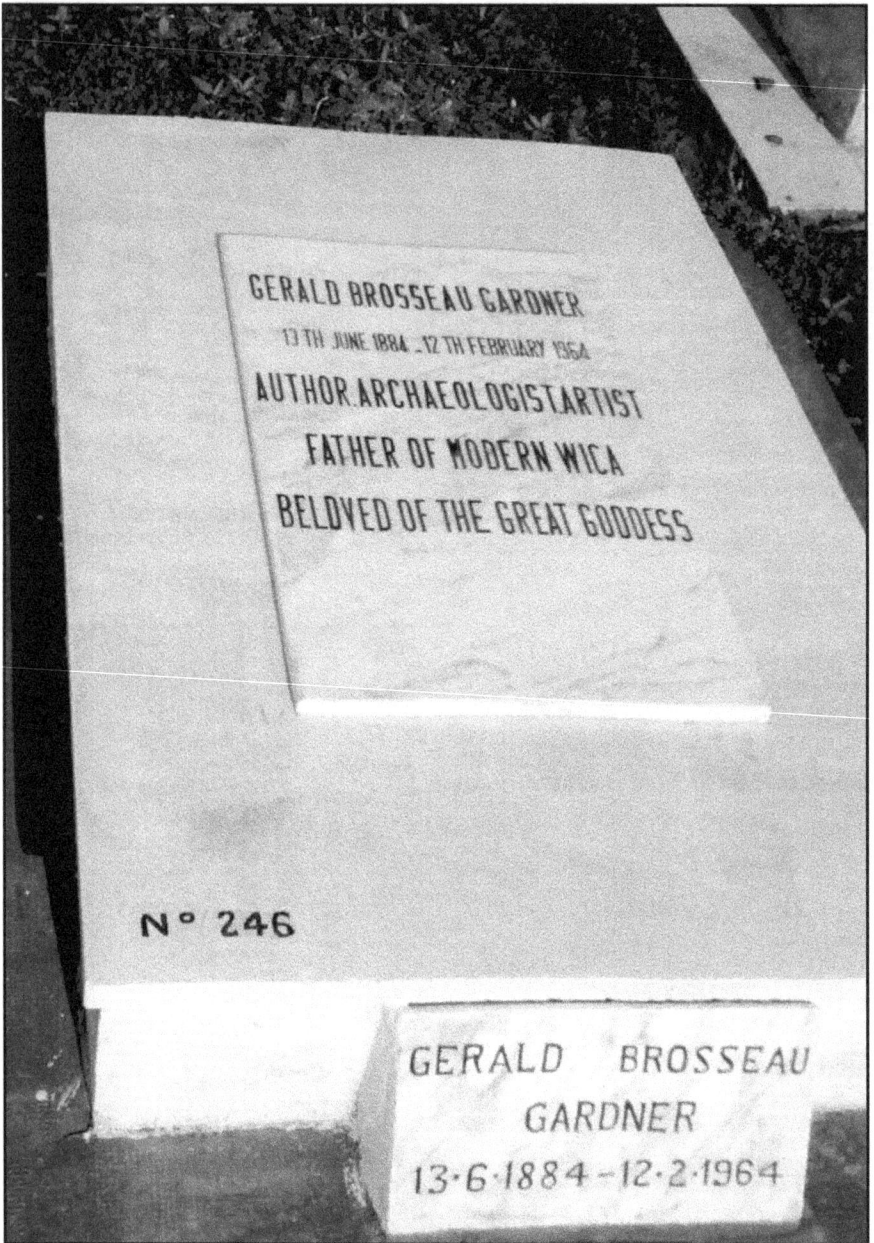

GERALD BROSSEAU GARDNER
13 TH JUNE 1884 - 12 TH FEBRUARY 1964
AUTHOR ARCHAEOLOGIST ARTIST
FATHER OF MODERN WICA
BELOVED OF THE GREAT GODDESS

N° 246

GERALD   BROSSEAU
GARDNER
13·6·1884 - 12·2·1964

48. Gerald's grave, Christian Cemetery (Cimetière de Borgel), Tunis

Frederick Lewis Maitland Boothby, had been a Wing Commander in the Royal Naval Air Service during the First World War and had become a C.B.E. and a Fellow of the Royal Aeronautical Society. Derek's mother, May Katherine Pery, was a daughter of the 3rd Earl of Limerick.

Boothby was a member of the coven when Dayonis and Jack joined. She describes him as being "a rather controlling person" and as being "very full of himself".[15] At some stage in late 1957, Boothby acquired some land not far from the village of Sarratt, in Hertfordshire, some six miles from Bricket Wood. This he called 'The Spinney'. It was a depression in the ground which seems to have been an old quarry or pit which had been completely overgrown with trees. In the middle of the site he had a hut which he lived in and used for witchcraft rituals, much to the disapproval of the local vicar. In December 1960 the hut was mysteriously burned down.

Boothby was later a founder member of the 1320 Club, which consisted of dissident Scottish nationalists. He was expelled from the Scottish National Party in 1968 after he had advocated raising a private army against the English. He died in Scotland in 1979.

Frederic Lamond says of himself: *I have ... lived through almost the whole of Wiccan history and am probably - since the death of Doreen Valiente - the oldest continuing practising Wiccan alive today.*[16] He was born in 1931 and, following the divorce of his parents when he was two years old, was taken on by his Jewish maternal grandmother. At the outbreak of World War II, they lived in French Switzerland where, at the age of twelve, he started to go for long solitary country walks. At the age of 16 he came to England, attending an Anglican High Church public school. He studied Economics at Cambridge and subsequently Planning at the University of Chicago. He has spent his working life in the computer industry, latterly as an independent consultant and lecturer.

However, in early 1956, when his story first intertwines with that of the Craft, he was a market researcher. Like most who are attracted to the Craft, he was able to think for himself and one way in which this manifested was in his membership of the Progressive League. This had been founded in 1932 by H.G. Wells,

---

15. Dayonis, interview with the author, February 2006.
16. Lamond, (2004).

C.E.M. Joad and others, primarily to unite progressive organisations against fascism. It promoted pacifism, European federalism, world government, socialism, progressive (i.e. non-authoritarian) education, nudism and free love. According to Katharine Whitehorn[17] one of the things they went in for was naked country dancing. According to Antonia Lister-Kaye, most of them seemed to live in or near Hampstead, in north-west London. She describes them as "poets and artists and sub-Bloomsbury" who "had conferences, and all got into each others' beds, which was quite something in those days."[18]

As one might expect from someone who was a member of such an organisation, Fred Lamond was an avid reader and it is likely that the title of a book by the anthropologist, Gordon Rattray Taylor caught his eye: *Sex in History*.[19] In it the author referred to the idea put forward by Margaret Murray that witchcraft in mediaeval times had been an actual religion of the country people. This excited him and he began reading other books about witchcraft, including Gerald Gardner's *Witchcraft Today*. On reading it, Lamond remarks "it contained enough hidden cues to ring all my spiritual bells."

Like Jack Bracelin before him, Lamond wrote to Gerald Gardner care of his publishers and soon afterwards received a letter from Gerald with an invitation to meet him at his flat in Holland Road. This first meeting took place in June 1956. His impressions of Gerald were that he was:

> ... a kind unassuming gentleman with a fine crop of white hair and a white barbiche. He was an excellent raconteur with a good eye for human eccentricity and the occasional absurdities of daily life, and had a fine sense of humour. His friendliness and childlike enjoyment of life inspired love and affection in all who knew him ... But for a man who was trying to revive the mysterious and awe-inspiring witchcraft tradition, I found him disappointingly lacking in charisma.[20]

17. *The Guardian*, 6 July 2006.
18. www.speakingforourselves.org.uk/uploads/interviews/lister4.doc.
19. Gordon Rattray Taylor, Sex in History, (Thames and Hudson, 1953).
20. Robert' (Frederic Lamond), "Witness to Wicca", (unpublished manuscript), "Chapter 2: Gerald Gardner", (Boscastle Museum of Witchcraft archives).

He tells me that:

... Gerald was already under pressure from the coven not to invite people on his own initiative, and had to discuss matters with the coven before issuing an invitation. The summer intervened and it was in September or early October that I was invited to meet the coven just before their next meeting. I then asked if I could bring with me Jacqueline, a friend from the Progressive League with whom I had often discussed our common interest in witchcraft. This was granted and so we both met the whole coven before their October, November and December 1956 meetings. These meetings took place at Gerald's Holland Park flat. We would interact with the coven socially during the early part of the evening, and would leave when they wanted to start their circle. It was during the December meeting that Jack Bracelin told Jacqueline and me that we had been accepted by the coven and would be initiated at the February Eve 1957 sabbath if we accepted, which we did. We were then given copies of High Magic's Aid to read, especially the description of a witch initiation, to check that ritual nudity and scourging didn't freak us out, which it didn't.[21]

Jacqueline and Fred were initiated, probably on the night of Saturday 2nd February 1957, in the Witches' Cottage, perhaps in the first ritual that had been held in the Cottage for a considerable time. He rightly does not give details of that initiation, but does say the following:

When the blindfold was removed from my eyes, and I found myself in a dark incense-filled candle-lit cottage surrounded by naked figures, I felt again the presence of ... divine power ... And when the acting High Priestess read The Charge of the Goddess, I felt this power welcoming me home![22]

Those who have experienced rituals in the cottage have testified to the atmosphere that was present. However, the building needed

---

21. Email, Frederic Lamond to the author, 17 April 2008.
22. Lamond, (2004), 7.

to be warmed up by portable heaters, as it was not insulated and its normal condition was one of penetrating cold and damp. Despite this, the atmosphere was overwhelming and, once the candlelight, incense and the magic contained in the very fabric of the building were activated, it became a very special place indeed. Patricia Crowther has very similar feelings: *There was a wonderful atmosphere in the cottage. It was like stepping back in time, and the aroma of incense seemed to permeate the very walls.*[23]

Fred Lamond continues: *Since meetings could last until fairly late, members without cars or with long distances to cover slept in a hut neighbouring the witches' cottage.*[24] This may originally have been a chicken shed. Jack lined it out with dry wall sheeting to make it habitable. It still exists and provides living accommodation for club members. He continues: *Gerald liked to cuddle up with whoever had been his high priestess: he was too old to engage in penetrative sex but would have enjoyed affectionate caresses. ... Dayonis ... had a very open relationship with Jack Bracelin and was temperamentally warm and affectionate. Cuddling up with her must have been ... enjoyable for Gerald ... and he became very fond of her."*[25] He tells me that others liked to cuddle up after coven meetings as well: *Through ritual nudity and mutual scourging we built up erotic energy, which is the "power" that we used in our healings and other magical workings. This had to be grounded at the end. Part of this was done by the all round hugs between every man and every woman in the circle. But the remainder was by magical partners sleeping together in the hut adjoining the witches' cottage, or in the witches' cottage itself. Magical partners were not necessarily the life partners one had outside the circle ...*[26]

❦

Rex Wellbye had owned a substantial part of the land now occupied by Five Acres Club for many years and for a long time he had been talking about selling it, either to the Club or to someone sympathetic to it. By the mid-1950s he was determined to do something about it. He was in his eighties and wanted to

---

23. Crowther, (1998), 46.
24. Lamond, (2004), 10.
25. Op. cit., 10-11.
26. Email, Frederic Lamond to the author, 17 April 2008.

retire from active involvement in the Club, to retain his house and a small amount of land next to it, but to dispose of the rest. The land that Rex was willing to sell was valued at £1900.

Gerald saw this as a way of getting more control, but I think he didn't like to be seen to be doing so too openly. So just as he had earlier persuaded Edith to act as if she were a financial backer, now he enlisted the services of a mystery woman whom he called 'Mrs. Z'. This turned out to be Doreen Valiente. Gerald showed himself in a typically misleading ploy in a letter to Rex[27] where he finally admitted that 'Mrs.Z' was actually Mrs. Valiente. He wrote: "...my wife has known her and her husband for years ...". Now, Donna undoubtedly had met Doreen on a few occasions since 1953, but it was through Gerald that she knew her, and Gerald met her first: she was Gerald's friend and, indeed, initiate. This is a typical example of Gerald saying something which is strictly true but is designed to mislead, in this case to the belief that Doreen was Donna's friend rather than Gerald's. Whether either of them ever met Doreen's husband, Casimiro, as claimed, is open to considerable doubt.

Doreen had never been well-off, had an ordinary office job and lived in a humble flat in Brighton. She would never have been in a position to act as a financial backer for the Club. It is clear that the money came from Gerald, which for his own reasons he wanted to conceal. As well as controlling things, he probably also wanted to make comments and attach conditions to the provision of funding while distancing himself from such remarks. Then again, he definitely enjoyed intrigue and deception.

The issue seemed to come to a head as both Gerald and Rex had severe criticisms of the way J.B. Mackee ("Mack") had been running the Club. He was Secretary of the Woodside Close Property Company, but whether he was actually a salaried administrator as Fred Lamond claims, is uncertain. Lamond states: *This man deliberately ran the club at a loss by setting unrealistically high requirements for membership, hoping thereby to persuade Gerald eventually to sell the club to him at a low price. By 1956 Fiveacres had only 40 members. But Gerald saw through the ploy[28]* ... Previously Gerald had given Mackee Power of Attorney, to act

27. Letter, Gerald Gardner to Rex Wellbye, 13 January 1957.
28. Lamond, (2004), 31.

for him when he was away, which he was quite a lot, either in the Isle of Man during the summer or 'wintering abroad', which he tended to do most years. This Power of Attorney Gerald now withdrew, which effectively removed Mackee's control of the Club.

The Annual General Meeting of the Woodside Close Property Company was held on 7th January 1957 at Gerald's flat in Holland Road. Mackee tendered his resignation as Secretary and Director, and Jimmy Garvey tendered his resignation as Director and Managing Director. This all seems to have been arranged beforehand. Garvey, for example stated: *I have told Gerald that I want to resign my Managership and I suggested his blue eyed boy, Jack, but whether he could do the job I wouldn't know.* Gerald proposed that Jack Bracelin, Dayonis, Doreen Valiente, and Derek Boothby be appointed as directors. Rex Wellbye seems to have severed his connection with the Company previously and, for the first time, it was now in the hands of those sympathetic to Gerald. Jack Bracelin was appointed Managing Director of the Woodside Close Property Co. and, according to Fred Lamond, took on administration of the Club. He took no salary, but Gerald told him that he could live off the Club's income, which encouraged him to expand the number of members from the very low level to which it had fallen.

Following the A.G.M., the resignation of Mackee and the appointment of Jack Bracelin as administrator there was a change in the membership policy of the club to try and get more members. One consequence of this is that several members of the coven were able to become members of the club. Probably they had either been rejected as unsuitable by Mackee or they had felt uneasy about joining a club which they felt was in some way hostile to their beliefs and practices. This all changed with the 'takeover' and, in the month or so following the A.G.M., membership applications were received and approved in respect of Ned Grove, Derek Boothby and Dennis Collings. Membership applications for Fred Lamond and Jacqueline followed shortly afterwards.

Gerald departed for his usual wintering abroad in February, but apart from the phrase "departing to foreign parts" I have no idea where he went. He was, however, back by mid March, for he attended a Folk-Lore Society meeting on the 13th.

Gerald and Rex having the personalities that they did, there was a lot of haggling over details of the sale documents, including last minute threats of withdrawal, but on 3rd April 1957, the sale was completed. Even then, there was much haggling over solicitors' expenses, which were inevitably more than they would have been precisely because of such activity on the part of both vendor and purchaser.

The land was now officially in the ownership of Doreen Valiente, as Gerald made clear in a letter to Rex: *The land is now as much private property as it was when it belonged to you. The only difference is you wouldent allow the Club to walk over the land, the new propriators dont mind them doing so.*

However, these were not the only changes that were afoot!

CHAPTER THIRTY

The Split

Some things build up slowly over the years, only coming to a head over a relatively minor incident. So it was with the split in the coven, which happened in March 1957. Some of the older members, including Doreen Valiente, Ned Grove and Derek Boothby, were becoming increasingly concerned about Gerald's publicity seeking and interviews he had given to the press which were distorted to give an unfavourable impression.

Lamond says that the coven split six weeks after his initiation and that there was only one full moon ritual before the split. Since he was initiated at February Eve 1957, probably on Saturday 2nd February, six weeks later takes us to Saturday 16th March, which is the date of the full moon. So one could imagine the 'rebels' just not turning up for that ritual, leaving Gerald with the younger members to carry on alone. Fred told me that:

The younger members – [Dayonis], Jack, [the anaesthetist], Jacqueline and myself – stayed with Gerald, on the grounds that but for Gerald's openness about witchcraft we would not have been in it. In my case, my initiation by [Dayonis] had created a strong spiritual bond and I decided to go where she went.[1]

After the split, Gerald was left with a problem. Dayonis was Maiden of the coven and could stand in for the High Priestess on a temporary basis, and indeed had done so on several occasions when Doreen had not been present. However, to become High Priestess on a permanent basis required her elevation to 2nd degree and, preferably, 3rd. Gerald felt that he needed some sort of confirmation that he was doing the right thing and so he arranged to take Dayonis and Jack down to Highcliffe so that Edith could give her opinion on their suitability to take on the roles of High Priest and High Priestess.

So Gerald, Jack and Dayonis visited Edith in the Austin A40 van which Gerald had given Jack. Dayonis remembers meeting Edith, whom she was introduced to as Dafo, and her impression was of a very nice gentle lady. It was a chat over afternoon tea and there was no mention of the Craft at all.

Edith obviously approved of Dayonis and Jack because shortly afterwards, possibly at the May Eve seasonal ritual, Dayonis was put through the 2nd and 3rd degree in one evening by Gerald and she then elevated Jack to 3rd. It was at this ritual that she was given her witch name of Dayonis, as was normal at that time.

Gerald did not seem to have been put off talking to the press and about this time he was interviewed by the well-known *Daily Mirror* journalist, Marjorie Proops. In what was basically a sympathetic piece, she gives a vivid description of him:

> *... with wild white hair and mesmeric eyes like blue marbles and arms tattooed all over with cabbalistic signs. He wore fancy costume jewellery - also dotted about with cabbalistic symbols - on wrists and fingers. And he'd brought with him to the luncheon witches' wands, beads, silver cups and saucers, swords and knives and other witch paraphernalia.*[2]

Shortly after this, on Friday 3rd May 1957, Gerald appeared on ITV on the programme *This Week*. He was interviewed by

---

1. Frederic Lamond, interview with the author, July 2006.
2. Marjorie Proops, "I Got the Low-down on this Witch Lark", *Daily Mirror*, 10 April 1957.

ex-Superintendent Tom Fallon, when he talked about the ritual the witches carried out in 1940 to help stop the threatened invasion. Margaret Murray was also interviewed, where she said that witch covens were harmless but romantic. The background to this is not known but it may have been something to do with May Day celebrations.

The split in the coven was not complete and absolute, however, and I think this was because Doreen and Ned, whilst they had left the coven, did feel a responsibility for the Craft as a whole and wanted to do what they could to limit what they saw as Gerald's harmful publicity-seeking and initiation of unsuitable people. They tackled Gerald, pointing out that his publicity-seeking was, as Doreen put it, "adding fuel to the fire of the national press witch-hunt". Gerald said that he would behave, but before long an article appeared in the popular illustrated magazine, *Weekend*, in its June 24-30, 1957 issue. Unusually, the article was actually written by Gerald, with the journalist, Barbara Stabler, being relegated to the role of listener or observer and, I would imagine, editor of the text.

The article was to my mind a reasonably positive view of witchcraft. Gerald relates the story of how the witches worked a ritual to stop a blackmailer and another to secure the purchase of Gerald's house in the Isle of Man. It also has an interesting story of the witches performing a healing ritual.

Doreen Valiente was not pleased with this article, however. She wrote that Gerald had "prattled away" to "a particularly silly popular magazine" and complained that he had "posed for a ludicrous picture which showed him sitting cross-legged in the magic circle and pointing a magic sword at what the caption called a 'weird image' of a bat-winged demon!"[3] She tackled Gerald about it, who claimed that the interviewers had been sent up to see him in the Isle of Man by his publishers, Riders. Doreen was sceptical about this and went to see Riders' manager, who confirmed that they had done nothing of the sort. She relayed that information to Gerald and received, in her words, "an incoherent and rather abusive letter which was notable only for its absence of straight answers about anything".

---

3. Valiente, (1989), 71.

It was at this point, the beginning of July 1957, that Doreen sent a letter to past and present coven members enclosing a copy of 'Proposed Rules for the Craft', which Ned had drafted. The way they saw it was that they had all been sworn to secrecy when they were initiated and here was Gerald apparently breaking that oath with abandon! There were, as befits a witchcraft document, thirteen rules. They refer, not just to members of the Craft (the coven members) but also the Elders. I'm not quite sure who is included here, but it clearly is intended to include Gerald himself, as well as Doreen and Ned. What is probably the first draft of the Rules went as follows:

[1] No member of the Craft will initiate any person unless that person has been interviewed by at least two Elders and accepted as suitable.

[2] No affairs of the Craft will be discussed by members in the presence of uninitiated persons, or in places where conversation is likely to be overheard.

[3] No copies of any papers relating to the Craft will be made or retained without the Elders' permission. Such papers as are permissible will be kept in a secure place.

[4] As it is essential for the successful working of ritual by a group that there should be unity of purpose and an harmonious psychic atmosphere, members who create dissention and discord within the Craft will be asked to resign.

[5] No member of the Craft will give any information or interview about the Craft to any journalist or writer, or cause any such information to be published in any way, without the approval of the Elders; nor will any of the Elders do so without the approval of the rest of the Elders.

[6] If any member of the Craft feels that he or she has reason to complain of the conduct of any other member in matters affecting the Craft, or of any misdemeanour towards any member whilst on Craft premises, he or she will bring the said complaint to the notice of the Elders as soon as possible. The Elders, after considering all available evidence, will, if they find the complaint justified, take appropriate action.

[7] No member will be present at any meeting where the working is that of a higher Grade than he or she has attained, except by

invitation of the Elders. These invitations will only be extended on very rare occasions where special circumstances exist.

[8] No member will disclose the name and address or telephone number of any other member to any person whatsoever, without the said other member's previous permission.

[9] Members will meet upon the traditional occasions, or as near to them as possible, and such meetings will be arranged by the Elders, or such Officers as the Elders authorise to do so. If the Elders be not present at such meetings, they will receive a report of them. Members may arrange other meetings for their private working if they so desire, but if more than two members be present at such a meeting, the Elders will receive a report of it. This report will take the form of a short letter to the elders, giving place and date of the meeting, names of members attending, and details of ceremonies carried out. Where convenient, verbal reports will be accepted.

[10] Members will endeavour to acquaint themselves with the traditions of the Craft, and will not introduce innovations into the working without the Elders' approval. Nor will the Elders give approval to any important innovation without first asking the approval of the rest of the Craft.

[11] In the event of any member resigning from the Craft, he or she will honourably observe the Oath of Secrecy taken at initiation, and will also return to the Elders any written matter relating to the Craft which may be in his or her possession.

[12] All members will receive a copy of these rules, and all new members will be given a copy of these rules upon initiation. New members, prior to initiation, will read these rules and declare upon their honour that they will abide by them in letter and in spirit.

[13] It will be understood by all members that these rules are equally binding upon all Grades of the Craft, including the Elders, and that serious and/or persistent breach of these rules will be grounds for expulsion.

Points to note about these are:

Rule 1: This was included because Gerald was in the habit of initiating individuals, particularly young women, without even telling the rest of the coven. This probably included Jack and Dayonis, and others whose names have now been lost.

Rule 4 suggests that there had been some disagreements which had spilled over into their rituals, with predictable undesirable consequences. This was clearly an important factor, since a revised version of the Rules adds the sentence: "Should they fail or refuse to do so they will be informed in writing by the Elders that they have been expelled."

Rule 9 seems to be a response to factional meetings organised by Gerald and kept secret from the rest of the coven.

Rule 10 seems to have been in response to innovations agreed between Gerald and the younger members of the coven, following the split, without consultation with Doreen and Ned. Such innovations could, for example, have included the introduction of the eight sabbats.

Rule 12 makes it incumbent upon members that they accept and abide by them "in letter and in spirit". The revised version of the Rules makes this stronger by adding: "This declaration will be made to the Elders in writing, and signed."

Rule 13 makes it quite clear, if there were any doubt, that the rules apply equally to Gerald and the other Elders as to the other members of the coven.

Doreen and Ned sent the document (probably in early July 1957) up to Gerald, who was in the Isle of Man. After a few weeks, Gerald replied, saying that there was no need for such a document since the Laws of the Craft already existed. His letter was accompanied by a document known as The Old Laws. These were typed but used archaic language and word forms, such as 'Alther' and 'loveth'.

Doreen's immediate thought was that these had been concocted by Gerald in response to Ned's "Proposed Rules for the Craft". Her scepticism increased when she read one of the 'Laws' on the first page, which read: *And the greatest virtue of a High Priestess is that she recognises that youth is necessary to the representative of the Goddess, so that she will retire gracefully in favour of a younger woman, should the Coven so decide in Council.*

It struck Doreen that this whole exercise was just a way in which Gerald could get rid of her. She tells of her own reactions to seeing the 'Laws':

> *We were apparently supposed to be overawed. Our actual reaction was to be extremely sceptical. None of us had ever set eyes on these alleged 'Laws' before, though we noticed that they incorporated a preliminary passage from the 'Book of Shadows' commencing: 'Keep a book in your own hand of write ...' (This passage is reproduced in Gerald's book Witchcraft Today.) If these 'Laws' were so ancient and authoritative, why had Gerald never given them to us before? We discussed these matters, realizing that the question had become, by Gerald's own actions, one of confidence in him – and the more we examined the alleged 'Laws', the less confidence we had in either him or them.*[4]

Ned wrote back to Gerald, saying that he and Doreen were of the opinion that Gerald had made 'the Laws' up for his own purposes.[5] According to Doreen, there then followed a heated exchange of letters between Gerald and Ned.

It has been said that by nominally placing all power and authority in the coven in the hands of the High Priestess, and by simultaneously requiring her office to be passed periodically to a younger woman, Gerald could exercise covert authority while avoiding responsibility for anything that might go wrong. In practice, this didn't happen, though he may well have intended it.

The Laws have been studied in great detail by such researchers as Aidan Kelly[6] and 'Oakseer'[7] and they are still the subject of controversy. I think it possible that Gerald had inherited some sort of basis for the Old Laws from Edith but it is very clear that he added to them substantially for his own purposes.

At the time when Fred Lamond joined the coven, meetings, known as 'Esbats', were held on the Saturday nearest the Full

---

4. Valiente, (1989), 70.
5. Op. cit., 71.
6. Aidan A. Kelly, *Inventing Witchcraft*, (Thoth Publications, 2007), Chapter 8.
7. Oakseer, "Gerald Gardner, Old Words and the Old Laws", www.newwiccanchurch.net/articles/ggowol.htm].

Moon. They were on Saturdays because people could stay late and generally wouldn't have to work the following day, though occasionally they met on Fridays.

Apart from these they celebrated the four Great Sabbats which they knew as Candlemas, Beltane, Lammas and Halloween. They were essentially open meetings although the coven sometimes had a private ritual beforehand. They were big bonfire parties at Five Acres where sympathetic friends were invited. Dayonis recalls these:

> *November time was the best because Jack would organise a sheep and cut it in half and spread it out and then that's when Boothby was in charge of cooking and barbecuing that. And we would have a gallon of red wine, white wine and pink wine. Somebody else would be in charge of the fireworks. We got French bread and what-have-you and just generally had a damn good party! It was lovely!*[8]

Gerald gives his own dramatic account of this, in the context of writing about pictures illustrating the works of opponents of witchcraft:

> *I was puzzled, at first, by the great number of these pictures which showed the skeletons of animals, usually with some fragments of flesh still on them. They are generally depicted as if they were alive and moving. I used to think these were simply to make the picture horrible until I was present at a witch party in a wood when they "Barbecued" a whole sheep over a bonfire (and mighty good it was too). This was roasted whole, on a huge iron spit, and when done the flesh was sliced off the bones. It was a weird sight, with the flames lighting up the trees, and I suddenly saw the framework of the sheep, through the bonfire, its ribs bare, the bones of the four feet hanging down. The flickering of the fire and smoke made it seem to move as if it were alive, and it was exactly as the old "Witch pictures" showed it, excepting this had no head, and it is quite possible that in the old days they may have barbecued it with the head on.*[9]

8. Dayonis, discussion with the author, February 2006.
9. Gardner, (1959), 123.

Fred Lamond gives a very vivid picture of being a member of the coven before and after the 1957 split:

In those days, binding and scourging was the only method we used for raising power, because it was the only one that worked for Gerald. The coven member who knew the person we were working for best knelt in the middle of the circle and was scourged by his or her partner while the rest of the coven just stood around them in a circle and contributed their power. ...

In the spring of 1958, after Gerald had left us to spend the summer on the Isle of Man, we decided that the B&S method of raising power was too damn boring. So we switched to the circle dance method of raising power, some-times with a transmitter still kneeling in the centre of the circle, sometimes without, as we all visualised the desired outcome while running around at an ever increasing speed. Someone mentioned that the Lakota Sioux dance for hours on end until they drop from exhaustion to raise power for their spells: we never managed more than 5 minutes at most, yet the spells still worked.

We also altered the "Purification" procedure at the opening of every circle. Whereas under Gerald each member was scourged individually by his or her partner while the rest of the coven looked on, we now decided all the men should be scourged simultaneously by their women partners, which was followed by all women being scourged simultaneously by their male partners.[10]

One of the most sensible statements about the 'Book of Shadows' that witches write and keep has been made by Fred Lamond when he recalls Gerald's own attitude to such a book:

"The Book of Shadows is not a Bible or Quran. It is a per-sonal cookbook of spells that have worked for the owner. I am giving you mine to copy to get you started: as you gain

___

10. Lamond, (2004), 20-21.

experience discard those spells that don't work for you and substitute those that you have thought of yourselves." Sound advice, but it was inconsistent with his attempt to make its contents look centuries old, with advice on what to do if one was caught by witch-finders and tortured, as well as occasional phoney archaisms, such as : "Keep your book in your own hand of write" and "At mine altars...".[11]

It bothered Gerald that we knew that he had put the Book of Shadows (BoS) rituals together with Doreen Valiente's help, because he dearly wanted us to believe they had an older provenance. So one day he told us with a sly look on his face: "Until recently witches were not allowed to write anything down, lest it incriminate them if their house was searched. When at last Books of Shadows were allowed, witches had to write their rituals and spells down in a jumbled manner, so that if any unauthorised person found the BoS and tried the rituals as written down they wouldn't work!"

In May or June 1957, Neville Stack, a reporter in the Manchester office of *The People*, received permission to come to London to carry out research into witchcraft for an article for the paper. Jack and Dayonis met and talked with him and were convinced of his sincerity, as was Fred Lamond when they met. Jack arranged to take Stack to the Witches' Cottage and perform a ritual for him and answer his many questions. However, the weather was such that it was decided that it would be better to hold the ritual somewhere more comfortable. Jack knew the proprietors of the Avoca Hotel in Belsize Park, Hampstead, and they were given the use of a top floor room. Jack telephoned Fred to ask whether he and Jacqueline would be interested in joining Dayonis and himself for the ritual in the presence of Stack and his photographer.

Fred told me: *At some stage Jack ordered some tea from Room Service. You should have seen the porter's face when he brought the tea and saw four naked figures being photographed together with an altar, candlesticks and so on.*[12]

11. Lamond, (2004), 14-15.
12. Email, Frederic Lamond to the author, 11 January 2009.

When Stack had completed his article he showed it to the coven, who considered it to be absolutely fair. The first of two reports appeared in the 27th October 1957 issue of *The People*. If the coven were expecting favourable publicity they must have been greatly disappointed. It seems as if, after it left Stack's hands, the copy writers got hold of it, altering it substantially and adding adverse comments. The article, which appeared under the title of "They call this Witchcraft", was even more biased against them than the article about Gerald in the same newspaper two years previously. It included reference to them as a "repulsive pagan sect", whose rituals were called "barbaric".

But, as with the article two years previously, not all readers were taken in by the approach adopted by the newspaper. One reader, in particular, thought it sounded interesting and contacted Gerald via *The People*. He subsequently joined the coven and, some years later, took on the role of High Priest. He is still in that role, over 50 years after his initial enquiry.

꧁

It is, I think, significant that, despite Doreen's break with the coven, there was no ownership crisis at Bricket Wood. This is a clear indication that the land was effectively in Gerald's control and the split made no real difference to this.

However, Gerald's health was causing concern and he was very conscious of his own mortality and wanted to ensure that the Club would remain in 'friendly' hands following his death. Whilst the informal arrangement with Jack was all right while Gerald was around, something more formal was needed that could be implemented after Gerald's death.

After obtaining legal advice from a friend who was a member of the Club, the first action was to wind up the old Woodside Close Property Company, which went into voluntary liquidation in July 1957. Gerald was then advised to form a new company in which ownership of the Club could be vested.

It was originally intended that shares in the new company should be held jointly by Gerald and Jack, so that Jack would inherit the whole property on Gerald's death. The new company was to be known as Ancient Crafts Limited. It was incorporated on 6th January 1958 and registered on 26th January. The Registered Office was 29 Oakwood Road, Bricket Wood, which in fact was the hut adjacent to the Witches' Cottage which still has the brass nameplate reading "Ancient Crafts Ltd., Registered Office". There were initially four directors, each of whom took one share: Gerald, Dayonis, Jack and the retired Army officer. The Objects of the Company are very wide and extensive, covering everything that it could possibly want to do, and obviously drafted by the legal advisor.

On 27th February 1958, an additional 400 shares of £1 each were allotted to Gerald, Jack, Dayonis, Edith, the retired Army officer and the anaesthetist. It was a strange and unequal allocation and the purpose of it is unknown. There was undoubtedly some reason that Gerald had for it, probably to do with the balance of power in some way. It is also almost certain that the money was actually all Gerald's; certainly neither Jack nor Dayonis could have afforded to buy the allocated shares.

In January 1958, Jack asked the coven to work a spell to lift an advertising embargo which had been placed on the Club by Ernest Stanley, a leading light in the Central Council for British Naturism. Fred Lamond writes that Stanley was a friend of Mackee, the administrator who had been sacked by Gerald, and he wanted an opportunity to get back at the Club. This opportunity arrived the same month, as Fred Lamond tells:

> *Events now took a strange turn. A year earlier the Danish naturist magazine Sun & Health had run a forum on sexual education for naturists' children.*
>
> *I contributed an article recommending linking sex and love in the minds of adolescents, but saying we should be consistent. When teenagers fell in love, they should be allowed to give their love a sexual expression subject of course to the usual contraceptive precautions. Although I had written it as far back as July 1957, Sun & Health published it in their January 1958 issue.*

This touched all of Ernest Stanley's most sensitive inhibitions. In the February 1958 issue of Health & Efficiency he published a libellous article accusing me of encouraging adult sexual abuse of children, and naming our club as a front for "witchcraft and black magic". Jack had a lawyer friend who promptly slapped an injunction on W.H. Smith and all magazine distributors to stop distributing the magazine on pain of being joined in the forthcoming libel suit. A day later, the offending issue disappeared from all newsagents' shelves.

Three weeks later, Jack received a letter from a firm of publishers informing him that they had bought Health & Efficiency from the previous owners and had put a new editorial team in charge. They offered him three months' free advertising for his club, and normal commercial terms thereafter, if he would please lift the injunction on the magazine's distributors. The club was saved.[13]

Meanwhile, Gerald's health continued to cause concern. On 17th January 1958, he was taken into hospital and had what Rex Wellbye describes as a "very severe operation (a big hole in his stomach with many complications)"[14] Apparently he was kept unconscious for a day or two afterwards, presumably to help the healing process.

Gerald seemed to make good progress, for he was well enough to be present for Lois Pearson's initiation, which took place at Candlemas that year, probably on the evening of Saturday 1st February, in the Witches' Cottage. She calls this "probably one of the most important ceremonies of my life".[15] It seems to have been a double ceremony, since Fred Lamond was raised to the 2nd degree. Jack and Dayonis told him that since he had been in the coven for a year and was competent at raising power, this was an appropriate step. Gerald was, however, not well enough to take his usual winter trip abroad, so he spent it in London.

---

13. Lamond, (2004), 31-32.
14. Letter, Rex Wellbye to Marjory, 20 January 1958.
15. Bourne, (1998), 21.

CHAPTER THIRTY–ONE

Curator, Writer and Artist

When the museum first opened in 1951 there was nothing available that could really be called a guide book. There was a folded leaflet entitled "The Folklore Centre of Superstition and Witchcraft, Castletown, Isle of Man, An Introduction to Visitors". This was largely written by Cecil Williamson and gave virtually no information on the exhibits beyond a hope that in the following season the upper floor would be opened up, which would have space for more exhibits and displays.

It is difficult to believe that when Gerald took over the museum in 1954 he waited four years before a guide book became available. I am sure that he would have produced something even if it only consisted of a few duplicated sheets. I have, however, never seen, nor seen reference to, such a guide, so at present it must remain a mystery.

The guide book which appeared in 1958 was published by the Photochrom Co. Ltd., of Tunbridge Wells, Kent. This was a firm which specialised in postcards and guide books and I imagine that Gerald had approached them about producing a guide book. He would undoubtedly have paid the full cost of production, to be recouped from sales, possibly over several years. The booklet is small in page size, just 4 ½ x 3 ½ inches, known as sextodecimo (16mo.), having 32 pages, and is printed in the sepia ink which characterised many of Photochrom's postcards.

When Gerald took over, the Mill and grounds still had a somewhat ramshackle appearance. By the time the guide book appeared in 1958 he had made various 'improvements', including a rustic 'gateway' structure, a large entrance sign reading 'The Witches Mill' with illustrations of a witch on a broomstick and a cat, some planting and the erection of 'Ye Olde Lucky Wishing Well'. These were all probably thought to, and no doubt actually did, attract visitors. They certainly gave the appearance of something light-hearted that would appeal to children rather than a sober academic institution.

The old granary, to the right of the entrance, was three storeys high. On the ground floor was the restaurant and kitchen. On the first floor were the two original exhibition rooms. On the top floor was the new Upper Gallery, which opened in 1952.

In the First Gallery, the contents of Case No. 1 are described in the guide book as follows:

> *A large number of objects belonging to a witch who died in 1951, lent by her relatives, who wish to remain anonymous. These are mostly things which had been used in the family for generations. Most of them are for making herbal cures. The herbs required to make charms or medicines had to be cut at the time when the moon or the planets were in the particular parts of the Zodiac "under the right astrological aspects", as a practitioner of the art would say; and the curved sickle or "boleen" was used for this purpose. She had a very fine ritual sword, which for many years was lent to the Druid Order which holds the annual Midsummer ceremony at Stonehenge, because it fitted exactly into the cleft in the Hele Stone.*

Doreen Valiente[1] assumed that the phrase "witch who died in 1951" was referring to Dorothy Fordham, who did indeed die in that year. However, a caption on that same cabinet as noted by

---

1. Doreen Valiente, "Appendix A: The Search for Old Dorothy", in Janet and Stewart Farrar, *The Witches' Way*, (Robert Hale, 1984), 283-293.

Daniel Mannix[2] in 1959 read: *"As a tribute to Aunt Agatha, one of our most outstanding witches, this collection of paraphernalia which she used is affectionately dedicated. Presented by her family in loving memory, 1951".* Note that there is no mention of her year of death in the caption, merely a date which, from the context, seems to be the year when the collection was presented by her family. Gerald often referred to Rosamund Sabine as "Aunt Agatha", perhaps as a private joke with Edith. Aunt Agatha was Bertie Wooster's overbearing and alarming aunt, a formidable figure who first appeared in P.G. Wodehouse's *The Inimitable Jeeves* in 1923. Patricia Crowther mentioned to me that, when she first met Gerald, he used to refer rather mysteriously to "Aunt Agatha".

I think on the basis of this caption we can reconstruct what happened. Rosamund Sabine (for I now think that it was her items in the cabinet) died in May 1948. Before she died, she had asked her husband, George, to pass her sword, and possibly some other ritual items, such as the scourge, to Edith, who lived just down Avenue Road from them. It is from that year that the sword starts to be used by the Druids at their midsummer Stonehenge rituals.

Then, George enters a nursing home and 'Whinchat' is put up for sale. He offers Edith other items of Rosamund's, including some books and the implements for the preparation of herbs. Whilst she had used the sword etc. occasionally for rituals, she had no use for the herbalist equipment and therefore stored them in a box, probably in her attic.

She obviously mentioned this to Gerald at some stage, because by April 1951 he was asking to borrow them for the museum. I told the story of the loan in Chapter 26. When the conflict with Cecil Williamson about the display of these items resulted in their removal from display, I suspect that Gerald retained them in his house or workshop until he took control of the museum, when they were moved back and again put on display.

Cases nos. 2, 3 and 6 contained the amulets that Cecil let Gerald have when he moved his collection out.

Case no. 4 probably consisted partly of items made specially for display rather than genuinely old, partly some of the 'Southern

2. Daniel P. Mannix, "Witchcraft's Inner Sanctum", *True Magazine* (August 1959), 78.

Coven' collection and partly of items from the 'Hopkins' box which Gerald had acquired in the late 1930s. Case no. 5 is clearly the remainder of the 'Southern Coven' collection.

In the Second Room, Case no. 7 contained the Golden Dawn notebooks rescued by Doreen Valiente, as recounted in Chapter 27. She either gave, or more likely lent, them to Gerald to display.

Case no. 8 contained items used for divination and fortune telling. These had been accumulated from contemporary sources to make an attractive and interesting display.

Case no. 9 contained both illustrations of witchcraft taken from a variety of sources and some of the material which Gerald had found during his researches into the history of witchcraft on the Island.

Case no. 10 contained mostly historic books on witchcraft which Gerald had acquired over the years. I suspect that most of them he had never read and he merely collected them because their titles indicated some connection with witchcraft. They are mostly now in the Toronto collection.

Case no. 11 contained more of the charms left by Williamson, including a baby's caul, plus items from Gerald's own collection of weapons, notably an example of the Malayan keris majapahit. It also contained items of dowsing and radiesthesia equipment.

The Upper Gallery on the top floor of the old Granary, opened for the 1952 summer season. It had seven new cases.

Case 12 included magical objects from Africa and Tibet, probably including several of the items Gerald brought back from his visits to West Africa.

Case 13 contained material relating to Aleister Crowley, including the Charter which is referred to in Chapter 21, books and other items.

Case 14 contained details of the origin of the three-legged Arms of the Isle of Man and also some objects lent by another coven of witches. The implication, to my mind, is that the exhibits were from a coven which met on the Island (probably what Gerald by then was calling "the Northern Coven") and it therefore may be worth looking at the description of these items. To quote from the booklet: *This includes a horned helmet as used by the male leader in certain rites. Also two most interesting examples of the "Green Man" symbol, sometimes called the Foliate Mask."*

Case 15 contained various items which could loosely be described as being connected with "Black Magic", although it also contained the form of Aleister Crowley's funeral service and a chalice from a magical fraternity. The only items that might be considered to be "Black Magic" are what is described as a curse prepared by Austin Osman Spare and a magical lamp supposedly owned by Sir Francis Dashwood who founded the Hell-Fire Club in the 18th Century.

Case 16 contained modern charms and talismans; Case 17 had articles used by astrologers and alchemists and associated books; Case 18 contained miscellaneous books on the subject of magic and some magical articles.

It is a great pity that much of this material has now been dispersed, apart from Gerald's library and other papers which are in the Toronto and Ripleys collections.

⁂

As befits someone who taught himself to read, Gerald made full use of the skill he had acquired solely through his own effort and accumulated, during the course of his life, a large and interesting collection of books in his own house. It appears that they were not arranged alphabetically in neat bookcases but in haphazard piles, to judge from the descriptions given by Bracelin[3] and Teare[4] that I quote in Chapter 25. Lois Bourne writes: *Hundreds of books lay in untidy groups: books on magic, witchcraft, psychical research, secret societies, folklore, archaeology, weapons – a lifetime's collection.*[5]

I have had the good fortune to be able to look through the bulk of the books comprising Gerald's library, as they are now part of the Toronto collection. I know that this is not the full extent of his library, however. I suspect that when it was sold to Ripleys several people including the Wilsons had already removed some volumes from the sale, though I don't know how

3. Bracelin, 7.
4. Teare, 197.
5. Bourne, (1998), 32.

many. Also, Ripleys retained several volumes when they sold the library to the James' in Toronto. But that is where the bulk of Gerald's library is now located.

We are also fortunate in that Oakseer has prepared a list of the books in Gerald's library, the contents of which comes to over 700, which is available online.[6] He writes in his introduction: "To know a person's library is to know something special about a person". So, what can we learn from the contents of Gerald's library?

We get a good idea of the range of subject matter covered by looking at the quotations above. A lot of books, as one might expect, have 'witch' or 'witchcraft' or 'magic' in their titles. There are also plenty to do with psychic phenomena, spiritualism, ghosts, healing, radiesthesia and esoteric matters generally. Then there are books covering Ancient British history, myth and folklore. And books on religion generally, with an emphasis on the unorthodox.

There is, however, a category of book which I will describe as 'antique', anything published before about 1850 including some dating back to the 17th Century. These all have titles that have something to do with witchcraft or magic. Many are in French. It is these books that were on display in Case no. 10 at the museum. In other words, Gerald didn't refer to them regularly or, indeed, I am inclined to think, at all. Many have pages still uncut. I think Gerald acquired them, presumably from second-hand book dealers or auctions, because he felt that he needed to have them, as the Director of a Museum of Magic and Witchcraft. It is my opinion that Gerald never even looked at the vast majority of these books.

In the days before websites such as AbeBooks, Gerald went to considerable lengths to find the out-of-print books that he wanted. I am informed[7] that the playwright, Bernard Kops, who at the time was supporting himself with an outdoor secondhand book kiosk in London, was one of those who was given a list of "wanted" books by Gerald, who asked him to find as many as possible.

There are very few works of fiction in Gerald's library. Those that are there mostly belonged to Donna. He was, however, keen on poetry, particularly Algernon Charles Swinburne (1837-1909);

6. www.newwiccanchurch.org/gglibrary/index.htm.
7. Email from CK to the author, 20 December 2009.

Rudyard Kipling (1865-1936) and William Sharp (1855-1905), who wrote under the pseudonym of 'Fiona MacLeod'.

꙳

During his time as Director of the Museum of Magic and Witchcraft, Gerald was not just reading, acquiring exhibits and talking to a variety of people. He was also writing another book. *The Meaning of Witchcraft,* as the book was to be called, has always been somewhat in the shadow of its better-known predecessor, but it is a good book in its own right, and Gerald explores themes at a greater length than he could in the earlier book.

As in *Witchcraft Today,* the amount of material that he claims came directly from those who initiated him is severely limited, and the bulk of the book is compiled from the wealth of information that Gerald had been in the habit of collecting, albeit in a disorganised way, about the history of witchcraft. It was a long way from being academically rigorous (Gerald's mind didn't work in that way and in any case he had never had formal training in any particular discipline) but what it lacked in rigour it made up for in quantity. I suspect that there was a lot of material that, for one reason or another, did not go into *Witchcraft Today,* possibly because of the publisher's stipulation on length. And Gerald did have insights – quite a lot of them – and he was prepared to look at things from an unorthodox viewpoint.

The opening sentences of *The Meaning of Witchcraft* show the context in which it was written and something of what Gerald was trying to achieve:

> *My Directorship of the Museum of Magic and Witchcraft at Castletown, Isle of Man, brings me a great deal of correspondence from all parts of the world; some interesting, some abusive (a very little, just enough to enliven matters), some fantastic, and some funny in all senses of the word. However, my more serious correspondents want to know the origin of witchcraft.*[8]

---

8. Gardner, (1959), 9.

Whilst Gerald was away from the resources of the big London libraries for most of the year, his own personal library had grown greatly in the years since 1945 and he was 'in his element' at the Museum, talking to visitors, exchanging ideas with them and adding to his stock of knowledge, which was centred around what could loosely be called 'the history of witchcraft'.

Gerald had always had help in getting his books into a form suitable for publication, sometimes considerably more than that, and *The Meaning of Witchcraft* was no exception. It is quite clear, on reading the book, that the individual helping him on this occasion was Doreen Valiente, whom Gerald had initiated in 1953. She writes:

> *For some time Gerald and I had been collaborating on a new book to follow* Witchcraft Today. *We proposed to call it* The Meaning of Witchcraft. *The book did eventually appear under that title, in 1959. I suggested to Gerald that we should incorporate in the new book a detailed analysis and debunking of all this newspaper sensationalism, showing how flimsy and lacking in real evidence it was. He agreed to this, and throughout 1956 I worked hard investigating and writing. I like to think that this book opened people's eyes about reporters' methods of cooking up a good story out of very scanty ingredients – and also of the way in which anything which did not fit in with the story was suppressed. But, alas, by the time the book appeared, Gerald and I had ceased working together.*[9]

This almost suggests that the book was originally intended to have a joint authorship. If so, the idea was implicitly abandoned following the split between Gerald and Doreen which occurred in March 1957. It is clear that Doreen did far more than just correct Gerald's spelling and grammar. Indeed, I strongly suspect that she wrote, not only the three chapters entitled "Some Allegations Examined", but parts of at least two others. I have not carried out any literary analysis, but the style of writing and the ideas expressed in some of the chapters are very similar to her later

---

9. Valiente, (1989), 68-69.

writing. I am fairly certain, for example, that the clear and concise summary of Aleister Crowley's life and work which appears on pages 101 to 103 is by her.

The timing is interesting. If we assume that the writing and research for the new book started in late 1954, following the publication of *Witchcraft Today*, we have the likelihood of collaboration during 1955 and 1956. Most of the references to up-to-date material are from those years or before. However, following the split, we have a period when Gerald had to manage the completion of the book on his own.

I imagine that he probably submitted the manuscript to Riders, the publishers of *Witchcraft Today*, which had been moderately successful in publishing terms, and they could reasonably have been expected to be interested in the new book. It seems, however, that they turned it down. Perhaps they were not entirely happy with Gerald's credentials. Also, whilst originally he had taken on *Witchcraft Today* and got it into shape, Gerald Yorke was Riders' 'literary advisor' by 1958 and his opinion of *Witchcraft Today* was that it was "a thoroughly bad book"[10] so perhaps he was unwilling to take on another book by the same author.

As late as the spring of 1958, Gerald had still not found a publisher. We know this because he wrote an undated letter to a Mr. Sheppard enclosing a copy of the Museum guide book (which was only published in 1958) in which he comments: "Unfortunatly Holy Church has intervened & scared publishers from touching my new book." So clearly he only found a publisher following the publication of the museum guide. The letter also hints that he may have had several rejections from publishers, although this is more likely to be because of the quality of the manuscript rather than the influence of the Church!

Gerald had to look elsewhere for a publisher and there were not many in those days who would take esoteric books. One of the few that did was the Aquarian Press. This started publishing in the early 1950s, focusing on spiritualist books by such authors as Cyril Scott, Ursula Roberts, F.W.H. Myers and Geraldine Cummings. It published several of Dion Fortune's novels and non-fiction books, and expanded in the occult field with books by W.E. Butler and others.

---

10. Letter, Gerald Yorke to Cecil Williamson, 11 April 1958.

Gerald was familiar with the Aquarian Press because he had been in the habit of buying second-hand books from their anti-quarian branch, the Aquarian Book Service. Indeed, there are over 30 books in his library containing their label. It was worth an approach, so he sent them the manuscript. Aquarian decided to take the book on and presumably provided the usual copy editing services, which would include correcting the spelling and gram-matical errors. It is clear, however, when looking at the book, that despite this it has been left in a rather incomplete state. The chap-ter headings, such as "Magic Thinking (Continued)" and "Some Allegations Examined – Part III" suggest that consideration given to such matters was minimal. The number of appendices, most of which could have been incorporated into the main text, is another indication of the lack of a clear structure to the book.

The book contains four different categories of material which, unfortunately, are not that well integrated. Firstly, there is some quite revealing information on what the witches who initiated Gerald did, particularly in the field of magical working. Secondly, Gerald continues the task which he started in *Witchcraft Today* of trying to chronicle, or re-create, the history of witchcraft from Palaeolithic times onwards, using a wealth of references, and interpreting events in his own distinctive way. Thirdly there is the section which Doreen wrote in which allegations in various news-papers about the witch cult are examined. And lastly, there is a chapter on how the author sees the future.

The first chapter, entitled "The Witch Cult in Britain" is a powerful exposition of the main elements of the craft into which Gerald had been initiated, particularly focusing on the working of magic. He refers to his personal experience when he writes: *I found ... what it was that made so many of our ancestors dare imprisonment, torture and death rather than give up the worship of the Old Gods and the love of the old ways.*[11] He does not spell this out more precisely, but it is clearly something which moved him deeply, quite rare for Gerald, who tended to have more of a practical nature. He expands on the witches' belief that *"the power" resides within themselves and that their rites serve to bring*

---

11. Gardner, (1959), 11.

it out.[12] This, he says, is the reason for ritual nudity; and he states that alcohol, fire and incense can all generate power, quoting scientific research which seemed to demonstrate the existence of the human aura and the concentration of such energy in such points as the eyes, the palms of the hands and the sexual organs.

The two chapters entitled "Magic Thinking" continue this theme of looking at what the witches who initiated Gerald actually did. Magic, he says, is the art of getting results. He writes of sympathetic magic and means of focusing the mind, and comments that ... *magic is knowing that certain things have certain effects, and how to make use of these effects to render people more sensitive to certain other influences. Combining half a dozen or more such influences – say dancing, chanting, incense, etc. – has effects ...* [13]

Gerald used the book as an opportunity to expound on the various topics which had attracted his enthusiasm, weaving them in to the story of witchcraft from remote prehistoric times onwards. For example, there are several pages about Stonehenge. He had been in the habit of attending the Druid ceremonies there and correspondence with the archaeologist and writer, T.C. Lethbridge, had stimulated Gerald's thoughts about its significance. Druidry, mystery religion in Greece and Rome, Arthurian and Welsh legend also feature strongly. Much of this is a romanticisation of the facts, but Gerald is, whether consciously or not, creating the 'myth' of witchcraft history, for which objective truth is relegated in importance.

There is an interesting chapter on church carvings. Following the work of Lady Raglan and others, Gerald claims that many of the carvings in mediaeval churches are likely to be essentially pagan, such as the shiela-na-gig and green man. This is a popular, though controversial, theme now, but was comparatively unknown then.

Towards the end of the book are three chapters entitled "Some Allegations Examined, Parts I, II and III". These were probably written by Doreen Valiente in late 1956 or early 1957 as a single report, which seems to have been incorporated into the book by Gerald relatively unchanged, having been subdivided into

---

12. Op. cit., 18.
13. Op. cit., 103.

three chapters for reasons of length. These chapters focus on certain of the hostile press reports which appeared in daily and Sunday newspapers, in the 1951 to 1956 period.

Doreen was ideally suited to this task, not least because from 1951 she had been keeping a scrapbook into which she put newspaper cuttings not just about witchcraft but on a wide range of occult, esoteric and other topics which interested her. I think she must have asked neighbours to pass their old newspapers on to her, since there is a wide range of publications represented. It is a valuable archive and resource.[14]

Early articles in the 1951-1955 period tended to confuse witchcraft with Black Magic and voodoo. The first chapter successfully demonstrated that there were very few facts behind reporters' allegations and that their accusations had no basis. In response to the *Sunday Pictorial's* June 1955 articles, Doreen submitted a reply on Gerald's behalf to the paper, but they refused to print it. It subsequently appeared in *Psychic News* under the title "Witchcraft in Britain" and it is reproduced in *The Meaning of Witchcraft*. This, as far as I know, is the earliest published writing by Doreen Valiente.

Gerald gives as an appendix an account of articles that appeared in October and November 1957 in *The People*. It is not clear why this is included as an appendix, since the articles are also referred to as a 'stop press' item at the end of the final chapter, incongruous with the subject matter of the rest of that chapter and a double reference which really emphasises the lack of any effective editorial control of the book as a whole.

The last chapter in the book is entitled "The Future". The style of writing and the topics it focuses on suggest to me quite strongly that part of it is by Doreen Valiente. For one thing, it goes on at great length about the so-called Aquarian Age, which was one of Doreen's favourite themes. It is certainly more hopeful than Gerald was when he wrote *Witchcraft Today* ("I think we must say goodbye to the witch"[15]). The view expressed, and I am pretty sure it was written by Doreen, is that the "craft of the Wica" can make a contribution because it is part of the coming Age of Aquarius.

---

14. I am grateful to Rufus and Melissa Harrington for allowing me access to this valuable resource.
15. Gardner, (1954), 129.

So, what are we to make of *The Meaning of Witchcraft*? It is fair to say that it has not had the impact of *Witchcraft Today* either in terms of its message or in sales figures. The reason possibly is that it is not saying anything fundamentally new. *Witchcraft Today* claimed that "the witch cult" still survived and that Gerald was a member of it. In a sense, *The Meaning of Witchcraft* is just "more of the same". Yet Gerald does provide us with insights which still have value fifty years later; the book is worth reading, and not just for its historical interest.

⁂

Gerald was skilled at making things, both practical and ritual objects. I suspect that this probably started from necessity when he was a 'creeper' in Ceylon. They would be a long way from the nearest supply stores and it was easier and a good deal cheaper to make things himself if at all possible. Tools and parts for equipment would be ingeniously made from the simple raw materials which were all that Gerald had at his disposal. These were skills that he would need throughout his working life, crafting tools and other items in both wood and metal. Following his retirement, these skills would be a great asset to his roles in the Home Guard and as an A.R.P. warden, particularly in getting some of his historic firearms into a serviceable condition.

After his initiation, Gerald began to use his skills in making ritual objects. The characteristic wide bracelets, such as the one with which he played the prank on Sullivan, were probably one of the first things that he started to make. These are perhaps three inches wide and usually have the owner's witch name inscribed in the Theban alphabet. He made them, not just for initiates but for female family members.

We have already seen from the report of the Druid Stonehenge Ritual that Gerald had constructed an oak-leaf crown, and I have seen other crowns in private hands that are likely to have been made by Gerald.

Swords were a little beyond him. He had inherited the sword which was lent to the Druids, but for any other swords needed, he cultivated a friendly blacksmith on the Isle of Man.

Gerald's woodworking skills were much in evidence while the museum preparations were being made. The solid tables in the restaurant and the altars and bookstands in the museum displays were all made by Gerald, or at least made to his design.

He was often extremely generous to those about to be initiated and made or acquired their magical tools, presenting them to the initiate at their initiation.

Gerald also became very skilled at model-making, probably wielding some of his early knife collection in making model boats and suchlike for himself during his winters in Madeira. He had certainly acquired those skills by the early 1930s when he was trying to demonstrate to the officials in the Raffles Museum the reality of the Malay ocean-going vessels. And we have seen how Laird-Clowes gave Gerald a room at the Science Museum where he made a replica of this. Edith's grandson remembers how Gerald, when visiting her in the 1950s, made him a large model ship, probably a brig with 12 guns, which became a valuable possession which he kept on a shelf for years. He seems to have been able to sit down with a bit of wood and carve something like a boat out of it, a skill at improvisation in model making which is, I am sure, reflected in this passage from *High Magic's Aid:*

> *"Fetch me a twig and a leaf." The child scampered away, returning with a leafy branch which she had torn from a neighbouring bush. Olaf broke off a twig, fixed a leaf to it by spearing it on in two places and deftly fitted the twig into the chip with the point of his dagger. He then replaced it on the water, a little ship with sail and mast.*[16]

❧

Gerald was also an artist, both in pen-and-ink, watercolour and engraving. His favourite subject matter was naked female witches flying on broomsticks!

Patricia Crowther has three of Gerald's paintings, including one which was reproduced in her book, *Lid Off the Cauldron*[17] and titled 'Off to the Sabbat', showing the aforementioned naked

---

16. Gardner, (1949), 46.
17. Patricia Crowther, *Lid off the Cauldron*, (Frederick Muller, 1981).

female witch astride a broomstick and about to fly up a chimney. The time shown is midnight.

Gerald painted a picture of Margaret Ine Quane and her son about to be burnt alive for witchcraft in Castletown, Isle of Man in 1617. It is set with Castle Rushen in the background with towns-people looking on. This was featured in the museum as the centrepiece of a memorial to those who died in witch persecutions over the years. A reproduction of this picture appears in *The Meaning of Witchcraft*.

My friend, the late Mériém Clay-Egerton, knew Gerald as a great conversationalist. Often when they were discussing things in a cafe he could become very animated: "He didn't mind criticism, but would want to discuss it with you in detail". She felt that his artistic skills had been rather neglected and that they were actually an important though relatively private and "dark" side to his life. She told me that there was an exhibition of his paintings in the early 1960s in Nuneaton Museum, but I have so far failed to get confirmation of that. The Curator was apparently a close friend of Gerald's and, in fact, gave Mériém a job as an archaeologist after Gerald put in a good word for her.

One picture which has been reproduced many times over the years and which was made into a postcard on sale at the museum, shows the tower of the Witches' Mill on the night of the full moon, with the ubiquitous naked female witch on a broomstick coming in to land at the mill. In an open door in the mill is what looks like a naked male waiting to greet her and on the ground floor is a fire around which they are planning to dance.

Gerald was also something of a cartoonist. One, which may have been directed at Cecil Williamson, is the draft of a Christmas card, reading "Wishing you a Very Merry Xmas at the Witches Kitchen". It shows a torturer in his torture chamber unwrapping a present from his wife, who appears to be a witch carrying a broom. The present is an Iron Maiden, a box in the shape of a woman, with spikes inside. He is saying to his wife: "Darling – Just what I wanted".

Gerald also adapted another Christmas card which the Williamsons had had printed. This was a cartoon of a witch flying on a broomstick looking displeased as her fellow witches look out at her from the windows of an aircraft! Gerald redrew this and, in the process, made the witches in the aircraft naked, making the flying witch even more haggardly and adding in the bottom left-hand corner a little thumbnail sketch of the Witches' Mill and a caption which reads: "Going to the Witches Mill. Up to date Witches fly by B.E.A.[18] " together with his "witch mark" and initials.

Gerald's drawings, particularly of the female form, are competent and characteristic, and show an understanding of how the human body moves. I have recently seen photographs of a Venus pentacle which has a naked female figure engraved upon it which I am certain is by Gerald, whose work is distinctive.

Whether Gerald continued his brief enthusiasm for photography I doubt. We have seen how he had a dark-room constructed at Southridge in the late 1930s and may have taken photographs of naked women, including Donna, which he was in the habit of showing to members of the Folk-Lore Society and to Kenneth Grant. However, by the time of his trips abroad in the 1950s, the photographs which have survived are not of particularly good quality and suggest that he used a simple camera and normal commercial developing.

⁂

Apart from his books and articles, Gerald seemed to be developing a skill in writing humorous short stories in the latter years of his life. "The Truth About George" was published[19] the month before his death. It concerned a Gremlin who had been persecuting him for years. It shows Gerald's rather quirky humour and I would like to see it performed some time. It ends:

> *"When yer 'as a proper certificate from a Gremlin as 'as given yer 'ell good an' 'earty for 25 years, it clears yer from 'ell when yer dies, and lets yer inter Fiddler's Green, where yer can drink and dance and fight all day and night. Now I got work to do".*

---

18. British European Airways.
19. Gerald Gardner, "The Truth About George", *New Dimensions*, (January 1964).

The voice stopped. And the electric light went out and I searched for a torch and wires and mended the fuse. But for the first time I didn't say, "damn George, biting through the fuses again".

There is in existence[20] an 80-page typed manuscript by Gerald entitled "Saints and Sinners, a Fairy Story for Slightly Older Children". It appears to be a novel, based on legends associated with St. George and Anatolia re-told from a pagan perspective.

Gerald had started writing a history of witchcraft in the Isle of Man. The Toronto collection contains sections of chapters and clearly he had quite a lot of work still to do on the book when he died. But I believe there is enough material to put together something interesting.

And I have what I consider to be reliable evidence that Gerald kept diaries over several years, some of which are certainly still in existence. The current owner of one of them has made a commitment not to release the contents while certain people are still alive, but there is certainly hope for the future that an additional insight into Gerald's life and character may one day become available.

---

20. Ripleys' Collection.

CHAPTER THIRTY–TWO

To the North and West

Ever since the museum opened in July 1951, Gerald had taken a prominent part in the activities, performing, as we have seen, the role of "resident witch". He enjoyed talking to all manner of visitors, most of whom were keen to know more about witchcraft. Some visitors came more than once, looking carefully at the exhibits and reading all the captions. And some had things to tell Gerald: these he listened to with particular interest. Eventually, one of them approached Gerald and told him that there were already witches on the Island and invited him to meet some of them. At least, that is how it could have been. There have been persistent rumours that Gerald had made contact with at least one traditional coven and, if such a group existed, this is quite likely. The mists are very thick, however, and it is uncertain exactly what was going on, by whom and where.

One of the first to contact Gerald was a boarding-house owner from Douglas, possibly the same woman that Gerald persuaded to impersonate Edith Woodford-Grimes in the incident which I mentioned earlier. Details are shadowy (which is probably as it should be) but she was apparently the High Priestess of two different covens which performed rituals robed. Their general philosophy seemed to be older and has been characterised as "an eye for an eye and a tooth for a tooth", a description which could apply to various traditional groups. Someone who knew of her writes the following: *One of the main points that was impressed to me many times over was how "she kept her vows". ... she was one of the Priestesses who remained true to the Art, practiced with the coven and shunned those that sought fame and fortune through the publishing of "what little they knew".*[1]

Gerald is reputed to have become a member of one of these traditional groups, and also of one which was known as the Mill Coven, which used to meet, not surprisingly, at the Mill. It may also have met in Gerald's temple on the upper floor of the barn attached to his house in Malew Street and, reputedly, at a member's property up in the hills. As late as 1959, Gerald told Daniel Mannix: "We still have our own coven here on the island".[2]

One prominent member was Angus McLeod (1920-1996), who lived at Scarlett, south of Castletown. He had moved to the Island from Bolton, Lancashire, in 1949 and at one time ran a small zoo at Glen Helen. He became knowledgeable about the Viking culture of the island and, while he was landlord of the Central pub in Peel, he played an important part in organising a Viking festival in the town. He was an engineer by profession, but gave this up, rented a cottage and made a modest living as an artist.

There was, however, another side to him. He quickly made friends with Gerald Gardner and worked, presumably part-time, at the museum. He may actually have managed it for a while. He became a member of the coven which met at the Mill. He also seems to have been the landlord of a pub in Castletown, "round the corner from the George", probably the Union. The coven frequented one of the two after their meetings. They were certainly the nearest two pubs to the Mill.

When Gerald was drawing up a version of his will, he wanted to leave the museum to Angus, whom he trusted as a reliable person. However, Angus didn't want it, so Gerald did not pursue that line further. He did, however, present Angus with the Book of

---

1. Email to the author, 12 November 2008.
2. Daniel P. Mannix, "Witchcraft's Inner Sanctum", *True Magazine*, (August-September 1959).

Shadows that he used from the mid-1950s onwards. It is known by researchers as 'Text D' and is now in the Toronto collection.

There are other members of the Mill Coven who are still alive and it would not be right to identify them. However, I can mention another prominent younger member of the coven: James Davies. He was initiated by the aforementioned High Priestess in the presence of Gerald Gardner. In an article which he wrote in the 1980s he gives his impressions of Gerald:

> *Along with the Witchcraft Museum in Castletown, Gerald operated a restaurant and dance club. In my pre-pubescent years, a day in the country (as we towneys referred to any outing which took us beyond the boundaries of Douglas) was not quite complete without a visit to the Witches Mill. For family outings, Sunday school picnics et al, here was a great spot to stop for lunch, a cup of tea, and for a bob or two, the chance to wander through the museum with its big glass cases full of the strange and curious. Everything from invaluable and ancient magickal artifacts, to what seemed to be blatant carney type hoaxes was to be found at the top of those dusty wooden stairs. Crucifix with knife concealed inside, Old Mother Shipton's mummified finger, Aboriginal pointing bones, roots, oils, talismans – all on display to intrigue and entertain. The restaurant itself was a veritable museum, complete with gigantic elephant skulls and walls decorated with old and unusual weapons from his rather vast collection.*
>
> *If you were really lucky, you got to meet the Witch, himself.*
>
> *The first time that I met Gerald, I was about 12 years old. He was standing at the bottom of the stairs leading up to the museum holding a broomstick. Pretty Scary! I (very nervously) asked the most obvious and probably tedious question. "Do Witches really fly on broomsticks?" Gerald slowly looked down and eyeballed me. "no..., he monotoned, we ride them!" Then grinning from ear to ear, he cackled at his private little joke. At the time, of course, I didn't understand.*

They both seemed the same to me. I wanted so much to see a demonstration of this most peculiar man flying (or riding, as he preferred to call it) around the restaurant, but unquestionable fear left the request unasked.

In my early teens, as a regular at the Saturday night dance, I got to know this strange man in a different light. He was not the story book Witch, and in spite of his odd sense of humour, he had a very serious side. A few years later, when I had entered my apprenticeship into engineering and showed a talent and interest in making knives, (along with my very real interest in the Craft) he opened doors for me that would change my life.

Gerald Gardner was an enigma. He was not a messiah, he was not a genius, nor was he the charlatan that many have tried to make him out to be. Gerald Gardner was a Witch. He passed along much of that which had been passed along to him and more, with the help of others he was able to gather around him. In spite of what one may think of this peculiar old man with the faded tattoos, he was a milestone in the Craft.3

❧

Some time in the 1950s, Charles Clark (1930-2002) from Salt-coats in Ayrshire, Scotland, made contact with Gerald, possibly originally through reading the British edition of the magazine, *Fate*, which described itself as the "Journal of Fantastic Reality". *Fate* topics included parapsychology, vanished civilisations, witchcraft, ufology, prediction, healing, spiritism, healing and radiesthesia. The British edition was published in Douglas, Isle of Man, by one Henri Leopold Dor.

Anyway, the two soon met and Charles Clark was initiated during a visit to the Isle of Man, taking the Craft name 'Selrach' ('Charles' backwards). The date for this is uncertain, but it could have been as early as 1954. He told his initiate, Melissa Seims, that

3. Astrophel (James Davies), "Gerald Gardner and the Isle of Mann".

both Gerald and Donna were present during the ritual. This is interesting, as Donna has generally been considered not to have been involved in the Craft. I think what probably happened is that Gerald wanted Clark to be initiated but had no convenient Priestess to perform such a task. He had yet to make contact with or to establish a coven on the Island and neither Edith nor Doreen were available or willing to come up. So, I suspect that Gerald initiated Donna and elevated her to a degree where she could perform an initiation. She may have felt that she had little choice in the matter and tended to go along with whatever Gerald wanted. It may also be significant that her gravestone[4] includes a triangle above a pentagram: the symbol of the third degree.

Clark was enthusiastic about promoting the Craft, particularly in Scotland, and as a result Gerald appointed him almost as a secretary, passing him correspondence that he had received at the museum, occasionally over 100 letters a week. By 1960 there was a coven established of which Melissa Seims writes:

> *Charles had managed to involve several students from the Universities at Glasgow, as well as a nurse, a butcher, an artist, and a few other people. Edith H., a librarian and student at the Scottish College of Commerce at Pitt Street, Glasgow, became his High Priestess. On occasion, Gerald Gardner would come over from the Isle of Man to attend the meetings of the Scottish Wica, bringing with him magical items to give to the various members. At that time, you couldn't just order a wand or an athame online like you can nowadays, but fortunately, Gerald, and others, had the necessary tools and skills to make magical equipment."[5]*

Gerald attended a meeting of the coven at Saltcoats on 30th April 1960, presumably a May Eve ritual. That same year, he passed on to Clark a letter from a Mr and Mrs Campbell Wilson, living in Perth. Melissa Seims writes:

> *Mrs Monique Marie Mauricette Wilson (née Arnoux) was born in 1923, in Haiphong, Vietnam to French parents. She*

---

4. In Malew Church new graveyard, Castletown.
5. Melissa Seims, personal communication with the author.

met her husband, Campbell 'Scotty' Wilson, when he was an R.A.F. Flight Lieutenant stationed in Hong Kong following the War. They subsequently moved to Perth, and Campbell went to work for the local gas board. Charles considered it particularly efficacious to initiate a couple as the two halves of a magical partnership were already in place with the polarity already established. He quickly elevated Monique, making her a High Priestess by 1961. As is customary she took a Craft name, 'Olwen', chosen by Charles. Her husband became 'Loic'. Charles encouraged the Wilsons to set up their own Coven in Perth and furnished them with the various Craft tools that they needed.[6]

By 1961, there seems to have been active covens in Saltcoats, Glasgow and Perth. However, shortly after this there was some difference of opinion between Clark and the Wilsons over the suitability of a candidate for initiation. This seemed to affect him deeply because he withdrew from any subsequent active involvement with the Craft for the rest of his life, apart from teaching a few magical students.

The Wilsons travelled down to Five Acres at the beginning of June 1961 and met Jack Bracelin, Fred Lamond and Lois Pearson.[7]

Following Clark's withdrawal Gerald and Lois took on the difficult task of taking over some of his students in Glasgow and establishing a 'coven by correspondence' whereby they went up to Glasgow to initiate new members and then sent them rituals and other parts of the Book of Shadows by post.

Monique Wilson, who had met him through Charles Clark, approached Gerald about continuing her training directly with him. He either re-initiated her and/or elevated her to 2nd and 3rd degree, and she seemed to take over from Clark in helping Gerald with correspondence.

⁂

In the autumn of 1956, Gerald received a letter from his old friend, Arnold Crowther. Their friendship dated back almost

---

6. Ibid.
7. Letter, Jack Bracelin to Gerald Gardner, 9 June 1961.

twenty years and they had kept rather loose contact after the time when they both went to visit Aleister Crowley in 1947. Arnold had some exciting news: he had met a young and good-looking woman named Patricia Dawson and they had fallen in love. They had met in London during rehearsals for the summer season at the Pier Casino, Shanklin, in the Isle of Wight, where they were performing in the same show. One day, Arnold came upon Patricia reading *Witchcraft Today* by one Gerald Gardner. He exclaimed that he knew the author and proceeded to tell Patricia something about him.

In order to be near her, Arnold moved up to Patricia's home town of Sheffield and obtained work as a performer in and around that city. But because of illness and work commitments it would actually be over three years before Patricia actually met Gerald. They finally visited him on the Isle of Man in June 1960:

> *When we arrived the housekeeper told us that Dr Gardner was very ill and could see no one. 'Let them come up', called a voice from within. We ascended the stairs quietly and entered his bedroom. Gerald was propped up in bed with huge pillows. 'Come in, come in, grand to see you.' He held out his arms to us, beaming. I looked into a pair of mesmeric blue eyes and felt the warm grip of his hands in mine. 'Darling, do sit down.' His white hair stood up in defiance of brush or comb, a fact which I learned later. A small, goatee beard and a weatherbeaten skin completed the picture.*

> *He told Arnold and me that the housekeeper had wanted our address in order to postpone our visit, but he had pretended that he couldn't find it. I was rather worried at his condition, but he assured me that now Arnold had arrived he would soon recover. He told us that he had been very ill in a hospital in London some years before, when Arnold had visited him. He had laughed so much by the time the visit ended that he had felt a great deal better. Sure enough, two days later Gerald was up and pottering about the house.*[8]

---

8. Crowther, (1981), 27.

Patricia describes her initiation in some detail in her books, *Witch Blood*[9] and *One Witch's World*.[10] Gerald was to initiate her first and then she, under Gerald's direction, would initiate Arnold, as it must be done male to female and female to male:

> *The blindfold was whisked away and I blinked in the gentle glow of candlelight. My initiation into the Mysteries of the Goddess had just taken place. With sword held high, my Initiator stood before me, his tall, sun-tanned body and snow-white hair, reflecting the lambent flames. He looked the very epitome of the consecrated High Priest.*
>
> *That night, as the wind buffeted against the windows of the barn, and the only other sounds were the slow, plop-plop of the paraffin stoves, his considerable age lay lightly upon him. Gerald Gardner looked at me, a smile upon his lips and questions in his eyes. I guessed that he was wondering how the ceremony had affected me and if I would be strong enough to overcome the tests that initiation always brings. ... I smiled back at the High Priest and suddenly knew him very well, indeed. A spark of recognition ignited between us; I had known this soul in the distant past. It was the awakening of old memories, evoked by the ritual. ...*
>
> *After a short rest I was required to initiate Arnold into the Mysteries. ... When all had been accomplished, the three of us sat in the now cosy atmosphere of the Circle, passing round the Communal Horn Cup. Gerald talked to us about magic, and that night I learned many things.*[11]

Later that year, Gerald flew over to attend Arnold and Patricia's wedding, which took place in Sheffield on 9th November 1960. The night before, he performed a handfasting for the couple. This is a traditional witch ceremony, although not legally binding in England. The wedding attracted the attention of the press, as Patricia recalls:

---

9. Patricia Crowther, *Witch Blood*, (House of Collectibles, 1974), 35-44.
10. Patricia Crowther, *One Witch's World*, (Robert Hale, 1998), 20-21.
11. Ibid.

In the city centre, newspaper vendors' placards proclaimed, 'The Witches are to Wed', and Gerald was highly amused at all the attention we were receiving and enjoyed himself, hugely. After the ceremony, the press followed us to the Grand Hotel, where a celebratory luncheon had been planned but, before we were allowed to eat, flash bulbs continued to pop merrily as yet more pictures were taken.[12]

Patricia gives another intriguing fact:

There could have been two weddings in our family, and fairly close together, because Gerald Gardner proposed marriage to my mother. He hastily reassured her it would be a union of companionship and friendship only, but, although my mother regarded Gerald as a close friend and someone upon whom she could rely, she did not want to leave her home and the environment in which she lived. They would go off together for tea in town, and got on like a house on fire. I know that she was very concerned about hurting her friend's feelings, but she felt unable to make such a major change at that late stage in her life.[13]

In December 1961, the first member was initiated into the Sheffield coven, which has now been in operation for well over 45 years.

·❦·

The previous month, following the Crowthers' appearance on the Granada television programme 'People and Places', they received a letter from an Alex Sanders saying that he had always wanted to be a witch but had so far not been able to contact anyone. They invited him to their house and he visited on three occasions. He did not impress the Crowthers and they did not consider him suitable for initiation into the Craft.

Sanders later started his own branch of the Craft, which became known as Alexandrian and which actively recruited

12. Op. cit., 31-32.
13. Op. cit., 30-31.

members, including notably Janet and Stewart Farrar, whose books brought many into the Craft.

I do not think that Gerald Gardner and Alex Sanders ever met, but there was some communication between the two. Patricia Crowther writes:

> On 27 August 1963 Gerald Gardner, who used to say that he heard things on the 'jungle telegraph' received a curious letter from Sanders which he forwarded to me. In this letter, Sanders said that he was invited to visit a witch whom he had met at my house, to explain a misunderstanding concerning the person's supposed part in his recent publicity, and that after the matter was cleared up his visit was prolonged for several days. He then went on to say that during his stay he met a High Priestess from Derbyshire, called Medea, and asked her to initiate him. She apparently agreed, as Sanders then states that the rite was performed on 9 March 1963[14]

Gerald was similarly not enamoured of Sanders, as Patricia recounts:

> On reading Sanders' sensational press stories, Gerald was horrified and commented to me, 'He'd better not come here – I don't want to be mixed up in anything to do with him. Sanders had better watch out. If he shows up he'll get the "Order of the Boot"!'[15]

Patricia continues with a story which reveals quite a lot of detail about Gerald's physical characteristics:

> A story went the rounds at that time that Alex was going to introduce Gardner at one of his gatherings. Gerald heard about this and was highly amused, he said, 'Now, I wonder, is Sanders going to get someone with a white beard and introduce him as Gardner? Of course, the impostor would have to have both forearms tattooed, also a small dagger on his left upper arm and a pixie dancing on his left leg. My

---

14. Crowther, (1998), 67.
15. Op. cit., 68.

*right thumb has had a bullet through it, and I have only a
sort of claw instead of a nail on it. All this would have to be
copied to make for a good impostor; I don't think he will be
too happy about it!*[16]

The Gardnerian and Alexandrian Books of Shadows are
remarkably similar and it is clear that the Alexandrian book was
copied from the Gardnerian book. Patricia tells the story of how
Sanders acquired a copy of the Book of Shadows.[17] She and
Arnold had taken some friends over to the Isle of Man and had
visited two members of Gerald's coven there. However, a short
time later, one of the visitors returned to the island and asked the
coven member, whom Patricia calls 'Fian', whether he could borrow his Book of Shadows to copy. Unfortunately, Fian agreed, and
very soon Sanders had a copy for himself.

Patricia waited until Gerald was visiting Arnold and herself
before telling him, as she wanted to break the news to him gen-
tly: *Gerald said it was very bad – very bad indeed, but some people
did do beastly things. He commented that he would never have
believed such a thing of Fian; it was totally out of character. I
agreed with that. Our friend looked very frail so we made light of
the matter and turned the conversation to happier things, but quite
suddenly Gerald's eyes gleamed fiercely and he barked, 'You know,
if I had caught that blackguard with the book, I would have let him
have both barrels of one of my guns!*[18]

※

In 1962, an Englishman, Raymond Buckland, had emigrated
to the U.S.A., settling in Bay Shore, Long Island, NY. While he was
still in England he had started corresponding with Gerald, receiving by post the typed "correspondence course" which by then had
been put in place. Things culminated in 1963 with his request to
be initiated and Gerald arranged for Buckland to spend 10 days on
an intensive course with Monique Wilson in Perth, at the end of
which he would be initiated, presumably to at least 2nd degree,

16. Ibid.
17. Op. cit., 68-71.
18. Ibid.

so that he could go home, initiate his wife, Rosemary, and start a coven. The visit is said to have started, but more likely probably finished, on 21st November 1963. The date may have been changed at Gerald's request because he wanted to meet Buckland when he visited the Wilsons prior to a visit to the Crowthers in Sheffield before setting out on what turned out to be his final voyage. Buckland took part in a ritual with the Wilsons and Gerald, who made quite an impression on him:

> *At our one-time meeting I found him truly delightful, with a wicked sense of humor ... He was also very sharp and very knowledgable on all things to do with religio-magic. I was especially struck by the strength of his voice in ritual; in contrast to his normal speaking voice.*[19]

He told me that Gerald was very keen to get the Craft started in America and pushed him to get it going. In this, he succeeded beyond Gerald's wildest expectations and the vast majority of witches in America can trace their origin, directly or indirectly, back to Raymond and Rosemary Buckland.

---

19. Email, Raymond Buckland to the author, 10 January 2008.

CHAPTER THIRTY–THREE

A Spy in the Camp

It was in 1958 that a new challenge to Gerald's credibility was launched, this time not by a newspaper, but by a self-styled consultant psychologist by the name of Charles Cardell. His influence on the Craft, though destructive, was of such a nature and so intertwined with that of Gerald Gardner, that it deserves a chapter to itself.

It is a well-known technique of newspaper reporters and sub-editors to make, as the saying goes, 'a virtue out of a necessity'. When they have failed in their task of finding information about a story they were investigating, how often do the headlines contain words like 'riddle', 'mystery' and even 'enigma'? I am tempted to use such terms when writing about Charles and Mary Cardell. Without them, this book would have been much more difficult to write, since they were partly the reason that the previous biography, *Gerald Gardner Witch*, was written.

Like many characters in our story, they are reputed to have changed their names: this always makes investigation more difficult, but when Charles, on one occasion in court was asked his age, replied "As far as I know I am 74", and since, six years earlier, he had given his age as 72, we realise that we have problems, but of a different sort to those of 'Com' and Dorothy Clutterbuck both wanting to appear younger out of vanity. With Cardell, he appears to be either wanting to appear older than his real age or to be genuinely unsure. Charles' original surname is said to have been Maynard and Mary's to have been Edwards. They are both reputed to have changed their names by deed poll to Cardell. Their early lives are still wreathed in mystery and I have so far failed to identify their Birth Records.

Following the publication of *Witchcraft Today* in 1954 and the subsequent series of newspaper articles about Gerald and the Bricket Wood coven, Cardell seems to have approached Gerald, probably in early 1958, wanting to buy his museum and move it to London, where he would find a suitable building for it: he had the idea of buying a cinema and fitting it up as a museum. This seems to have been a common ploy of Cardell, as he used it unsuccessfully against a national organisation devoted to psychic studies which he wanted to take over.

Gerald, despite being very ill at the time, was not interested and refused to sell the museum to him. However, Cardell persisted as well as making other claims: *One optimist tried to find out the secrets of the witch-cult in an original way from witches initiated by Gardner. The whole rituals were, he said, already known to him. They had actually been published in a book; and it was from this book that Gardner had copied them. Gardner, however, it was claimed, only had a part of the book. The rest (or a complete copy) was with the claimant.*

The story became rather too confused when it was being asserted by the same man that (1) the rituals were forged; (2) they were real. Then he demanded to see the witches' rituals for "purposes of comparison".[1]

It has been suggested that Gerald did pass Cardell the Book of Shadows to copy but I think this is unlikely as the following year Cardell made considerable efforts, with the help of Olive Greene, to obtain one.

Cardell also claimed to have inherited some witch-relics, but when Gerald examined these he discovered that they were "of the

1. Bracelin, 178.

theatrical kind, and had neither intrinsic value nor witchcraft associations."[2] He also claimed to have been a practising psychologist since the 1920s.

Charles and Mary Cardell first came to public notice in July 1958 with an article entitled "The Craft of the Wiccens" in the quarterly journal *Light*. This had a venerable history, having been founded in 1881. It is still published today by the College of Psychic Studies, as a 'Review of Spiritual and Psychic Knowledge'. It had, however, been almost defunct in the mid 1950s, but was taken on and revived by Francis Clive-Ross of Aquarian Press. Cardell said subsequently that he had written the article specifically to attract the attention of Gerald Gardner. Alongside the article was a full-page advertisement from Cardell inviting genuine members of the Craft to get in touch with him. What other contacts he made as a result I have no way of knowing, but Jack, Dayonis and Fred responded immediately and, in return, Cardell invited them to his luxury flat at 63 Queen's Gate, South Kensington. He appeared to be very affluent.

Dayonis remembers that to start with they were taken into the room where he had his ceremonies. She says: " ... it was the deadest room I've ever entered, as dead as a doornail, and it was obvious that nothing of significance had been going on there."[3] She was also unimpressed with a golden goddess statuette which he showed them. He gave them a very nice meal and then sat down to talk to them. He played them a tape recording of himself purportedly talking to the editor of the *Sunday Pictorial* referring to Jack, Dayonis and Fred and pleading with him: "Please leave these nice young people alone. They've had a big shock. Please leave them alone". This was following a raid on Five Acres in October 1958, to which we will return shortly. Cardell then said to them: "This is what happens when you get yourselves involved with a fraud like Gerald Gardner, who knows absolutely nothing. I'm the real McCoy. I have a good deal of magical knowledge. Why don't you join me? My group is really secret, so you wouldn't be bothered by the press in the future".

---

2. Op. cit.. 194.
3. Dayonis, discussion with the author, February 2006.

After they had been sitting down for some time, Dayonis remembers that she heard "a terrible humming whining noise" and it was obvious to her that they were being recorded, so they just started speaking nonsense.[4]

Fred Lamond summed up their conclusions: "... *we didn't like the man: he was a creep"*.[5] He added: ... *he didn't inspire us with any confidence, and we weren't going to join a man who had instigated this mess, nor abandon Gerald for whom we all had a great deal of affection for all his faults.*[6] Dayonis' conclusion about Cardell was that: ... *he was a rogue, and we really didn't trust him as far as we could throw him.*

Doreen Valiente and Ned Grove also read the article and responded to the request for genuine members of the Craft to get in touch with Cardell. Probably in early July 1958, they both, independently, met him and had long talks with him. At first they were open-minded about him and Ned was convinced that he was genuine. Cardell tried to recruit them, but, as they found out more about him, they became disillusioned, particularly when he suggested that they pool their respective traditions. This was clearly what Cardell wanted: the "secrets of the Craft". Whether his own tradition of the 'Wiccens' was genuine or just something he and his acquaintances had made up is probably irrelevant for the current purposes, but in the end he failed to get anything out of either Doreen or Edith, who sent a typically circumspect reply to Cardell, which in part read:

> *I have come to the conclusion that no useful purpose could be served by our meeting either at my home or in London; furthermore, dissention is maintained at such a pitch throughout certain circles that I have no wish to be party to it.*[7]

In a letter to Doreen, Edith was almost as guarded, though she says: ... *all this dissention makes me very sad: serious study in occult matters should give great happiness ...*[8] She was, however,

---

4. Ibid.
5. Frederic Lamond, discussion with the author, July 2006.
6. Lamond (2004), 36.
7. Letter, Edith Woodford-Grimes to Charles Cardell, 26 July 1958.
8. Letter, Edith Woodford-Grimes to Doreen Valiente, 25 July 1958.

subtly critical of Cardell: *From what I gather from Mr. Cardell's articles in "Light" if you join forces with him you may have to scrap some of your beliefs but that is as it should be and the great thing is that you can be happy in the company of your friends, learn something and help others: in passing, I may say that I think on the whole that has always been Gerald's idea.*9

⚜

Interest by the Press intensified when on Monday 27th October 1958, the influential BBC television programme, *Panorama*, hosted by Richard Dimbleby, featured interviews with Gerald Gardner and a female witch, although the latter was in shadow and veiled and identified only by her witch name, Tanith.

Earlier in 1958 there had been a radio broadcast. I am uncertain as to who was being interviewed on that occasion, but it included someone whose witch name was 'Tanith'. I understand that 'Tanith' was Lois Pearson's witch name. Her voice was thought by the BBC to be particularly good and when the possibility of a television broadcast to coincide with Halloween was being discussed, it was suggested that she should appear. However, she would only agree to this if her face did not appear and if she would not have to meet any press reporters.

There was some advance publicity in the morning papers. One piece by Leslie Watkins was headed "Two witches will confess" and described Gerald as "no stranger to viewers". It referred to 'Tanith' as "a mystery woman" and added "Even the BBC don't know who she is. Producer Christopher Burstell told me: 'It was the only condition under which she would appear'."

So, on the Monday before Halloween 1958, Gerald and 'Tanith' arrived at the television centre. They were first taken to a private dining room for a buffet supper, 'Tanith' was then shrouded in a thick silk veil and they entered the 'Panorama' studio.

The total length of the item was little more than four minutes and it was really in the nature of a semi-humorous piece to mark Halloween.

9, Ibid.

The interviewer was John Freeman, best known for his series of revealing interviews, 'Face to Face' and for his aggressive interviewing technique. He was later to become British Ambassador to the USA. His questions to Gerald were along the lines of whether a witch was an ugly old woman on a broomstick, whether witches performed the black mass and why they were naked in their rituals. Gerald's answers were good concise responses to such questions, but he had brought along various magical tools and, in response to a question about what happens in witch rituals, he tried to demonstrate with the sword and athame. Unfortunately, the camera operator seemed not to be aware that this was going to happen and was thus slow to respond with the new camera angle that was needed. Valuable time was lost in what can best be described as a shambles.

'Tanith' was so heavily veiled and in shadow that she was effectively camouflaged. She spoke about her witch ancestry and the benefits that being a witch provided. It sounded as if, underneath her veil, she was reading from a prepared script.

The item ended with John Freeman commenting: "Broomsticks are ready at the door"!

Gerald's conclusion after the programme was that it had been cut short, that 'Tanith' had not been given enough time, and that very little was shown of the witch tools. He had received comments that the handling of the item had been odd and bitty. The explanation is probably that it was a fill-in piece seen as being fairly light-hearted and that if any of the other items on the programme over-ran, it could be cut short, which seems to have been what happened. Television programmes tended to be a lot more amateurish in those days, anyway, certainly in England!

There was much excitement after the programme, however. Gerald was taken to a room where he was bombarded with questions from the press, particularly about 'Tanith', for three-quarters of an hour. When the press conference ended, they all crowded around the car that had come for Gerald, hoping to get a glimpse of 'Tanith'. However, Jack had his van ready inside the building and was able to slip out with 'Tanith' without being observed.[10]

---

10. Bracelin, 209.

In contrast, a few days later, and probably as a direct result of the *Panorama* interview, there was a very positive piece in the *Daily Mail* in a regular column, The Robert Muller Interview. Entitled 'The private life of a witch', it is a serious and measured account of an interview with Dayonis. Her statements give quite a vivid picture of the Craft, or rather the one coven which we know existed, in 1958. To quote extracts:

> "I am a witch ... an initiate into witchcraft. I worship a god and goddess who are the male and female principals of Life. ... Witchcraft is a religion. I believe in reincarnation, and I hope when I die I will be reborn as a witch. It will be like a home-coming. I have to keep our activities secret because we witches are persecuted. If my acquaintances knew I were a witch they wouldn't come near me. I would lose my job. My employer would think that he'd been made a fool of. I have one of the best jobs in the locality and I don't want to lose it. I don't cast spells in the old-fashioned sense. ... But I do generate a power, a Life Force, and can channel it to a specific purpose. I can heal sick persons, I can influence people. To some extent I can make wishes come true. If I want something desperately enough I know I can make it happen.

> ... It is true that we work in the nude. We meet once a month, and as high priestess I draw a circle and consecrate it. Then I bring the other witches into this circle. We worship our god and goddess. ... Towards the end of the ceremony we have a symbolic feast. Cake and wine. But there is no trans-substantiation. Just jolly good food.

> The atmosphere is one of friendliness. We use incense. There is a sort of agenda. We ask if anybody has anything they want done. We talk it over and decide the best way to do it. Then we do it.

> ... Mine is a beautiful religion. I have a habit of talking to the god and goddess in bed. No other religion could satisfy me. It means Belonging. Being a witch has helped me

tremendously, it has made me grow up, and I wouldn't change my life for the world. I am content to be a witch until the end of my days."[11]

A much less sympathetic approach to the Craft was, however, just around the corner. Throughout 1958, the sensationalist Press were building up to a big 'exposure', which came at the beginning of 1959. They had a lot of clues to go on. Names and addresses of the shareholders of Ancient Crafts Ltd. could be obtained from Companies House.

At some stage, probably in late 1958, it seems likely that a national newspaper, the *Sunday Chronicle*, was contacted with information about the Craft, the coven members and their rituals. It was strongly suspected that it was Cardell who gave them the information, suggesting that Gerald was a fraud who had invented a non-existent witchcraft cult to get some publicity. The paper was keen to do some sort of exposé of the coven and, probably on the night of Halloween 1958, the next ritual date according to the Book of Shadows which they had somehow got to see, a reporter and photographer climbed over the gates of Five Acres Club and, in the dark, managed to find the Witches' Cottage. However, it was deserted and it was clear that nothing was happening. This was unsurprising as the coven had probably performed their ritual the previous Saturday, as was their custom. Fred Lamond recounts what happened next:

The reporter and photographer now visited Gerald in his Holland Park flat and bullying accused him of deceiving the public in his interviews by claiming to have a coven with members that didn't exist. To defend himself Gerald weakly named a few coven members, including our anaesthetist member. After they had left, Gerald realised he had broken his oath of secrecy, had a severe attack of asthma and fled to Jersey, leaving Jack to clear up the mess.

Jack immediately instructed all coven members to refuse to talk to the reporters, thereby refusing them the corroboration they required. But the reporters inveigled one of our

---

11. Robert Muller, "The Private Life of a Witch", *Daily Mail*, 3 November 1958.

woman members into talking, saying it would be better for her if they printed just what she had told them instead of them engaging in more lurid speculations. They now had the corroboration of Gerald's names that they needed.[12]

The coven discussed the matter urgently. Some members' careers would be seriously vulnerable if it became known that they were witches, particularly the anaesthetist. It was decided to take a bold step and offer a story to a rival Sunday paper in the hope that the original story would thus become "old news". Jack asked members of the coven who felt invulnerable: he put himself forward. Dayonis and Fred came forward, as did Lois Pearson.

Jack approached a rival Sunday newspaper, *The People*, the very one which had published hostile articles in the past. So, only a few days into the New Year, Peter Bishop, a reporter with *The People*, approached Dayonis outside the Witches' Cottage, almost certainly by prior arrangement, and challenged her to admit that she was a witch. This she did, and gave some sensible replies to his questions. However, she did express to him her concern that she would lose her job if her identity as a witch became known.

A few days later an article appeared in the next issue of *The People*.[13] It gave Dayonis' name and identified her as the private secretary to the managing director of a local firm. The article also identified Jack Bracelin, Fred Lamond and Lois Pearson by name and giving addresses. The article was as biased against the witches as earlier articles in that newspaper. It refers to the Craft as "a repulsive sect" and calls the witches' beliefs "disgraceful rubbish" and insisted on putting such titles as "high priestess", "high priest" and "witch maiden" in inverted commas. The article states "... they dare to call their heathen cult "religion". And they have had the effrontery to register their temple as a place of worship." The article was accompanied by a photograph of Jack and Dayonis, and of the Witches' Cottage. It also included another photograph from their archive of the ritual at the Avoca Hotel.

The story was obviously taken up by the daily papers the following day. The *Daily Sketch* reporter could not find Dayonis or

---

12. Lamond, (2004), 35.
13. Peter Bishop, 'Now I will Lose my Job' says Girl who Revels in Nude Rites", *The People*, 11 January 1959.

Lois, so naturally the headline read: "Girl-Witches in Pagan Cult go into Hiding"! Their reporter did manage to speak to Jack Bracelin, however, who, if accurately reported, said:

> *They meet once a month to worship the god and goddess of fertility. They dance and chant in the nude round an altar and burn incense before pairing off. ... We follow a pagan rite which existed in Britain before Christianity. The sex act is part of the rite – but it doesn't take place in public. We have no super-natural power, but we worship the life force. That is why we wear no clothes so as to bring out all possible power from our bodies.*[14]

With regard to membership, Jack is reported to have said:

> *Many people try to join our coven. Only two have succeeded in the last two years. We don't admit married people singly – but we do allow married couples. We have two such couples. If we admitted married men and women singly we could foresee difficulties – perhaps in the divorce courts. Then all our secrets would come out.*[15]

This must have been a slight distortion of the truth, since under those rules Gerald himself would have been excluded!

The result of the publication of these two articles was that the revelations which the *Sunday Chronicle* were planning became 'used goods', in Lamond's phrase, and the article was abandoned.

Dayonis' fear of losing her job very quickly came to pass: there were no anti-discrimination laws in those days! She recalls that one day following *The People* report, she was tracked down at work by the newspaper reporters:

> *... one evening I was hounded by the press, and I couldn't leave until I'd got hold of Jack to come and pick me up, because I wasn't going to go out there and have people trying to talk to me or flash bulbs or anything like that, so I never did. But it was quite terrifying, the end of that job, and it was a nice one!*[16]

---

14. Daily Sketch, 12 January 1959.
15. Ibid.
16. Dayonis, discussion with the author, February 2006.

I think Gerald felt responsible for Dayonis being out of a job and he arranged for her both to live at Five Acres, in the hut adjacent to the Witches' Cottage, and to be employed as book-keeper there. She said to me:

> .. *I'd been doing all the books before and I had been doing all the typing ... for people who wanted to come in and be members of Five Acres. I had been doing that, so I just stayed up there. I never took any money: I was just kept. Whatever food was bought for afternoon teas, there was always a bit more bought for me.*[17]

⁂

By the end of 1958, Cardell realised that he had failed to find anyone to tell him the secrets of the Craft, and he therefore needed to find some other way of finding out about the coven. It seems most likely that he did this by finding someone to infiltrate and to 'tell all'.

The infiltrator was one Olive Greene (born Olwen Armstrong Maddocks in Cumberland in 1919), who at the time was the wife of Edward R. Greene, the chairman of the Brazilian Chamber of Commerce in Britain. She had written an article about the Peacock Angel in *Light* under the name of Olwen Armstrong.

There are different versions of the events, and one must ask whether Cardell sent Olive Greene to try to infiltrate the coven or whether she approached him after having been initiated and become disillusioned. The publication, *Witch*[18] strongly implies the second. The story that Cardell gives in the introductory section, which went by the somewhat grandiose title of "Rex Nemorensis Draws His Sword", was that Olive Greene (who is not named in the book, merely going by her witch name, Florannis) came to see him in 1957 after having been initiated as a witch by Gerald Gardner. Cardell goes on:

> *When the true facts of what witchcraft really was, with its beastliness, superstition, and sheer downright roguery, became clear to her it was a terrible shock, as it would be to*

---

17. Ibid.
18. Rex Nemorensis (Charles Cardell), *Witch*, (Dumblecott Magick Productions, 1964).

any girl of a sensitive nature. Yet the oaths she had sworn,
and the threats of spells and curses to be put upon her should
she divulge the secrets to outsiders, prevented her from leav-
ing. Her suffering was intense, and at last led to a complete
breakdown for which she dared not tell the reason.[19]

Cardell than claims that she made contact with him and that:
It required two years of psychological effort on our part for this
young girl [in 1957 Olive Greene was 38 years old] *to again arrive*
at a degree of emotional normality and physical health[20]

This story is at variance both with the known dates for Olive
Greene's contact with Gerald and the coven (early 1959) and with a
mysterious letter written by Cardell to Olive, as if he had never met
her. This is in the Toronto collection and is dated 11th May 1959, i.e.
two years later than Cardell claimed, in *Witch*, to have first met
her. Starting characteristically "Dear lady", it runs, in part: "I should
indeed be very happy to meet you and discuss the things we seem
to have as a common interest." This wording strongly implies that
it was written in response to an initial approach from Olive and
that the two had not yet met. How the letter came to be in Gerald's
possession is a mystery: presumably either Olive or Cardell passed
it to him in order to demonstrate that she was not a 'spy' sent by
Cardell to infiltrate the Craft. But was it genuine?

There were rumours, as early as March 1959 that one of Gerald's new pupils was a spy acting for Cardell. If this is true, it
means that at least as early as February 1959, Olive Greene (for it
could be no-one else) was already committed to supplying
Cardell with the information which eventually appeared in
Witch. If this is the case, then the 11th May 1959 letter cannot be
what it seems and was a deliberate fake designed to fool Gerald
into thinking that Olive and Cardell were not already in contact.

Fred Lamond confirms this when he writes: *He* [Cardell]
induced one of his patients, an unstable woman called Olive Green,
to write to Gerald and ask him to train her.[21] Dayonis adds to this
when she says that Olive was specifically sent to seduce Gerald.

---

19. Op. cit., 3.
20. Op. cit., 3-4.
21. Lamond, (2004), 35.

And we have Olive's own account, "Florannis Speaks", which was published by Cardell in *Witch* after Gerald's death.

It was probably in late 1958 or, more likely, very early 1959 that Olive Greene wrote to Gerald, probably c/o his publishers or via the Museum, and received a letter from him in reply asking her to visit him in his flat at 266 Elgin Avenue, into which he had moved in 1958.

Olive gives a detailed description of her first visit, which was probably in February 1959, for Fred Lamond says: "After six months she terminated the training"[22] and we know that happened in August of that year.

> *When first I met Gerald Brosseau Gardner he was a very sick man, sitting propped up in bed in his North London flat. His bedroom was a strange hotchpotch of study, workshop and sick-room. On a carpenter's bench lay half finished models of ancient galleons, and strange weapons, which I later learned he was in the process of making for his "Witchcraft". Piles of dusty old books spilled out of open bookcases, and overflowed onto tables, chairs and the floor, mixing in confusion with countless bottles of medicines and pills, and all the sick-room paraphernalia of a not very fastidious old man. Oil paintings of voluptuous, nude witches, coyly riding broomsticks, hung over his bed. These pictures he had painted himself."[23]*

And, in contradiction of the tale told in the introduction to the book, she also admits that the 'spy' story is the correct one: *In my role of investigator it was my task to achieve initiation into a Coven, and become the High Priestess.*[24]

Her description of Gerald, "huddled in innumerable grey shawls", is vivid:

> *Rheumy eyes blinked at me out of a waxy emaciated face. His hair stood on end in long tufts of grey thistledown, and above an uncombed goatee beard his lips twitched in a strange, nervous smacking sound, like some gourmet*

---

22. Ibid.
23. Rex Nemorensis, 44.
24. Ibid.

tasting a new gastronomical delight. Here was no picture of power and evil, but just a rather querulous invalid.[25]

She continues:

He welcomed me courteously and with obvious pleasure. His grotesquely long fingers, gnarled and talon-like with black rimmed nails, grasped my hand, and held it for just that fraction longer than politeness demanded. We were left alone together, and I found him quite eager to be drawn out about his work. Our conversation consisted of my flattering him on his writings and knowledge of witchcraft, and he on his part paying me rather arch compliments. It did not take very long before I was obviously accepted as a most promising candidate for Initiation.

I invented a grandmother whom, on rather thin evidence, I thought might have been a witch. I had been warned before that he always liked his priestesses to have come from "a long line of witches". Also on previous advice I let it be known I was interested in nudism. From this moment we never looked back! Gardner became very garrulous on the subject of Nudist Clubs, and all his past adventures whilst visiting them. He obviously enjoyed his reminiscences. It was not long before he wove into the conversation the information that in "The Craft", as he called it, it was sometimes necessary to remove one's clothes. He carefully watched my re-action to this statement.[26]

The conversation clearly ranged widely, covering, according to Olive, Black Magic, the "Hell Fire Club", Aleister Crowley and flagellation.

Before she left, Gerald told her that he would have to get the approval of the coven, and so it was arranged that Gerald would take her to Bricket Wood to meet them.

This meeting is told in another account, in *Gerald Gardner Witch*, which was written shortly after Olive's repudiation of the

25. Ibid.
26. Op.cit., 44-45.

Craft. It was written with hindsight and Lois Bourne[27] mentions that certain salient facts about Olive's activities were deliberately altered. However, it is worth quoting:

> *One woman, trying very hard to appear "well-connected", "superior" and all the rest, gave the witches one of their best jokes for years. She wrote several times, saying how interested she was, as the descendant of a witch, to hear that the faith survived. She wanted to join, had to join. Could she not just be taken in, even on probation? Now, Gardner and most other witches are convinced that they can often tell by intuitive methods whether a candidate is sincere or not, if there is any doubt. In this case Gardner and I [i.e. Jack Bracelin] both thought that there were indications that this was some kind of stunt. We had not had a joke for some time. We would invite her and see what we would see ...*
>
> *She came to a hut, which had been carefully prepared to give the impression of disorder, a certain amount of dirt and no mean affluim [sic] of cats. The senior coven-member slouched in, looking rather less respectable than this obviously dainty person would be expected to welcome. She was all smiles, gushing, a little too guileless. Speaking of the unique experience it was for her, she begged to be allowed to be initiated.*
>
> *Her preoccupation with her supposed social prominence was more than enough to overcome any qualms that we might have felt as [at] the practical joke which we were about to play upon her. In any case, her pretensions were in bad taste, and probably were connected with an inferiority-feeling. Before long we found through our own sources that she had been sent by someone who wanted a spy in the camp: a would-be witch-leader who wanted the secrets of the Craft in order to set himself up as some sort of witch-king. She certainly knew how to turn on a kind of bourgeois charm, but its insincerity and superficiality were almost painful.*

---

27. Bourne, (1998), 29.

Her story, quite apart from her undercurrent of unease, was, as Gardner said, "rather too slick". She wanted to have what she called a private initiation. If she could have this, she would bring all sorts of important and well-connected people into the Craft. ... word had come back from another direction that she had been sent by someone who was anxious to get the secrets of the Craft in order to encompass its downfall in some way. So [s]he had her "initiation", and was able to take all the alleged secrets back to her employer. It was not until much later that he found out that she knew - precisely nothing.[28]

This account is clearly somewhat unreal in that it implies that everyone, including Gerald, knew, right from the start, that Olive was not to be trusted and that no true secrets of the Craft were therefore passed to her. It is clear that neither assumption is correct.

Lois Bourne describes her as "somewhat oleaginous" (a memorable word!) and Olive equally found disfavour with the rest of the coven, who did not like her and would not have her as a member.

But Gerald, as was her intention, seems to have become infatuated with her, for the next time she visited him, he told her: "I will rush you through the three grades of Initiation as quickly as possible".[29] The reason, apparently, that he gave to her for this was that he always spent the summer season at his museum on the Isle of Man and that he wanted to make her a High Priestess before he went. It is perhaps typical of Gerald, as "an old man in a hurry", to use Fred Lamond's description, that he was looking ahead with regard to Olive, who wrote:

Gerald was very anxious to know what plans I had for the future, when I was a fully fledged High Priestess. He wanted to know where I planned to start a new coven, and asked if I had any influential friends who would be interested in the Craft ... Already he started to plan coming to my new coven and lecturing the members, and encouraging them to start new covens themselves.[30]

28. Bracelin, 195-196.
29. Rex Nemorensis, 46.
30. Op. cit., 47.

Whilst in many ways it is intended to be hostile to Gerald, Olive's account of her initiation is very well observed and revealing of Gerald's environment and way of working. I therefore think it is worth quoting at length:

> *... Gerald opened the door to me himself. The whole flat reeked of incense, thin wreaths of smoke curling from under the drawing-room door. Gerald was very excited, and danced about like a small boy on Guy Fawkes' Night. He disappeared for what he called "finishing touches", and left me alone to prepare for the ordeal.*

> *It was a strange sight which greeted me when I entered the drawing-room. All the furniture had been pushed against the walls, and there was Gerald, specially scrubbed and talcum powdered for the occasion, standing in the middle of the room beside a small table, which had been arranged as an altar. On this altar lay a confusion of dishes, flasks, weapons and a carved figure with horns. Propped on a book-rest in the middle of it all was an ancient volume with tattered pages. Gerald had already told me about this book, and said that it contained all his secrets. Under the altar was placed a long sword.*

> *A circle was roughly marked out with blue silk cord, but it was a very haphazard affair. Gerald was obviously rather short of cord, and he had filled in the gaps round the circumference with political books with titles such as; "The Left is Never Right", and "The Party Never Runs Away".* [These were probably The Left Was Never Right by Quintin Hogg (Faber 1945) and The Party That Runs Away. A Floating Voter Sums Up the Socialists by Cedric Garth (Hutchinson 1940). These titles have been used by some writers, such as Ronald Hutton, to indicate Gerald's political affiliation, though it is perhaps significant that they do not appear in the collection of Gerald's books that was later purchased by Ripleys. They may have belonged to the owner of the flat at 266 Elgin Avenue.] *A large sofa*

blocked our path whilst I was being led round the Circle and introduced to the Gods. "Just pretend it isn't there, dear," said Gerald, "after all in our world it really isn't there, so just draw the Circle right through it." As we barked our shins on it every time we trotted round, this statement was a little hard to believe.

Our work in the Circle was always done at a strange jog-trot, with Gerald muttering odd rhymes into his beard. He very soon got out of breath and would hop around very shakily, looking like an elderly hobgoblin. Using red cord he tied my wrists behind my back, the cord then went round my neck, and down again to be tied to my left knee. A separate cord was tied round my right ankle. It was all very uncomfortable, and I felt very foolish, but Gerald called it, "warlocking and warricking", and said it was most important. Thus he led me round the Circle, waving a dagger at the various points of the Compass.

The general technique in the Circle was the same at this first Initiation as at the following ones. Every move was accompanied by a kiss, and the scourge was made use of at every possible opportunity. I was only flicked lightly, but Gerald liked the strokes hard and strong. I was very nervous of administering such harsh punishment. Having had no experience of such things I started by tentatively flicking the scourge across him, believeing it to be a purely symbolic action. But Gerald became very excited. First I had to warrick and warlock him, and he liked to be very tightly tied, so that the cords cut into his flesh. He then knelt at my feet, with his head bowed down and resting on the altar table. He was pathetically thin and emaciated. I felt one hard lash of the scourge and he would snap in two. But all the time he kept crying; "Harder, dear, harder. I can't feel it at all. You must make the blood course." He swayed as he knelt, and each time he felt the scourge, his head knocked the table and rattled all the tools on the altar. He kept multiplying the number of strokes to make it more and more. He said the reason for this was magical.

In between the kissing and the scourging (work in the Circle, I soon realised, was primarily made up of the [five-fold kiss] and the [scourge]), we sat on the floor by the altar table and rested. We drank the consecrated wine and ate Peak [sic] Frean's assorted biscuits. The wine was a fearsome brew - Uncle had added special ingredients of his own.

It was at these resting times that he delivered cosy chats on magic. The gist of it all was that you must hold in your mind the image of what you desired, and then work yourself up to it. Hence the witches' dances, and the scourge. "You must get the blood to course" was a favourite statement. Gerald said that you must never use magic for wicked ends or your own power. For example, it was all right to work magic in order to desire a new house. But you must be prepared to pay a fair price for it: not desire to get it cheaper! ...

Gerald instructed me that my personal Witch Book was very important. I had to write everything in it in my own hand, and never let it out of my keeping. He hinted at terrible retribution if I did."[31]

It has been assumed by many that it was just such a thing that Olive Greene did, by passing her Book of Shadows to Cardell to copy. To continue Olive's narrative:

The question of my Witch Name now arose. I suggested "Flora" as a pretty name, and as she was Goddess of Spring I thought it suitable. But Gerald said it was "a little girl's name", and he wanted me to be a Goddess. I must be called "Florannis"; it sounded more impressive and dignified.[32]

Very quickly after her first degree initiation, Olive received the Second Degree, probably in February 1959:

It was during the Second Initiation that he presented me with the rest of my working tools. These included a bell with a carved phallic handle, my witch's bracelet with my new

---

31. Op. cit.
32. Op. cit.,52.

name engraved on it in Theban, an ivory handled scourge, cords and various other articles. Some of these Gerald had made himself, and must have spent hours of work on them. He was an excellent craftsman.

By now the kisses in the Circle had become more passionate, and the scourging more intense. I was now his "own Witch and Goddess". Bound in cords he fell down on his knees before me and begged my forgiveness as Goddess, for having "put through the Initiations too quickly the woman I love."

He told me that one could call down the Goddess in three different aspects: Lucina, Goddess of Love; Diana, chaste and cold; Hecate, Goddess of Death. He always chose to call down Lucina.

By now he trusted me implicitly and began to reminisce about his past High Priestesses and Witch Queens. Apparently they all became very jealous of each-other. The incongruity of the "Perfect Love" and "Perfect Trust" of the Circle turning into plain jealousy did not seem to strike him. According to him one lady in particular had betrayed him. He always referred to her as "Traitor Witch". At the same time he admitted to having been very fond of her. She had been very "naughty", but very firm with him when he was "naughty", and had penalised him heavily with the scourge whenever he forgot the ritual in the Circle, or did the wrong thing. He sniggered and giggled as he remembered these past pleasures.

He loved having "a bit of fun" in the Circle, and remarked how roguish I looked when a lock of hair fell over my eye. Childish games of forfeits gave him immense joy; the forfeit invariably being the scourge, laced with kisses. Although some of the ritual itself was beautifully worded Gerald never spoke of The Craft in a romantic way. He always made it sound rather footling and idiotic. It was all in the nature of a frolic. Quite apart from the complete lack of any profound spiritual significance in his teachings, there was not even a grain of plain, simple common sense.

When I asked serious questions about witchcraft having a religious meaning based on old traditions, he immediately became very evasive. He would either nod his head in a very sagacious manner and say; "It's a secret, dear, you are not yet advanced enough in The Craft to know", or he would volunteer some odd unrelated information, such as that all the mightiest Gods lived in the North because of the Aurora Borealis, but that the gods of the East were the oldest."[33]

Olive had less to say about her Third Degree initiation, which followed soon afterwards:

When I arrived for this crowning achievement, I found the sofa plumb in the middle of the Circle. Gerald was drooling with excitement. Bathing had never been his strong subject, but to-day he had obviously done his best, and had even combed his hair.

He had spoken much about the Great Rite: either in "token" or in "reality". Luckily for me I had known before I met him that he was quite impotent, and he, himself, had confided to me sadly that he wished he were thirty years younger. So I had no fear of the "reality". However, on the sofa had to be acted out the "token". Much fuss was made of the exchange of kisses and names, and he finally wished that when I formed a new coven I would find "a handsome High Priest who would do me justice." And that was that."[34]

The initiation rituals took place in the afternoon and they were always followed by another sort of ritual - afternoon tea!

... at 4.30 o'clock to the dot, Gerald became ravenously hungry for Tea. The Circle was closed and the Mighty Ones dismissed rather abruptly. We hurriedly dressed in different rooms, and then I was rushed downstairs for an enormous, nursery style tea."[35]

---

33. Op. cit., 52-54.
34. Op. cit., 55.
35. Op. cit., 54.

Olive also mentions an incident which occurred at a seasonal ritual following her initiation. It confirms that Gerald was not the sole owner or occupier of the flat:

> *I remember well the only time we were late for tea. It was the time of the Spring Equinox. The altar was decorated prettily with Forsythia, and Uncle was trotting round the Circle carrying a long pole with a large phallic symbol on the end. This pole, incidentally, had been carved specially for him by a Jesuit priest, an alleged friend of Gerald. In the Circle was a large copper cauldron of fire, burning merrily, and we were supposed to dance round and leap over it. Unfortunately, Gerald did not leap high enough, and kicked over the flaming cauldron. Fire spread quickly over the drawing-room carpet. He panicked and flung on it anything that came to hand; the consecrated water and oil, and even the special brew of wine. The latter obviously did the trick and the flames subsided. But Gerald was in a terrible state of agitation, as he was terrified that the large scorch mark on the carpet would be discovered, and he would get into trouble. We rubbed away at it with the wet altar cloth, and hoped to make the mark look like part of the pattern. Then like two naughty children we moved the sofa over to cover it.*[36]

In many ways, I think that Olive Greene's account of her encounters with Gerald is surprisingly accurate, with a lot of circumstantial detail and characteristic insights into Gerald as a person. Even though it was written to try to discredit him, and it does emphasise some of the less favourable aspects of his personality, it is nevertheless one of the most vivid pictures that we have of Gerald Gardner and one that I feel justified in having quoted at some length.

Lois Bourne[37] mentions that Olive was given a key to his flat by Gerald while he was in hospital for an operation for a digestive obstruction, and thus had access to all his private papers.

On 19th August 1959, Gerald wrote a very friendly letter to Olive. He had been occupied with an American visitor, probably

---

36. Op. cit., 54-55.
37. Bourne, (1998), 28.

Daniel Mannix, whose visit to the Isle of Man was subsequently recorded in an article that appeared in *True* magazine (subtitled 'The Man's Magazine') in late 1959. Gerald's letter starts "The Yank has gone ...". He proceeds to answer questions which Olive has put to him, presumably in an earlier letter. She had obviously asked Gerald about Charles Cardell, because, after discussing the etymology of the word 'witch', he goes on:

> *Question 2. Ross says that Mr. Cardell has admitted that he is Rex Nemorensis, and that he signs letters with this name. He should know whether he is or not.*

This could be a reference to Ross Nichols, who helped Gerald with *Witchcraft Today*, but it is more likely to be Francis Clive-Ross, editor of the journal *Light*, which published more than one of Cardell's articles.

Olive had then asked about the question of fakes. Whether she was thinking of Charles Cardell or Gerald Gardner or both of them in this context is unclear.

It was towards the end of August 1959 that Olive dropped her bombshell. She wrote a letter to Gerald. I have not seen it, but it was clearly a complete repudiation of Gerald and the Craft, and in the strongest possible language. Some think that it was actually dictated by Cardell. Fred Lamond writes[38] that the letter was extremely wounding to Gerald, calling him a fraud and a pervert.

Gerald's reply is very poignant. Writing from his house in Castletown on 28th August 1959, it runs: *My dear Olive. Now, the main thing I have to say is, "You say I Stink". Well, I do not think that this is so, And I do not think I am frightned either. But if you think "I STINK" I do not think it is worth saying anything more. Yours sincerely. May you be blessed. Gerald.*

Gerald was obviously very upset by the letter from Olive. Lois Bourne writes:

> *When all this was discovered Gerald was quite mortified, and Jack was incandescent with sheer rage, his language becoming even more colourful than usual. In Jack's opinion, Gerald was a loose cannon (Gerald once confessed to me, 'I*

---

38. Lamond, (2004), 35.

*am unfortunately no judge of character' and this sad fact led to many fiascos in his life).*39

It was during this period, probably after Olive's wounding letter, that Gerald and Doreen Valiente were reconciled, probably in August 1959. I would imagine that, following his disillusionment with Olive, Gerald would have written to Doreen a reconciling sort of letter, to which she would have replied in the same way. Apparently they met "in friendly fashion, due to the good offices of Ray Bone".

There was also an increasingly acrimonious exchange of letters between Gerald and Cardell. Fred Lamond remembers Jack Bracelin saying "I am letting those two get on with it on their own; I'm not getting involved".40

❧

Subsequent to Olive's initiations by Gerald, there was, in May 1959, an attempt at rapprochement between the Bricket Wood coven and the breakaway group, for Jack Bracelin received a letter from Derek Boothby "saying that he thought it was about time that the fighting was over and contact was re-established".41 So the coven went over to Sarratt at Derek's invitation, but apart from Derek, there were only two other members of his coven present. Dayonis reported to Gerald that things were not going well for the group:

> *Oh. Boy! did we hear tell a tale of rows and fights. It was incredible. Firstly, Derek and Ameth rowed and decided not to talk to one another. And then Derek and Ned/Muriel rowed and decided not to talk to each other and so the only other two people we saw were Claude and Joan - who were so fed up with the whole business that they were thinking of chucking the whole thing up. Derek, of course, suggested, well nearly so, that we join forces again, but we had been bitten once before, and did not make any comment."*42

---

39. Bourne, (1998), 28.
40. Email from Fred Lamond to the author, 16 January 2009.
41. Letter, Dayonis to Gerald Gardner, 28 June 1959.
42. Ibid.

Something positive did come out of the visit, however, and that was a suggestion by Derek for a gathering of both covens at the Rollright Stones in Oxfordshire on Midsummer Eve. These are a circle of prehistoric standing stones adjacent to an area of woodland on the Oxfordshire/Warwickshire border. Dayonis' account is very evocative of the atmosphere of the gathering:

> *... about fourteen of us went up, travelling from Bricket wood in two cars and a van, meeting Derek and reaching the Rollright round about 11.30 at night. We all walked solemnly round the stones at first, talked quietly, looked at the moon, (which was also full), had a picnic in the middle of the circle and then somehow, some sort of wildness seemed to come into to us, because we started dancing round, first of all hand in hand and then splitting into pairs and leaping around. It was wonderful. I felt I wanted to roll over and over - like a young animal. and then we lit a small bonfire with sticks we had brought with us, joined hands and went leaping around the fire singing Eko, Eko Azarak and shouting at the tops of our voices. I've never felt so excited and wonderful at the same time. The atmosphere of the place is terrific and none of us wanted to go home, but alas we had to, so at about 1.30 on Midsummer Day, we piled back into the assorted vehicles and off we went and at about 3.30 there was the sun to greet us on our way. Gerald, it truly was a wonderful night and something that we must do again."*[43]

It may have been on this occasion that a 'souvenir' of a large stone over a foot in diameter was apparently removed from the circle and taken back to the Witches' Cottage, where it was placed adjacent to the altar. What happened to it subsequently I do not know, but it was still there in 1964. One can only hope that it was eventually returned to its rightful place in the Rollright Stones.

⚘

---

43. Ibid.

Probably only three weeks after Olive's "bombshell", Gerald received another bombshell, this time from Dayonis. She wrote a letter to Gerald, resigning as High Priestess, resigning from the Craft, and resigning from Five Acres: she was getting married and emigrating. Her husband-to-be was introduced to the Club by Fred in the spring of 1959. He obviously liked what he saw, for he became a member of the Club in early May 1959. He and Dayonis were mutually attracted, as she tells Gerald in late June:

> *Life is very good as far as I am concerned, I've got a new love (mind you I don't know how long this one will last, but I think a good deal longer than that funny bod. you met last summer) and he's coming into the Craft and has joined the club too! So cross your fingers for me, I do want to produce at least one potential witch before its too late!"*[44]

They became engaged to be married in August 1959 and, as his work took him abroad, they arranged to emigrate following their wedding in late September. The relationship did indeed last a fair time, for I had the pleasure of meeting Dayonis and her husband, still happily married, some 47 years later!

This all came as a complete shock to Gerald, who replied immediately to Dayonis' letter from his home in Castletown:

> *My dear .... I got your letter at midday. well it has been an awful shock, after what you said to me a few days ago. I am still trembling and its past six. and poor Jack was crying when he wrote to me.*
>
> *I suppose thers some reason for what you are doing. I mean, what you have said. looking at your letter again. I see that you want to speak to me somtime. Well, I know, you can say things, which its impossible to put on paper. I am trying to get a flight down. but theyre all booked up. but there is a possibility of somthing being cancelled. You see dear. If you had only said it and given us a chance to make some arrangements. well, thers no use saying anything.*

---

44. Ibid.

*Well, you know I have always been very fond of you in a
fatherly way. and I do hope that you will be very happy in
your new life.*[45]

Unfortunately, Dayonis never received that letter. The first
she heard from Gerald was a cheque for £30, intended as a wedding present. However, in isolation, without the context of his
letter, she saw the money as being the equivalent of "30 pieces of
silver" and she thought that Gerald saw her resignation as an act
of betrayal. She told me: ... *I sent it back, because I didn't want him
to have given me something that was like 30 pieces of silver, and I
felt that this is what he felt about it, that I was giving it all up and
deserting.*[46] It was only in the 1990s, when she was shown a copy
of Gerald's letter, that she understood Gerald's true feelings. Such
events might be taken straight from a novel by Thomas Hardy!

Anyway, with Dayonis' departure, Lois Pearson became High
Priestess of the coven.

⁂

From time to time, various people, mostly those who had read
his books, made contact with Gerald and he used to bring them
to meet the other members of the coven. It sounds as if there had
been quite a succession of these, mostly young women, whom
Gerald brought along. Quite frequently, the coven didn't think
much of Gerald's choice, as with Olive Greene, but one exception
was Monica English (1920-1979), who appeared, probably some
time in 1960. She grew up in Buckinghamshire, and her father
had been a professor of mathematics. At the time she made contact with the coven, she was living in Gayton, Norfolk, where she
was supposedly a member of a traditional witch coven. There had
been a bit of publicity about the Bricket Wood coven and apparently she had been sent to check it out.

Fred Lamond told me that he considered her to be a brilliant
woman who, when the coven circled to raise power, used to run
"like blazes" and "gave out shrieks and whoops of joy and raised
more power herself than the whole of the rest of the coven".

---

45. Letter in the Toronto collection.
46. Dayonis, discussion with the author, February 2006.

Monica withdrew from the coven following one of the bouts of press publicity, but kept in touch with Lois Bourne, who calls her "Margo" in her book, *Dancing with Witches*.[47]

Eleanor ('Ray') Bone (1911-2001) had apparently been initiated into a witch tradition in Cumberland in 1941. She was matron of the Brackenburn Rest Home in Tooting and approached Gerald in late 1959 or early 1960 asking to be initiated. He invited her for a chat with the coven, but after two or three meetings they decided that they couldn't have her in the coven, probably because she was considerably older than the others and because she did not appreciate the obscene songs and limericks that the others were keen on. Basically, she didn't fit in.

Gerald, therefore, arranged for her to have a private initiation and later invited her to the Isle of Man for a month of intensive training, at the end of which he put her through the second and third degrees. Thereafter, he encouraged her to establish a new coven in Tooting, which she did, to the extent that many present-day witches can trace their lineage back to Eleanor Bone.

On Saturday, 31st October 1959, Jack was warned by telephone, probably by *The People*, who, Fred Lamond writes, "obviously regarded us as their own preserve",[48] that reporters and photographers from at least three newspapers would be attempting to raid the Witches' Cottage together with the local police on the grounds that something illegal was taking place there.

Three car-loads of press did indeed turn up about 9pm, followed by a car-load of police. Jack spoke to the police, who advised him to contact them if any more reporters turned up. Later, more press did indeed turn up and attempted to take photographs over the gate of an empty car park by search light. At 11.30pm, the press were still there laying siege to the place, so Jack phoned the police, but by the time they arrived the press had left.

No report of the evening's activities appeared in any paper.

※

Olive's letter to Gerald in August 1959 was not her last. From an examination of letters from Gerald's solicitors, it seems clear

---

47. Lois Bourne, *Dancing with Witches*, (Robert Hale, 1998).
48. Email, Frederic Lamond to the author, 17 January 2009.

that both Gerald and Donna continued to receive letters from Olive of an abusive or threatening nature. These particularly upset Donna, and Gerald's solicitors agreed that they may have been a contributory factor in her death, which occurred on 30th January 1960.

Gerald's solicitors had obviously had previous dealings with Olive, for on 12th February 1960, they wrote to him: *We have had letters from this woman threatening going to the Law Society for unethical conduct and all sorts of other nonsense. We do not know whether she is mad or bad but when we wrote to her in consequence of Mr Bracelin's instructions to ascertain what she meant by "horrible practices" we received a reply giving no information. We have since ignored her letters in accordance with your subsequent instructions.*

They then suggested: *Do you not think, now that your dear wife has passed on, that the right course would be to put an end to this stupid woman's activities by writing to her in the terms that unless she stops communicating with you, you will be compelled to apply for an Injunction to restrain her?*

Whether this was done, I do not know, but, just over a week later, Gerald received another letter from Olive: *It was only yesterday that I learned the news of Donna's death. It came to me as a great shock, + I felt I must write + send you my sympathy. I know how terribly you must miss her. Also there were times in the past when she showed me personally much kindness. It is in memory of those times that I write to you."*[49]

Gerald replied: *Thank you very much for your kind letter. She liked you very much, and told me you were true, and she was very distressed when you turned against her. Thanking you again for your letter, and may you be blessed.*

It is clear that Cardell also sent his condolences for Gerald writes to him: *I have indeed lost a loved and loyal companion.*[50]

Charles Cardell died in October 1977. Mary Cardell died in October 1984. Olwen Greene died in August 1994.

---

49. Letter, Olive Greene to Gerald Gardner, 21 February 1960.
50. Letter, Gerald Gardner to Charles Cardell, 5 March 1960.

CHAPTER THIRTY–FOUR

A Charismatic Biographer

O ne individual who had a major influence on Gerald Gardner was Sayed Idries Shah. He was born in Simla, India on 16th June 1924 into a distinguished Hashemite family which traces its ancestry back to the Prophet Muhammad. His father was Sirdar Ikbal Ali Shah, who, while a medical student in Edinburgh, met and married a Scotswoman. He then took her to live in Paghman in the Afghan Highlands, which was the Shahs' ancestral home-land. During this time he wrote a book, *Occultism, Its Theory and Practice*.[1] This was the result of a lot of research into systems of magic from Jewish, Egyptian, Babylonian, Arabian, Iranian, Indian, Tibetan, Chinese and Japanese traditions. It included thoughts on the mechanisms and processes involved.

Idries and his brother, Omar Ali Shah (1922-2005) were brought up in England, at first in Sutton and then Oxford. Idries seems to have inherited his father's interest in the occult, and, in the mid 1950s, the first two of his many books were on this sub-ject: *Oriental Magic*[2] and *The Secret Lore of Magic*.[3]

---

1. Sirdar Ikbal Ali Shah, *Occultism, Its Theory and Practice*, (Castle Books New York, 1929).
2. Sayed Idries Shah, *Oriental Magic*, (Rider and Co. 1956)
3. Sayed Idries Shah, *The Secret Lore of Magic*, (Frederick Muller, 1957).

An obituary in *The Guardian* gave a vivid picture of Idries Shah: *He was immensely articulate and caustic, gentle and funny. His range of information on so many subjects was prodigious and he was an excellent raconteur who used humour to challenge his listeners' assumptions. His circle of friends was vast and often colourful ...*[4]

Shah is known today largely as a writer and teacher of Sufism, a mystical and pantheistic Muslim philosophy, though his own particular approach to Sufism was as something which, in essence, pre-dated Islam and was more universal in nature. He was Director of Studies of the Institute for Cultural Research, which studied cross-cultural thought and practice. Idries Shah died on 23rd November 1996 at the age of 72.

It was almost certainly through Jack Bracelin that Gerald Gardner got to know Shah and it is likely that Jack met him at a restaurant in Swiss Cottage, north west London, known as 'The Cosmo'. This was situated on Northways Parade, on the east side of Finchley Road and is now occupied by the Eriki Indian Restaurant. 'The Cosmo' had a very distinctive atmosphere.

The poet and writer, Dannie Abse "admits that he doesn't know what would have happened to him if Swiss Cottage hadn't been there. His life was transformed by the table talk of the Cosmo and post-war continental coffee bars and cabarets ..."[5] He gives a vivid impression of 'the Cosmo' in his novel *The Strange Case of Dr. Simmonds and Dr. Glas*:

> There is something old-fashioned about the old Cosmo restaurant. It is as if the clock had stopped, not in 1950 but in pre-First World War Vienna. On the wall are prints of one of our local refugee artists, Topolski, and one has the feeling of not being in England. This is partly due to the foreignness of the waiters and waitresses. Before they left their country they probably had been violin or cello players in some great Austrian orchestra or professors of Ichthyology. The menu, too, suggests Vienna: Rheinische Sauerbraten with dumplings and red cabbage; or Wiener Schnitzel; or

4. David Wade and Edward Campbell, "To teach the way of the Sufi", *The Guardian*.
5. Gerald Isaaman, "The Doctor Poet and His 80 Years of Rage", *Camden New Journal*, 25 September 2003.

Zwiebel Hockbraten; or Zwiebel Rosbraten Viennoise; or Karlsbraten Veal Goulash. And those who eat at the restaurant are frequently not British.[6]

It was in the Annexe, which has been described as a "Spartan coffee-bar" that meetings, mostly impromptu, were apt to take place. Abse describes the ambience as being quite different: "It was only a few steps from the main restaurant to its adjacent annexe but, in taking them, one moved from the Past to the Present".

The Cosmo was a meeting-place for the literary and intellectual inhabitants of that part of post-war London, particularly refugees. One phrase repeats itself in several accounts of the place, and that is "holding court". These were informal meetings, but it was somewhere where people came to listen to the often remarkable individuals who would issue forth on any subject in which they were knowledgeable and their listeners interested.

One such individual 'holding court' every Tuesday evening in the late 1950s was Idries Shah and one interested listener was Jack Bracelin. Jack had developed a keen interest in ceremonial magic and was much taken with Sufism, which Shah was expounding. Such a meeting of minds had implications not just on the history of the Craft but in a very real way on the life of Gerald Gardner.

Fred Lamond recounted his personal experience of Shah to me, contrasting him with Gerald:

Did that man have charisma! Was he impressive! He was tall and had this presence, what the Arabs call 'baraka', basically an aura of authority about him. But he wasn't snobbish at all: he was an extremely funny man. The stories he used to tell and pranks he got up to …! If I'd met him before I got involved in the Craft I might have become a pupil of his and sat at his feet for five or ten years. I remember contrasting him with Gerald, because Gerald did not have charisma. He was a very lovable man, but he did not have charisma! And he did not have this aura of spiritual authority.[7]

Lamond writes: *When he [Jack Bracelin] mentioned that he was the right-hand man to Gerald Gardner in the witchcraft*

---

6. Dannie Abse, *The Strange Case of Dr. Simmonds and Dr. Glas*, (Robson Books 2002).
7. Frederic Lamond, personal discussion with the author, July 2006.

revival, Idries asked to meet Gerald and then offered to interview him and write his biography.[8]

Whilst there is really no doubt that Shah wrote substantial parts of the book which became *Gerald Gardner Witch*, it is undoubtedly equally true that Jack Bracelin did a lot more than just put his name to it, as I shall show.

I am sure that in practice the decision to write the biography was not quite as quick or one-sided as that seemed to imply. Anyway, the meeting took place, probably in early 1959. The main motivation behind a biography was Gerald's growing belief that he was nearing the end of his life and his need to chronicle it in some way. Probably he was encouraged by others, certainly including Shah, who felt that Gerald's life was sufficiently interesting to merit some permanent record.

Another reason for writing the biography seems to have been to counteract the activities of Charles Cardell. Lois Bourne, without naming him, states the following: ... *the whole purpose of the book was to infuriate the psychologist - who nevertheless continued to persecute Gerald in articles in England and abroad, even after his death. It would appear that this man, despite being a psychologist, had serious problems of his own.*[9]

To counteract the claim that he was making it all up, Gerald would have to give more details about the witches who initiated him. And so the idea for a biography began to take shape. Also Jack asked the members of the coven to try to remember any events connected with Gerald and to write it all down. He co-ordinated this and collected all the material together.

There is a persistent rumour that Idries Shah was for a time Gerald Gardner's secretary. Lois Bourne makes clear that there is no basis for such a rumour. However, I have an idea of how such a rumour might have started. Gerald was such a disorganised individual and spoke rapidly once he was in his stride that the only way that Shah was going to make sense of the accounts of his life was to make tape recordings of their sessions. It is clear that this was the method adopted because there are passages in the book which the author acknowledges are quoted verbatim

8. Lamond, (2004), 19.
9. Bourne, (1998), 29.

from Gerald. One example is the account of the ritual known as "Operation Cone of Power", where the author says of it: "This is documentarily an important enough part of the history of witchcraft to quote verbatim from Gardner's own mouth."[10] There then follows a paragraph in quotation marks describing the ritual and it is clear from the context that these are Gerald's actual words. The only way this could be achieved is if a recording had been made, or if someone who knew shorthand had been present. I have no evidence that either Shah or Bracelin fell into that category. Despite the book's limitations, I think that Shah and Bracelin did quite a good job of putting Gerald's rambling accounts into some sort of order.

It is a pity that these tapes can no longer be found for, as well as being a fascinating record of Gerald's voice and presence, they would undoubtedly have provided further detail, in Gerald's actual words, of some important events in the history of the Craft.

The book is obviously the result of several sessions with Gerald, and I suspect that, once the project was agreed, Shah went up to the Isle of Man to stay with Gerald, perhaps undertaking one session per evening over a period of a few weeks. Because of his tendency to be secretive, Gerald would probably not want it generally known that a biography was being written, and so he invented the 'cover story' that Shah was acting as his secretary. He may even have done some secretarial work for Gerald while he was there, so the story may not have been entirely false, though it was at most a subsidiary role to the main reason for Shah being on the island.

In early 1960, Shah was at a crucial point in his career. He was moving away from ceremonial magic and had got rather tired of it and everything to do with it. As he got to know Gerald better, he became more and more disillusioned with him. Fred Lamond recalls a conversation he had with Shah after the material for the book had been largely accumulated:

As he was coming to the end of his research Idries came one day to have tea with my wife Gillian and me, accompanied by his girl friend and Jack Bracelin. He seemed to have become somewhat disillusioned with Gerald because he

---

10. Bracelin, 167.

said: "When I was interviewing Gerald I sometimes wished I was a News of the World reporter. What marvellous material for an exposé! And yet" - here he looked thoughtful - "I have it on good authority" (I assume he meant the inner planes) "that this group will be the cornerstone of the religion of the coming age. But rationally" - and here he looked despairingly at us sincere but by his standards woefully ignorant young people - "rationally I can't see it!"[11]

But can the authorship be ascribed so firmly to Shah? Morgan Davis [12] has drawn attention to something which, like all the best discoveries, is obvious when it is pointed out but which certainly remained below the surface of my consciousness for many years. And that is that the character of the first part of the book, up to the crucial Chapter 13 – 'Into the Witch Cult', is very different from the character of the remainder of the book. As Davis puts it:

I noticed that at some point between Chapter 11-13, the writing and organizational skill of the author seems to change dramatically. The first two thirds of the book seem well thought out and organized with a specific pace, an engaging language, and occasions where the author really succeeds in bringing Gardner alive on the page. On the other hand, the last third of the book is sort of a helter-skelter mish-mash that looks to me like someone wove a thin narrative structure around a set of notes. The occasional vividly described sequences or well-turned phrases that brought the book alive were absent.[13]

I am sure that Morgan Davis has hit on the truth and that Shah had far less input into the latter third of the book.

Francis Cameron has studied *Gerald Gardner Witch* for some years and has applied his considerable experience with manuscripts, interpolations and changes of style to the text. He writes:

When I eventually came to really study the biography, instead of just skimming through it for factual information,

---

11. Lamond. (2004), 19.
12. Morgan Davis, personal communication with the author, 12 August 2008.
13. Ibid.

*I noticed at once the rather flowery language of the open-
ing: "The East Wind whirls over the Pennines .. &c". Then
later in the book, this level of description is lacking even
though the events being described would merit equal treatment with Shah's vision of GBG's situation on the Isle of
Man. It gives me the impression of a writer beginning to
polish an original script but giving up before working
through to the finish.*[14]

He speculates:

*It was intended that Idries Shah should write GBG's biogra-
phy. He began the work but felt unable to continue. That is
why it was published with Bracelin's name as author. I find
three levels of writing. The descriptive prose of Shah – especially in the opening chapters. Some passages worked up,
which I take to be Bracelin. Other passages seem to be
Gardner's own words.*[15]

There are certainly several section in the latter part of the book
where the author refers to himself in the first person and it is quite
clear from the context that it is Jack Bracelin who is meant. Moreover, at least two of the passages contain details known by Bracelin
but of which Shah would be unlikely to be aware:

*I read the attack upon Gardner on that Sunday afternoon
with mounting incredulity. If something as unfair as I
realised this to be was being projected with such unbelievable force, this man Gardner might be someone worth con-
tacting. I had for several years been reading about fertility
religions and the ancient mysteries. Ploughing through
book after book, I realised that people with the academic
background of Sir James Frazer and Professor Murray do
not spend a lifetime in research for nothing.*[16]

This conforms with the account which I give in Chapter 29 of
how Jack first became involved with the Craft. Another statement

14. Email, Francis Cameron to the author, 13 August 2008.
15. Email, Francis Cameron to the author, 12 August 2008.
16. Bracelin, 187-188.

is clearly not just written as if by Bracelin; it could only have been written by an initiate:

> *As far as his* [Gerald's] *mission to enrol others into the fold of the deities of fertility is concerned, one cannot say that there is one Craft member who does not feel that his or her membership of the Cult is anything but a fulfilment; a "coming home". Speaking for the present generation of witches, at least, this is perhaps enough coming from one who has been through this experience.*[17]

I think what probably happened is that, as Lamond indicates, Shah began to have doubts about his involvement with the whole project. He was moving towards Sufism and he didn't think it would really help where he wanted to go to if his name appeared as the author of a book about witchcraft. He certainly fully intended to go ahead with publishing the book which he had clearly spent much time over, but he ceased to have personal involvement in the project after having written some of the chapters. He handed his notes over to Gerald, who had to find someone to complete it. Jack was the obvious choice. He it was who had first introduced Shah to Gerald and he almost certainly welcomed the idea of being involved in a biography of the man who had been a profound influence on the course of his life. So Jack and Gerald between them were able to finish the project, albeit with considerable editorial help, for neither were good at spelling.

There is, however, no doubt in my mind that Shah was involved in writing a substantial part of the book, for there is evidence within the text itself in the form of a highly unusual sentence structure which occurs frequently both in *Gerald Gardner Witch* and in other books definitely written by Shah. It is better demonstrated than described. The following sentences from *Gerald Gardner Witch* are typical:

> *The pay was only £16 a month - but there were the compensations of a free bungalow, a houseboy for the domestic work.*[18]

---

17. Bracelin, 214.
18. Bracelin, 29.

He read papers on the kris and the Scottish dirk, was enter-
tained at the Palace.[19]

They seemed rather brow-beaten by the others, kept them-
selves to themselves.[20]

The common structure of these sentences is clear: the author
adds a final phrase separated by a comma where normal usage
would require it to be separated by the word "and" or another
conjunction. A similar structure can be found in sentences in
books where there has never been any doubt about Shah's
authorship. For example:

I picked up Robot Two-point-Eight, weighed it in my hand.[21]

Snakes bring good fortune, guard souls and hidden trea-
sures, form the outlet for occult utterances.[22]

Scholars - frequently at State expense - systematized the
teachings of Aristotle and the other Greek writers, summa-
rized ancient histories, organized the codes of law, religion
and ethic.[23]

It may, in the climate of the times, have been a difficult book
for which to find a publisher. Both Gerald Gardner and Idries
Shah had had books published in the previous few years by Rider
and Co., *Witchcraft Today* and *Oriental Magic* respectively. It is
hard to imagine that they would not have tried Riders, who obviously turned them down. The publisher of Gerald's 1959 book,
The Meaning of Witchcraft, Aquarian Press, presumably turned
them down also.

In the end, they fell to their own resources. Just as he had
done three times previously, Gerald almost certainly financed
publication himself. He knew he would not live more than
another few years and he had no dependants. He might as well
spend his money on this as anything else.

---

19. Op. cit., 152.
20. Op. cit., 164.
21. Sayed Idries Shah, *Destination Mecca*, (Octagon 1969), 13.
22. Shah, (1956), 4.
23. Op. cit., 76.

It is clear that Shah did not abandon the project completely, as he arranged for the book to be published by the newly-established Octagon Press, which was an enterprise run by Shah and, I understand, his sister. In fact, *Gerald Gardner Witch* was the very first book that they published and it may even be that Octagon Press was set up specifically to publish the book and only later became a well-established firm publishing books by Shah and others on Sufism and similar religious and esoteric themes. To quote from its current publicity material : "Octagon Press has built a bridge between West and East and ... has made available many of the greatest texts of Eastern thought, psychology and literature. Our aim is to connect the Orient to the Occident ..."

The book, the title of which was settled on as being *Gerald Gardner Witch*, was, to be honest, rather amateurish. The pages look as if they have been produced by an electric typewriter rather then properly typeset, and the proof-reading leaves much to be desired. The reproduction of the photographs is also rather poor. However, the book was nicely bound in red cloth and it had quite a striking dust-jacket in black, red and white. The book was demy 8vo size (pages roughly 8ins x 5ins), 232 pages long and contained 17 illustrations. It was for sale at 25/- per copy.

There was a book launch in September 1960. Where the launch took place, I really do not know, although it could well have been at Atlantis Bookshop. It probably took place on 20th September, as Gerald sent a copy to his sister in law, Louise (wife of his brother, Robert Marshall Gardner), known to Gerald as "Loo", which was inscribed both by Jack Bracelin on the 20th and by Gerald the following day. In the letter which accompanied the book, Gerald gave some more details of how it was written:

> *My dear Loo, I am sending you a copy of the book wh has been written about me, wh I hope you will find amusing. Rember I dident write it, I only told a lot of stories, wh he has used in his own way, and put in things other people have told him. If I were writing it I wd have treated it in a differnt way. Also, Its a first book, and he is not a good proof reader. Well, its all fun anyhow. With all love. By the way, an Auther gets*

only 6 free copies. I get one only. So if anyone else wants some, they can buy them. All love. Yours ever Gerald [24]

He gave some more details about the book in a post-script to that letter:

He jumps about in time for some reason, which I find rather disconcerting. Rember its his first book. And, as I say, I told him stories over a number of years, and other people have told him stories, and he has picked out what intrested him, & put it together, then when, as all do, he found he had written far too much, he cut down rather indescriminatly. [25]

Gerald Gardner Witch was the only biography of Gerald Gardner to be published before the present volume. It has proved most useful to me in providing leads to follow and clues in tracking down some of the essential facts in Gerald's life. Indeed, it has been my constant companion for several years. That is not to say that it is always entirely accurate, but I have found that in essence it is usually broadly correct, the inaccuracies resulting in the main either from Gerald's less than perfect memory or misinterpretations on the part of the authors which were either not picked up by Gerald or left in out of a sense of mischief or mystification!

The first time I read the book was many years before I started my researches into the history of the Craft. I had ordered the book via inter-library loan and can still remember leafing through it that first time. Over half of it seemed to be the adventures of an Englishman in his working life "out East". The latter part seemed to be largely philosophising about the Craft. What I really wanted was to find out how Gerald Gardner had come into the Craft, to read about the witches he had met and about what they believed and did. My gaze thus focused almost entirely on one chapter and one chapter only - appropriately Chapter 13: Into the Witch Cult. This was the heart of the book and, as if to demonstrate it, in the days before photocopiers were readily available, I typed the whole of that chapter out on my Olivetti

---

24. Letter, Gerald Gardner to Louise Gardner, 18 September 1960, in Gardner Family archives.
25. Ibid.

portable: a labour of love, and one which I still possess, though the typewriter is long gone.

The slow and laborious progress of such an enterprise helped, I am sure, to instil in me the importance of the actual words used rather than others' (sometimes superficial and inaccurate) versions of those words.

Here, in Chapter 13, was certainly the heart of the book but, even on first reading, I felt it was inadequate, glossing over or omitting facts that seemed to me then, and still seem to me now, to be vital for a full understanding of the story of how Gerald came in contact with the witches and what they taught him. Perhaps in a very real sense the seeds of the present volume were sown by my first reading of *Gerald Gardner Witch*.

⁂

Gerald did not winter abroad in 1959/60 because, as already mentioned, Donna, his wife for over 30 years, died in Nobles Hospital, Douglas on 30th January 1960. She had been painfully afflicted with osteoporosis for several years.

Jack Bracelin and Lois Pearson immediately flew over to be with Gerald and to try and find a housekeeper for him. This was eventually achieved, and Lois stayed on for about ten days to comfort Gerald. He asked her to help him sort through all his papers to decide what should be kept and what could be got rid of. However, Lois commented:

> In the months following Donna's death Gerald's behaviour became, as Jack Bracelin described it 'even more bizarre', and Jack was very worried. Donna had been a stabilizing influence in Gerald's life, she preserved him from his worst excesses and I suspect kept watch on the suitability or otherwise of his friends. Without her he was like a ship drifting helplessly without a rudder; an elderly man by his own confession, not a student of human nature nor a good judge of it, a prey to self-seeking people, as Jack graphically described the situation.[26]

---

26. Bourne, (1998), 66.

Lois suspected that it was because Gerald was lonely that he was making contact with some rather undesirable people. When she could she went over to spend a few days with him. He was, however, dwelling on his own mortality and asked Lois whether she would take over the museum after his death. However, family circumstances meant that she could not take up this offer.

A few months later, Gerald received an invitation to attend a garden party at Buckingham Palace on Thursday 12th May 1960. Many thousands of people attend these events in the course of a year, so it was probably not the significant recognition that some have suggested. He was probably there because of his membership of the Royal Asiatic Society and the Royal Anthropological Society, or possibly because he was a Council member of the Folk-Lore Society. He was certainly not there as a witch.

Following the publication of *Gerald Gardner Witch*, Gerald wrote a letter to Arnold and Patricia Crowther (probably some time in December 1960. He was somewhat erratic about dating letters - sometimes he did and sometimes he didn't!). This went, in part:

> *I am just off, to Majorca, for two or three months. At least, Ime going off with Sayed Idries Shah. Majorca first stop. When you go with him you never know where you will end up. He writes on Magic, and he always tries to do the flying Carpet trick. He dosent like the cold. That's why we're getting out of England.*

In not liking the cold, Idries was certainly at one with Gerald. The letter implies that Gerald had been on trips with him before. Certainly by New Year 1961 they were in Majorca, for Shah wrote a letter to that well-known Majorca resident, Robert Graves, poet and author of *The White Goddess*.[27] He expressed his admiration for Graves, mentioned his own work on magical practices, ecstatic religions and ingestion of hallucinogenic mushrooms, all subjects which he knew would interest Graves. In his letter, Shah wrote that he had: ... 'written various books on the diffusion of magical practices, published in Britain and elsewhere'; and that at the moment he was 'studying ecstatic religions', and had been

27. Robert Graves, *The White Goddess*, (Faber and Faber, 1948).

'attending ... experiments conducted by the witches in Britain, into mushroom-eating and so on'.[28]

It was certainly true that some of the witches in the early 1960s were experimenting with drugs: they had used mescalin and LSD, I understand as a control group for the psychiatrist, R.D. Laing, who was experimenting on possible treatments for schizophrenia. In early 1960, Graves had had some correspondence with Derek Boothby, who told him something of what his coven was doing and that he was trying to allocate the Witch festivals to the 13-month calendar and generally thanking him for his advice. Whether this advice was in letter form or just generically in *The White Goddess* is not clear. Boothby does, however, mention that he has "a medical team from the membership of several covens" (which is almost certainly an exaggeration) which was to carry out experiments on *Amanita muscaria* and *Panaeolus papilionaceus*, which contains the psychoactive drug psilocybin. He later gave Graves reports on the results of those experiments.

Shah, in his letter to Graves, continued:

I am accompanied at the moment by Dr Gerald Gardner, who is the chief man among the British witches, and Director of the Museum of Magic and Witchcraft in the Isle of Man. He proposes to spend some months here in some secluded spot, to work on a book. He asks me to mention that he would be greatly honoured if it were possible for him to be received by you...[29]

Grevel Lindop writes: "Shah had baited his hook skilfully".[30] Shah knew that Graves had recently become interested in the use of hallucinogenic fungi and its implications for ecstatic religious experience. He continues:

Idries Shah's other masterstroke was to combine mushroom-eating with 'the Witches of Britain'. Graves had long

28. Letter, Idries Shah c/o wagons-lits Palma Majorca to Robert Graves, 3 January 1961, quoted in Richard Perceval Graves, *Robert Graves and the White Goddess*, 1940-1985, (Weidenfeld and Nicolson, 1995), 326.

29. Letter, Idries Shah to Robert Graves, 4 January 1961.

30. Grevel Lindop, "From Witchcraft to the Rubaiyyat: Robert Graves and the Shah Brothers", in *The Art of Collaboration: Robert Graves and his Contemporaries*, edited by Dunstan Ward, (Collectio Estudis Anglesos, Universitat de les Isles Balears, Palma, 2008), 187-205.

been interested in witchcraft, and had corresponded with the aged Margaret Murray, author of The Witch Cult in Western Europe *and* The God of the Witches, *whilst writing* The White Goddess. *Murray's theory, that witchcraft was the survival of a preChristian fertility cult, naturally appealed deeply to Graves and was easily conscripted into the worldview of* The White Goddess. *How could Graves fail to jump at the chance of meeting someone who could tell him about the use of magic mushrooms by British witches?*[31]

Graves' interest in witchcraft dated back several years. It had probably been stimulated by reading *Witchcraft Today* because just a month after its publication, on 1st December 1954, he had a humorous short story entitled "An Appointment for Candlemas" published in the magazine, *Punch*. It showed in some of the details given that he had some knowledge of members of the Craft. Indeed, Graves says in the Introduction to his *Collected Short Stories*,[32] in which "An Appointment for Candlemas" is included, that he cannot claim to have invented the factual details in the story, so it seems as if Graves may actually have met a witch some time before late 1954, when the story was first published!

Graves also wrote an essay on modern witchcraft in 1964 which has appeared in several different publications[33] since that date. The article, written just after Gerald Gardner's death, includes a brief history of witchcraft, including Margaret Murray's writings and his own interpretation of them. He is quite clear and perceptive when he states:

I am not a witch myself and have never assisted at a Sabbath. Although most English witches of my acquaintance are honest idealists, the craft attracts hysterical or perverted characters and, there being no longer a Grand Master or Chief Devil to discipline them, schisms and dissolutions are frequent in covens.[34]

31. Ibid.
32. Robert Graves, *Collected Short Stories*, (Cassell. 1965).
33. Robert Graves, "Witches in 1964", *Virginia Quarterly Review XL*, (1964), 550-559.
34. Op. cit., 553.

He is also perceptive enough to observe *..his* [i.e. Gardner's] *doctorate came from no University*[35] and went on to comment: *Dr. Gardner was first initiated into a Hertfordshire coven whose traditions had, it seems, been reinterpreted by a group of theosophists before being aligned with his own views of what young witches need in the way of fun and games.*[36]

This may well be directly from what Gerald told him at their meeting, though I strongly suspect that the mention of Hertfordshire is a misremembering or misinterpretation on Graves' part for what should have been Hampshire. He ends the article with his own assessment of the modern witchcraft revival:

> ...the craft seems healthy enough in 1964, and growing fast, though torn by schisms and Dr. Gardner's death. It now only needs some gifted mystic to come forward, reunite and decently reclothe it, and restore its original hunger for wisdom. Fun and games are insufficient.[37]

Anyway, to return to Majorca in early 1961, the prospect of meeting two such apparently fascinating characters as Idries Shah and Gerald Gardner did indeed prove too much for Graves to resist, so they arranged to meet at the Granja Reus in Palma at 4 o'clock in the afternoon of Tuesday 17th January 1961. Exactly what was discussed is not known, but Graves invited them to visit him the following Sunday at his home at Canelluñ in Deyá.

Researchers such as Richard Perceval Graves and Grevel Lindop have shown that Shah clearly had his own reasons for meeting Graves. Cleverly feeding his own ideas back to him mixed with the traditional teachings of Sufism, Shah quickly became one of Graves' trusted friends. He probably used Gerald to make the initial contact, but once it was made, he was to some extent dropped rather unceremoniously. Certainly after the first two meetings with Graves, Gerald was left to fend for himself while Shah got to know Graves much more closely. Indeed, it seems that Graves did not take to Gerald at their initial meeting and friendship did not develop as it did with Shah.

---

35. Ibid.
36. Ibid.
37. Op. cit., 559.

Lindop is very perceptive about Shah's motives in getting to know Graves:

Shah was a good listener. A lively, resourceful and highly intelligent man, he was full of charm. He had a wide knowledge of literature and world religions. Whatever bits and pieces he and Gardner had to tell Graves about the British Witches, his main intention was to get to know Graves, to gauge his interests and enthusiasms and to appeal to Graves's curiosity by conveying an impression that he possessed hidden knowledge from Eastern sources, which he might in due course be able to impart to Graves.[38]

The whole relationship between Shah and Graves is fascinating, as Shah appears to use some of the same techniques on Graves that he had earlier used on Gerald - reflecting his own ideas back to him, making himself indispensable and playing him at his own game.

One of the great controversies surrounding the relationship of Robert Graves and Idries Shah and his brother Omar was in connection with an old manuscript of the Rubaiyyat of Omar Khayyam which was supposed to be in the Shah family possession. Omar gave Graves a prose version from which Graves produced a poetic translation which was published in 1967. The book never received critical acclaim and it is highly likely that the original manuscript never existed. It is clear that the Shahs had a long history of deception and subterfuge, which makes their relationship with Gerald Gardner more understandable.

It is, perhaps, a slight exaggeration to say that Shah dropped Gerald like a stone for I am sure they both visited places of interest on the island together during the rest of January and the beginning of February. Towards the end of February, however, Gerald was beginning to get a little lonely, and in early March he wrote to Lois Pearson inviting her to come out and join him, which she did.

They stayed in a hotel in the old part of Palma, a typical Spanish style building with a courtyard with Moorish arches and plenty of vegetation. They both liked sunbathing, so spent quite a lot of time doing that, though Gerald insisted on telling Lois about the history

---

38. Lindop, op. cit.

of the island until she was suffering from 'cultural indigestion'!39 Gerald took Lois on trips to look at ancient sites and museums. Idries joined them when he was not ensconced with Graves. Lois also reports that Gerald's health improved while he was in Majorca: he had put on some weight, became suntanned and, she wrote, "his eyes sparkled".40

One of the places they visited was Porto Cristo, a fishing village. Gerald particularly wanted to visit the nearby Cuevas de Drach (Caves of the Dragon). Lois reports that Gerald "was ecstatic and, like a small, endearing child, gave voice to his delight at the sight that met his eyes."41 A musical performance was laid on for members of the public, involving musicians in a gondola playing as they floated across the underground lake. Lois recounts an amusing incident when the lights were extinguished and silence fell upon the audience. At this point, she recalls, "... Gerald piped up in a loud voice, 'Oh, where was Moses when the lights went out?'", at which she and Idries Shah burst into uncontrollable laughter!

While in Majorca, Gerald carried out some research into the reported abilities of the early islanders to throw stones by means of slings.

Gerald, Lois and Idries then took the plane to Madrid, where Shah had arranged to meet Robert Graves and his friend, the film actress Ava Gardner. While in Madrid, one of the places they visited was the world-famous Prado museum, upon which Gerald proved to be extremely knowledgeable. He told Lois that he had a photographic memory and didn't need a guide book.

Next was the ancient city of Toledo, in which Gerald was particularly interested as it was a centre of decorative art and the home of the painter El Greco.

Whilst being no admirer of Spain's ruler, General Franco, Gerald wanted to see the memorial to the dead in the Civil War which lies in the Valle de los Caidos (the Valley of the Fallen). Gerald predicted, correctly, that it would become a mausoleum for Franco himself after his death.

39. Bourne, (1998), 69.
40. Op. cit., 70.
41. Op. cit., 73.

The place that Gerald most wanted to visit was the monastery of El Escorial, which was also a palace for Philip II as well as a library, art gallery and college. According to Lois, he was particularly impressed with the Panteón de los Infantes, a 20-sided mausoleum of white marble containing the remains of royal children.

I think Gerald enjoyed his trip to Majorca and other parts of Spain very much and he seems at some stage to have gone on another trip with Lois, this time to Greece. This may have been in the winter of 1962/63, which was another very severe one in England.

Just as Shah was providing tempting bait for Graves, I think that at a certain stage during the trip, he decided that, as Gerald had lost his usefulness to him, he would play Gerald at his own game and wind him up with an elaborate story with very little basis in truth. His name for Gerald was 'Mali', which means 'gardener' in Hindi.

Shah told Gerald a story, or interlocking series of stories, which appealed to all Gerald's weaknesses, for status, excitement, subterfuge and secrecy. These probably developed over long evening chats in the hotel at Palma. The story quickly became both elaborate and mystifying. On returning to England, Shah had a bout of 'flu but, on his recovery, he wrote a very strange letter to Gerald. This involved some sort of dispute involving the Prime Minister of India and the prospect of settlement. He mentions that his brother, Omar (whom he calls "Mo") is flying out to talk about a new scheme to get agreement between the main parties involved. The whole letter is full of intrigue and excitement: just the sort of thing to appeal to Gerald. It may or may not be of some significance that the letter is dated 1st April!

The affair grew in complexity over the coming months. It was a strange mixture of psychological warfare, spying, and general intrigue, involving a projected trip to India. I think Gerald realised deep down that this was all a hoax on Shah's part. Yet it had all the themes that attracted Gerald - mystery, adventure, intrigue - and he was willing to be taken in.

He certainly seems to have started on a trip to India. He had been in Shrodells Hospital, Watford in November 1961. When he was discharged, he left with Eleanor Bone, who told the hospital people that she was his niece, in order that they would release him. Gerald stayed with her for a while and then she took him down to Highcliffe to stay with Edith for a few days.

From there he got a ship (probably from Southampton) which was bound for Bombay. This was all very exciting for Gerald. He believed he was being pursued and had to throw people off his trail (he had done the same back in 1927 when he was wanting a spiritualist consultation). Anyway, Gerald seems to have abandoned the adventure in Genoa in Italy and, presumably, returned home.

The whole thing seems to have started when Shah was doing some research into Gerald's family background for the biography he was writing. He had looked up the various Gardners mentioned in the Dictionary of National Biography and was particularly struck by the life and exploits of Colonel William Linnaeus Gardner, better known as 'Gardner of Gardner's Horse'. As I mention in Chapter 1, he had just the sort of exciting action-packed life that would have appealed to Gerald. However, the episode in his life which Shah drew particular attention to in his discussions with Gerald was the fact that William Linnaeus Gardner had married an Indian princess who was a descendant of Ghengis Khan. Shah wove a story to the effect that it was the custom in the princess's family that anyone marrying into them, plus all their family, were automatically ennobled. Gerald was therefore, according to Shah, entitled to the rank of Indian Prince, but he needed to go to India in person to claim the title.

I think in the end Shah decided he had played Gerald at his own game long enough and that he should end it. He persuaded him not to go to India because he said there were political disturbances threatened. As a post-script to this, Shah told Gerald that the family was entitled to bear the Moghul standard of sacred yaks' tails, but he couldn't find any in Britain, so reluctantly abandoned the idea.

Shah later seemed to make up for this whole business because, according to Lois Bourne, Gerald was made an honorary Sufi: ...*in gratitude for certain kindnesses, Idries Shah presented Gerald with the accoutrements of Sufi ritual. I was there when this took place.*[42] Indeed, I have seen and held the Sufi wand which was given to him on that occasion and which is now in private ownership.

---

42. Letter, Lois Bourne to the author, late April 1999.

The relationship between Gerald Gardner and Idries Shah was a strange one. It could be seen in terms of exploitation and trickery on Shah's part. Yet he did do a lot of work on Gerald's biography and injected a degree of excitement and adventure into his life at a time when Gerald probably needed it.

CHAPTER THIRTY–FIVE

A Resting Place Near Carthage

In her book, *Lid Off the Cauldron*, Patricia Crowther mentions that Gerald had told her that something of great importance had happened in his life every nine years. Whether this was strictly true is perhaps of less significance than the fact that Gerald believed it to be true. Patricia continues: *He confided to Arnold and me in 1963 that the following year would be another nine year and added, 'I suppose I shall pop off then, as I can't think of any other important thing that could happen to me.'*[1]

Lois Bourne writes about the last coven meeting that Gerald ever attended. She puts it in January 1964, but it must been earlier, as Gerald embarked on his last voyage in November 1963. She writes that he was ... *very pale and drawn, and I sensed that he was exhausted. He admitted that he felt very tired ...*[2] Gerald told Lois about a dream which he had had concerning a tree in Islamic legend whose leaves are inscribed with people's names. The leaves of those who were to die during the following year would fall to the ground. He had seen his name on a falling leaf. Lois continued: *He was depressed about the dream because he felt that, if only he*

---

1. Crowther (1981), 29.
2. Bourne (1998), 92.

*could recover from this extreme tiredness, he could make plans for an innovation he planned for his museum. In order to recover his energies he had made arrangements to take a cruise in the sun.*3

In mid-November 1963, Gerald went up to Perth to visit the Wilsons and to meet Ray Buckland who was training with them. He then took the train down to Sheffield to stay with Arnold and Patricia Crowther. On Thursday 21st November 1963, Arnold and Patricia took Gerald by car from their house in Sheffield over the Pennines to the inland port of Manchester, which is linked to the sea via the Manchester Ship Canal. Here Gerald boarded a cargo boat, which Patricia described to me as beautifully laid out, with a lot of polished and shining wood. Arnold and Patricia were the last members of the Craft to see Gerald. She describes the parting as follows:

> *It was pouring with rain as we helped him with his luggage up the steep, iron steps on to the ship. Tears mingled with the raindrops on my face, as we waved him good-bye. I was very upset about him going so far on a boat which had no doctor on board, as he wasn't at all well. I could see no reason for such a long journey, when he could have flown to a warmer clime much more quickly.*4

It was a momentous weekend in more ways than one. The following day brought the assassination of John F Kennedy and the Saturday saw the very first broadcast of the television series, 'Dr. Who', still running almost 50 years later!

However, the ship did not leave: it stayed moored in Manchester for a fortnight! Perhaps it reminded Gerald of his experience over 50 years previously waiting in Singapore harbour! When it did depart, it made a detour to Ireland, but finally made its way slowly to Lebanon, probably stopping at various ports on route.

In a letter to Gerald dated 12th December 1963, Monique Wilson writes: *If you arrived as scheduled you will have been in the Lebanon six days now. Did you have a good trip? Do you like Beirut? How are Marie and Zouhair?* I do not know who Marie and Zouhair are, but they are obviously residents of Beirut who were

---

3. Ibid.
4. Crowther, (1981), 29.

known to Gerald and Monique before Gerald's trip. Possibly he had arranged to stay with them while he was in Beirut. It has been suggested[5] that they were members of a coven which had been founded earlier.

What with the delay, Gerald probably did not arrive in Beirut until shortly before Christmas 1963. We know that on 2nd January 1964 he signed a new version of his will, which was witnessed by the Vice-Consul and a clerk in the British Embassy in Beirut. It seems highly likely that Gerald had had this typed up according to his instructions by the Westminster Bank on the Isle of Man, which he had appointed as his executor and trustee. However, he had not signed it then and there on the Isle of Man but had taken it with him on his trip. This strongly suggests that he wanted to ponder over it as he was not sure whether it provided for what he really wanted.

Anyway, the will was finally signed. From Gerald's estate in England, which was later valued at £21,688, he bequeathed a total of £9000 to various of his friends and colleagues: £3000 to Patricia Crowther; £1500 to Edith Woodford-Grimes; £1500 to Monique Wilson; £1000 to Lois Pearson; £1000 to Jack Bracelin; £500 to Donna's sister, Victoria Rosedale; £300 to Mrs. A. Jones, his housekeeper; and £200 to Doreen Valiente. He left his shares in Ancient Crafts Ltd to Lois Pearson and all his Scottish regalia to his sister-in-law, Miriam Gardner. He left his home, 77 Malew Street, and another house in Castletown, 22 Queen Street, to Monique Wilson. He left 19, 21 and 23 Mill Street to the caretaker of the Museum, William Worrall. He allowed Victoria Rosedale to take any family portraits and pictures which she wanted to keep.

It is clear that Gerald wanted the museum to continue and to be in good hands. He had mentioned to various people the possibility of setting up a trust to manage the museum and its collection after his death, and was really searching for someone to take it over. We have already seen that he asked both Angus McLeod and Lois Pearson to take it on but neither felt able to. In an earlier will, he had bequeathed the museum to Patricia Crowther, and Eleanor Bone had also been "sounded out" about taking it on.

---

5. Arcanus, "The Arrival of Modern Witchcraft: a Personal Reminiscence", www.somersetpagan.org/dem_personal_rem.html.

Gerald clearly wanted the caretaker, William Worrall, to continue running the museum, mill and outhouses subject to keeping it in good condition and paying rates and insurance. If he died within five years or was in breach of any of the conditions, then the museum would revert to Monique Wilson. Gerald left her the contents of the Museum provided that she allowed Worrall to display the items. In the event, Worrall did not wish to continue running the museum, and both buildings and contents passed to Monique Wilson. If she had died before Gerald, then the museum would have gone to Patricia Crowther.

There have been various criticisms of the way in which the Wilsons acted, suggesting that they influenced Gerald to change his will in their favour, with allegations of blackmail and worse. This is not the place to elaborate on such comments. I am sure that at some stage a biography of the Wilsons will be written which will put these matters into their proper perspective.

While he was in Lebanon, Gerald received a letter from Monique giving news of how things were going in the U.S.A. following Raymond Buckland's initiation:

The American group is formed. Delightful people! And they are taking to the Craft like ducks to water. I have had to lead and teach everyone I brought in, but Robat & Rowen [Raymond and Rosemary Buckland] came with complete faith and delight in our rituals. They just love everything about us. We sent Robat back as HP [High Priest] with nearly a complete set of tools. He will bring in Rowen, and they are starting with a group of 8. I have also handed over all my American correspondence and they will handle it.[6]

This was probably one of the last letters Gerald received and it is good that he knew before he died that the seed sown in America was beginning to grow.

In the Toronto collection is probably his last piece of writing. It goes, in part:

I write this in Beirut in the Lebanon. ... everything is under deep snow, all the roads are cut off. and this weather is

---

6. Letter, Monique Wilson to Gerald Gardner, 5 December 1963.

exceptuanall for this time of year. mid january. so I have no chance to check the statement made that rere is a village here in Lebanon where annually carry out the usual rites of astoreth and this observance is reguarded as a ussl part of the ... Though the local Arabs still tell tales of Astorooth they know that she ... in ancient times, and speak of her still exist-ing. but as the most part of [them are] Roman catholics, or else Muhamaden. and some are jews. so it is natural they dont want to speak about it. And, owing to the cold and all the roads being blocked it is impossible to travel about look-ing for it. nor is it likely that any can be celebrated this year, unless there is an extreme change in the weather.

Some roads were cut off for three weeks by frozen snowdrifts. It was unfortunate for Gerald that the inclement weather had enveloped Lebanon: just the sort of thing he was hoping to escape for a month or two! It can't have been very good for his health. Indeed, I suspect that he cut his stay in Beirut short for, probably no later than the beginning of February, he managed to secure a cabin on the *S.S. Scottish Prince*, which was due to return, indirectly, to England.

The *Scottish Prince* had been built in 1950, appropriately enough in Burntisland in Scotland, and was owned by the Prince Line. It had accommodation for 12 passengers as well as carrying considerable cargo. One of its former captains, Laurie Scott, described it as follows: *We carried twelve passengers on the Mediterranean Trade, mainly retired teachers, hoteliers and restau-rateurs, enjoying a holiday after a busy summer season. ... We also had an extensive library and an excellent choice of food which we all appreciated.*[7]

It seems as if the Scottish Prince and its sister ships did round trips from England to the eastern Mediterranean of about six weeks. Some of the ports they visited included Alexandria, Latakia, Iskenderun (Turkey), Famagusta (Cyprus), Beirut and Tunis, plus ports in Israel, which fact they tried to

---

7. http://patmedia.net/iscott/Captainscottslog/Story%20n.htm.

conceal because it would not go down well with some of the other port authorities!

⚘

Gerald Brosseau Gardner died on Wednesday 12th February 1964. He was on board the *Scottish Prince*, had just had breakfast and was sitting down reading a book on magic (possibly one from the ship's library or more likely one of his own), when he collapsed and died. He had had a cerebral haemorrhage, in other words a stroke.

A myth has grown up that the ship was in the middle of the Mediterranean and put in to the nearest port for Gerald's body to be taken for burial. However, his Death Certificate is quite clear: the ship was already on a scheduled stop in Tunis Harbour when the death occurred.

Gerald's body was taken ashore and was buried with the minimum of ceremony the following day at the Christian Cimetière du Belvédère in the Bab El Khadra quarter of the city. It is rumoured that the ship's captain was the only witness.

Just over four years later, Eleanor Bone was on holiday in Tunis and took the opportunity to look for Gerald's grave. What she found was rather disturbing: the Chaplain in charge of the cemetery informed her that the Government was turning it into a public park, but that, if she wanted to, she could disinter Gerald's remains and move them to another cemetery. Very quickly she raised the necessary sum from witches back in Britain and the reinterment was accomplished on 24th October 1968. In fact, the cemetery did not actually close until 1979, when it was incorporated into the Parc du Belvédère, the largest park in Tunis, which had been opened originally in 1892 on the site of an olive grove.

As part of the closure procedures for the Cimetière du Belvédère, a Christian extension to the existing Jewish Cimetière du Borgel was created, and it was to this cemetery that Gerald's body was moved. It now lies in the Christian Cemetery (formerly known as the Cimetière du Borgel), on Keiredine Pacha Street (across from the Pacha Centre) in Tunis. The grave is in Section F,

Carre 4, Plot 246 (Conservator's reference number: 4 F 246). The precise location of the grave is 36.82462 degrees N; 10.19073 degrees E.

For almost 40 years, Gerald's grave lay undisturbed but unmarked, gradually becoming overgrown and rubble-strewn. However, in 2007, a meeting took place between Patricia Crowther and Larry Jones, a member of the Craft from Washington State, U.S.A. Larry told Patricia that he was working in North Africa, and Patricia took the opportunity to charge Larry with finding the grave. Taking a short break from his work to visit Tunis, he started making enquiries and managed to track down the location of the grave. In the short time available to him, Larry arranged for the ground to be cleared and for a gravestone to be erected. This is now in position and reads, in the words of Patricia Crowther:

GERALD BROSSEAU GARDNER
13TH JUNE 1884 - 12TH FEBRUARY 1964
AUTHOR, ARCHAEOLOGIST, ARTIST
FATHER OF MODERN WICA
BELOVED OF THE GREAT GODDESS

CHAPTER THIRTY–SIX

An Assessment of Gerald Gardner

What, then, are we to make of Gerald Gardner? As we try to understand the workings of a complex if fascinating character, what themes can we discern? To use a colloquial phrase, what made Gerald Gardner tick?

Whatever one's thoughts on the validity of astrology, it is undoubtedly true that the generally recognised character of those born with the Sun in Gemini, as was Gerald Gardner, fits him very well. His mind was very active. He read, thought and talked a lot, ranging widely in those activities over many subjects, noting connections that others had ignored. He retained the most obscure facts in his mind, and seemed, according to Lois Bourne, to have a photographic memory.[1]

In the classic children's story, *The Wind in the Willows*, by Kenneth Grahame, first published 1908, there is a character, Toad, who has enthusiasms which he suddenly drops when a new thing to be enthusiastic about comes to his attention. Gerald was very much like this, but it is significant that, though it waned to some extent at times, he never lost his enthusiasm for witchcraft from the moment he was initiated until the end of his life.

---

1. Lois Bourne, *Dancing with Witches*, (Robert Hale, 1998), 75.

Gerald seemed to combine a delicate state of health with a robust and active lifestyle, which continued right through to his final adventure in the Mediterranean. Asthma was certainly a key element in the direction of the whole of Gerald's life. It prompted decisions which ultimately led to his working life 'out East' and to the pattern of his activities following his retirement.

As with many Europeans, he contracted malaria in Borneo and its associated black-water fever, which, against all the odds, he overcame. His asthma came back badly following the momentous ritual in the New Forest in 1940, and for the last 20 years of his life he had several spells in hospital and more than once expressed the view (somewhat exaggerated) that he was on his last legs.

Whilst he was ever ready to express to others this idea that he would not last long, he was nevertheless always planning for the future, right up until just before his final voyage.

One of the most important consequences of Gerald's asthma was that he was never sent to school and, indeed, had no formal education of any sort, since I am quite sure that Com never provided any.

Gerald had an inquisitive mind, however, and assimilated a lot of experiences during his trips with Com. The most notable thing was that he taught himself to read, and I think as a result he valued knowledge gained in that way: he had achieved it by his own efforts and this resulted in an eclectic approach to his reading rather than a structured academic approach. He followed his natural inclinations and this is reflected, for example, in his library.

A negative consequence of Gerald's lack of formal education combined with his mercurial character is that he seemed incapable of spelling. He tended to spell words phonetically and, as a result, needed a great deal of help in getting things ready for publication. It also, I think, whether rightly or wrongly, affected how academics who received letters from him tended to respond.

One positive aspect of the lack of formal schooling was Gerald's ability to tackle things in his own, perhaps unorthodox, way. He didn't know that certain things were not done, so he did them! He made contact with native people in an age where this was considered eccentric, and he proposed down-to-earth explanations for so-called 'supernatural' events.

Indeed, he was very practical, from necessity, making parts for machinery in areas where one could not conveniently go to a nearby supply depot. This was later manifest in his skills and enjoyment in model-making and in the creation of ritual equipment and museum exhibits.

We don't always know why we become interested in particular things and I doubt whether Gerald would have been able to explain his fascination for weapons, and particularly knives. I don't think he actually ever used them as weapons, but there was a lifelong obsession with collecting them. Perhaps Gerald felt the subconscious need to defend, with all the means at his disposal all that was of most value to him, as in the central theme to *A Goddess Arrives* and in the 1940 'Operation Cone of Power'. This may be why he was particularly attracted to the cast circle, in both witchcraft and ceremonial magic ritual and why the sword and the athame (witch's knife) have such a prominent place in those rituals.

Gerald was always interested in history, or what we may call the dimension of time, or how things got to be how they are. In this, as in much else, he was prepared to think for himself and ask previously unasked questions in order to get to what he saw as the truth. Probably because he had no formal training in historical investigation, he was prepared to use unorthodox methods and come up with his own, often very closely thought-out explanations, such as the origin of the keris in the stingray barb.

An awareness of the reality of 'the other worlds' was something which came to Gerald at a young age, possibly because of his asthma - 'the occultists' disease', and remained with him for the rest of his life. Florence Marryat's writing fell on fertile ground and Gerald was clearly sufficiently attuned, sensitive to and sympathetic to the beliefs about the 'supernatural' of the native peoples that he encountered. If he had not been convinced before, his experiences with some of the London mediums in 1927 convinced him in a very personal way of the reality of survival beyond physical death.

So, when he came across the Crotona Fellowship and, through them, the group into which he was initiated, he was familiar with and accepted such things as reincarnation and psychic vision through such techniques as scrying and psychometry.

The other side of the coin from psychic awareness is magic, the ability to influence things on the subtle realms. Again, Gerald had had practical experience of the reality of magic through attending 'séance' sessions in Borneo and Malaya and was thus in a receptive frame of mind when he was introduced to the magical techniques of the witches.

Despite his awareness of the psychic dimension and magical techniques, Gerald was actually very much of a materialist, trying to find material explanations for supposed 'supernatural' events. It is one of the themes of *A Goddess Arrives* - that the emergence of Aphrodite from the waves could actually have been merely a woman swimming in from a ship from which she had just escaped.

I don't think that Gerald actually ever believed that spirits were really conjured by means of elaborate magical rituals, but included them in *High Magic's Aid* merely for their dramatic effect and because he wasn't allowed to write about any witch magic. And, whilst he definitely accepted that witch magic existed, because he had seen it work on more than one occasion, I don't think he was ever able to really work magic himself. For this, he relied on others.

Indeed, he really didn't, I think, have any of what we might call 'spiritual' feelings: at any rate, he never wrote about any. What he did write about, when it wasn't the purely intellectual, which formed the bulk of his writings, was relationships, particularly with his fellow members of the witch cult. If anyone had a "mystical goddess experience", it was not Gerald but someone like Katherine Oldmeadow.

Fred Lamond told me: "Gerald did not have charisma. He was a very lovable man, but he did not have charisma! And he did not have this aura of spiritual authority."[2] This is very rare amongst those who have founded new religions or championed old ones. Indeed, it was only years after reading *Witchcraft Today* that I realised the central place which Gerald had been given by those who were writing about the Craft. Indeed, in that book he wrote: *I must make it clear - I am a humble member of a coven. I am not its head or leader in any way, and I have to do what I am told.*[3] In

---

2. Frederic Lamond, discussion with the author, July 2006.
3. Gardner, (1954), 138.

practice, of course, this was only true of the 'Southern Coven' in Highcliffe and not of any later covens, such as in Bricket Wood, where Gerald definitely was 'in charge'.

Gerald was a trickster and had perfected this to a fine art. Dayonis says of him that he was "a barrel-load of monkeys". As has been said of the veteran politician, Denis Healey, he had an "... extraordinary ability to convey an impression that was frequently in direct contradiction of the truth."[4] Gerald was not above telling deliberate untruths, as when he claimed to have been born in Scotland, but he much preferred to speak the literal truth while giving a totally misleading impression.

Yet we would be wrong if we were thereby to discount everything that Gerald said or wrote. There are things about which he was truthful and things about which he was not necessarily truthful, and it is important to distinguish between them. Where he was writing about his emotional response to things and about his friendships he was sincere and honest. When writing about the history of the Craft he often got carried away by what he would have liked the truth to have been, or how he imagined things had been, rather than how things actually were. One might call this romanticisation.

There are so many aspects of Gerald's personality that it is difficult to sum him up in a few paragraphs. He was very much his own man, not following any 'party line'. And it is to be hoped that the major religious movement that he helped into being remains a home for those of like mind and that it will never become a rigid structure following the handed-down words of "Saint Gerald". I hope that this book will help in some way to reveal the true Gerald Gardner: the one who enjoyed life and was always open to new experiences.

---

4. Leader, *The Guardian*, 3 December 2008.

≫ PART IV ≪

Bountiful Harvest

Gardner's Legacy

When Gerald Gardner died in 1964, there were, perhaps, a few hundred at most initiated witches in England, Scotland, Wales and the Isle of Man. One coven had just been established in America, and there were isolated individuals in Australia and one or two other places, and that was it.

In 2001, the American Religious Identification Survey estimated that there were 134,000 adults in the USA who identified themselves as Wiccan. Isaac Bonewits writes:

> ... I've seen what I consider reasonable estimates for the number of self-identified, practicing Neopagans (including Wiccans) running from half a million to several million people in the USA and Canada. Certainly there are more of us than there are members of many other religions such as Unitarian Universalists, Quakers, Christian Scientists, or Spiritualists.[1]

In Britain, Paganism is now the eighth largest religious grouping, with 40,000 people identifying thus in the 2001 Census, of

---

1. Isaac Bonewits, "How Many "Pagans" Are There?", www.neopagan.net/HowManyPagans.html.

which 7000 identified as 'Wicca'. It has been estimated that by the time of the 2011 Census, this figure could reach a quarter of a million.

All this has come, directly or indirectly, from Gerald Gardner. There is a poignant passage in *Witchcraft Today*, which reveals his feelings in 1954:

> *... I think we must say good-bye to the witch. The cult is doomed, I am afraid, partly because of modern conditions, housing shortage, the smallness of modern families, and chiefly by education. The modern child is not interested. He knows witches are all bunk - and there is the great fear. ... The other reason is that science has displaced her; good weather reports, good health services, outdoor games, bathing, nudism, the cinema and television have largely replaced what the witch had to give. Free thought or spiritualism, according to your inclinations, have taken away the fear of Hell that she prevented, though nothing yet has replaced her greatest gifts: peace, joy and content.*[2]

Yet he didn't want this to happen. His whole life following initiation was devoted to ensuring that it didn't happen. In Fred Lamond's telling phrase, he was "an old man in a hurry". Perhaps, as a result, he did initiate some unsuitable people and make unwise decisions about the future of the museum. And yet, by the time of his death, things were beginning to turn. He would have been, I am sure, overjoyed by the 'Bountiful Harvest' that his life's work has now achieved.

---

2. Gardner, (1954), 129.

Appendices

APPENDIX A

Chronology

1884 June 13th: Gerald Brosseau Gardner born at Ingle Lodge, Serpentine North, Blundellsands, Great Crosby, near Liverpool, Lancashire, England.

1888-1890: Wintering in Nice with 'Com'

1891-92: Wintering with 'Com' in Canary Islands, Accra and Madeira

1892-1896: Wintering with 'Com' in Madeira

1897/98: Wintering with 'Com' in Madeira and South Africa

1898-1900: Wintering with 'Com' in Madeira

1891 December: Working on the Ladbroke tea estate, Ceylon

1904: Working on the Non Pareil tea estate, Ceylon

1907 April–December: Trip to England

1910 May 23rd: Entered Apprentice Degree at Sphinx Lodge No. 107, Colombo
June 20th: Fellow Craft Degree
June 27th: Master Mason Degree

1911 May 18th: Grand Lodge Certificate

1911: Working at Mawao Estate, Membakut, North Borneo

1912: Working at Sungkai, Perak, Malaya

1912: Working at Bidor

1912: Bought estate at Bukit Katho, Bidor

1916 April-October: Visit to England and Wales

1921: Trip to England
1921: Working for Public Works Department
1923 September: Appointed Inspector of Rubber Plantations
1926: Appointed Inspector of Chandu Shops
1927: Visit to England
1927 August 16th: Married Dorothea Frances Rosedale (Donna)
1928-1932: Excavations at Johore Lama
1932: Visit to England
    August: Attends International Congress of Prehistoric and Protohistoric Sciences - London
1934: Visit to China
1936 January 29th: Retires from post with Johore Civil Service
1936 March: *Keris and Other Malay Weapons* published
1936 April: Returned to England - living at Flat 10, 26 Charing Cross Road, London
    April: Attended Vaabenhistorisk Selskab conference in Denmark
    December: Living at 23a Buckingham Palace Mansions, Victoria, London
1936/37: Wintering in Cyprus
1937 April: Volunteered as an Air Raid Warden
1937 September: Obtains PhD from the Meta Collegiate Extension of the National Electronic Institute
1938 January–April: Wintering in Cyprus
    July: Moved to Southridge, Highcliffe, Hampshire
    August: Attended performance of *Pythagoras* at the Garden Theatre, Christchurch
1939 February: Elected member of the Folk-Lore Society
    September: Initiation into the Witch Cult
    December: *A Goddess Arrives* published
1940 August 1st: "Operation Cone of Power" in the New Forest
    August 13th: The "Magna Carta" letter appeared in the *Daily Telegraph*
    August 17th: Marriage of Rosanne Woodford-Grimes and 'Tommy' Thompson
1944: Moved to 47 Ridgmount Gardens, London
1945 June: Acquires Witch's Cottage from J.S.M. Ward

July: Purchases land at Bricket Wood

1946 February: Elected to Council of the Folk-Lore Society

May: Became member of the Society for Psychical Research

June 19th: Gave talk on "British Charms, Amulets and Talismans" to the Folk-Lore Society

August 29th: Ordained Priest of the Ancient British Church

December: Attends Winter Solstice meeting of Ancient Druid Order

1947 May 1st: Visited Aleister Crowley in Hastings with Arnold Crowther and Eda Collins

June 21st: Housewarming of Witch's Cottage at Five Acres Club

July: Attended International Conference of Folk-Lore in Paris

November 29th: left Liverpool for visit to U.S.A.

1948 March: returned to England

July: Attended Congress on Folk-lore, Ethnography and Archaeocivilisation in Paris

December: Wintered in Cyprus and Lebanon

1949 July: *High Magic's Aid* published

December: Wintered in Spain

1950: Initiation of Barbara and Gilbert Vickers

November: met Cecil Williamson at Atlantis Bookshop

1951 February to March: Wintering in Gibraltar with Edith

April 14th: BBC Television appearance

June 22nd: The Fraudulent Mediums Act became law

July 8th: Attends Summer Solstice ritual at Stonehenge

July 29th: Grand Opening of the Folklore Centre, Castletown, Isle of Man

August 27th to 31st: Attends International Congress of European and Western Ethnology in Stockholm and Uppsala

1952 January to March: Wintered in Italy

January: publication of Pennethorne Hughes' *Witchcraft*

March: left 47 Ridgmount Gardens and moved to 77 Malew Street, Castletown, Isle of Man and 145 Holland Road, London

September 27th: article "Witchcraft in Britain" by Allen Andrews in *Illustrated*

December: Wintered in West Africa

1953 March: returned to England

June: Doreen Valiente initiated

1954: Wintered in West Africa

April: Took over Museum

June 5th: Opening of the Museum of Magic and Witchcraft

September 24th: meets Austin Osman Spare

November 1st: *Witchcraft Today* published

1956 March: Jack Bracelin and 'Dayonis' initiated

1957 February 2nd: Fred Lamond initiated

March: The Split in the coven

July: "Proposed Rules for the Craft"

1958 January 6th: Incorporation of Ancient Crafts Limited

1959 February: *The Meaning of Witchcraft* published

1960 January 30th: Death of Donna

June 6th: initiation of Arnold and Patricia Crowther

September: *Gerald Gardner Witch* published

December: Wintering in Majorca

1961 January 17th: meets Robert Graves with Idries Shah

March: visits Spain with Lois Bourne

1963 November: meets Ray Buckland in Perth with Monique and Scotty Wilson

November 21st: embarks on last trip to Lebanon

1964 January 2nd: signs latest version of Will

February 12th: dies aboard the *Scottish Prince* in Tunis harbour

APPENDIX B

Gerald Gardner Bibliography

BOOKS

Keris and Other Malay Weapons, (Edited by B. Lumsden Milne) (Progressive Publishing Company, Singapore), Limited Edition 150 copies, March 1936; Second Edition, April 1936. Republished by EP Publishing Limited, East Ardsley, Wakefield, Yorkshire, England 1973. 138 pp. Republished Orchid Press, Thailand 2009, 144 pp.

A Goddess Arrives, (Arthur H Stockwell Ltd., London), December 1939, 382 pp. I-H-O 2000, 296 pp.

High Magic's Aid, (Michael Houghton, London) July 1949, 352 pp.; Weiser 1975; Pentacle Enterprises, (Foreword by Patricia Crowther), 1993; Godolphin House, Hinton WV, 1996, 238 pp; I-H-O 1999, 218 pp.

Witchcraft Today, (Rider and Company, London), November 1954, 163 pp.; The Citadel Press, New York, 1955, (First US Edition); Edwin Self/Pedigree Books, 1960, 191 pp; Arrow Books, 1966, 192 pp; Jarrolds, 1968; Citadel, 1970 and 1971; Arrow Books, 1970;

Arrow, 1975 192pp; Magickal Childe, New York, 1982 and 1988; Mercury Publishing, 1999; I-H-O, 1999, 135 pp; Kensington Pub Corp. 2004; Citadel, 2004, 197 pp (Fiftieth Anniversary Edition. Foreword by Judy Harrow).

The Museum of Magic and Witchcraft: The Story of the Famous Witches' Mill at Castletown, Isle of Man, (The Photochrom Co. Ltd., Tunbridge Wells, Kent), 1958, 32 pp.

The Meaning of Witchcraft, (The Aquarian Press, London), February 1959, 288 pp.; reprinted 1971; Mercury Publishing, 1982 and 1999; Magickal Childe 1982, 1988, and 1991; I-H-O 2000, 290 pp; Red Wheel/Weiser, 2004.

Gerald Gardner Witch by J. L. Bracelin, (The Octagon Press), September 1960, 224 pp.; I-H-O 1999, 202 pp.

ARTICLES

"Notes on Some Ancient Gold Coins from Johore River", *Journal Malayan Branch Royal Asiatic Society,* Vol. XI, Part II, Dec. 1933, pp 171-176.

"Notes on Two Uncommon Varieties of the Malay Kris", *Journal Malayan Branch Royal Asiatic Society* Vol. XI, Part II, Dec. 1933, pp 178-182.

"Ancient Beads from the Johore River as Evidence of an Early Link by Sea between Malaya and the Roman Empire", *Journal Royal Asiatic Society,* 1937, pp 467-470.

"Le Problème de la Garde de l'Epée Cypriote de l'Age du Bronze" *Bulletin de la Société Préhistorique Française* No. 12, 1937.
"More Coins from the Johore River", *Numismatic Chronicle,* 5th Series, Vol. xix, 1939, pp 98-103.

"Witchcraft", *Folk Lore*, Vol. 50, June 1939, pp 188-190.

"British Charms, Amulets and Talismans", *Folk Lore*, Vol. 53, II June 1942, pp 95-103.

"The Hazel as a Weapon", *Folk Lore*, Vol. 55, No 4, (Dec. 1944), p 177.

"The Museum of Magic and Witchraft" [sic], *Humana Studia*, Serie II, Anno VII, Fasc I, 1955.

"The Truth About George", *New Dimensions*, January 1964.

"Witchcraft in the Isle of Man", *New Dimensions*, March 1964, pp 6-11.

APPENDIX C

General Bibliography

Abse, Dannie, *The Strange Case of Dr. Simmonds and Dr. Glas,* (Robson Books, 2002).

Beatty, Charles, *Gate of Dreams,* (Geoffrey Chapman, 1972).

Billingsley, John, *The Day The Sun Went Out,* (Northern Earth, 1999).

Bourne, Lois, *Dancing with Witches,* (Robert Hale, 1998).

Bracelin, J. L., *Gerald Gardner Witch,* (Octagon, 1960).

Buchan, John, *The Moon Endureth,* (Hodder and Stoughton, 1912).

Buddicom, Jacintha, *Eric and Us: A Remembrance of George Orwell,* (Leslie Frewin, 1974; revised edition Finlay Publisher, 2006).

Carr-Gomm, Philip, *In the Grove of the Druids - The Druid Teachings of Ross Nichols,* (Watkins, 2002).

Chamot, Mary, Farr, Dennis and Butlin, Martin, *The Modern British Paintings, Drawings and Sculpture, Vol. I,* (Oldbourne Press, 1964).

Childers, Erskine, *The Riddle of the Sands,* (Smith Elder, 1903).

Churchill, Winston S., *The Second World War, Volume II: Their Finest Hour,* (Cassell, 1949).

Collum, V.C.C., *The Tressé Iron-Age Megalithic Monument,* (Oxford, 1935).

Colquhoun, Ithell, *Sword of Wisdom,* (Neville Spearman, 1975).

Crowther, Patricia, *Witch Blood,* (House of Collectibles, 1974).

Crowther, Patricia, *Lid off the Cauldron,* (Frederick Muller, 1981).

Crowther, Patricia, *One Witch's World,* (Robert Hale, 1998).

Crowther, Patricia, *From Stagecraft to Witchcraft,* (Capall Bann, 2002).

Domhoff, G. William, *The Mystique of Dreams: A Search for Utopia Through Senoi Dream Theory,* (University of California Press, 1985).

Endicott, Kirk Michael, *An Analysis of Malay Magic,* (Oxford, 1970).

Farrar, Janet and Stewart, *The Witches' Way,* (Robert Hale, 1984).

Ferguson, John, *Ceylon in 1883: the Leading Crown Colony of the British Empire,* (Sampson Low, 1883).

Fortune, Dion, *The Goat-Foot God,* (Williams and Norgate, 1936).

Fortune, Dion, *The Magical Battle of Britain,* (Golden Gates, 1993).

Frey, Edward, *The Kris: Mystic Weapon of the Malay World,* (Oxford University Press, 1986).

Gardner, G. B., *Keris and Other Malay Weapons,* (Progressive Publishing Company, 1936).

Gardner, G. B., *A Goddess Arrives,* (Arthur H. Stockwell, 1939).

Gardner, G. B., *Witchcraft Today,* (Rider, 1954).

Gardner, G. B., *The Museum of Magic and Witchcraft: The Story of the Famous Witches' Mill at Castletown, Isle of Man,* (Photochrom, 1958).

Gardner, G. B., *The Meaning of Witchcraft,* (Aquarian, 1959).

Gilbert, Martin, *Finest Hour: Winston S. Churchill 1939-1941,* (Heinemann, 1983).

Gilbert, R. A., *The Golden Dawn Companion,* (The Aquarian Press, 1986).

Gombrich, Richard F., *Buddhist Precept and Practice: Traditional Buddhism in the Highlands of Ceylon,* (Kegan Paul, 1971).

Grant, Joan, *Winged Pharaoh,* (Arthur Barker October, 1937).

Grant, Kenneth, *Nightside of Eden,* (Frederick Muller, 1977).

Grant, Kenneth, *Images and Oracles of Austin Osman Spare,* (Fulgur, 2003).

Grant, Kenneth and Steffi, *Zos Speaks! Encounters with Austin Osman Spare,* (Fulgur, 1998).

Graves, Richard Perceval, *Robert Graves and the White Goddess 1940-1985,* (Weidenfeld and Nicolson, 1995).

Graves, Robert, *Collected Short Stories,* (Cassell, 1965).

Greenfield, T. Allen, *The Secret History of Modern Witchcraft,* (1996).

Haeckel, Ernst, *A Visit to Ceylon,* (Peter Eckler, 1883).

Haggard, H. Rider, *Allan and the Ice Gods,* (Hutchinson, 1927).

Heselton, Philip, *Wiccan Roots,* (Capall Bann, 2000).

Heselton, Philip, *Gerald Gardner and the Cauldron of Inspiration,* (Capall Bann, 2003).

History of Joseph Gardner & Sons Limited, Liverpool and London, 1748-1948.

Howard, Michael, *Modern Wicca: A History from Gerald Gardner to the Present,* (Llewellyn Publications 2009).

Hughes, Pennethorne, *Witchcraft,* (Longmans Green, 1952).

Hull, Roger C., *Social Differentiation in a North Liverpool Suburb: The Case of Great Crosby and Waterloo 1841-1901,* A Thesis Presented to the University of Liverpool for a Master of Arts Degree (in Local History), September 1989.

Hutton, Ronald, *The Triumph of the Moon,* (Oxford University Press, 1999).

Kelly, Aidan A., *Crafting the Art of Magic: Book I: A History of Modern Witchcraft 1939-1964,* (Llewellyn Publications, 1991).

Kelly, Aidan A., *Inventing Witchcraft,* (Thoth Publications, 2007).

Kershaw, Eva Maria, *A Study of Brunei Dusun religion: Ethnic Priesthood on a Frontier of Islam,* (Borneo Research Council 2000).

King, Francis, *Ritual Magic in England,* (Neville Spearman, 1970).

King, Francis, *The Magical World of Aleister Crowley,* (Weidenfeld and Nicolson 1977).

Kingsley, Mary H., *Travels in West Africa,* (Macmillan 1897).

Laird-Clowes, G. S., *Sailing Ships: Their History and Development as Illustrated by the Collection of Ship-models in the Science Museum,* (HMSO, 1932).

Lamond, Frederic, *Fifty Years of Wicca,* (Green Magic, 2004).

Laver, James, *Nymph Errant,* (Heinemann 1932).

Laver, James, *Nostradamus, or The Future Foretold,* (Collins, 1942).

Le Marchant, Denis, *Report on the Proceedings of the House of Lords on the Claims to the Barony of Gardner,* (Henry Butterworth, 1828).

Lewis, James R., *Magical Religion and Modern Witchcraft,* (SUNY Press, 1996).

Louÿs, Pierre, *The Adventures of King Pausole,* (Privately Printed for William Godwin, Inc. in New York in 1933).

Mackay, Derek, *Eastern Customs: The Customs Service in British Malaya and the Opium Trade,* (The Radcliffe Press, 2005).

Manwaring, G.E. and Dobrée, Bonamy, *Mutiny: The Floating Republic,* (Geoffrey Bles, 1935).

Marryat, Florence, *There is No Death,* (Kegan Paul, 1891).

McIntosh, Christopher, *The Rosicrucians: Their History, Mythology and Rituals of an Esoteric Order,* (Weiser, 1997).

Mee, Arthur, *The King's England: Hertfordshire,* (Hodder and Stoughton, 1939).

Murray, Lynda J., *A Zest for Life: the Story of Alexander Keiller,* (Morven Books, 1999).

Murray, Margaret, *The Witch Cult in Western Europe,* (Oxford 1921).

'Nemorensis, Rex' (Charles Cardell), *Witch,* (Dumblecott Magick Productions, 1964).

Newman, Paul, *The Tregerthen Horror,* (Abraxas, 2005).

Oldmeadow, Ernest, *The North Sea Bubble,* (Grant Richards, 1906).

Oldmeadow, K. L., *Madcap Judy,* (Collins, 1919).

Oldmeadow, K. L., *Ragged Robin,* (Collins, 1920).

Oldmeadow, K. L., *Princess Charming,* (Collins, 1923).

Oldmeadow, K. L., *Princess Anne,* (Collins, 1925).

Oldmeadow, K. L., *When George The Third Was King,* (Hutchinson, 1934).

Oldmeadow, K. L., *The Folklore of Herbs,* (Cornish Brothers Limited, 1946).

Pearson, Joanne, *Wicca and the Christian Heritage,* (Routledge, 2007).

Pickford, Doug, *Cheshire: Its Magic and Mystery,* (Sigma Leisure, 1994).

Pitcairn, Robert, *Criminal Trials in Scotland,* (Edinburgh, 1833).

Pocock, Geoffrey A., *One Hundred Years of the Legion of Frontiersmen,* (Phillimore, 2004).

Priestley, J. B., *They Walk in the City,* (William Heinemann, 1936).

Proceedings of the First International Congress of Prehistoric and Protohistoric Sciences, (Oxford, 1934).

Richardson, Iseult, *No Shadows Fall,* (Coast and Country Naturist Publications, 1994).

'Scire' (G. B. Gardner), *High Magic's Aid,* (Michael Houghton, 1949).

Shah, Sirdar Ikbal Ali, *Occultism, Its Theory and Practice,* (Castle Books New York, 1929).

Shah, Sayed Idries, *Oriental Magic,* (Rider, 1956).

Shah, Sayed Idries, *The Secret Lore of Magic,* (Frederick Muller, 1957).

Shah, Sayed Idries, *Destination Mecca,* (Octagon, 1969).

Skinner, Julia (compiler), *Did You Know? Southport: A Miscellany,* (Francis Frith, 2006).

Smith, Dr. Geoffrey Basil, *Knights of the Solar Cross,* (1981-83).

Smyth, Frank, *Modern Witchcraft,* (Macdonald, 1970).

Sutin, Lawrence, *Do What Thou Wilt: A Life of Aleister Crowley,* (St. Martin's Press, 2000).

Taylor, Gordon Rattray, *Sex in History,* (Thames and Hudson, 1953).

Teare, T. D. G., *Folk Doctor's Island,* (Times Press, Douglas, 1964).

Thomas, David A., *The Illustrated Armada Handbook,* (Harrap, 1988).

Twain, Mark, *A Yankee at the Court of King Arthur,* (Chatto and Windus, 1921).

Valiente, Doreen, *Witchcraft for Tomorrow,* (Robert Hale, 1978).

Valiente, Doreen, *The Rebirth of Witchcraft,* (Robert Hale, 1989).

Ward, J. S. M., *Gone West,* (Rider, 1917).

Ward, J. S. M., *A Subaltern in Spirit Land,* (Rider, 1920).

Ward, J. S. M., *Freemasonry and the Ancient Gods,* (Simpkin Marshall, 1921).

Ward, J. S. M., *Who was Hiram Abiff?* (Baskerville Press, 1925).

Ward, J. S. M., *The Orthodox Catholic Church in England,* (Showing its History and the Validity of its Orders), (1944).

Ward, J. S. M. and Stirling, W. G., *The Hung Society: or the Society of Heaven and Earth,* (Baskerville Press, 1925).

Index

A selection of other titles by Thoth Publications

THE TREASURE OF THE SILVER WEB
By Marian Green

Magic is a subject which fascinates many people, both young and old. Popular books may have drawn it to the attention of a new generation, yet magical tales of quest and mysteries, of symbols and discoveries seem to go back through human history.

The Treasure of the Silver Web is the story of friendship, discovery and magic set in the simpler times of the pre-computer age. It reveals secrets of the countryside the gifts of nature as well as describing magical arts and methods still used today. Readers will have to decide for themselves where the facts stop and fiction begins.

Marian Green is well known for her many books on folklore, occult philosophy, modern magic and witchcraft so her approach to these matters, even in a story book setting, are based on many years of practical experience and study.

ISBN 978-1-870450-77-5 eBook
ISBN 978-1-870450-78-2 paperback

A MODERN MAGICIANS HANDBOOK
By Marian Green

This book presents the ancient arts of magic, ritual and practical occult arts as used by modern ceremonial magicians and witches in a way that everyone can master, bringing them into the Age of Aquarius. Drawing on over three decades of practical experience, Marian Green offers a simple approach to the various skills and techniques that are needed to turn an interest into a working knowledge of magic.

Each section offers explanation, guidance and practical exercises in meditation, inner journeying, preparation for ritual, the arts of divination and many more of today's esoteric practices. No student is too young or too old to benefit from the material set out for them in this book, and its simple language may help even experienced magicians and witches understand their arts in greater depth.

ISBN 978-1-870450-43-0

THE GRAIL SEEKER'S COMPANION
By John Matthews & Marian Green

There have been many books about the Grail, written from many differing standpoints. Some have been practical, some purely historical, others literary, but this is the first Grail book which sets out to help the esoterically inclined seeker through the maze of symbolism, character and myth which surrounds the central point of the Grail.

In today's frantic world when many people have their material needs met some still seek spiritual fulfilment. They are drawn to explore the old philosophers and traditions, particularly that of our Western Celtic Heritage. It is here they encounter the quest for the Holy Grail, that mysterious object which will bring hope and healing to all. Some have come to recognise that they dwell in a spiritual wasteland and now search that symbol of the grail which may be the only remedy. Here is the guide book for the modern seeker, explaining the history and pointing clearly towards the Aquarian grail of the future.

John Matthews and Marian Green have each been involved in the study of the mysteries of Britain and the Grail myth for over thirty- five years. In the Grail Seeker's Companion they have provided a guidebook not just to places, but to people, stories and theories surrounding the Grail. A reference book of Grail-ology, including history, ritual, meditation, advice and instruction. In short, everything you are likely to need before you set out on the most important adventure of your life.

This is the only book that points the way to the Holy Grail Quest in the 21st. century.

ISBN 978-1-870450-49-2

THE HIDDEN VALUES OF THE GOLDEN DAWN
Volume One: **We call thee to the Gentle Light**
By Rick Falconer
Forward by Charles Chic Cicero and Sandra Tabatha Cicero

These volumes are indispensible for any with a genuine interest in the Golden Dawn. They are no beginner's guides, for you are no beginner. *The Hidden Values of the Golden Dawn* is a series of Psycho/Spiritual Magical treatise aiding transformation to a Higher Magical Awareness. The Adept, student, and all with an interest in the Golden Dawn will find aspects of themselves within these volumes. They each form experiential and insightful importance, revealing an alchemical infusion and a depth shaping magical undercurrents to ever take you deeper into your spiritual journey with a gradual potential of Divine perfection.

Rick Falconer is an Adept of the Golden Dawn System and a member of various Rosicrucian and Esoteric bodies. Living in England he is a lifelong student of more than thirty years involvement in Hermeticism, including Golden Dawn, Esoteric, Pagan, Theosophical, Psychical Research and Spiritualist Organisations. He began his magical and spiritual vocation at the age of 11 with three Middle England Spiritualist Mediums in the mid 1970's.

ISBN 978-1-870450-88-1 paperback
ISBN 978-1-870450-89-8 eBook

PRACTICAL MAGIC AND THE WESTERN MYSTERY TRADITION
Unpublished Essays and Articles by W. E. Butler.

W. E. Butler, a devoted friend and colleague of the celebrated occultist Dion Fortune, was among those who helped build the Society of the Inner Light into the foremost Mystery School of its day. He then went on to found his own school, the Servants of the Light, which still continues under the guidance of Dolores Ashcroft- Nowicki, herself an occultist and author of note and the editor and compiler of this volume.

Practical Magic and the Western Tradition is a collection of previously unpublished articles, training papers, and lectures covering many aspects of practical magic in the context of western occultism that show W. E. Butler not only as a leading figure in the magical tradition of the West, but also as one of its greatest teachers.

Subjects covered include: What makes an Occultist
Ritual Training
Inner Plane Contacts and Rays
The Witch Cult
Keys in Practical Magic Telesmatic Images Words of Power
An Explanation of Some Psychic Phenomena

ISBN 978-1-870450-32-4

PRACTICAL OCCULTISM
By Dion Fortune supplemented by Gareth Knight

This book contains the complete text of Dion Fortune's Practical Occultism in Daily Life which she wrote to explain, simply and practically, enough of the occult doctrines and methods to enable any reasonably intelligent and well balanced person to make practical use of them in the circumstances of daily life. She gives sound advice on remembering past incarnations, working out karma, divination, the use and abuse of mind power and much more.

Gareth Knight has delved into the Dion Fortune archive to provide additional material not available before outside Dion Fortune's immediate circle. It includes instruction on astral magic, the discipline of the mysteries, inner plane communicators, black magic and mental trespassing, nature contracts and elemental shrines.

In addition, Dion Fortune's review of The Literature of Illuminism describes the books she found most useful in her own quest, ranging from books for beginners to those on initiation, Qabalah, occult fiction, the old gods of England, Atlantis, witchcraft and yoga. In conclusion there is an interpretation by Dion Fortune's close friend Netta Fornario of The Immortal Hour, that haunting work of faery magic by Fiona Macleod, first performed at Glastonbury.

ISBN 978-1-870450-47-8

SPIRITUALISM AND OCCULTISM
By Dion Fortune with commentary edited by Gareth Knight

As well as being an occultist of the first rank, Dion Fortune was an accomplished medium. Thus she is able to explain the methods, technicalities and practical problems of trance mediumship from firsthand experience. She describes exactly what it feels like to go into trance and the different types of being one may meet with beyond the usual spirit guides.

For most of her life her mediumistic abilities were known only to her immediate circle until, in the war years, she responded to the call to try to make a united front of occultists and spiritualists against the forces of materialism in the post-war world. At this point she wrote various articles for the spiritualist press and appeared as a speaker on several spiritualist platforms

This book contains her original work Spiritualism in the Light of Occult Science with commentaries by Gareth Knight that quote extensively from now largely unobtainable material that she wrote on the subject during her life, including transcripts from her own trance work and rare articles from old magazines and journals.

This book represents the fourth collaborative work between the two. An Introduction to Ritual Magic, The Circuit of Force, and Principles of Hermetic Philosophy being already published in this series.

ISBN 978-1-870450-38-6

DION FORTUNE AND THE INNER LIGHT
By Gareth Knight

At last – a comprehensive biography of Dion Fortune based upon the archives of the Society of the Inner Light. As a result much comes to light that has never before been revealed. This includes:

Her early experiments in trance mediumship with her Golden Dawn teacher Maiya Curtis-Webb and in Glastonbury with Frederick Bligh Bond, famous for his psychic investigations of Glastonbury Abbey.

The circumstances of her first contact with the Masters and reception of "The Cosmic Doctrine" The ambitious plans of the Master of Medicine and the projected esoteric clinic with her husband in the role of Dr.Taverner.

The inside story of the confrontation between the Christian Mystic Lodge of the Theosophical Society of which she was president, and Bishop Piggot of the Liberal Catholic church, over the Star in the East movement and Krishnamurti. Also her group's experience of the magical conflict with Moina MacGregor Mathers.

How she and her husband befriended the young Israel Regardie, were present at his initiation into the Hermes Temple of the Stella Matutina, and suffered a second ejection from the Golden Dawn on his subsequent falling out with it.

Her renewed and highly secret contact with her old Golden Dawn teacher Maiya Tranchell-Hayes and their development of the esoteric side of the Arthurian legends.

Her peculiar and hitherto unknown work in policing the occult jurisdiction of the Master for whom she worked which brought her into unlikely contact with occultists such as Aleister Crowley.

Nor does the remarkable story end with her physical death for, through the mediumship of Margaret Lumley Brown and others, continued contacts with Dion Fortune have been reported over subsequent years.

ISBN 978-1-870450-45-4

AN INTRODUCTION TO RITUAL MAGIC
By Dion Fortune & Gareth Knight

At the time this was something of a unique event in esoteric publishing - a new book by the legendary Dion Fortune. Especially with its teachings on the theory and practice of ritual or ceremonial magic, by one who, like the heroine of two of her other novels, was undoubtedly "a mistress of that art".

In this work Dion Fortune deals in successive chapters with Types of Mind Working; Mind Training; The Use of Ritual; Psychic Perception; Ritual Initiation; The Reality of the Subtle Planes; Focusing the Magic Mirror; Channelling the Forces; The Form of the Ceremony; and The Purpose of Magic - with appendices on Talisman Magic and Astral Forms.

Each chapter is supplemented and expanded by a companion chapter on the same subject by Gareth Knight. In Dion Fortune's day the conventions of occult secrecy prevented her from being too explicit on the practical details of magic, except in works of fiction. These veils of secrecy having now been drawn back, Gareth Knight has taken the opportunity to fill in much practical information that Dion Fortune might well have included had she been writing today. In short, in this unique collaboration of two magical practitioners and teachers, we are presented with a valuable and up-to-date text on the practice of ritual or ceremonial magic "as it is". That is to say, as a practical, spiritual, and psychic discipline, far removed from the lurid superstition and speculation that are the hall mark of its treatment in sensational journalism and channels of popular entertainment.

ISBN 978-1-870450-26-3 Soft cover edition

PRINCIPLES OF HERMETIC PHILOSOPHY
By Dion Fortune & Gareth Knight

Principles of Hermetic Philosophy was the last known work written by Dion Fortune. It appeared in her Monthly letters to members and associates of the Society of the Inner Light between November 1942 and March 1944.

Her intention in this work is summed up in her own words: "The observations in these pages are an attempt to gather together the fragments of a forgotten wisdom and explain and expand them in the light of personal observation."

She was uniquely equipped to make highly significant personal observations in these matters as one of the leading practical occultists of her time. What is more, in these later works she feels less constrained by traditions of occult secrecy and takes an altogether more practical approach than in her earlier, well known textbooks.

Gareth Knight takes the opportunity to amplify her explanations and practical exercises with a series of full page illustrations, and provides a commentary on her work

ISBN 978-1-870450-34-8

THE STORY OF DION FORTUNE
As told to Charles Fielding and Carr Collins.

Dion Fortune and Aleister Crowley stand as the twentieth century's most influential leaders of the Western Esoteric Tradition. They were very different in their backgrounds, scholarship and style.

But, for many, Dion Fortune is the chosen exemplar of the Tradition - with no drugs, no homosexuality and no kinks. This book tells of her formative years and of her development.

At the end, she remains a complex and enigmatic figure, who can only be understood in the light of the system she evolved and worked to great effect.

There can be no definitive "Story of Dion Fortune". This book must remain incomplete and full of errors. However, readers may find themselves led into an experience of initiation as envisaged by this fearless and dedicated woman.

ISBN 978-1-870450-33-1

THE FORGOTTEN MAGE
The Magical Lectures of Colonel C.R.F. Seymour.
Edited by Dolores Ashcroft-Nowicki

Charles Seymour was a man of many talents and considerable occult skills. The friend and confidant of Dion Fortune, he worked with her and his magical partner, Christine Hartley, for many productive years.

As one of the Inner Circle of Dion Fortune's Society of the Inner Light, Seymour was a High Priest in every sense of the word, but he was also one of the finest teachers of the occult art to emerge this century.

In the past, little of Seymour's work has been widely available, but in this volume Dolores Ashcroft-Nowicki, Director of Studies of the Servants of the Light School of Occult Science, has gathered together a selection of the best of Seymour's work. His complex scholarship and broad background knowledge of the Pagan traditions shine through in articles which include: The Meaning of Initiation; Magic in the Ancient Mystery Religions; The Esoteric Aspect of Religion; Meditations for Temple Novices; The Old Gods; The Ancient Nature Worship and The Children of the Great Mother.

ISBN 978-1870450-39-3

THE WESTERN MYSTERY TRADITION
By Christine Hartley

A reissue of a classic work, by a pupil of Dion Fortune, on the mythical and historical roots of Western occultism.

Christine Hartley's aim was to demonstrate that we in the West, far from being dependent upon Eastern esoteric teachings, possess a rich and potent mystery tradition of our own, evoked and defined in myth, legend, folklore and song, and embodied in the legacy of Druidic culture.

More importantly, she provides practical guidelines for modern students of the ancient mysteries, 'The Western Mystery Tradition,' in Christine Hartley's view, 'is the basis of the Western religious feeling, the foundation of our spiritual life, the matrix of our religious formulae, whither we are aware of it or not. To it we owe the life and force of our spiritual life.'

ISBN 9781913660154

www.ingramcontent.com/pod-product-compliance
Lightning Source LLC
Chambersburg PA
CBHW020407100426
42812CB00001B/230